# Radical Inequalities

For Bill—
Thank you for your interest
and support. Best,
N—

HARVARD EAST ASIAN MONOGRAPHS 383

# Radical Inequalities

*China's Revolutionary Welfare State
in Comparative Perspective*

## Nara Dillon

Published by the Harvard University Asia Center
Distributed by Harvard University Press
Cambridge (Massachusetts) and London 2015

The Harvard University Asia Center publishes a monograph series and, in coordination with the Fairbank Center for Chinese Studies, the Korea Institute, the Reischauer Institute of Japanese Studies, and other facilities and institutes, administers research projects designed to further scholarly understanding of China, Japan, Vietnam, Korea, and other Asian countries. The Center also sponsors projects addressing multidisciplinary and regional issues in Asia.

The Harvard University Asia Center gratefully acknowledges a generous grant in support of publication of this work from the Chiang Ching-kuo Foundation for International Scholarly Exchange.

Library of Congress Cataloging-in-Publication Data

Dillon, Nara.
   Radical inequalities : China's revolutionary welfare state in comparative perspective / Nara Dillon.
       pages cm. -- (Harvard East Asian monographs ; 383)
   Includes bibliographical references and index.
   ISBN 978-0-674-50431-8 (hardcover : alk. paper)  1.  Welfare state--China--History--20th century. 2.  China--Social conditions--1949- 3.  China--Economic conditions--1949- 4.  China--Social policy. 5.  China--Economic policy. I. Title.
   HN733.5.D55 2015
   361.6'509510904--dc23

                        2014033426

Index by the author

 Printed on acid-free paper
Last figure below indicates year of this printing
25 24 23 22 21 20 19 18 17 16 15

For
Dave Dillon
&
Judith Braden Dillon
for all their support and guidance

# Contents

*List of Tables, Maps, and Figures*     ix

*Acknowledgments*     xi

*List of Abbreviations*     xii

Introduction: The Paradox of China's Unequal
Welfare State     1

**PART I  THE POLITICS OF FOUNDING CHINA'S WELFARE STATE**

1   China's Place in the Globalization of the Welfare
State, 1880s–1980s     39
2   The Nationalist Origins of the Chinese Welfare
State, 1943–49     78
3   The Communist Foundations of the Chinese Welfare
State, 1948–51     118

**PART II  THE POLITICS OF EXPANDING CHINA'S WELFARE STATE**

4   The Soviet Model: Transitional Welfare in the First
Five-Year Plan, 1952–54     157

5 Chinese Austerity: Transitional Restraint in the Urban
  Revolution, 1955–58                                        192
6 Mao's Communes: Universal Welfare in the Great Leap
  Forward, 1958–62                                           229

  Conclusion: China's Narrow Welfare State in Comparative
  Perspective                                                268

  *Bibliography*                                             297
  *Glossary*                                                 323
  *Index*                                                    325

# Tables, Maps, and Figures

## Tables

I.1 Conditions Shaping the Founding of the Chinese Welfare State 32

I.2 Conditions Shaping the Expansion of Welfare Coverage 33

2.1 Shanghai Worker Welfare Implementation, December 1947 104

2.2 KMT Unemployment Relief, 1945–48 111

2.3 Shanghai Welfare Coverage, 1945–49 115

3.1 Shanghai Unemployment Relief, 1947 versus 1951 136

3.2 Shanghai Worker Welfare and Labor Insurance Implementation, 1947 versus 1951 143

3.3 Shanghai Welfare Coverage, 1949–51 152

4.1 Shanghai Transitional Welfare Program Enrollees, 1951–54 179

4.2 Shanghai Relief Handouts, 1951–54 183

4.3 Shanghai Permanent Welfare Program Enrollees, 1952–54 187

4.4 Shanghai Welfare Coverage, 1952–54 188

5.1 Shanghai Unemployment Programs, 1954–57 201

5.2 Shanghai Relief Handouts, 1954–57 202

5.3 Shanghai Labor Insurance and Contract Coverage, 1955–57 218

5.4    Shanghai Welfare Coverage, 1955–57    226

6.1    Shanghai Commune Meals and Relief Handouts, 1958–63    247

6.2    Shanghai Unemployment Programs, 1958–63    250

6.3    Shanghai Labor Insurance and Contract Programs, 1958–63    261

6.4    Shanghai Welfare Coverage, 1958–62    264

C.1    Conditions Shaping the Expansion of Welfare Coverage    281

## Maps

I.1    Broad and Narrow Welfare States    13

## Figures

1.1    Welfare Legislation around the World, 1880s–1980s    40

2.1    Shanghai Soup Kitchen Providing Relief in the 1940s    97

3.1    Shanghai Unemployment Relief in the Early 1950s    137

C.1    Shanghai Food Distribution Programs, 1945–65    279

C.2    Shanghai Welfare Coverage, 1945–65    280

# *Acknowledgments*

This research would not have been possible without the assistance of the dedicated staff of the Shanghai Municipal Archives; the faculty at the Shanghai Academy of Social Sciences; and the librarians in the Shanghai Municipal Library, the Hoover Institute Library, the Harvard-Yenching Library, and the Fung Library. It was also made possible by the financial support of the University of California at Berkeley, the Social Science Research Council, and Bard College. Guidance from my teachers has been fundamental; they include Henry Brady, Hong Yung Lee, Tom Gold, Christopher Ansell, and Gail Hershatter. Henrietta Harrison provided invaluable suggestions on revising the manuscript. Colleagues at both Bard College and Harvard University have been very helpful as well: Rob Culp, Omar Encarnacion, Wilt Idema, Rod MacFarquhar, and Rudolf Wagner. I also want to thank my anonymous reviewers for their thoughtful criticism.

This book is dedicated to my parents for their steady support throughout my life. The rest of my family and friends have also been encouraging throughout the years that this project has taken. Most of all, my deep gratitude goes to Liz Perry for her unwavering support in life and scholarship.

# *Abbreviations*

| | |
|---|---|
| BBC | British Broadcasting Company |
| CCP | Chinese Communist Party |
| CIO | Congress of Industrial Organizations |
| CNRRA | Chinese National Relief and Rehabilitation Administration |
| KMT | Kuomintang, Chinese Nationalist Party |
| ILO | International Labour Organization |
| PLA | People's Liberation Army |
| SMA | Shanghai Municipal Archives |
| SSA | Social Security Administration |
| SSB | Social Security Bureau |
| UNRRA | United Nations Relief and Rehabilitation Administration |
| WFTU | World Federation of Trade Unions |

# INTRODUCTION

## *The Paradox of China's Unequal Welfare State*

Laying the foundations of a modern welfare state was one of the most significant achievements of the 1949 Chinese Communist Revolution. But as important as this new pillar of the Communist state was to the millions of ordinary Chinese citizens who enjoyed its security and protection, it also served to deepen long-standing inequalities in Chinese society that the revolution sought to eliminate. Even at its peak, this workplace social insurance program reached only a minority of the Chinese population: party cadres, government employees, and permanent workers in large factories. Within that privileged minority, there were significant variations in benefits and security. But more important than this inequality within the welfare state was the fact that the vast majority of the Chinese population was excluded. The narrow reach of the Maoist welfare state served to increase the gaps between city and countryside, industry and agriculture, and men and women. One of the bitter ironies of the Chinese Communist Revolution is that the most important social program for workers did not eliminate inequality; it entrenched it.

Understanding this paradox at the heart of the Maoist welfare state and the Chinese Communist revolution is the goal of this study. How did the welfare state, one of the most effective tools ever developed to promote economic equality, become instead a force for increasing inequality in Chinese society? Why did the Chinese Communist Party (CCP), which under Mao Zedong's leadership was one of the most ruthlessly egalitarian revolutionary forces in world history, end up betraying one of its most deeply held commitments?

The labor insurance program that constituted the core of the Maoist welfare state was adopted in 1951, less than two years after the Chinese Communist Party seized national power. Not surprisingly for a major social program implemented by a fragile new regime, this program was by no means perfect. Its greatest strength was that it provided a comprehensive array of benefits; retirement pensions, health insurance, disability benefits, and paid maternity leave were among the most important. The greatest weakness of the new program was its limited coverage, since only permanent employees of large factories and other big employers were eligible for the program. Although the program was reformed many times during the Mao era, it never overcame its initial limitations. Coverage was extended to a significant share of the urban labor force, but never reached all urban residents—much less the peasants who constituted the vast majority of the Chinese population. Adding to this injustice, the rural majority ended up subsidizing the welfare state that excluded them. Because China's command economy extracted resources from the countryside and redirected them into industry, the high industrial profits that sustained the Maoist welfare state came at the expense of the rest of the economy.

As a result, the Maoist labor insurance program further deepened the gulf between city and countryside. Economists estimate that, by the end of the Maoist period in 1976, the urban-rural wage gap favored the average urbanite, with double to more than triple the income of the average peasant.[1] Labor insurance and other benefits dramatically increased the gap. When welfare benefits and subsidies are added on top of wages, the difference between average urban and rural incomes doubled again to a differential of five or six times. The consequences of these gaps were profound. One rough measure of the impact of these differences in living standards is life expectancy. The health care and

---

1. Selden, *Political Economy of Chinese Socialism*, 163; Riskin, *China's Political Economy*, 240–42; Parish and Whyte, *Village and Family*, 53; Lardy, *Economic Growth and Distribution*, 175.

income security provided by the Maoist welfare state made an important contribution to one of the most rapid gains in life expectancy in human history. In urban China average life expectancy jumped from forty to seventy-two years during the Maoist era. The improvement in rural China from forty to fifty-seven years was significant, but only half as large as the gain in the cities.[2]

Inequalities within Chinese cities were not as severe as the rural-urban gap, but the Maoist welfare state exacerbated these differences as well. The most fundamental cleavage among urban residents was between permanent employees in the state-owned and the collective sectors. Workers in collectively owned enterprises earned on average only three-quarters the income of workers in the state sector, and enjoyed few welfare benefits to soften the impact of illness or old age. Since women were much more likely to work in the collective sector, this institutionally defined inequality had a gender dimension as well.[3] Even within state-owned enterprises there were cleavages between permanent and temporary workers. Temporary employees tended to earn significantly less than permanent workers and uniformly lacked welfare benefits as well, even though their "temporary" status was usually a long-term condition.[4] In addition, different generations of workers within the same enterprises received different wages and welfare benefits, with older workers doing significantly better than their younger counterparts.[5]

A decade after the market reforms began, the Chinese welfare system inherited from the Mao era still increased the income gap between rich and poor by one-third, placing it among the most regressive welfare states in the world.[6] These inequalities were recognized by the ordinary Chinese people whose lives were shaped by them and by the Communist leaders who struggled to eliminate them. Given the Communists' commitment to egalitarianism, the persistence of these

2. Selden, *Political Economy of Chinese Socialism*, 163; World Bank, *China: The Health Sector*, 3, 113.

3. Whyte and Parish, *Urban Life*, 31–32.

4. Walder, *Communist Neo-Traditionalism*, 43–48.

5. Davis, "Unequal Chances," 223–42.

6. Gao, "Redistributive Nature," 13.

inequalities is puzzling. The Chinese Communist Party (CCP) success-
fully engineered a massive redistribution of wealth in the 1950s. Why
would the redistribution of income prove so much more difficult? Why
did their own welfare programs run counter to their goals?

## *The Debate over Workplace Welfare in China*

The paradox of an unequal communist welfare state is a striking legacy
of the Chinese revolution, so it is not surprising that, long after Mao
passed away and revolutionary ideals lost their urgency, scholars still
debate how and why the Maoist regime failed to achieve one of its
central aims.[7] To explain the limits of the Maoist welfare state, China
specialists first pointed to the conditions its founders faced in the early
days of the revolution as well as the regime's political and economic
priorities. The problem of scarce resources in a war-torn country with
an agricultural economy was an important constraint on the Chinese
welfare state.[8] The CCP's ideological preference for the working class
and its development strategy of building and expanding heavy industry also affected its priorities.[9] Although poverty, ideology, and development strategies all shaped the Chinese welfare state, they provide
incomplete explanations for its narrow reach. To varying degrees, all
communist regimes faced these kinds of pressures and priorities, yet
most managed to achieve nearly universal coverage in their welfare
programs.[10] Indeed, comprehensive welfare states came to be seen as a
defining feature of communist regimes.

In the search for the reasons the Chinese welfare state was so
different from those in the rest of the communist world, many China

---

7. See Walder, *Communist Neo-Traditionalism*; Frazier, *Making of the Chinese Industrial Workplace*; Bian, *Making of the State Enterprise System*; Bray, *Social Space and
Governance*; Lü and Perry, *Danwei*.
8. Kallgren, "Social Welfare."
9. Dixon, *Chinese Welfare System*; Ahmad and Hussein, "Social Security," 249.
10. ILO, *World Labour Report 2000*, Statistical Annex, table 11; Buckley and Donahue,
"Promises to Keep," 254–56; Adam, "Social Contract," 3; Müller, *Political Economy of
Pension Reform*, 63, 95.

specialists have focused on its unusual institutional structure. Workplace provision of social insurance, housing, and other public services was taken to an extreme in Maoist China, surpassing the level found in other communist countries.[11] Indeed, some scholars have gone so far as to argue that the Chinese term for the workplace, *danwei*, cannot be adequately translated because the institution is uniquely Chinese.[12] Furthermore, the institutional boundaries and hierarchies of the workplace largely overlapped with the inequalities of the Maoist welfare state. Many have interpreted this overlap as evidence of a causal relationship, arguing that the institutional structure of the Chinese workplace defined and limited the Maoist welfare state.

Debate in the field has also turned to explaining the origins of workplace welfare. Broadly speaking, two schools of thought can be distinguished: a historical institutional school and a comparative communism school. Their debate boils down to the question of whether the *danwei* was an unintended consequence of preexisting institutional constraints or the result of the clash between communist modernizing strategies and the harsh realities of China's premodern economy.

The historical institutional school looks to the legacies of the prerevolutionary era for explanations. Mark Frazier emphasizes the weight of institutional inertia, claiming that workplace welfare programs established during the Second World War survived the Communist revolution with many of their capitalist organizational hierarchies intact.[13] Elizabeth Perry points to the impact of the long history of exclusive labor guilds on the Communist labor movement, especially the strong influence of the radical but elitist skilled artisans who built the trade unions.[14] Xiaobo Lü offers another variation of this argument by emphasizing the history of the Communist Party, especially the development of comprehensive supply and rationing systems for cadres working in the revolutionary base areas in the 1930s and 1940s.[15] These

---

11. Ferdinand and Gainsborough, *Enterprise and Welfare Reform*; Rein, Friedman, and Wörgotter, eds., *Enterprise and Social Benefits*.
12. Bray, *Social Space and Governance*, 3.
13. See Frazier, *Making of the Chinese Industrial Workplace*; Bian, *Making of the State Enterprise System*; Bray, *Social Space and Governance*.
14. Perry, "From Native Place to Workplace."
15. Lü, "Minor Public Economy."

three sources of hierarchy and exclusivity in companies, labor unions, and the Communist Party itself provide complementary explanations for the development of limited and inegalitarian workplace welfare programs in the Maoist era.

The comparative communism school is more skeptical about historical continuities in the context of a sweeping social revolution and focuses instead on the problems the Chinese revolutionaries faced in constructing a communist regime and a command economy in an agricultural country.[16] Andrew Walder identifies an inherent conflict in Leninist organizations between the demands of political loyalty and economic production, which in the Chinese case was exacerbated by the undeveloped state of the economy. According to Walder, this Leninist dilemma was resolved in China by resorting to ostensibly "traditional" patterns of authority relations such as paternalism and clientelism. This solution used personal loyalties to buttress the power of the Communist Party and grease the wheels of the command economy but at a cost to the larger goals of the revolution.[17] Barry Naughton makes a similar but more narrowly focused argument. He maintains that the mature *danwei* system emerged out of ad hoc efforts to stabilize China's political system and revive the economy after the crisis of the Great Leap Forward (1958–62).[18] Both authors share the conviction that the shortcomings of the Maoist welfare state were one aspect of a larger compromise between the ideals and reality of Communist rule in China rather than prerevolutionary institutional legacies.

Both schools have found considerable enterprise-level data to support their claims, making it difficult to settle the debate over the origins of the *danwei* without more evidence. But a shift in perspective suggests that their consensus that the structure of the workplace is responsible for the limits of the Chinese welfare state may be premature. From a comparative perspective, the most notable parallels to the inequalities of the Maoist welfare state are not with prerevolutionary Chinese institutions or with other communist regimes but instead with other welfare states in the developing world. Although welfare state

16. Kaple, *Dream of a Red Factory*.
17. Walder, *Communist Neo-Traditionalism*.
18. Naughton, "Danwei."

programs have been adopted by the vast majority of countries today, in most places they have not had the effect of reducing poverty or ameliorating inequality, as they have done in the advanced industrial countries. The paradox of an unequal welfare state is not a uniquely Chinese problem, even though few other regimes were as committed to reducing inequality as the Chinese Communists under Mao's rule.

This study builds on earlier research on workplace welfare, but takes a different tack. China's social insurance program for workers is placed in the context of other welfare programs created for the urban poor. The focus on inequality in urban welfare highlights some of the limits of the current debate. Both schools of thought on the origins of the *danwei* share a common analytical focus on industrial relations. From this shared perspective, welfare is one aspect of a broader relationship between workers and the party-state that also encompasses wages, the organization of production, and the structure of political authority in state-owned enterprises. Left in the background, however, is the role of outsiders in the construction of the welfare state. Not only does China's peasant majority fade from view, but so too do the urbanites who were never lucky enough to make it onto the factory floor. Broadening the focus beyond the factory walls promises a clearer view of the redistributive struggles in Chinese society. It also connects the Chinese case to the large body of comparative research on the development of the welfare state in other parts of the world. This shift in perspective is necessary to unravel the paradox of the Maoist welfare state: how and why a radical communist regime created a deeply unequal welfare state.

## Redefining the Problem: Unequal Welfare States in the Developing World

China's welfare state is not alone in failing to reduce poverty or income inequality. Regressive welfare states are all too common in the developing world, presenting a fundamental contrast to welfare states in advanced industrial countries. The extensive literature on welfare states in these industrialized countries tends to focus on the variations among them rather than their basic similarities. But one important characteristic they all share is that they reduce poverty, regardless of how much they ameliorate inequality.[19] Comparable data on income, taxation, and transfer payments are hard to come by, but the best research to date shows that the welfare state in advanced industrial countries has had a clear impact on the distribution of income at the bottom end of the scale. Even the American welfare state, long maligned for its many shortcomings, reduces the incidence and severity of poverty by boosting the incomes of the elderly and many families at the lowest reaches of the income ladder.[20] The relevant question for welfare states in the advanced industrial countries is how progressive they are—the degree of redistribution they provide.

The contrast with regressive welfare states in the developing world is stark.[21] Several reasons for their failure to reduce poverty and inequality have been identified. As in China, one leading cause is limited population coverage. When only a minority of the population is targeted for income protection, the welfare state is only effective as an antipoverty program if that minority is the poorest group in society. In most developing countries, however, the poorest citizens are excluded from the welfare state, and there are often no social assistance or poor relief programs in place to help them.[22] Another source of inequality stems from the financing mechanisms for welfare state programs. The tax systems that fund these programs are often regressive in developing countries, placing a heavier burden on the poor.[23] In addition, employers can often pass on the costs of their contributions to welfare state programs to consumers. When limited coverage and

19. Alesina and Glaeser, *Fighting Poverty*; Smeeding, Rainwater, and Burtless, "U.S. Poverty"; Esping-Andersen, *Three Worlds*.
20. Kenworthy, "Do Social Welfare Policies Reduce Poverty?"; Smeeding and Phillips, "Social Protection for the Poor."
21. Huber and Stephens, *Democracy and the Left*; Rudra, *Globalization and the Race to the Bottom*; Midgley, *Social Security and Inequality*; Paukert, "Social Security and Income Redistribution"; Mouton, *Social Security in Africa*, 153; Abel and Lewis, "Exclusion and Engagement," 24.
22. Rudra, *Globalization and the Race to the Bottom*; Mesa-Lago, *Changing Social Security*; Weyland, *Democracy without Equity*.
23. Paukert, "Social Security and Income Redistribution," 125–26.

regressive financing are combined, the poorest members of society are forced to subsidize the welfare state programs from which they are excluded.

Limited coverage that fails to target the poor is arguably the most important source of inequality in the global welfare state. More than half of the global workforce lacks any social security protection at all.[24]  It may also be the source of inequality most amenable to solution, since expanding population coverage could immediately improve the lives of the most vulnerable groups in society. For these reasons, the primary focus in this study is on coverage rather than more direct measures of poverty and inequality, for which reliable data are difficult to find for most developing countries. Although coverage only indirectly captures the impact of the welfare state on inequality, it does center attention on the most important cleavage created by a limited welfare state: the  division between protected insiders and excluded outsiders.

## Toward a New Typology: Universal, Broad, and Narrow Welfare States

To draw useful cross-national comparisons among welfare states, the concept of the welfare state itself needs to be carefully specified. The term "welfare state" has become so popular since it was coined during the Second World War that it has been used to refer to almost any kind of social program, from social insurance to public education, as well as to abstract principles such as social rights or equality of opportunity.[25] Here the term refers more narrowly to the income maintenance programs that have been at the core of the welfare state in most countries in the world. These programs provide income and access to health care to those who are unable to work owing to old age, disability, maternity, illness, or unemployment. Because old-age pension programs have

24. Gillion et al, *Social Security Pensions*, 194.
25. Briggs, "The Welfare State in Historical Perspective"; Alber, "Continuities and Changes."

become the largest, most expensive part of the welfare state in most countries, they are the focus of this study.

Four different program designs for old-age pensions have been adopted around the world. Citizen pensions provide the same basic pension to all elderly citizens.[26] Originally, these programs were limited to those elders who passed a "needs test" showing that they lacked sufficient income. For the most part, citizen pensions have been financed from general tax revenues. In contrast, social insurance provides retirement pensions pegged to a worker's income that are guaranteed for his or her lifetime. Social insurance is financed through dedicated payroll taxes levied on both employers and workers, sometimes with additional subsidies and guarantees from general tax revenues. In developing countries, a third program design is also popular: provident funds. Mandatory savings programs with dedicated payroll taxes similar to social insurance, provident funds typically disburse the accumulated savings to workers as a lump-sum payment at retirement without providing any guarantee of lifetime protection. More recently, a fourth program design has been developed: privatized old-age pension programs with individual savings accounts, which represent a variation on the provident fund design.

This study uses a straightforward conceptualization of the reach of these welfare programs: *population coverage*, which refers to the proportion of the total population or the total labor force eligible for benefits.[27] Because data on coverage have not been routinely collected until very

26. This program design has a bewildering variety of names: social pensions, noncontributory flat-rate pensions, demogrant pensions, social assistance pensions, and others. I am using the term "citizen pensions" to differentiate it clearly from social insurance and am including both means-tested and universal programs in this same category.

27. The concepts of solidarity and social exclusion are alternative possibilities for conceptualizing the dependent variable. Both overlap with population coverage but encompass far more than coverage alone. Solidarity incorporates a shared perception of risk or a sense of membership in a national community (see Baldwin, *Politics of Social Solidarity*). Social exclusion also encompasses all other institutional and cultural barriers that prevent people from participating fully in their society (see, for example, van Ginneken, ed., *Social Security for the Excluded Majority*). The narrower concept of population coverage has the advantage of focusing on a single dimension of a single program.

recently, and often reflect varying definitions of program participation, they must be treated with caution. Even with these limitations, however, population coverage provides a basis for rough comparisons of how the reach of the welfare state has changed over time and, to some degree, across countries. In light of the lack of consistent standards for welfare coverage data, for cross-national comparisons this study classifies welfare states into three general categories, *universal, broad,* and *narrow,* to capture the most basic distinctions in levels of coverage.

Welfare states that make all citizens eligible for benefits as a social right can be classified as *universal.* Short of this clear standard, drawing meaningful distinctions is more ambiguous. However, the International Labour Organization's (ILO) minimum standard for social security coverage, 75 percent of the labor force, provides a yardstick that has achieved considerable international consensus.[28] This study defines *broad* welfare states as covering 75 percent or more of the workforce but lacking universal social rights to benefits. *Narrow* welfare states have less than 75 percent of workforce participation in the program. Although this labor force standard may sound high, it actually sets a relatively low threshold for a broad welfare state, since the labor force in most countries ranges from one-third to half of the total population. Coverage of employees' families varies widely, so meeting the ILO minimum standard can still mean that less than half the total population is covered by the welfare state, leaving the majority unprotected.

Although the existing comparative research on coverage is preliminary, it does show the prevalence of narrow welfare states in the contemporary world. In one of the first large studies of coverage, the World Bank reported that only 19 percent of the 63 countries examined met the ILO minimum standard in 1990.[29] Although the World Bank sample was selected for the availability of data and was not representative, it included countries from all regions of the world and every level of development (including China). More recent data collected by the ILO on coverage rates in 122 countries around the world show a similar pattern fifteen years later, with only 16 percent of them achieving broad cover-

28. Gillion, et al., eds., *Social Security Pensions,* 400; ILO Convention 128 (1967) (NORMLEX database).
29. World Bank, *Averting the Old Age Crisis.*

age.[30] These large-scale data collection efforts are also supported by many regional and single-country studies documenting limited coverage in developing countries.[31]

Surveying this evidence suggests that the problem of narrow coverage has a distinct geography (see map I.1). Europe stands out as the lone region of the world with extensive population coverage. The universal welfare states of Western Europe provide all citizens social security protections as a social right. Even without those guaranteed rights, most of the formerly communist countries of Eastern Europe and the former Soviet Union provide broad coverage of their populations.

The Americas present a mixed picture. North America also features broad, nearly universal coverage in the United States and Canada, whereas Mexico's narrow coverage is much more similar to the pattern found in most Latin American countries. Brazil, Argentina, Uruguay, Costa Rica, and Cuba have achieved broad coverage. Most other Latin American countries, however, have failed to achieve the ILO minimum standard in their primary pension programs. Like the Americas, Asia and the Pacific are marked by diversity. Japan, Australia, and New Zealand have universal coverage, whereas South Korea, Taiwan, and Singapore have broad coverage. The rest of the region features very narrow coverage, including India and China, which together account for more than one-third of the global population.

The Middle East and Africa are dominated by narrow welfare states. Israel, Botswana, and Mauritius stand out in these regions with their universal welfare states, while South Africa is the only large country in these two regions with broad coverage. More typical are countries such as Nigeria and Chad, with social security programs that reach less than 3 percent of their labor forces. The pockmarked map of Asia, Africa, and Latin America suggests that broad welfare states are possible in the developing world, but narrow welfare states are far more common.

---

30. ILO, *World Social Security Report 2010/11*, 240–43.
31. Mouton, *Social Security in Africa*; Abel and Lewis, "Exclusion and Engagement"; Mesa-Lago, *Social Security in Latin America*; Mesa-Lago, *Social Security and the Prospects for Equity*; Mesa-Lago, *Ascent to Bankruptcy*; Barrientos, *Pension Reform in Latin America*; van Ginneken, ed., *Social Security for the Excluded Majority*; Rofman, "Social Security Coverage in Latin America."

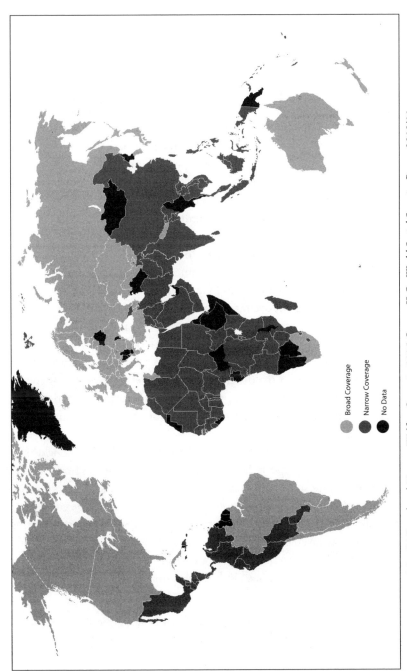

*Map I.1* Broad and Narrow Welfare States in 2005 *Source:* ILO, *World Social Security Report 2010/11.*

Narrow coverage has long been viewed as a transitional problem in the development of the welfare state. However, the failure to make any significant gains in the twenty years between the World Bank study and the ILO report of 2010–11 suggests that most welfare states have plateaued at low levels of coverage for decades, and case studies show that coverage levels have stalled for generations in some countries. For example, in 1990, forty years after the Communist revolution, China's welfare state reached only 24 percent of the labor force, which amounted to 12 percent of the total population.[32] Despite economic growth and significant reforms in the 1990s and 2000s, coverage was still only 23 percent of the labor force fifteen years later.[33] Other developing countries have experienced significant erosion in coverage. For example, Colombia and Peru experienced very slow growth in population coverage over the first thirty or forty years of their social security programs only to see coverage erode since the 1980s under the pressure of sharp economic recessions and government cutbacks.[34]

Since the level of welfare state coverage can decline or plateau at low levels for decades, we must consider the prospect that narrow welfare states can be economically and politically stable. Narrow welfare states may constitute a new type of welfare state rather than a transitional stage in the development of universal coverage. If so, we need a better understanding of the conditions that give rise to narrow welfare states as a first step toward overcoming their limits and addressing the inequalities they create.

From a comparative perspective, the debate in the China field over workplace welfare appears less relevant for explaining the limits of the Chinese welfare state than characteristics that China shares with other developing countries. Furthermore, China can and should be considered an important case for comparative research on the welfare state. In terms of population coverage, the conventional wisdom should be turned upside down: the Chinese welfare state is a typical case, whereas the universal welfare states of the advanced industrial countries are outliers.

32. World Bank, *Averting the Old Age Crisis*; Cuban Economic Research Project, *Social Security in Cuba*, 47; Mesa-Lago, *Ascent to Bankruptcy*, 50.
33. ILO, *World Social Security Report 2010/11*, 241.
34. Barrientos, *Pension Reform in Latin America*, 167.

# Research on Welfare Coverage

Previous research in three areas provides a starting point for understanding the development of narrow welfare states. First is recent research from policy analysts who have tried to identify obstacles to the expansion of welfare coverage and formulate new policy interventions to overcome them. Second is a small body of comparative research that turns the frame of analysis around to focus on policies to expand coverage as one dimension of welfare state expansion. Third is comparative research on the politics behind the adoption of those reforms that produced today's broad and universal welfare states. All three approaches are useful for analyzing the Chinese case.

## POLICY RESEARCH: OBSTACLES TO THE EXPANSION OF WELFARE COVERAGE

The assumption that narrow welfare states are a transitional stage of development has shaped the way the problem has been approached in policy research.[35] Most analysts have tried to identify key obstacles standing in the way of the expansion of welfare coverage, implying that removal of these barriers will allow narrow welfare states to assume a more "normal" course of development. Analysts have identified at least three common problems: low levels of economic development, economic incentives that discourage program participation, and weak state capacity.

The economic hurdles to expansion have attracted the most attention. The striking pattern of broad and universal welfare states in most of the advanced industrial countries and narrow welfare states in most of the developing world has led many researchers to conclude that the overall level of economic development is the main variable affecting welfare coverage.[36] For example, World Bank researchers estimate that

35. The ILO acknowledged this assumption at its 2001 conference on social security. See ILO, *Social Security: A New Consensus*, 33.
36. van Ginneken, ed., *Social Security for the Excluded Majority*; Gillion, et al., eds., *Social Security Pensions*; James, "Coverage under Old Age Security Programs"; Holzmann et al., eds., *Closing the Coverage Gap*.

94 percent of the variation in coverage is accounted for by a country's level of economic development.[37] An earlier generation of researchers who studied the expansion of the welfare state among the advanced industrial countries also initially focused on economic development as the driving force.[38] But their cross-sectional studies showing a correlation between the level of economic development and welfare expansion were not supported by subsequent longitudinal studies of either welfare spending or the adoption of new welfare programs.[39] Similarly, these cross-sectional studies on coverage cannot account for developing countries with stagnating coverage during periods of sustained economic growth. Put together, these findings suggest that economic development may be a necessary but insufficient condition for the expansion of welfare coverage.

Researchers have also focused on microeconomic obstacles to explain narrow coverage. The payroll taxes that finance social insurance and provident funds have been identified as a serious disincentive for program participation, especially at lower ends of the pay scale. These disincentives are compounded for the self-employed, who often bear the costs of both employee and employer contributions.[40] In addition, casual or temporary workers may not be able to sustain contributions for a long enough period ever to qualify for benefits. For these kinds of workers, avoiding the program altogether may be a rational cost-benefit calculation. The evidence for the cumulative impact of these incentives, however, is weak. Today's broad welfare states overcame individual disincentives to participation. Moreover, the experience of countries with privatized old-age pension programs designed to eliminate these disincentives has been disappointing, since coverage rates have continued to stagnate and in some cases have declined since the reforms were put in place.[41]

37. World Bank, *Averting the Old Age Crisis*, 39.
38. Cutright, "Political Structure, Economic Development, and National Social Security Programs"; Wilensky, *Welfare State and Equality*.
39. Mares, "Social Protection"; Collier and Messick, "Prerequisites vs. Diffusion"; Hicks, *Social Democracy*.
40. World Bank, *Averting the Old Age Crisis*; James, "Coverage under Old Age Security Programs," 155; van Ginneken, eds., *Social Security for the Excluded Majority*, 11.
41. Barrientos, *Pension Reform in Latin America*, 172, 193; Gil et al., *Keeping the Promise*.

The third important obstacle identified in the policy literature is weak state capacity.[42] The demands of administering national income maintenance programs are high, and many states in the developing world have not proven capable of rising to the challenge. However, the data on administrative hurdles come from single-country case studies that often do not identify what the specific shortcomings were or explain how they became long-lasting constraints.[43] Without identifying what these failures of state capacity are, it is difficult even to compare them let alone overcome them.

Policy research into the problem of narrow welfare coverage in the developing world is relatively new, present-oriented, and focused on technocratic solutions. Given the limited evidence available on obstacles to the expansion of coverage and uncertainty about any "normal" process of growth, the finding from this preliminary research that seems most widely applicable is the relationship between economic development and welfare coverage. State capacity must also be important to the expansion of welfare coverage, but the research is too preliminary at this point to provide much guidance about its impact.

## COMPARATIVE RESEARCH: POLICIES TO EXPAND WELFARE COVERAGE

There is good reason, however, to doubt that the problem of narrow coverage can be solved without questioning the political and institutional underpinnings of the welfare state. Coverage is ultimately a political question: who is included and who is excluded from the welfare state is as important politically as who pays and who benefits. If we step back to consider the comparative research on welfare state development, it is clear that politics plays a crucial role in expansion.

Most of the comparative research on the development of the welfare state does not examine population coverage as a separate dimension of its growth and instead focuses on new programs and new spending.

---

42. Gillion, et al., eds., *Social Security Pensions*, 200–201; van Ginneken, ed., *Social Security for the Excluded Majority*, 13; Ghai, "Social Security: Learning from Global Experience," 142.
43. van Ginneken, ed., *Social Security for the Excluded Majority*, 11.

This focus makes sense for the advanced industrial countries, where these three dimensions of the welfare state grew in tandem. Since the data on programs and spending are more reliable and more comparable across countries than the data on population coverage, focusing on these more easily measured aspects has led to rapid advancement in our understanding of the welfare state in these countries. The handful of studies that examine coverage as one among several dimensions of welfare state development provide some insight into the political struggles surrounding coverage.

Peter Flora and Jens Alber show considerable variation in the timing and pace of the expansion of population coverage among European welfare states, even if they achieved similar results in the end. One basic and important finding from this research is that legislation has been central in the expansion of welfare state coverage in Europe.[44] Job and income growth provide one avenue for expanding coverage, but welfare reforms to extend coverage to new groups have also been necessary. Flora and Alber identify reforms to extend coverage to new groups as driving expansion before the Second World War, followed by more ambitious reforms to achieve universal coverage in the postwar period.

Peter Baldwin takes this research a step further in his study of the development of solidarity in European welfare states. Because universal coverage is a prerequisite for solidarity, Baldwin's history explores the expansion of welfare coverage in detail. He identifies two institutionally defined paths to universal coverage, each of which was established by the founding legislation of the welfare state.[45] In Europe, two alternative program designs were popular for this founding legislation: citizen pensions and social insurance. Choices between the two have usually been framed as a trade-off between income security and poverty prevention, since social insurance typically provides higher benefits that come closer to replacing a worker's income, whereas citizen pensions are more effective at providing a safety net. In addition to these different policy outcomes, the institutional structures of the two programs define distinct paths of expansion.

44. Flora and Alber, "Modernization, Democratization and the Development of Welfare States," 54.
45. Baldwin, *Politics of Social Solidarity*, 113.

Countries that first adopted citizen pensions expanded vertically, starting from the poorest members of society and then including more people until all citizens were made eligible as a social right. The legislative reforms to expand coverage in a citizen pension program focus on loosening eligibility restrictions or eliminating them entirely. Countries that adopted social insurance as their founding welfare state legislation expanded horizontally, from the industrial workers who were initially targeted for protection, to other occupational groups, and then finally to people outside the workforce.[46] Reforms to expand social insurance focus on extending coverage to new economic sectors as well as creating the administrative framework to reach people outside formal employment. Not only did the reform policies for these two program designs differ fundamentally, but the people affected and the nature of their political conflicts differed as well.

The Soviet and Eastern European communist regimes developed a new variation to expand coverage in social insurance welfare states. Cheaper, temporary welfare programs such as unemployment relief were targeted to welfare state outsiders to ease the transition to a command economy and the eventual expansion of social insurance.[47] Another variation on this strategy emerged in Latin America in the 1970s: cheaper, permanent programs targeted to key groups of welfare state outsiders.[48] These citizen pension or social assistance programs operate side by side with the existing social insurance program, expanding coverage significantly but at the same time institutionalizing inequality within the welfare state.

The findings from this research help explain why economic development alone is insufficient to achieve broad welfare coverage. Most of the income maintenance programs that have been adopted around the world were never designed to achieve broad, much less universal, coverage.[49] As a result, reform is required to overcome these limitations.

46. Ibid., 248–49.
47. Buckley and Donahue, "Promises to Keep," 253–54; George and Manning, *Socialism, Social Welfare and the Soviet Union*, 38–42.
48. Mesa-Lago, *Social Security in Latin America*; Malloy, *Politics of Social Security*; Huber and Stephens, *Democracy and the Left*.
49. The few exceptions are countries that adopted their welfare state legislation after the Second World War with the explicit goal of achieving universal coverage, such as Switzerland and Israel.

Furthermore, different program designs create distinct, institutionally defined paths of expansion and require different policies to expand coverage.

If these coverage reform policies failed to spread very far, limited diffusion could help explain the prevalence of narrow welfare states in the developing world. Although no research has been done on the diffusion of welfare reforms to expand coverage, studies of the global spread of the original welfare state policies and recent privatization reforms show that international influence has long played an important role in welfare politics. Regional demonstration effects and international organizations have been important mechanisms for welfare policy diffusion.[50] More recently, global economic competition has also been identified as a contributing factor.[51]

COMPARATIVE RESEARCH: THE POLITICS OF
EXPANDING WELFARE COVERAGE

Comparative research on the politics of welfare state expansion addresses coverage only tangentially, in conjunction with the expansion of benefits and programs. This research portrays welfare expansion as relatively straightforward compared to founding a welfare state, which entails restructuring the economy and initiating redistribution. In fact, conservative critics have argued that it is difficult to slow down the expansion of the welfare state.[52] More neutral observers have shown that the welfare state strengthens its constituencies over time, giving it remarkable staying power in the face of rapidly changing economic and political conditions.[53] The prevalence of narrow welfare states today, however, suggests that the assumption that founding new institutions is more difficult than expanding existing ones needs to be questioned. Although this assumption may make sense for other dimensions of

50. Collier and Messick, "Prerequisites vs. Diffusion"; Strang and Chang, "ILO and the Welfare State"; Usui, "Welfare State Development"; Orenstein, *Privatizing Pensions;* Ewig, *Second-Wave Neoliberalism*; Weyland, "Theories of Policy Diffusion."
51. Brooks, "Interdependent and Domestic Foundations"; Madrid, *Retiring the State.*
52. Wolf, *Markets or Governments*, 43.
53. Pierson, *Dismantling the Welfare State?*

welfare state expansion, such as benefits and programs, the politics of coverage are quite different since expansion does not benefit the welfare state's constituencies, and may impose new costs on them.

Two political forces have received the most attention in comparative research on the expansion of the welfare state: state officials who take the initiative in welfare reform and class coalitions among potential welfare beneficiaries. State officials have initiated welfare reform in many countries in the absence of popular pressure.[54] International influence often affects state officials most directly. Top-down political mobilization has been another reason for state activism in nondemocratic regimes, using welfare as a tool to recruit or pacify popular constituencies. Economic development strategies have provided another compelling motive. Stephan Haggard and Robert Kaufman identify import-substitution industrialization strategies as providing a logic for including organized labor in the welfare state while excluding farmers. In contrast, they argue that export-led development strategies put a premium on limiting welfare for both workers and farmers in favor of investing in higher priorities, such as education. Finally, they argue that communist development strategies put the first priority for inclusion in the welfare state on workers, but the collectivization of agriculture then led to the incorporation of farmers at a later point.[55] This research shows that state officials often have their own motives for promoting welfare reform, but these reasons vary so widely that it is difficult to predict whether and how they might take action.

The role of class coalitions among potential beneficiaries in welfare reform has received much more attention from scholars, but their findings are sometimes contradictory. Peter Baldwin argues that farmers and urban middle classes played key roles in the expansion of coverage in Europe. Because each of these classes includes diverse subgroups with different interests in the welfare state, Baldwin maintains that they blunted and complicated the more clear-cut conflict between capital

---

54. See, for example, Malloy, *Politics of Social Security*; Ewig, *Second-Wave Neoliberalism*. Similar claims have been made for European welfare states, especially in the early years of founding welfare states. See Heclo, *Modern Social Politics*; Steinmetz, *Regulating the Social*.

55. Haggard and Kaufman, *Development, Democracy, and Welfare States*, 9–10.

and labor, facilitating the formation of coalitions for expansion.[56] The coalitions varied for different program designs, but they were all cross-class alliances of potential welfare beneficiaries. When workers joined forces with farmers, citizen pension programs were adopted. Reforms to expand coverage in citizen pension programs extended the politics of redistribution, but also created win-win bargains in which taxpayers gained coverage and beneficiaries suffered less stigma attached to being identified as poor. When workers pressed for welfare state programs on their own, social insurance programs were created instead. Reforms to expand coverage in social insurance programs also extended the politics of redistribution. But they added new layers of complexity on top of the conflict between workers and employers, including redistributive conflicts between welfare state insiders and outsiders as well as conflicts among diverse groups of welfare state outsiders.[57] Once organized labor and middle class employees forged alliances, the expansion of coverage in social insurance welfare states followed.

In contrast, scholars who examine class politics in developing countries have viewed internal divisions within social classes as obstacles rather than catalysts to welfare state expansion. In a study of inequality among the social insurance welfare states of Latin America, Carmelo Mesa-Lago argues that Latin America's internally divided social classes engaged in welfare politics as distinct occupational subgroups that functioned more like interest groups than class organizations.[58] Mesa-Lago maintains that this segmentation undermined coalitions, since powerful occupational subgroups sought inclusion in the welfare state on preferential terms, leaving less organized groups without the same kind of political leverage to fend for themselves. The contrast between Baldwin's and Mesa-Lago's analysis of internal class divisions suggests that more than the institutional structure of the welfare state is at stake: the broader context in which coalitions are formed is also important.

---

56. Baldwin, *Politics of Social Solidarity*, 289–90.
57. Because they are also targeted toward workers and financed in similar ways, provident funds and privatized pension programs expand in a similar manner to social insurance.
58. Mesa-Lago, *Social Security in Latin America*, 270.

Some scholars have focused on the economic context to reconcile these contradictory views on class divisions, arguing that high levels of inequality undermine the incentives for cross-class cooperation among potential welfare beneficiaries.[59] Others counter with the opposite argument that inequality promotes redistribution since the majority stands to gain from it, at least in democratic regimes. Due to data limitations, most empirical research to test these competing hypotheses has focused on the advanced industrial countries, showing that their broad welfare states do promote greater redistribution in response to rising inequality.[60] Whether rising inequality also affects the expansion of coverage in developing countries starting with much higher levels of inequality remains an open question.

Other scholars have focused on the political context for coalition formation, arguing that democratic regimes offer better prospects for expansive welfare reform.[61] Evelyne Huber and John Stephens' study of recent welfare coverage reforms in Latin America shows that their adoption was shaped by the length of time that democracy had been in place, combined with the election of leftist parties.[62] Similarly, in research on all three dimensions of welfare state expansion (benefits, programs, and coverage), Haggard and Kaufman argue that longer-lasting democracies are the most likely to expand their welfare states. Both studies exclude communist regimes, however, making it difficult to determine if limited coverage is a byproduct of the institutional structure of the regime or of the right-wing governments that were common in the regions studied.[63] Moreover, studies that examine the impact of a wider range of regime types on social spending have yielded ambiguous results.[64]

59. Baldwin, *Politics of Social Solidarity*, 296; Mares and Carnes, "Social Policy in Developing Countries," 108.

60. Kenworthy and Pontusson, "Rising Inequality"; Remington, *Politics of Inequality*, 21.

61. Haggard and Kaufman, *Development, Democracy, and Welfare States*; Huber and Stephens, *Democracy and the Left*.

62. Huber and Stephens, *Democracy and the Left*; Haggard and Kaufman, *Development, Democracy, and Welfare States*; Wong, *Healthy Democracies*.

63. This exclusion is surprising since Haggard and Kaufman include communist Eastern Europe in other aspects of the study, while Cuba, China, and other Asian communist countries are excluded entirely.

64. Ross, "Is Democracy Good for the Poor?"; Avelino, Brown, and Hunter, "Effect of Capital Mobility"; Kaufman and Segura-Ubiergo, "Globalization, Domestic

A closer look at the politics of welfare reform reveals considerable variation in the coalitions formed within these broad regime types. Examining the variation among democratic welfare states, for example, reveals that cross-class political coalitions are not always expansive; they can also lead to welfare state exclusion. Sometimes the exclusion is deliberate, as was the case for the alliance between organized labor and southern white landowners in the United States. This coalition pushed for the enactment of social security with exceptions for farm workers and domestic servants to exclude African American participation in the South.[65] At other times the exclusion is implicit, resting on assumptions that policy makers and ordinary citizens alike may not acknowledge or even realize. The assumption that men are breadwinners for their nuclear families served to exclude women from many welfare states or to incorporate them on unequal terms.[66] Democratically engineered exclusion suggests that simple assumptions about economic interests in the welfare state and coalition formation can be misleading.

 Taken together, this research suggests that state officials and social forces play important roles in welfare reform. But more work needs to be done on welfare politics in different contexts before reliable generalizations can be drawn. In that effort, shifting the level of analysis from broadly defined regime types to focus on specific policy-making institutions offers a way to develop mid-level generalizations by spotlighting the interactions between state officials and social forces. Political coalitions are often institutionalized in ways that simultaneously structure and limit popular access to the policy-making process. Furthermore, many welfare state programs around the world have been formally established as tripartite corporatist institutions administered jointly by workers, employers, and government officials. Whether operating in democratic regimes open to the formation of new coalitions or authoritarian regimes that limit them, corporatist welfare programs institutionalize coalitions for welfare reform.

Politics, and Social Spending"; Mulligan et al., "Do Democracies Have Different Public Policies?"

65. Quadagno, *Color of Welfare*.

66. Gordon, ed., *Women, the State, and Welfare*; Skocpol, *Protecting Soldiers and Mothers*; Ewig, *Second-Wave Neoliberalism*.

Research on the politics of expanding coverage shows that these reforms are contentious because they extend the politics of redistribution, recapitulating and complicating some of the same struggles that surrounded the founding of the welfare state. Both government officials and cross-class coalitions can play important roles in welfare reform. The economic, political, and institutional context shapes the politics of welfare reform, but research on coverage is too preliminary to provide much guidance on which factors are most important.

## A New Analytical Framework

Bringing together these three areas of research that address welfare coverage directly or tangentially offers a few basic conclusions. First, welfare reform is a prerequisite for a broad welfare state. Economic growth, exposure to international policy advice, and the context for welfare politics seem to shape the adoption of these reforms, but little is known about which variables are most important, or how they influence the politics of state officials and potential welfare beneficiaries. Given the preliminary nature of these findings, the first step is to develop an analytical framework to guide further research.

### THE CONTEXT FOR WELFARE REFORM

Because policy decisions are so fundamental to the politics of welfare coverage, *international influence* on those choices is an important element in the context for welfare reform. International influence on the choice of founding legislation for the welfare state can leave a lasting legacy on welfare politics. After that point, the diffusion of knowledge about the importance of reform in expanding coverage as well as the appropriate policies to achieve it are preconditions for the expansion of coverage.

Another important element in the context for welfare reform is the *program design* of the founding welfare state legislation, which shapes the expansion of coverage by defining different institutional paths of development. Coverage in citizen pension welfare states expands vertically, from the poor to all citizens. Reforms to expand coverage in citizen pension programs extend the politics of redistribution between taxpayers and beneficiaries, but they can also create win-win bargains in which both sides gain from reform. In contrast, social insurance expands horizontally to workers in different sectors of the economy and then ultimately to people outside it.[67] Reforms to expand coverage in social insurance programs also extend the politics of redistribution. But they add new lines of conflict beyond the struggle between workers and employers, including redistributive conflicts between welfare state insiders and outsiders as well as conflicts among diverse groups of welfare state outsiders.

Once the core welfare state legislation is in place, economic and political conditions also shape the politics of welfare reform. The *level of economic development* shapes welfare state expansion through the size and growth of the formal sector and government revenues. Ample resources ease the politics of redistribution, lowering the stakes in the conflict and facilitating policies to buy off political opposition. There does not seem to be a threshold of economic development necessary for achieving broad welfare coverage, but the small number of broad welfare states in the developing world suggests that low levels of economic development make expansion more difficult.

Political institutions can also shape the mobilization and incorporation of social groups in the policy-making process. Different patterns of *preferential incorporation* can promote or hinder the expansion of coverage. Preferential incorporation of political opponents of the welfare state can limit its expansion. Similarly, if only a few of the social groups that could benefit from the welfare state are organized and incorporated into the political arena, then the privileged groups who become welfare state insiders first may use their leverage to prevent redistribution to outsiders.

---

67. Because they are also targeted toward workers and financed in similar ways, provident funds and privatized pension programs expand in a similar manner to social insurance.

## THE DYNAMICS OF WELFARE REFORM

Within this context, the dynamics of welfare reform are shaped by more immediate causes. Political pressure for expansion can come from two sources: state and society. Top-down pressure for welfare reform stems from multiple motives, such as international influence, economic development policy, and political mobilization strategies. As a result, it is impossible to predict from the outside whether state officials will promote welfare reform or whether those reforms will expand or restrict population coverage. Instead, empirical research is necessary to determine the direction and the strength of state-led reform efforts.

Bottom-up pressure for the expansion of the welfare state is more consistent and easier to predict because potential welfare beneficiaries have a clear economic motive with long-term consequences. Cross-class coalitions of potential welfare beneficiaries are more likely to expand coverage, while the absence of coalitions or the exclusion of potential beneficiaries are likely to inhibit it. But whether these potential beneficiaries perceive their interests and have the power to act on them is an open question. Although theorists often assume that workers and other popular social classes have shared goals in welfare reform, in reality there has been tremendous variation in whether and how these groups perceive their interests and their common ground. As with state actors, empirical research is necessary to understand the mobilization of social groups, their perception of their interests, and the formation of coalitions for welfare reform.

In nondemocratic regimes that establish corporatism and other limited forms of political participation, top-down and bottom-up pressures meet in these political institutions. Top-down mobilization of social forces defines political actors and the arenas they can operate within. Members of these social groups can accept or reject the role offered to them, but they have little leverage to define the role themselves. In these contexts, political regimes are not simply structures that shape the conditions for coalition formation, they also define the political actors who operate within institutions, making them dynamic elements of the reform process itself.

Significant expansion of coverage is most likely when both top-down and bottom-up pressures promote it. In addition to the strength of reform pressures, the *political incorporation* of potential welfare beneficiaries such as farmers, the middle classes, and the urban poor needs to be taken into account. Expansive reforms are more likely if welfare state outsiders are given equal or preferential access to the policy-making process. A broad cross-class coalition of organized social groups actively pressing for inclusion is most likely to overcome political opposition and expand coverage. Anything short of that is likely to leave groups behind: internal divisions, disorganization, and discrimination are some of the political obstacles that can block the expansion of coverage.

This model of the politics of coverage predicts that there are multiple routes to broad welfare states, none of which is easy or straightforward to traverse. Social forces provide the most consistent and strongest pressure to expand coverage, but only if they perceive their interests in the welfare state, are mobilized as a political group, and are incorporated into the political arena. With that foundation in place, they can form coalitions to change welfare coverage. State actors can play an important role in shaping these political coalitions as well as promoting welfare reform for their own reasons. But top-down forces for expansion can prove to be weak or fickle on their own if they are not accountable to social forces providing bottom-up pressure for inclusion. The best chance for expanding coverage is when both forces are pushing in the same direction.

Since research on the expansion of coverage is limited, additional variables may be important, but we do not know enough yet to understand how they affect welfare politics. State capacity is inherently important in welfare programs, but we do not know which capacities or how they shape program development. The structure of economic inequality might also affect the politics of welfare reform, although it is not clear whether high levels of inequality help or hurt the expansion of coverage.

## Research Strategy

In an era of war and revolution, China's domestic politics provides a laboratory of sorts for analyzing the interaction of different political and economic factors in the development of the welfare state. Single-country case studies have been justly criticized for failing to provide structural variation, focusing attention on immediate, short-term causes at the expense of more fundamental but slow-moving changes. Revolutionary China, however, presents considerable structural variation in a very short period of time. These changing conditions provide a way to narrow the focus of analysis to a few key variables while holding constant the other social, historical, and cultural differences that vex cross-national comparisons.

The Chinese case is also useful for exploratory research on the development of narrow welfare states. China is exceptional in many ways, including its vast size, distinctive culture, and unusually radical politics. But in other ways China is a typical developing country, with a low level of economic development throughout the postwar period. Moreover, China's politics have been nondemocratic and marked by considerable political instability. These economic and political conditions make China more similar to the majority of countries in the world than the advanced industrial countries that provide the basis for most theories of the welfare state.

Moreover, conditions in China seemed favorable for welfare state expansion. China has been open to international influence from the early twentieth century onward. Both the Nationalist (KMT) and Communist (CCP) parties pursued ambitious state-building agendas and economic development strategies. The Communists in particular were committed to improving the welfare of the people and creating a more egalitarian society, and their expropriation of the capitalist class in the mid-1950s eliminated one of the most powerful opponents of welfare state expansion. Finally, China's record of economic growth in the Maoist period was favorable for gradual expansion of the welfare state. Even considering the dislocations of war and the Great Leap Forward, China's average growth rates in the postwar period matched those of the advanced industrial countries in Western Europe in the period when they achieved broad coverage.[68]

These advantages make China a critical test case for the study of the constraints that limit the reach of the welfare state in the developing world. If the Chinese failed to expand welfare coverage with active state leadership, relatively good economic growth, and a revolution that eliminated many sources of political opposition to redistribution, then perhaps the constraints on the expansion of the welfare state in the developing world are more fundamental than studies of the advanced industrial countries have led us to believe.

THE CONTEXT FOR WELFARE REFORM IN CHINA

To understand the conditions that shaped China's welfare reforms to expand coverage, the first step is to place China in the context of the globalization of welfare state policies, since both the original welfare programs and the policy goals of universal coverage were imported to China from Europe and the Soviet Union. International influence helped to define the parameters and the content of Chinese policy debates.

The founding of the Chinese welfare state also defined the domestic context in which China's reform attempts were carried out. The critical decision on program design in the initial labor insurance regulations defined the longest-lasting constraint on the development of China's welfare state. Why did Chinese policy makers choose social insurance over citizen pensions or some other program design?

In addition to the institutional structure of the welfare state, the timing of this social insurance initiative also shaped the context for welfare reform. China's low level of economic development in the early 1950s ensured that economic constraints on welfare reform would be significant. Moreover, the Communist revolution was still under way

---

68. China averaged an annual growth rate of 2.86 percent in per capita GDP from 1950 to 1973, faster than the U.S. average of 2.45 percent in the same period. Although this was lower than Western Europe's postwar growth rates (4.08 percent), China's rate was much higher than prewar Western European growth rates, which averaged 0.76 percent from 1913 to 1950. Maddison, *World Economy*, 265.

and the process of regime change unfinished. Why was the Chinese welfare state founded under such difficult economic and political conditions? Most important, what legacy did these decisions leave for the welfare state reformers who followed in their footsteps?

A comparison of the Nationalist and Communist regimes during and after the Chinese Civil War (1946–49) provides a way to assess the impact of challenging economic and political conditions on the founding of the welfare state. Both political parties faced dismal economic conditions in this period of unending warfare, starting with the Second Sino-Japanese War (1937–45) and followed by the Chinese Civil War and the Korean War (1950–53). Even as they fought those wars, rebuilt the state, and transformed their political institutions, each party tried to implement major new welfare programs for workers. Although the Nationalist welfare programs were not as ambitious as the Communists' labor insurance program, they targeted the same groups and provide a baseline for comparison.

Bottom-up demand for welfare was relatively low in this period, despite the dislocation and suffering caused by war. For the most part, Chinese workers had never heard of the kinds of welfare policies that policy makers were advocating. Moreover, there were no precedents of government welfare programs to create any expectation that the state might provide a solution to their problems.

Despite the revolutionary struggle between the Communists and the Nationalists, there were also some fundamental similarities between their political strategies in this period. Both parties sought to incorporate capitalists and workers into a cross-class, corporatist regime. In addition, they reached out to mobilize one key group among the urban poor: unemployed industrial workers, who were incorporated into the official labor unions in this period. Within these broadly similar strategies, however, the Nationalists gave capitalists more policy-making power in corporatist institutions. In contrast, the Communists limited capitalists' scope of action in welfare politics and instead gave labor preferential access (table I.1).

Comparing welfare politics under these different regimes offers a way to assess whether the preferential incorporation of capital and labor shaped the founding of the welfare state. It also provides an

*Table I.1.* Conditions Shaping the Founding of the Chinese Welfare State

|  | KMT 1945–49 | CCP 1949–51 |
|---|---|---|
| Political conditions | civil war | civil war and Korean War |
| Level of development | low | low |
| Political regime | state corporatist | communist corporatist |
| Top-down pressure | high | high |
| Bottom-up demand for welfare | low | low |
| Preferential incorporation | capitalists | labor |

opportunity to evaluate whether the enormous political and economic challenges that both parties faced during the war left any long-lasting legacies for the Chinese welfare state. Did the sharp reversal in the sources of international influence on Chinese policy makers have an impact? Did the constraints imposed by such a poor economy limit the new welfare state? Did the weakness of bottom-up demand for welfare make the new program fragile?

THE DYNAMICS OF WELFARE REFORM IN CHINA

Cross-regime comparisons between the KMT and the CCP become more problematic after the Civil War and the Nationalist retreat to Taiwan, given the difference in scale and resources between Taiwan and the mainland. But the urban revolution and the sheer variety of different economic development strategies tried in the 1950s provide wide variation in economic and political conditions in mainland China alone. At least three major efforts to expand the Chinese welfare state were attempted in the 1950s, each tied to a different economic development strategy: first, a Stalinist industrialization strategy; second, a Chinese adaptation of this approach featuring greater fiscal austerity; and, third, a Maoist strategy that sought to accelerate industrialization even further. Because of these changing development strategies, top-down pressure for welfare reform was high through most of the 1950s, although there was a brief phase of short-term restraint in the mid-1950s.

Political conditions also changed quickly in the 1950s. Bottom-up demand for welfare spiked soon after the implementation of the welfare state, as workers and the urban poor began to see and understand the value of the new benefits it offered. But the biggest changes stemmed from the way these classes were incorporated into the political arena. Capitalists became the targets of political campaigns in the early 1950s, and then the urban revolution in 1956 expropriated the capitalist class and ended the earlier experiments in cross-class corporatism. The urban poor also experienced dramatic changes in political status in the 1950s. The unemployed went from being incorporated into the labor unions, to being forced out, to being incorporated into the urban communes a few years later. Examining how these changes affected the leverage of welfare state proponents and opponents provides a starting point for analyzing the politics of welfare (table I.2).

The revolution also provides an opportunity to examine how inequality affected the formation of cross-class coalitions for the expansion of coverage. In the early 1950s, Chinese society was extremely unequal, even if war had eroded some of the wealth of China's capitalists. The socialization of industry in the mid-1950s redistributed wealth and standardized wages, making Chinese urban society among the most egalitarian in the world. Similarly, rapid gains in state capacity in the 1950s provide a way to assess that factor's impact on the development of the Chinese welfare state.

*Table I.2.* Conditions Shaping the Expansion of Welfare Coverage

|  | *Soviet transitional reforms 1952–54* | *Chinese austerity reforms 1955–57* | *Maoist commune reforms 1958–62* |
|---|---|---|---|
| Top-down pressure | high | mixed | very high |
| Political incorporation | labor and urban poor in equal coalition | preferential access for labor; urban poor excluded | labor and urban poor in unequal coalition |
| Predicted outcome | major expansion | no expansion | minor expansion |

## A SHANGHAI CASE STUDY

A local case study is a first step toward understanding the evolution of the Chinese welfare state. [69] Although power was highly centralized in this period, the impact of social forces was felt at the local level. Capitalists, workers, and the urban poor had little or no access to the policy-making process that took place within the Nationalist and Communist parties, both of which were Leninist political parties that dominated the state apparatus. People outside the parties interacted with each other and the state at the grass roots, where they could have an impact on the implementation of new programs and their subsequent administration. Both individually and collectively, people had the power to cooperate with policies they supported and the power to resist policies they opposed. Another reason for focusing on grassroots politics stems from the structure of the Chinese welfare state. Labor insurance was so decentralized that one scholar coined the apt term "mini-welfare state" to describe the Chinese workplace welfare system. [70] Because of this, the factory floor was an important arena for welfare politics. Moving one level up from the factory to the city as the unit of analysis captures the politics of welfare on the streets as well as within the workplace.

Shanghai was chosen not because it is representative of Chinese cities—it most definitely is not. Instead, Shanghai offers the advantage of being critically important, both economically and politically. As China's premier industrial city, Shanghai was home to the country's largest working class, wealthiest businessmen, and most ambitious political leaders. Because the city was so important to the national economy and its revenues were a key pillar of the national state, implementing major policy initiatives in Shanghai had to be a high priority for any political regime. If the party-state could not achieve its stated objectives in Shanghai, then either the policy was only a propaganda exercise or the sources of opposition to the policy within the city were too powerful to overcome. Shanghai should therefore be considered a "most likely case" rather than a typical Chinese city. [71]

69. Snyder, "Scaling Down."
70. Gu, "Dismantling the Chinese Mini-Welfare State?"
71. Eckstein, "Case Study and Theory."

Because this is an urban case study, it focuses on urban inequality rather than the much deeper urban-rural gap. Unemployed workers stand in for the much larger category of the urban poor who were excluded from labor insurance. But unemployed workers were actually better off than the rest of the urban poor, and much better off than their rural counterparts because so many different kinds of welfare programs for the unemployed were tried in the 1940s and 1950s. These programs included emergency relief, long-term relief, job training, political education, public works employment, and job placement services. Conflicts between welfare state insiders and outsiders in this context were defined by different levels of privilege rather than complete inclusion or exclusion.

## Preview of the Argument

Political struggles between reformers, workers, and welfare state outsiders defined the narrow reach of China's welfare state. Sustained international influence shaped the founding of the Chinese welfare state as well as its reform. Strong state leadership and enthusiasm for the welfare state among workers and the urban poor compelled repeated attempts at welfare reform in the 1950s. But the challenging constraints posed by China's low level of economic development and the high cost of expanding social insurance coverage proved to be too difficult to overcome.

The urban revolution and China's radical experiments with policies to expand coverage help identify some of the most important political obstacles to achieving a broad welfare state. Labor's preferential incorporation into political coalitions for welfare reform turned into one obstacle. The lack of state capacity to regulate the expansion of the welfare state to ensure its economic viability proved to be another.

This study shows that labor plays a contradictory role in the formation of welfare states. Preferential incorporation of labor ahead of other social classes, especially capital, facilitates the founding of the welfare state. But the preferential incorporation of labor can pose an obstacle to the expansion of welfare coverage after that point. Slow job growth or budget cuts that make people concerned about protecting their interests in a time of scarcity can lead to politics of rationing. In this context, the redistributive struggle between welfare state insiders and outsiders over who gets welfare protection first and who is forced to wait is heightened, taking on the dynamic of a zero-sum struggle. Once the politics of rationing develops, labor uses its extra leverage in the policy-making process to direct new resources to benefit welfare state insiders rather than to extend coverage to new groups. Each gain made by labor in this context only increases the gap between welfare state insiders and outsiders, and further entrenches the politics of rationing. This vicious cycle may produce stable narrow welfare states in which the expansion of coverage stalls indefinitely, even as spending continues to escalate.

But the Chinese case also shows that the politics of rationing can undermine the sustainability of the welfare state. The key state capacity required for the successful expansion of welfare coverage is the ability to regulate the supply and demand for welfare. Soft budget constraints can be destabilizing in a context of scarcity, opening up opportunities for welfare state insiders and outsiders alike to press for rapid, unsustainable growth of the welfare state. The end result of this dynamic can be the bankruptcy of the welfare state. The failure to expand coverage can stem from trying too hard as much as from not trying hard enough.

PART I

*The Politics of Founding China's Welfare State*

## CHAPTER I

# *China's Place in the Globalization of the Welfare State, 1880s–1980s*

International influence on the Chinese welfare state was profound. Both social insurance and universal coverage were European inventions, and their globalization defined the social agendas of Chinese reformers and revolutionaries alike. But as European ideas and global policy debates were translated by Chinese intellectuals and government officials for a domestic audience, they were also transformed in the process.

Policy diffusion is usually measured using the year a new policy is adopted in new legislation, compressing the spread of knowledge and the entire policy-making process into the moment they both culminate in success. But in the Chinese case, this process of diffusion took decades. Information about welfare policy reached China by the 1920s, but welfare state legislation was not adopted for nearly thirty years. As if to make up for lost time, reforms to expand population coverage of the nascent Chinese welfare state began almost immediately afterward. Given the long gap between the arrival of these ideas and the adoption of the policies to enact them, this chapter will focus primarily on the diffusion of knowledge, leaving analysis of China's adoption of these policies to later chapters.

The history of the welfare state began in northern Europe in the 1880s. Its diffusion over the next century was an unusually successful

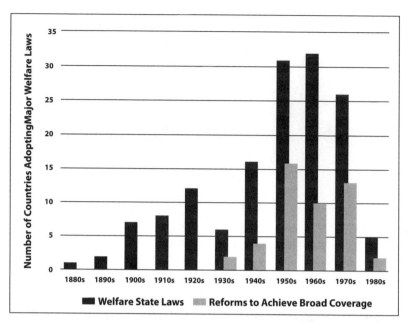

*Figure 1.1.* Welfare Legislation around the World, 1880s–1980s. *Sources:* Flora, *Growth to Limits*; SSA, *Social Security Programs 1961*; SSA, *Social Security Programs 1979*; SSA, *Social Security Programs 1999*; SSB, *Outline of Foreign Social Insurance.*

example of policy globalization. More than 90 percent of the countries in the world had adopted welfare state legislation by the 1980s.[1] China's adoption of labor insurance regulations in 1951 places it within the global peak of welfare state adoption in the 1950s and 1960s, when most developing countries founded their welfare states (fig. 1.1). During the sixty-year period it took for the policy to travel from Germany to

1.  Orenstein, *Privatizing Pensions*, 19–24; SSA, *Social Security Programs 1999*. Other scholars have used occupational injury programs to trace the diffusion of welfare state legislation because they were typically the first programs adopted (see Collier and Messick, "Prerequisites vs. Diffusion"). But because the financial and administrative requirements of those programs were minor in comparison to the other social insurance programs, they required much less commitment. Furthermore, in many developing countries, including China, there was a long gap in adoption between the first occupational injury program and the rest of the social insurance programs that composed the welfare state. See Orenstein, *Privatizing Pensions,* for a similar approach.

China, two processes of diffusion can be distinguished: an initial European process of diffusion from the 1890s through the 1910s, followed by a more global process that began in the 1920s after the institutionalization of new conduits for policy dissemination. It was the second process of global diffusion that spread detailed knowledge of welfare state policies to an educated public in China.

The first welfare reforms to achieve universal population coverage emerged in the mid-1930s in response to the crisis of the Great Depression. The idea of universal welfare states spread much faster than knowledge of the original welfare state policies, reaching almost every country in the world in the 1940s. But policies to achieve broad or universal coverage did not spread nearly as far after that point. Although the majority of countries with welfare state legislation in place have adopted reforms to expand population coverage, only one-third tried to achieve broad or universal coverage in the first century of the welfare state. China was part of the minority of ambitious welfare state reformers, and its expansive welfare reforms adopted in the 1950s also coincided with the global peak of reforms to achieve broad or universal coverage.

This chapter traces the diffusion of knowledge about these policies from the European home of the welfare state to China, starting with the first Eurocentric period of diffusion from the 1880s to the 1910s, followed by the globalization of welfare policy that began in the 1920s and 1930s. This diffusion reached a turning point during the Second World War, and then peaked during the Cold War from the late 1940s through the 1980s. China was drawn into the globalization of these policies from the 1920s onward. The impact of international influence on Chinese welfare politics was decisive: setting the policy agenda and at the same time narrowing the scope of debate.

## Early Diffusion of Welfare State Policies, 1880s–1910s

The diffusion of the welfare state began almost immediately after its invention. Germany and Denmark pioneered the two main kinds of income maintenance programs for the elderly that formed the core of the modern welfare state. Germany adopted social insurance for the elderly in 1889, and Denmark followed with citizen pensions for poor elders in 1891. From those starting points, welfare state legislation spread to neighboring countries in Europe and to European settler colonies in the Americas and Australasia. At the same time, countries such as France experimented with alternative policies, such as providing government subsidies to encourage voluntary insurance and mutual aid societies.[2] This early period in the diffusion of the welfare state was characterized by extensive experimentation and rapid diffusion of knowledge, followed by more gradual adoption of different welfare state programs according to rhythms set by domestic politics.

Informal networks among social policy experts along with inspection tours, international conferences, and exhibitions helped to spread knowledge about these early welfare state programs in Europe and its settler colonies.[3] The networks of policy experts in this early period were overlapping and uneven, including some countries but not others. For example, when British policy makers debated the United Kingdom's first income maintenance programs for the elderly in 1908, there was extensive consideration of the Danish and New Zealand citizen pension programs but almost no discussion of Germany's social insurance system, which was deemed "un-British" at the time.[4]

Demonstration effects among countries with extensive interaction led to the diffusion of different program designs within Europe. Social insurance spread from its home in Germany across most of continental Europe, while citizen pensions spread from Denmark to the rest of Scandinavia, Britain, and Australasia.[5] Initially, citizen pensions were particularly attractive to countries where a large proportion of the workforce was self-employed, such as the predominantly agricultural economies of Scandinavia and Australasia. But this fit between program design and economic structure was not an obstacle to the adoption of citizen pensions in the United Kingdom despite its highly

2. Rodgers, *Atlantic Crossings*, 227.
3. Ibid., 60–61; Heclo, *Modern Social Politics*, 179–81.
4. Rodgers, *Atlantic Crossings*, 230.
5. ILO, "ILO and Social Insurance," 781; SSA, *Social Security Programs 1961*.

industrial economy. Similarly, poor agricultural countries in Central Europe such as Romania adopted social insurance. [6] These patterns suggest that sources of international influence were more decisive in shaping policy choices than the fit between economic structure and program design.

Sweden provides a fairly typical example of early European patterns of diffusion. The spread of policy ideas to Sweden predated the first welfare state pioneers, since Swedish reformers were part of international policy circles that also included their counterparts in Germany and Denmark in the 1870s and 1880s.[7] Swedish legislators first began researching and debating welfare state proposals in formal study commissions in 1884, when they evaluated Germany's first social insurance programs.[8] After the resulting proposal failed to win passage, Swedish welfare reformers began studying the Danish alternative. Swedish study commissions not only carried out detailed investigations of the early programs, they also gathered the statistical data necessary for actuarial estimates of the long-term cost of both program designs for the Swedish population. Legislators debated new proposals in 1895, 1898, 1905, and 1907 before a bill finally passed in 1913.[9] The key change that led to the success of the 1913 proposal was the electoral reform in 1907–1909 that fully democratized Sweden's constitutional monarchy. The prospect of forging a majority coalition in parliament encouraged labor unions to give up their preference for social insurance to compromise with farmers' associations on a new citizen pension program with supplemental contributory insurance.[10]

Sweden's pattern of immediate diffusion of policy knowledge followed by nearly thirty years of research, debate, and negotiations over welfare state legislation was lengthier than many of its European neighbors, but the process was similar elsewhere. Experts involved in European research and policy debates helped to spread the ideas, but electoral and interest-group politics shaped the timing of their

6. ILO, "ILO and Social Insurance," 781.
7. Heclo, *Modern Social Politics*, 179–81.
8. Baldwin, *Politics of Social Solidarity*, 85; Heclo, *Modern Social Politics*, 181.
9. Baldwin, *Politics of Social Solidarity*, 87–88.
10. Ibid., 90–91.

adoption. Even in monarchies such as Sweden and Germany, gradual democratization and the incorporation of workers and farmers into politics provided the fuel that kept policy debates active. Democratization also allowed the formation of voluntary associations, including new class organizations, professional associations, nonprofit mutual aid associations, and religious charities. These groups jockeyed to advance their interests in debates about whether welfare state legislation should be adopted, what kind, and involving how much redistribution.

This early Eurocentric period of welfare state diffusion took place during the peak of European imperialism, although the welfare pioneers were not themselves major world powers. This high point of European power coincided with the precipitous decline of the Chinese empire. China's descent began in the mid-nineteenth century with the imposition of semicolonialism after the Opium Wars and then accelerated in the face of large-scale peasant rebellions that severely weakened China's imperial regime. By the 1890s, moreover, the Chinese state faced a new and much closer threat from a modernized and aggressive Japanese military. China's loss in the First Sino-Japanese War in 1895 precipitated a crisis within the monarchy and stimulated nationalist political reform movements outside of it. A political revolution in 1911 succeeded in bringing down the imperial regime but failed to establish a viable new central government. After briefly wavering between democracy and military rule, China devolved into the chaos of regional warlordism in the 1910s.

European imperialism was not a conduit for information about welfare policy innovations; European colonial bureaucracies deemed the colonies too poor for modern European social policies.[11] Semicolonialism in China had a similar effect, since the colonial governments in China's treaty port concessions were conservative in the realm of social policy. Although their policies for workhouses, policing, and public health were influential in China, the foreign concessions did not turn out to be channels for European welfare innovations.[12]

---

11. Havinden and Meredith, *Colonialism and Development*, 91, 198–204. The British Empire, for example, did not create a welfare division in the Colonial Office until 1937 or adopt any colonial welfare legislation until 1940.

12. Chen, *Guilty of Indigence*; Rogaski, *Hygienic Modernity*.

Even in the face of political turmoil and semicolonialism, the interest of Chinese intellectuals in Western political, economic, and social policy did not flag. The central Chinese government was too weak after the fall of the imperial regime to sponsor formal study commissions to go to Europe or North America, but this lack of official leadership was more than made up for by the diversity of individual and institutional initiatives that surged across China in the wake of its political crises.[13] Spearheaded by individual scholars who studied abroad and buttressed by the support of new Chinese institutions such as publishing houses and universities, these diverse efforts led to the collection of foreign-language books in Chinese libraries and translation projects to make key texts from Europe, North America, and Japan accessible in Chinese.[14] These efforts laid the foundation for the diffusion of knowledge about European welfare policy.

## *The Globalization of Welfare State Policies, 1920s–1930s*

Knowledge about welfare policies spread more widely and deeply around the world in the 1920s and 1930s. In addition to the ongoing process of diffusion among countries with extensive interaction, the end of the First World War accelerated and internationalized the process. The Russian Revolution in 1917 and the global strike wave in 1919 pushed "the social question" to the top of the political agenda in many countries around the world. Another impetus for diffusion was the creation of the International Labour Organization (ILO). Founded in 1919 with an explicit mandate to standardize social policy and working conditions worldwide, this new international organization provided a centralized, institutionalized mechanism for diffusing information and expertise on social policy.

13. Lee and Nathan, "Beginnings of Mass Culture."
14. Chiang, *Social Engineering*; Reed, *Gutenberg in Shanghai*. For a wide-ranging bibliography of English-language texts on social policy available in China, see Lamson, *Social Pathology*. It lists many books on welfare policy published in the 1900s and 1910s from the United States and the United Kingdom. (My thanks to Rudolf Wagner for recommending this source.)

From the founding of the ILO, the organization's staff included a Social Insurance Division to carry out research and provide technical advice to member countries.[15] The economists who staffed this office in the 1920s quickly developed an informal but strong preference for social insurance, which they viewed as better at preserving incentives to work and save.[16] This informal position was soon reinforced by the first international standards for old-age pension programs in 1933. These welfare state conventions were adopted after seven years of debate at the ILO's annual labor conferences, which essentially marked the end of the European debates over program design.[17] The higher benefits and greater security of social insurance won out over the broader reach and more effective safety net of citizen pensions. The ILO also endorsed a comprehensive set of programs for work injury, old age, disability, survivors, and health insurance.[18]

Even if the debate on program design for the welfare state was closed in Europe, new innovations in welfare policy continued to emerge. First Sweden in 1935 and then New Zealand in 1938 eliminated the means test that limited enrollment to the poorest members of society, making their old-age pension programs a universal right of citizenship.[19] During the Great Depression, news about these policy innovations spread much farther than the limited group of countries with citizen pensions similar to the Swedish and New Zealand programs. For example, the first American ILO Regional Labor Conference held in Chile in 1936 discussed these reforms and endorsed the principle that social insurance should be extended to the entire workforce, including the self-employed. However, the policies to achieve this goal in the very different program structure of Latin America's social insurance systems were not specified.[20]

15. ILO, *ILO and Social Insurance*, 15.

16. Endres and Fleming, *International Organizations and the Analysis of Economic Policy*, 136–37.

17. ILO, *ILO and Social Insurance*, 18; ILO, "Sixteenth Session"; ILO, "Seventeenth Session."

18. Conventions on Workmen's Compensation (1925), Health Insurance (1927), Old Age (1933), Disability (1933), and Survivors Benefits (1933) were all passed. For the policy on old age pensions, see ILO, NORMLEX Database, Convention No. 35.

19. Castles, ed., "Working Class and Welfare," 25–26.

20. Cohen, "First Inter-American Conference on Social Security," 6–8.

Comparative research shows that participation in ILO conferences and other activities increased the likelihood of welfare policy adoption.[21] The pace of welfare state adoption accelerated in the 1920s and the 1930s, reaching most of Europe and making significant headway in the Americas. Even with a five-year hiatus of welfare program adoptions in the depths of the Great Depression in the late 1920s and early 1930s, twice as many countries founded a welfare state in the interwar period than during the first thirty years of the welfare state. Even more striking was the policy convergence in this period, as social insurance became the overwhelming favorite in program design.[22]

Although it was dominated by Europeans, the ILO helped to spread detailed knowledge about welfare state policies far beyond Europe and its settler colonies. The ILO set lower labor standards for colonies and non-Western countries (labeled "special countries" by the ILO), but participation at the annual ILO labor conferences also provided a direct source of information about European policies for all members.[23] For example, Indian reformers first learned about social insurance from their delegates at the ILO rather than from the British Colonial Office. India's first welfare legislation, the Indian Workers' Compensation Act, was adopted in 1923 in response to the first ILO convention on work injury programs.[24] The Indian colonial government also began considering a social insurance program for health care in 1928, following the policy debates at the annual ILO labor conference in 1927 (and ignoring the standards for special countries). But the Indian health care proposal was shelved by the colonial authorities, who saw the problems in collecting data to plan for the program as an indication that India lacked the economic and political conditions necessary to carry out the program.[25]

China had an official role in the ILO, but the weakness of the Chinese central government limited its impact for much of the 1920s. As a minor participant in the First World War on the French and British

21. Usui, "Welfare State Development," 269; Strang and Chang, "ILO and the Welfare State," 235–62.
22. Dixon, *Social Security in Global Perspective*, 124; SSA, *Social Security Program 1961*.
23. Ayusawa, *International Labor Legislation*, 219–20.
24. Agarwala, "Social Security Movement in India," 569.
25. Ibid., 573.

side, China was signatory to the Versailles Peace Treaty in 1919 and a founding member of the new international organization created by the peace treaty. But because China could afford only to send its diplomats stationed in Europe to the annual ILO labor conference in Geneva, the interaction was limited at that point.

By the late 1920s, this chaotic period of semicolonialism and warlord rule in China had begun to stabilize. The Nationalist and Communist parties forged an alliance in the mid-1920s to defeat the warlords and reunify the country. Although the alliance fell apart in a bloody purge of the Communists in 1927, the Nationalist Party succeeded in defeating the warlords to reestablish an effective central government in a new national capital in Nanjing in 1928. As a result, political and economic conditions in China were improving for the first time in generations just when the Great Depression led to the collapse of financial markets and international trade in the rest of the world.

Despite the global economic crisis, the consolidation of a new central government in China accelerated the importation of foreign ideas. The new Nationalist government sponsored large-scale translation and publication projects on various aspects of public policy, including welfare policy.[26] In addition, China's relationship with the ILO grew much closer. The director of the ILO, Albert Thomas, toured China's main industrial centers in 1928 and urged the new government to establish basic labor standards and a labor inspection system.[27] The KMT responded to this advice quickly, given that its hold on power was still tentative. One response was to begin sending full delegations to the annual international labour conference in 1929. Although the new employer and labor delegates were party officials rather than independent representatives as stipulated in ILO conventions, the new KMT delegations provided much more effective communication between Geneva and Nanjing in the 1930s.

The Nationalist government sought a seat on the ILO's governing board and pressed the ILO to establish a Correspondent's Office in

26. For some examples from two government-sponsored translation projects, see Guomin zhengfu, *Shehui baoxian*, a translation of part of Commons and Andrews, *Principles of Labor Legislation*; Horie, *Shiye wenti*.
27. Thomas, À *la recontre*.

China to supplement the other Asian regional offices. Although the Chinese delegates failed to win election to the ILO governing body, they did succeed in getting the ILO to open an office in Nanjing in 1930. The office collected data on Chinese labor conditions, published reports and journals in Chinese, and provided technical assistance to the Nationalist government on an ongoing basis.[28]

By the 1920s and 1930s, academic research and participation in the ILO provided detailed knowledge about welfare policies and programs around the world to a small, highly educated public in China. University professors, political activists, and government officials were actively debating welfare state policy and its application to China. In addition to revealing their sources of information about the welfare state, their publications provide a window into their policy preferences. As conduits for the importation of welfare state ideas, these intellectuals and government officials played a key role in the diffusion process by establishing the framework for Chinese domestic policy debates.

## TRANSLATING INTERNATIONAL WELFARE DEBATES FOR A CHINESE AUDIENCE

One common theme in this policy literature is strong advocacy for establishing a welfare state in China. In addition to describing the welfare policies of the advanced industrial countries, many Chinese authors went further to make the misleading claim that the welfare state was universal in the Western world by the 1920s.[29] For example, Ma Chaojun, a KMT labor official who published a major volume on labor and social policy, praised the United States for having the most comprehensive labor insurance program among the advanced industrial countries, even though the United States was considered a welfare state laggard in Europe.[30] This portrayal of welfare states as standard in the Western world set up the contrast to China, which these authors described as backward not only for failing to establish a welfare state, but also for lacking any sustained news coverage or popular debate over welfare policy.

28. Wagner, *Labor Legislation*, 182.
29. Ma Chaojun, *Zhongguo laogong wenti*, 95; Li Baosen, *Laodong baoxian fa ABC*, 7.
30. Ma Chaojun, *Zhongguo laogong wenti*, 96.

Chinese authors portrayed the welfare state as an integral part of an industrial economy, thereby providing another important reason for its adoption in China as it industrialized.[31] For example, Fudan University professor Lu Zhushu described labor insurance as serving the interests of all involved: protecting workers from the risk of impoverishment, helping employers maintain productivity, and promoting economic growth for the larger society.[32] In their books on labor policy, Ma Chaojun and Li Baosen also added the urgency of protecting workers from the dangers of industrial work as an additional reason for establishing a welfare state.[33] Only Ren Yuanyuan, among these authors in the 1920s and 1930s, suggested that there were any preconditions for establishing a welfare state in China. Ren argued that China first needed to regain control over its foreign trade in order to ensure its industries could compete with the advanced industrial countries before adopting labor insurance.[34] The other authors called for the immediate creation of a welfare state in China.

Program design received little attention in this policy literature. Even before the ILO standards were set in 1933, few Chinese authors identified any significant choices in program design—social insurance was the only model described, and often the German program was the only real-world example analyzed in detail.[35] The books that cite their sources in footnotes or bibliographies make it clear that this narrow focus on social insurance was a deliberate choice, since their foreign sources analyze the pros and cons of different program designs in considerable detail.[36] The handful of Chinese books on social policy that raised the question of program design did so briefly and made

31. Lu Zhushu, *Shiye wenti yanjiu*, 87; Ma Chaojun, *Zhongguo laogong wenti*, 95; Li Baosen, *Laodong baoxian fa ABC*, 3–5; Ren Yuanyuan, *Shehui baoxian lifa*, 7.
32. Lu Zhushu, *Shiye wenti yanjiu*, 87.
33. Ma Chaojun, *Zhongguo laogong wenti*, 95; Li Baosen, *Laodong baoxian fa ABC*, 3.
34. Ren Yuanyuan, *Shehui baoxian lifa*, 116.
35. Lu Zhushu, *Shiye wenti yanjiu*; Chen Shousun, *Shehui wenti cidian*; Li Baosen, *Laodong baoxian fa ABC*; Jin Yufan, *Laodong baoxian fa*.
36. These sources are mostly English-language (predominantly American) books as well as a few French and Japanese sources. For example, Lu Zhushu, *Shiye wenti yanjiu,* and several other Chinese authors cite I. M. Rubinow's *Social Insurance* and Carlton, *History and Problems of Organized Labor,* both of which compare social insurance and citizen pensions in some detail.

the author's preference for social insurance clear in the process. Ma Junwu, for example, devoted eighteen pages of *Relief Policy for the Unemployed and Poor* to a detailed description of the German social insurance system but only two sentences to note that Britain and Australia employed a "completely different" (*quanyi*) kind of pension program that covered all elderly citizens who needed assistance. This brief mention provided no explanation of how this was accomplished or what the trade-offs might be.[37] Similarly, Ren Yuanyuan briefly described the New Zealand citizen pension program in *Trends in Social Insurance Law* but then went on to note accurately that social insurance had proven to be a far more popular program around the world.[38]

Policy choices about population coverage were presented within a social insurance framework. Authors pointed to two key decisions: first, whether programs should be public or private, and, second, whether participation should be mandatory or voluntary. This formulation reflected debates that had taken place in Europe and North America, but the Chinese literature did not recapitulate those debates.[39] Instead, the Chinese authors presented public programs with mandatory participation as optimal, providing broader coverage and more sustainable financing.[40] Jin Yufan went one step further in his *Primer on Labor Insurance Law* to claim that voluntary programs could only work in advanced industrial societies and that a backward country like China needed compulsory insurance (reversing the claims made for these policies in Europe and North America).[41]

Another strong point of agreement in the Chinese literature centered on the kind of people that social insurance should first target for protection—industrial workers. Some authors treated this question as a given, not requiring explanation or justification.[42] Most authors

---

37. Ma Junwu, *Shiyeren ji pinmin jiuji zhengce*, 41–59.
38. Ren Yuanyuan, *Shehui baoxian lifa*, 3–5.
39. Baldwin, *Politics of Social Solidarity*; Tone, *The Business of Benevolence*.
40. For summaries of the debate, see Lu Zhushu, *Shiye wenti yanjiu*, 82, 86–87; Chen Shousun, *Shehui wenti cidian*, 183–84. See also Ma Chaojun, *Zhongguo laogong wenti*, 100; Ma Junwu, *Shiyeren ji pinmin jiuji zhengce*, 52; Li Baosen, *Laodong baoxian fa ABC*, 6; Jin Yufan, *Laodong baoxian fa*, 18–24.
41. Jin Yufan, *Laodong baoxian fa*, 24.
42. Lu Zhushu, *Shiye wenti yanjiu*; Ma Junwu, *Shiyeren ji pinmin jiuji zhengce*.

defended the choice, arguing that industrial labor deserved special protection because the work was exhausting and dangerous.[43]

The other major policy decision described in this literature regarded which risks to loss of income deserved protection in the welfare state. Most Chinese authors identified work accidents, health, old age, disability, and survivors' insurance as the core set of programs that advanced industrial countries had adopted.[44] In addition to advocating this comprehensive set of programs for China's welfare state, most also recommended unemployment insurance as part of the core package of programs. In this regard, the Chinese consensus was stronger than its international counterpart, since many advanced industrial countries resisted unemployment insurance in this period.[45] In contrast, most Chinese authors did not advocate including maternity benefits in the Chinese welfare state, even though they were far more common than unemployment insurance at the time.[46]

An interesting lacuna in this literature is politics. Not a single source mentions political opposition as a potential obstacle to establishing social insurance in China. A range of political influences can be discerned in this literature, from conservative approaches showing the mark of American and Japanese debates about the impact of welfare on market incentives to openly socialist analyses employing Marxist class categories and praising the Soviet welfare state. Some authors even synthesized conservative and progressive approaches, framing discussions about how to preserve economic incentives to work and save within a broader Marxist historical narrative.[47] Regardless of the political orientation of the author, these books all treat social insurance

---

43. Ma Chaojun, *Zhongguo laogong wenti*, 95–96; Ren Yuanyuan, *Shehui baoxian lifa*, 2.
44. Lu Zhushu, *Shiye wenti yanjiu*; Ma Chaojun, *Zhongguo laogong wenti*; Chen Shousun, *Shehui wenti cidian*; Ma Junwu, *Shiyeren ji pinmin jiuji zhengce*; Li Baosen, *Laodong baoxian fa ABC*; Jin Yufan, *Laodong baoxian fa*; Ren Yuanyuan, *Shehui baoxian lifa*.
45. Lu Zhushu, *Shiye wenti yanjiu*; Ma Chaojun, *Zhongguo laogong wenti*; Chen Shousun, *Shehui wenti cidian*, 184; Li Baosen, *Laodong baoxian fa ABC*, 45; Ren Yuanyuan, *Shehui baoxian lifa*, 124
46. Chen Shousun, *Shehui wenti cidian*, 625.
47. For a conservative perspective, see Lu Zhushu, *Shiye wenti yanjiu*; for a socialist slant on welfare, see Ma Chaojun, *Zhongguo laogong wenti*; for a synthesis, see Li Baosen, *Laodong baoxian fa ABC*.

as a problem of social engineering rather than a political struggle over redistribution.

A final point of agreement in the Chinese literature is the level of analysis. The sources are quite striking in their focus on the big picture: the purpose of social insurance, the history of its development, and broad policy principles.[48] More practical concerns about program administration and finance are examined only briefly and in broad brush. For example, many sources recommended government administration of social insurance without going into much detail about the variety of alternatives that the advanced industrial countries had employed. Similarly, the few sources that do discuss financing do not go beyond identifying who should contribute—including employers, workers, and the state. There is no detail on the level of their contributions, much less any actuarial analysis of the long-term obligations that social insurance entails. In keeping with this focus on the big picture, data about program performance in the advanced industrial countries are missing, as are estimates of the scope and cost of a Chinese program.

The consensus among Chinese intellectuals surrounding social insurance was strong—stronger than the international consensus. In all of the writings, the question of program design was settled, with social insurance the foregone conclusion. Similarly, the question of timing received little attention. Few authors discussed when China should adopt social insurance or under what conditions. They pressed for creating a welfare state in China soon, and several even asserted that social insurance was already long overdue.[49] Only one author identified obstacles to the adoption of social insurance in China: lack of control over China's foreign trade due to semicolonialism resulting in the inability to protect domestic industries from competition with foreign-owned factories in the foreign concessions.[50] The small group

48. Since some of this literature catalogs minute details of European social insurance law, it is possible to argue that this generalization does not hold. But the detail is so overwhelming that it is difficult to see how it could influence political debates or policy making. The more analytical introductions to these catalogs seem more likely to influence informed public opinion, but this hypothesis is open to question.

49. Ma Chaojun, *Zhongguo laogong wenti*, 95; Li Baosen, *Laodong baoxian fa ABC*, 7–8.

50. Ren Yuanyuan, *Shehui baoxian lifa*, 116–20.

of Chinese experts on social policy was diverse in both occupations and political orientations, but they shared a remarkable agreement that China needed a comprehensive welfare state as soon as possible.

## FORGING A POLITICAL CONSENSUS IN CHINA ON SOCIAL INSURANCE

If there was an expert consensus on welfare policy in China by the 1920s, how did Chinese political leaders with the power to act on these ideas respond? Although China had been effectively drawn into global policy debates in the late 1920s and 1930s, its unstable domestic politics continued to pose an obstacle to social reform. However, when we turn to examine the two most powerful political parties in the Republican period, the KMT and the CCP, it is clear that they also contributed to the early consensus surrounding social insurance, even before they had any measure of political power to do something about it.

The CCP called for an industrial accident program as early as 1922, just a year after the party was established. By 1925, the Communists advocated comprehensive social insurance for work injuries, illness, unemployment, and old age.[51] The KMT first proposed social insurance during its First National Congress in 1924, when the party was reorganized into a Leninist party on the advice of Sun Yatsen's Soviet advisers. This pledge was renewed at subsequent KMT party congresses and in the party platform, along with other labor policies such as an eight-hour workday, a minimum wage, and the abolition of child labor.[52] In addition to the influence of Chinese policy experts, the agreement between these two revolutionary political parties on social insurance was also partly attributable to Soviet influence, which shaped their alliance during the Nationalist Revolution (1924–28) against the warlords.

Even after their violent split in 1927, however, both parties continued to advocate social insurance, suggesting that there was more to their early consensus on welfare policy than a temporary alliance. In most policy arenas, the rival Nationalist and Communist parties grew

51. Zhongyang dang'anguan, ed., *Zhonggong zhongyang wenjian xuanji*, 567, 636–37.
52. Wagner, *Labor Legislation*, 98–99; Xie Zhenmin, *Zhonghua minguo fashi*, 1308; Liang, *Kuomintang and the Chinese Worker*, 21.

increasingly polarized during the Nanjing decade (1927–37), when the Nationalists ruled the country and the Communists were forced to try to survive as a guerrilla force. The differences between them were especially stark in the realm of labor policy. The KMT underwent a sharp reversal, seeking to demobilize labor and other progressive social forces that had helped it achieve power.[53] In contrast, the CCP continued its radical strategy of mobilizing underground labor unions to spearhead armed uprisings in the cities. At the same time, the CCP was organizing soviet governments in its mountain hideouts.

While pursuing diametrically opposed labor policies, both parties continued to call for social insurance throughout this period of bitter conflict. If the goal remained the same, their strategies for achieving that goal diverged in the 1930s. The KMT pursued an ambitious social policy agenda but repeatedly postponed implementation. In contrast, the CCP quickly moved to experiment with much more modest welfare policies in the limited territories under its control.

The Nationalist government's 1929 Factory Act began this pattern of adopting the highest international standards in legislation but then postponing implementation until the KMT's political preconditions were met: the end of semicolonialism and reunification of the country.[54] The Factory Act featured full ILO standards, such as an eight-hour workday and an occupational injury program, eschewing the lower standards proposed for China by the ILO Commission for Special Countries. But the Factory Act was never fully implemented, even in Chinese territory under the control of the Nationalist government, because the factories in the foreign concessions were exempt. Even after this precedent of inaction was clearly established, China began ratifying ILO conventions in the 1930s, quickly ratifying 20 percent of the total number of conventions that had been adopted since the founding of the international organization.[55]

The ILO was probably more important as an arena for the new regime's diplomatic efforts to combat imperialism than for labor politics in this period. The Chinese delegates to the international labor

53. Perry, *Shanghai on Strike*, 92–93; Dirlik, "Mass Movements."
54. Wagner, *Labor Legislation*, 188.
55. Ibid., 187–88.

conferences concentrated their efforts on proposing resolutions that challenged key provisions of the unequal treaties that defined semicolonialism in China. For example, in 1929 the Chinese delegation submitted a draft resolution to enforce Chinese labor laws without regard to extraterritoriality, and in 1930 it submitted a proposal to limit the extraterritorial privileges of foreign ships in Chinese waters. Opposition from the imperial powers ensured that these resolutions were watered down or rejected outright, but Chinese delegates persevered in their efforts to use the ILO's agenda of harmonizing labor policy around the world to promote their own national goals of regaining sovereignty over China's foreign trade and colonial concessions. Drafting ambitious legislation that the Nationalist government had no intention of implementing fit with this larger diplomatic effort.

In this context, the KMT began consideration of the ILO's 1932–33 conventions on social insurance in 1934. The Chinese government reported to the ILO that it agreed in principle to the social insurance conventions and that it was in the process of drafting new legislation on that basis.[56] The resulting bill made it to the KMT's Central Political Council by 1935 but stalled in that key policy-making body before the party referred it to the Legislative Yuan.[57] The bill effectively died there in 1937, when the Japanese invasion temporarily pushed social policy off the party's political agenda. Throughout its brief ten-year rule over China, the Nationalist government was a conduit for importing, but not implementing, the most advanced ILO policies.

In the 1930s, the CCP also continued its advocacy for social insurance even as it faced the intense pressure of the Nationalist suppression campaigns. The new soviet governments that the CCP established in its rural base areas adopted rudimentary versions of social insurance. For example, the Huang'an County Soviet in Jiangxi established a Social Insurance Bureau to collect "social insurance fees" from local factories and handicraft workshops in 1930.[58] Subsequently, the regional Jiangxi Soviet Government incorporated a similar vaguely defined social insurance program in its 1931 Labor Law. The programs were

56. *ILO Yearbook 1934–35*, 266.
57. *ILO Yearbook 1935–36*, 228; Li Qiong, "Minguo shiqi shehui baoxianchu," 84.
58. Ye Zhonghao, "Huang'an xian suweiai zhengfu shehui baoxianju."

too basic to be considered real social insurance programs, since they were unemployment relief programs that did not provide any defined benefits to program participants. But the use of social insurance rhetoric connected these experimental welfare programs to the CCP's larger social policy platform.

The CCP's improvisational welfare policy proved premature, however, since even these simple unemployment relief programs could not be sustained in the revolutionary base areas. By June 1933, Liu Shaoqi, chairman of the CCP labor union federation, openly criticized soviet social insurance policies for bankrupting factories with burdensome taxes and thereby increasing unemployment. He argued that the rural base areas had not yet reached a level of economic development appropriate for these kinds of welfare initiatives. Before the year was out, the soviet Labor Law was revised to eliminate the program until economic conditions improved.[59] By the mid-1930s, the CCP ended up in the same place as the KMT but by a different route.

The degree of political consensus surrounding welfare state policy in the 1920s and 1930s stood out in a period of deep division in Chinese politics. This consensus was no doubt nurtured by the broader agreement among Chinese intellectuals as well as the ongoing contacts each party sustained with international advocates for social insurance, such as the ILO and the Soviet Union. The question in this period was not so much if but when social insurance should be adopted. Most intellectuals called for establishing a Chinese welfare state as soon as possible, while the two political parties were more cautious. The KMT set political preconditions for implementation of its social policy agenda: elimination of the colonial concessions and the complete reunification of China under its control. The CCP, in contrast, set economic preconditions for the welfare state: achieving a sufficient level of economic development. For both parties, such preconditions were far beyond their control, meaning that the delay in founding a welfare state was a long-term proposition.

In contrast to the decades of study and political debate that separated the diffusion of knowledge and the adoption of the welfare programs in countries like Sweden, Chinese policy makers quickly reached a

59. Wang Yongxi et al., eds., *Zhongguo gonghui shi,* 224–27.

consensus on the welfare state. The decades of delay between knowledge and action in China were due to more fundamental constraints.

## The Turning Point in the Globalization of Welfare Policies: The Second World War

The Second World War was a catalyst for the diffusion of welfare policies. In contrast to the First World War and the Great Depression, diffusion of welfare state policies gained speed in the Second World War even as it crossed longer distances. The process of diffusion in Europe and its settler colonies was largely completed in this period. Latin America led the way, with multiple countries founding welfare states during and after the war. Adoption of welfare state legislation reached a new peak in the 1940s, and again social insurance was the overwhelming favorite in program design. At the same time, the diffusion of welfare state policies also began to overlap with the diffusion of new ideas about universal coverage.

Tracing the diffusion of the idea of universal coverage from Europe to China is not difficult. Instead of the long, circuitous route that initial knowledge about welfare state policies took from Berlin to Geneva, then Moscow and finally to Nanjing and the Jiangxi Soviet, Chinese officials were involved in the rapidly forming international consensus surrounding the idea of a universal welfare state almost from the beginning. The 1937 Japanese invasion and the Second World War that followed led to vast destruction and the division of China into Japanese, Nationalist, and Communist territory. Representing a major theater in this global conflict, China's diplomats were vaulted into the central arenas of international diplomacy among the Allied Powers. Their main goal was to secure military and economic aid for the war against Japan, but Chinese officials also played an active role in the newly emerging international policy consensus on the welfare state.

The acceleration of welfare policy diffusion was not due to the ILO. The organization was forced to evacuate from Switzerland to the safety of Canada, and its labor conferences became smaller and more infrequent. But the Allied powers' public diplomacy more than made up for the ILO's reduced stature. Portraying the welfare state as the democratic alternative to the fascist "warfare" states of the Axis powers, the Allies incorporated welfare policy into wartime propaganda. Great Britain's wartime diplomacy was especially important in this process, with its multinational campaign to publicize the 1942 Beveridge Report, *Social Insurance and Allied Services*. An unlikely candidate for bestseller status, the Beveridge Report was a highly technical, 299-page proposal to expand the British welfare state to provide universal coverage and comprehensive protection. Citizen pensions were at the heart of Beveridge's proposal, combined with social insurance contributions.[60] Although the complexity of Beveridge's policy recommendations made the report almost impenetrable, its message of universal coverage was simple and extremely popular. More than 600,000 copies of *Social Insurance and Allied Services* were sold to the public in Great Britain, and the British Ministry of Information launched an international public relations campaign to spread the idea that the "purpose of victory is to live in a better world than the old world."[61]

The BBC spread the message far beyond the battlefield, broadcasting news about the Beveridge Report in twenty-two languages.[62] In addition, the British Foreign Ministry took on the task of translating and distributing a shortened version of the report to the other Allies, shipping copies to the United States and translating it into Chinese for distribution to the public in Nationalist territory in Southwest China.[63] The report's key recommendations were summarized in the KMT's official party newspaper, the *Central Daily News*, and journal articles soon appeared with titles asking "What is the condition of China's Beveridge Plan?"[64]

Wartime diplomacy spurred the diffusion of welfare state policies, especially among the countries on the sidelines of the fighting. Anglophile Argentine reformers, for example, described the Beveridge Report

60. Beveridge, *Social Insurance and Allied Services*.
61. Timmins, *Five Giants*, 24.
62. Ibid., 23–25.
63. Yingguo zhu Hua da shiguan, *Beifolizhi shehui baoxian*.
64. Ma, "Chinese Beveridge Plan," 337.

as receiving an enthusiastic response in Buenos Aires and facilitating the passage of major pension programs in 1944 and 1946.[65] Similarly, Indian reformers were "inspired" by the Beveridge Report, claiming that reading it made it "psychologically possible for India to take a path-breaking step in regard to social security."[66] Social insurance initiatives that had been shelved since the late 1920s were suddenly dusted off and seriously considered again when the Indian government established new social insurance study commissions in 1943 and 1944.[67]

In addition to accelerating the diffusion of welfare state legislation, British propaganda spurred efforts to forge a new international consensus on universal welfare states. The first initiative was the 1944 ILO conference in Philadelphia, one of the many international conferences sponsored by the Allies from 1943 to 1945 to plan for the postwar period. The scope and ambition of the Philadelphia conference was much more ambitious than the ILO's prewar annual labor conferences, even if attendance was more limited. In the words of the U.S. secretary of labor, the purpose of the Philadelphia conference was "to lay one of the foundation stones of the great peace, the stone of social justice, on which human hope and human life can be built."[68] More concretely, the conference agenda focused on three major issues: first, defining the future of the ILO and its relationship to the newly formed United Nations; second, finding ways to maintain employment in the transition from war to peace; and, third, establishing a new consensus on social policy.

The concept advanced to summarize this new policy approach was "social security," which connoted far more than the limited American social insurance program that popularized the name.[69] Although definitions of social security varied widely in this period, they commonly included an integrated, comprehensive social insurance program with broad or even universal coverage, as well as Keynesian economic poli-

---

65. Lewis, "Social Insurance in the Argentine," 186.

66. Agarwala, "Social Security Movement in India," 575.

67. Government of India, *Report on Health Insurance.* India's first social insurance program for health care was adopted in 1948, just a year after liberation from British rule. Agarwala, "Social Security Movement in India," 576–79.

68. ILO, "Twenty-sixth Session," 1.

69. Gillion et al., eds., *Social Security Pensions,* 396–97

cies designed to maintain full employment.[70] Rather than using an insurance metaphor, with emphasis on contractual obligations and risk management, social security was based on concepts of social rights. The new emphasis on universalism was evident in the 1944 "Declaration of Philadelphia," which committed the ILO to advancing ten specific goals, including "the extension of social security measures to provide a basic income to all in need of such protection."[71]

Chinese diplomats took advantage of the country's new wartime status as an Allied "power" to participate actively in the international organizations that were key arenas for forging the new approach to social policy. At the Philadelphia conference, China's labor representative, Zhu Xuefan, strongly supported the emerging consensus.[72] The Chinese government delegate, Xie Zhengfu, went on from the ILO conference to work with the newly organized United Nations Relief and Rehabilitation Administration (UNRRA) and to help found the Chinese National Relief and Rehabilitation Agency (CNRRA).[73]

Both Nationalist and Communist labor leaders played an active role in the new World Federation of Trade Unions. KMT labor leader Zhu Xuefan led the Chinese delegation to the founding congress of the World Federation of Trade Unions in 1945, when he became a vice president of this predominantly European organization.[74] Liu Ningyi, the head of the CCP's union federation in the base areas, assisted Zhu Xuefan at the congress, becoming integrated into its global policy networks at the same time. The World Federation of Trade Unions echoed the ILO's call for social security at its founding congress, passing a resolution "that a single and comprehensive program of State social insurance should be established in every country."[75]

Public diplomacy put welfare on the agenda in international politics during the Second World War. The war also had an impact on

---

70. ILO, "Twenty-sixth Session," 19–21.

71. Ibid., 39.

72. Lu Xiangxian and Liu Songbin, *Zhu Xuefan*, 127.

73. Ma, "Chinese Beveridge Plan," 335.

74. Lu Xiangxian and Liu Songbin, *Zhu Xuefan*, 203. The results are recounted in the Ministry of Social Affairs social work journal *Shehui gongzuo tongxun*: Shehui bu, "Yingguo shehui anquan jihua"; Shehui bu, "Jianada shehui anquan zhidu."

75. WFTU, *Report of Activity*, appendix 1, 15.

policy diffusion through the creation of new international organizations such as the United Nations and the World Federation of Trade Unions. These organizations broadened global policy networks significantly, giving Chinese policy experts new opportunities to participate in international policy debates. Although China was by no means a leader in social policy, the aspirations of its leaders to great power status reinforced the importance placed on fully participating in international arenas.[76] Instead of lagging behind Europe's welfare pioneers, China now endorsed the same policy goals at the same time.

Most important for the globalization of the welfare state, the war weakened the foundations of imperialism, opening up new possibilities for a fundamentally different world order. The sudden collapse of the Japanese empire in 1945 liberated China from semicolonialism and marked the beginning of the end of imperialism in the rest of the world.

## Diffusion of Welfare Policies during the Cold War

The Cold War started gradually in the late 1940s. In China, it started as a hot war almost as soon as the Second World War came to an end. The Nationalists and Communists raced to take over Japanese-occupied territory, and this jockeying for position in 1945 soon escalated into open warfare in 1946, when the Chinese Civil War officially began. The conflict between the United States and the Soviet Union emerged in 1947 in the controversy over the Marshall Plan. The conflicts quickly began to fragment the global policy networks forged during the Second World War. Despite these divisions, the surge of adoption of welfare state legislation that began during the Second World War reached its peak in the postwar period, doubling the pace of adoption and reaching every continent in the process.

Once the European, American, and Japanese empires were dismantled, most newly created countries adopted major welfare state legisla-

76. Ma, "Chinese Beveridge Plan," 342.

tion soon after their liberation. China's adoption of labor insurance regulations in 1951 fit squarely within these larger trends. In the 1950s, 78 percent of all welfare state adopters were newly independent countries or colonies undergoing reform in preparation for greater autonomy. In the 1960s, the proportion of newly independent countries among welfare state adopters rose to 86 percent.[77] The Cold War reinforced these trends as welfare policy was incorporated into the foreign policy of the superpowers, becoming an arena of competition between the communist and capitalist worlds.

If welfare state legislation and the ideal of universal coverage were embraced so widely around the world, why did the policies to achieve broad coverage fail to spread as far? China was part of the minority of ambitious welfare state reformers who sought to expand population coverage significantly in the postwar period. This group of ambitious reformers accounted for one-third of the countries in the world that had welfare state programs in place in the postwar period. Diffusion of reforms to achieve broad coverage was much more successful on the communist side of the Cold War: more than 90 percent of communist countries with welfare states adopted these reforms, while only 27 percent of capitalist countries attempted them.[78]

The stark difference was not due to Cold War politics. Even with the clash in ideology and new divisions in global policy networks, both sides agreed on the broad contours of welfare policy. In addition, political competition kept both sides of the Cold War engaged in promoting the idea of a universal welfare state.

The ILO began the work of forging a policy consensus about how to achieve universal coverage in social insurance welfare states in the late 1940s. The 1947 ILO Asian Regional Conference in New Delhi proved to be influential because it went beyond statements of principle to lay out more concrete plans for welfare state expansion appropriate for developing

77. Flora, *Growth to Limits*; SSA, *Social Security Programs 1961*; SSA, *Social Security Programs 1979*; SSA, *Social Security Programs 1999*; Haggard and Kaufman, *Development, Democracy, and Welfare States*; Mesa-Lago, *Social Security in Latin America*.
78. SSA, *Social Security Programs 1961*; SSA, *Social Security Programs 1979*; Flora, *Growth to Limits*; Haggard and Kaufman, *Development, Democracy, and Welfare States*; Mesa-Lago, *Social Security in Latin America*.

countries. Bao Huaguo, in charge of planning for the new Nationalist Social Insurance Commission, led a delegation of fifteen Chinese government, business, and labor representatives to India.[79] The advice they heard at the meeting codified the pattern of development that had been forged by the advanced industrial countries: first establishing benefits sufficient to protect people's basic income, second expanding the risks covered until a comprehensive set of programs was in place, and then gradually expanding the population covered, all according to a long-term plan of legislation.[80] But the actual policies to accomplish the expansion of coverage were not specified, and the trade-offs between increasing benefits and expanding coverage were not acknowledged.

When the United Nations elevated income maintenance to the level of a human right in 1948, the Nationalist government's delegates to the UN Human Rights Commission participated actively in the drafting process for the universal declaration.[81] Zhang Pengjun was vice-chairman of the Human Rights Commission, which Eleanor Roosevelt chaired. China was also represented on the drafting committee along with delegates from seven other nations. Although the Chinese delegation did not put special emphasis on social or economic rights, China's draft declaration included a provision that made social security a human right. In the final version, the Chinese delegation also voted to endorse a more detailed version of this new right to social security: "Everyone has the right to . . . security in the event of unemployment, sickness, disability, widowhood, old age or lack of livelihood in circumstances beyond his control."[82]

The Soviet Union and Eastern European members of the international organization abstained from voting to endorse the Universal Declaration of Human Rights, but there was no disagreement about the goal of a universal welfare state. While the Chinese Communists were excluded from the UN, their role in the World Federation of Trade Unions grew after unions from capitalist countries withdrew from the organization to form the rival International Federation of Trade Unions

79. Guoji laogong ju, *Yazhou laogong*, 156–57.
80. ILO, "Post-War Trends," 670.
81. Svensson, *Debating Human Rights*, 201–3.
82. ILO, "Post-War Trends," 669.

In 1949. For example, China hosted the first Asian regional meeting of the World Federation in Beijing in December 1949, receiving fourteen union delegations from Asia and Australia.[83]

In 1952, as the Cold War heated up, the ILO debated and then adopted a formal resolution on social security that established new international standards. These new minimums defined the lower limits of a comprehensive welfare state, including the kinds of programs offered, the benefits provided to a "standard beneficiary" of a male worker with a wife and two children, and the proportion of the population covered. The minimum level of coverage established in the 1952 convention was 50 percent of the workforce or 20 percent of the total population.[84]

Cold War competition continued to ratchet up the standards. For example, the World Federation of Trade Unions continued to press the issue of universal coverage after its capitalist members withdrew. In 1953, the federation convened an International Conference on Social Security in Vienna with its remaining communist members, including a full Chinese delegation. The organization endorsed a proposal for making social insurance a right of citizenship and providing comprehensive benefits for all major risks to loss of income, from maternity to old age. Furthermore, the proposal explicitly advocated universal coverage of the labor force, including seasonal workers, casual workers, apprentices, farmers, and students.[85] This 1953 conference was followed by a formal WFTU resolution advocating universal coverage as an international standard by 1961.[86] Although a Chinese delegation also attended the conference and endorsed the new standard, the Sino-Soviet split in 1960 relegated the Chinese to the back benches.

On the capitalist side of the Cold War, the Council of Europe also became involved in this competition over welfare state standards. In 1964, the council adopted the European Protocol for Social Security.[87] In addition to reinforcing the ILO standards as minimum requirements

83. *World Federation of Trade Unions*, 64.
84. ILO, "Thirty-fifth Session," 289–91.
85. Bras, "15th Anniversary," 2; Shanghai Municipal Archives (SMA), C1-2-1118.
86. *World Federation of Trade Unions,* 104. China remained a member of the World Federation until the beginning of the Cultural Revolution in 1966.
87. Villars,"Social Security Standards," 343.

for its members, it also set higher goals for the region. For example, it raised the standard for population coverage to 80 percent of the labor force or 30 percent of the population. In addition, it endorsed the policy principle that coverage be extended to employees' dependents. Soon afterward, the ILO raised its minimum standards for coverage again. In 1967, a new convention increased the standard for old-age pension coverage to the current level of 75 percent of the labor force. Two years later, the standard was increased to the same level for health insurance.[88]

If both sides in the Cold War kept confirming their commitment to the goal of broad coverage, why did the diffusion of reforms to achieve this goal diverge so widely? One reason may have been the lack of consensus about which reforms provided the best way to achieve broad welfare states. The policies that Sweden and New Zealand used to achieve universal coverage were inapplicable to the much more complicated problem of expanding social insurance. Both the higher cost of social insurance and the reliance on employers in the financing and administration of the program posed obstacles to incorporating the poor and reaching people outside formal sector employment. Similarly, Beveridge's policy recommendations were far more controversial than his vision of a universal welfare state, since he combined the least popular aspect of each program: the high payroll taxes of social insurance and the low, flat-rate benefits of citizen pensions. Few countries adopted his proposals, even as they endorsed his goals.[89] The shift in focus in international debates from policies to goals did not help clarify the problem.

DIFFUSION OF POLICIES TO ACHIEVE BROAD
COVERAGE IN THE CAPITALIST WORLD

Given the almost universal popularity of welfare state legislation among capitalist countries during the Cold War, the more limited diffusion of policies to expand coverage is puzzling. Although political opposition to welfare may have been more common in capitalist countries, the fact that so many countries with ostensibly pro-welfare governments

88. Gillion, et al., eds., *Social Security Pensions*, 612.
89. Hills, Ditch, and Glennerster, "Introduction," 8.

failed to adopt the reforms suggests that there were additional obstacles to their diffusion. The Nationalist government in Taiwan, for example, did not follow through on the KMT's 1947 endorsement of broad coverage for another fifty years. Although the Nationalists did adopt reforms to extend coverage to discrete groups in 1953, 1956, 1958, and 1965, they did not add up to anything close to broad coverage.[90] While American influence on the KMT may have changed its approach to welfare during the Cold War, India claimed to be a socialist country following a "third way" between the Cold War superpowers. India's First Five-Year Plan set the goal of achieving full coverage of the industrial sector in the provident fund program, but the government passed no major legislation to expand coverage. As a result, it never achieved even this modest goal.[91]

The consensus on goals masked a complete lack of agreement on policy among capitalist countries. The ILO sidestepped the question of policy. Moreover, successful models of reform varied widely. Rather than a single reform policy, the most common route to broad or universal coverage in social insurance welfare states in the capitalist world involved multiple rounds of reform to reach different kinds of workers. These reforms faced political opposition at every step.

Germany, for example, first started debating reforms to achieve broad coverage after the Second World War. Even during the occupation, Social Democrats and other political parties and interest groups began pushing for the same kind of universal welfare state that their occupiers were creating back home.[92] Major welfare reforms were required in 1948 and again in 1957 to revive and stabilize the bankrupt German welfare state. On both of those occasions, universalistic proposals were advanced to expand coverage to all citizens.[93] Both

---

90. SSA, *Social Security Programs 2012–13*, 193; Dixon and Kim, *Social Welfare*, 326–27; Haggard and Kaufman, *Development, Democracy, and Welfare States*, 131.

91. India, Planning Commission, *First Five-Year Plan*, 221.

92. Interestingly, secondary sources on the postwar reforms do not mention outside influences on Germans reformers (indeed, pressure from the Allied Occupation was seen as an obstacle), despite the Cold War competition with East Germany and the standards set by the European Community. For example, see Baldwin, *Politics of Social Solidarity*, and Flora, *Growth to Limits*.

93. Baldwin, *Politics of Social Solidarity*, 197–205; Flora and Alber, "Modernization Democratization and the Development of Welfare States," 53.

times, these proposals were defeated by the opposition of two powerful groups that limited expansion to more modest increases. The first
source of opposition came from workers already covered by the welfare
state, who opposed expansion out of fear that the program's resources
would be redistributed to lower-income workers and reduce their own
benefits in the process. The second source of opposition came from
professionals and small business owners, who also opposed redistribution created by their being incorporated into the welfare state along
with low-income workers outside the formal sector, such as farmers and
domestic servants.

The German welfare state finally achieved universal coverage with
the 1972 Pension Reform Act.[94] Political opposition was overcome by
buying off workers with benefit hikes and building a coalition with
different segments within the middle classes, whose interests were
changing with the rapid expansion of formal sector employment in this
period. Altogether it took four rounds of reform and the ambitious 1972
legislation to incorporate almost the entire West German population
into the welfare state.

The developing countries that tried to achieve broad or universal
welfare coverage in the postwar period did not have rapidly growing
formal sectors to change the interests of the middle classes or ample
resources to buy off the opposition. Their route to broad coverage was
different. For example, Costa Rica, after a series of minor reforms to
expand coverage in the 1950s, adopted a constitutional amendment in
1961 mandating universal welfare coverage within ten years.[95] Bills to
expand coverage significantly were defeated in 1965 and 1969 owing to
the opposition of physicians who opposed expansion of the national
health service as well as resistance from highly paid employees, such
as bank workers and civil servants. Under the pressure of the constitutional deadline, the Costa Rican president pressed for major reforms in
1971, even in the face of a physician strike. The physicians were bought
off with an 83 percent pay hike, but the reformers were able to compel

94. Baldwin, *Politics of Social Solidarity*, 281–83.
95. Gonzalez-Vega and Cespedes, "Costa Rica," 101–3; Rosenberg, "Social Security
Policymaking," 125–26.

high-earning employees to help finance a major expansion in coverage for poor workers.[96]

The politics of welfare reform may have been similar in Germany and Costa Rica, but the solution to narrow coverage proved to be different. Costa Rica achieved broad coverage with another initiative in 1974 that created a separate citizen pension program for rural farm workers and other poor citizens, financed in part through new payroll taxes on employers.[97] Benefits in the new pension program were significantly lower than those provided by the existing social insurance program, institutionalizing a fundamental inequality within the Costa Rican welfare state. But almost a decade after the self-imposed deadline, Costa Rica achieved broad coverage through the combination of the two programs.[98]

These two examples show that expansion policies required sustained political commitment to achieving the goal of broad coverage over years and even decades of reform. Moreover, there was no consensus about the best policies to achieve a broad welfare state. There was no single solution to creating a universal social insurance welfare state. The combination of the vagueness and complexity of the reforms to achieve universal coverage posed an additional obstacle to their diffusion.

DIFFUSION TO CHINA AND THE REST OF THE
COMMUNIST WORLD

In contrast to the limited diffusion of welfare reforms to achieve broad coverage in the capitalist world, most Communist countries with welfare programs adopted these reforms during the Cold War. Both politics and policies help explain such wide diffusion. The politics of welfare reform was simplified in all these countries, since their social revolutions had eliminated major sources of political opposition to the

---

96. Rosenberg, "Social Security Policymaking," 127–28; Gonzalez-Vega and Cespedes, "Costa Rica," 105.
97. Rosenberg, "Social Security Policymaking," 128; Durán-Valverde, "Anti-Poverty Programmes," 14–16.
98. Durán-Valverde, "Anti-Poverty Programmes," 22; Mesa-Lago, *Ascent to Bankruptcy*, 40–41.

expansion of the welfare state, such as capitalists and professionals. Another contributing factor was the Soviet Union, whose diplomacy promoted both the idea of a communist welfare state and the policies to achieve it.

China was incorporated into communist welfare diplomacy even before the Sino-Soviet Friendship Treaty was signed in 1950. In addition to training Chinese Communist leaders in the Soviet Union in the 1930s and 1940s, Soviet advisers began going to China in large numbers in the 1950s. There were also multilateral exchanges of trade union delegations among China, the Soviet Union, and Eastern Europe. Chinese policy makers were more tightly integrated into these transnational policy networks than ever before, although they were no longer actively participating in the formation of a new policy consensus. Soviet power and influence set the agenda, even as both China and the Soviet Union adopted similar reforms to expand coverage at the same time.

These contacts helped spur a surge of new publications in the early 1950s that introduced Soviet and Eastern European social insurance policies to a wider Chinese audience. The new official Chinese Communist labor union established a Russian translation service that published Soviet social insurance regulations, Soviet trade union manuals, and compilations of articles from Soviet trade union journals.[99] Books on social insurance in Eastern European countries such as Czechoslovakia and Romania also appeared.[100]

The surge in publications about Soviet and Eastern European welfare policy provide a window into the kind of advice Chinese policy makers were given in this period. Although the new Chinese policy literature of the 1950s continued to present welfare as a problem of social engineering rather than political struggle, it focused more closely on administrative issues than the broad policy overviews of the 1920s and 1930s. Another difference was that the Chinese sources from the 1950s did not describe the parameters of international policy debates and instead presented a complete consensus on communist welfare

99. See, for example, Quanguo zonggonghui, *Guojia shehui baoxian*; Quanguo zong-gonghui, *Sulian gonghui*.

100. Li Rongting, *Shehui baoxian gailun*; Yang Zhi, *Sulian laodong baoxian zhidu*; Zhang Yongmao, *Jiekesiluofake de shehui baoxian*.

policy. This consistency was as much a product of propaganda as of the coherence of the policies themselves, but the repetition reinforced the perception of their importance and integration as a policy package. The model for communist social insurance was often defined in contrast to capitalist social insurance programs, whether prerevolutionary programs in Russia and Eastern Europe or more contemporary American and British models. Such comparisons highlighted the idea that welfare was integral to a communist regime. Four key differences between communist and capitalist welfare states were identified: the range of income maintenance programs provided, their administrative structure, their sources of financing, and the extent of population coverage.

Communist social insurance programs were depicted as comprehensive, covering all risks of income loss, from maternity to disability to old age. In contrast, capitalist programs were portrayed as incomplete: Russia's prerevolutionary social insurance program, for example, only provided health and disability benefits and made no provision for old age.[101] Similarly, the American welfare state was described as "backward" for lacking any provision for health insurance.[102] The fact that almost all advanced capitalist industrial countries had comprehensive welfare states by that point was not mentioned. The one exception to the characterization of communist social insurance as comprehensive was unemployment insurance, which some sources described as transitional and others as simply unnecessary. Instead, they argued that structural unemployment was an inherent feature of capitalism, whereas Soviet-style planned economies eliminated the root cause of the problem by expanding the economy to the point of full employment.[103] For this reason, the socialist alternative to unemployment insurance was to establish a constitutional right to work for all citizens.

According to the Chinese sources, the second key difference between communist and capitalist social security stemmed from the way they were administered. Communist social insurance was unified in a single national program in contrast to the capitalist pattern of

---

101. Quanguo zonggonghui, *Sulian gonghui*, 2.
102. Li Rongting, *Shehui baoxian gailun*, 50.
103. Ibid., 15–16.

multiple programs for different occupational groups, each with different services and benefits. The blame for multiple programs was placed on capitalists and their agenda of dividing and weakening the working class.[104] The other key feature of communist social insurance administration was the central role of the trade union, which was characterized as a form of direct democracy. The Soviet system of direct administration by the trade union was presented as ideal, but the Eastern European pattern of trade union participation in corporatist institutions was also characterized as an improvement over capitalist forms of corporatism, which was portrayed as dominated by government bureaucrats and/or capitalists themselves.[105] Sources emphasized that communist trade unions drafted major social insurance reforms themselves rather than having an indirect influence on the legislative process as in capitalist democracies.[106] They also highlighted union provision of benefits and supervision of program finances as a form of working-class democracy.[107]

The difference in the financing of communist and capitalist social insurance lay in who shouldered the burden of financing the program. According to the Chinese sources, in capitalist countries workers provided most of the financing through deductions levied against their already low wages. In contrast, communist social insurance demanded no financial contribution from workers at all and was instead entirely financed by the state and/or the employer.

The final important difference between communist and capitalist social insurance in the Chinese accounts was population coverage. Prerevolutionary social insurance programs were all characterized as having very limited coverage. For example, the 1912 Russian social insurance program was criticized for covering only 15 percent of the workforce.[108] Similarly, capitalist social insurance was described as targeting only manual laborers and often only industrial workers.[109] Communist social insurance reforms, in contrast, were portrayed as

104. Zhang Yongmao, *Jiekesiluofake de shehui baoxian*, 4.
105. Quanguo zonggonghui, *Sulian gonghui*, 2, 15.
106. Zhang Yongmao, *Jiekesiluofake de shehui baoxian*, 6.
107. Quanguo zonggonghui, *Sulian gonghui*, 15.
108. Ibid., 2.
109. Li Rongting, *Shehui baoxian gailun*, 24.

extending coverage to the entire working population and, through them, their dependents as well. In different combinations, construction workers, shop clerks, the self-employed, intellectuals, seasonal workers, farm workers, tenant farmers, and even farmers who owned their own land were described as targets for inclusion in communist social insurance programs.[110] The only distinction between this kind of broad coverage and the universal coverage established by citizenship rights was the emphasis on every able-bodied citizen's duty to work. The logic behind the distinction was that the combination of a constitutional right to work and social insurance rights earned on the job together preserved work incentives while ensuring broad, practically universal coverage.[111]

This simplified and idealized portrayal of welfare states in the Soviet Union and Eastern Europe provided a clear goal for Chinese policy makers. These sources also offered a roadmap to get there by following the example set by the Soviet Union but with shortcuts along the way. Avoiding some of the circuitous routes the Soviet Union had been forced to take as a pioneer in social reform, Chinese reformers would be able to achieve the same ends without incurring the same costs and delays.[112]

According to these Chinese accounts, the Soviet Union initially took a cautious approach to welfare in response to the economic problems growing out of the Russian Civil War and the foreign interference that came with it. The first Soviet program mentioned in these sources from the 1920s covered only a few risks, providing little or no protection for disability or old age. Furthermore, coverage remained limited to factory workers, which is why it was initially called a labor insurance program. The Chinese sources portray Stalin's First Five-Year Plan as a turning point in the development of the Soviet welfare state. The industrialization drive was key. First, it eliminated unemployment and expanded coverage within the original program through massive expansion of the formal sector. Second, it yielded the resources necessary for new reforms to expand coverage outside

110. Ibid., 30; Quanguo zonggonghui, *Sulian gonghui*, 3.
111. Li Rongting, *Shehui baoxian gailun*, 25.
112. See, for example, ibid., 118.

the initial program. In the short term, new unemployment relief programs eased the transition into the new economy for the urban poor and rural migrants. Although the benefits were lower than labor insurance, these programs were temporary measures. By the end of the First Five-Year Plan, the Soviet Communist Party had been able to expand labor insurance into social insurance and extend coverage to employees outside the factory.[113]

In Chinese books on Eastern European welfare states, the nearly twenty-year process of development in the Soviet Union was described as telescoped into a few years immediately following the Second World War. Like Russia, these countries also had preexisting social insurance programs in place before their "people's democratic revolutions" in the late 1940s. But without facing the same kind of foreign invasion that the Soviets had suffered after the Russian Revolution and by drawing on the lessons of the Soviet experience, they were able to accomplish nearly as much in just two or three years. According to these accounts, comprehensive reform programs that unified preexisting social insurance programs and standardized benefits provided the foundation for a dramatic expansion in coverage to everyone who earned a living, whether wage workers, salaried employees, or the self-employed. New constitutions prominently featured an array of social rights, especially the right to work and the right to social security. These sweeping reforms punctuated industrialization drives and the nationalization of industry at the end of transitional two- or three-year economic plans. Almost every Eastern European country reported completely eliminating unemployment in this period.[114]

Much is forgotten from these accounts. Most important, failures are erased, such as the unsustainable initial social insurance program of the War Communism period of the Russian Revolution, which offered generous benefits and extremely broad coverage.[115] Differences are also obscured by the overdrawn contrast between commu-

113. Quanguo zonggonghui, *Sulian gonghui*, 5–6; Yang Zhi, *Sulian laodong baoxian zhidu*, 3.

114. Zhang Yongmao, *Jiekesiluofake de shehui baoxian*, 5–7; Li Rongting, *Shehui baoxian gailun*, 68–73; WFTU, *Report of Activity*, 136–62.

115. Rimlinger, *Welfare Policy and Industrialization*, 259–60.

nist and capitalist social insurance, leaving the variation among communist countries unclear. In this depiction, agricultural Romania is portrayed as eliminating unemployment as rapidly as industrialized Czechoslovakia. This portrayal also overstated the progress made in the Soviet Union, suggesting that it had already completed the process of expansion. In the early 1950s when translated works were published in China, the Soviet Union still had a narrow welfare state. Like most capitalist countries, the Soviets required multiple rounds of reform to achieve broad coverage. In 1956, a major Soviet reform expanded coverage to all employees and their dependents (a reform described in the Chinese literature as taking place in 1932). Nearly universal coverage was only achieved in 1964, when farmers were finally incorporated into the Soviet welfare state.[116] Whether by omission or design, the message to Chinese policy makers was clear: comprehensive welfare reform at the end of the First Five Year Plan was the route to a broad welfare state.

The cumulative impact of this international influence was visible soon after the 1949 Chinese Communist Revolution. When the CCP adopted its social insurance program in 1951, it also endorsed the goal of creating a broad welfare state. This commitment was evident in the preamble to the labor insurance regulations, calling for the program's expansion as soon as wartime conditions eased. This promise was spelled out in more detail in the official labor union newspaper, *Labor Gazette* (*Laodong gongbao*), which devoted most of its May Day issue to publicizing the new program. In one article, a Labor Department official in the East China regional government described the CCP's strategy for expanding coverage in some detail. Announcing the goal of covering all people who supported themselves entirely or even partially from wages (including seasonal and other temporary workers with their own land in the countryside), he explained that it would take time to achieve that goal. The unfinished war, the struggling economy, and the half-built union organization were cited as factors that temporarily limited the scope of the labor insurance program. These 1951 policy decisions made China a typical developing country in the timing of its adoption of the welfare state, as well as in its choice of program design.

---

116. George and Manning, *Socialism, Social Welfare and the Soviet Union*, 42.

It was a pioneer in the developing world, however, for following the communist model and quickly adopting ambitious reforms to achieve broad coverage.

## *The Long View: The First Century of the Globalization of the Welfare State*

The globalization of welfare policies accelerated rapidly during the twentieth century, as international policy networks were broadened and institutionalized. In the first half of the twentieth century, imperialism was one of the most significant constraints on the diffusion of the welfare state. The Second World War was a catalyst in the process of diffusion, both by inserting welfare into international relations and by undermining the foundations of imperialism. When decolonization removed this key obstacle, newly sovereign nations quickly moved to adopt welfare legislation. As a result, international politics played a far more important role in shaping the diffusion of the welfare state in the developing world than domestic politics or economic development.

Even though the Cold War divided many of these policy networks, political competition between the capitalist and communist sides sustained the momentum in welfare policy diffusion. But patterns of diffusion diverged, with almost all communist countries adopting ambitious reforms to expand coverage, but only about one-fourth of the capitalist world following suit. Political differences help explain these outcomes, but the nature of the coverage of the reform policies developed on each side was also important. The Soviet Union promoted a relatively simple, standardized welfare reform policy that facilitated its spread through the communist world. There was no comparable policy package for the capitalist countries.

Chinese officials and policy experts were first drawn into international policy networks in the 1920s, and took on a more active role in the 1940s and 1950s. Although these networks grew increasingly open, they were dominated first by the imperial powers and then by the Cold War superpowers. Welfare policies achieved broad consensus in China because they had been endorsed as the gold standard in social policy in Geneva and Moscow, not because they had strong support from Chinese citizens. In this unequal global context, Chinese policy experts' main impact on the diffusion of these policies lay in the way they translated and framed international debates. They not only limited the range of policies considered, but helped shape a strong political consensus in China in favor of creating a social insurance welfare state with broad population coverage.

CHAPTER 2

# The Nationalist Origins of the
# Chinese Welfare State, 1943–49

Understanding how international influences shaped the adoption of new welfare policies in China requires examining the evolution of welfare politics in the 1940s and early 1950s. The KMT began advocating for social insurance in the 1920s and considered social insurance legislation in the 1930s (see chapter 1). But this early embrace of the idea of a welfare state was tempered by an equally strong sense of caution that China's political and economic difficulties militated against concrete action to create a welfare state until conditions improved. Semicolonialism and lack of national unity were seen as obstacles to major welfare initiatives any time in the near future.

After twenty years of pragmatic caution, however, the Nationalists suddenly reversed course. In the depths of the Second World War in 1943, the Nationalist government adopted China's first national welfare programs for workers: the Worker Welfare and Unemployment Relief programs. By committing the central government to the welfare of China's workers, these programs set an important precedent for the welfare state initiatives that followed in 1951. The adoption and implementation of wartime welfare programs raise fundamental questions. Most immediately, why did the Nationalist regime abandon its caution to take the initiative in welfare policy precisely when it was at the nadir of its power? Moreover, did challenging wartime conditions limit the scope of the Chinese welfare state?

To understand why the KMT reversed course, we need to examine the political forces behind welfare reform in the 1940s. International influence on the KMT escalated dramatically after the Second Sino-Japanese War widened into the Second World War in 1941. Once China joined the Allied Powers, it began receiving policy advice and economic assistance from Great Britain and the United States (as discussed in chapter 1).

Even more important was the pressure that came from within the Nationalist regime. The war's reversals pushed the KMT to launch new political reforms to reinvigorate its control over Chinese society, including a shift to authoritarian state corporatism. Different factions within the KMT responded to the political opportunities opened up by political reform by stepping up their own competition for dominance within the Nationalist regime. This factional conflict promoted bold policy initiatives even as it undermined their implementation.

Bottom-up demand for welfare was probably never higher in the sense that war and the Japanese occupation created widespread unemployment and a massive refugee crisis. But the scale and intensity of the human suffering was not matched by political demand for welfare.[1] Strikes and protests were much less frequent in Nationalist territories during the Second World War, and when they did occur they tended to focus on resisting Japanese aggression rather than making new claims on the state.[2] Similarly, there were few strikes, protests, or other forms of pro-welfare mobilization in the territories under Japanese or Communist control.[3] Although bottom-up pressure was not a major factor in policy making, its role in postwar implementation was more significant.

The combined forces of factional conflict and bottom-up demand help explain the KMT's surprising policy reversal in the Second World War. They also help explain the limitations of program implementation during the Chinese Civil War that followed. This chapter explores the politics behind the KMT's new national welfare initiatives, first examining the policy-making process at the national level leading up to the

1. Janet Chen, *Guilty of Indigence*, 129–30, 171–72.
2. Epstein, *Notes on Labor Problems*, 80–89; Howard, *Workers at War*, 188.
3. Perry, *Shanghai on Strike*, 110–14.

1943 initiatives and then focusing on implementation in Shanghai from 1945 to 1949. In addition to establishing a baseline for comparison to the Communist welfare state, this chapter addresses the question of whether the wartime origins of the Chinese welfare state left a lasting legacy that contributed to its narrow reach.

## Welfare Policy and the Shift to Authoritarian Corporatism

The Second Sino-Japanese War was China's most severe crisis in nearly a century of crises. The Nationalist government lost the eastern half of China to Japanese control and was forced to retreat to remote southwestern mountains to try to outlast the war. Not surprisingly, this military debacle loosened the KMT's dictatorship. The war with Japan allowed the CCP to survive, by bringing an end to the KMT's military suppression campaigns. The war also loosened the KMT's authoritarian controls over civil society in the territories still under its control. In almost every way, the war had a devastating impact on KMT power.

KMT controls on civil society had begun to erode in the lead-up to the 1937 Japanese invasion. Japanese aggression first began to undermine Chinese national unity in 1931, with the takeover of Manchuria in northeastern China and the creation of a nominally independent kingdom under Japanese control. From that stronghold, the Japanese military gradually encroached southward in the early 1930s by provoking border conflicts with Chinese troops. In 1935, Chinese activists across the country responded to Japanese aggression by organizing a national protest movement to resist Japanese imperialism and oppose KMT leader Chiang Kaishek's short-term strategy of appeasement until he could build up China's military power. Reaching its high point of mobilization in 1936–37, this "National Salvation" movement (*jiuguo yundong*) marked an important first step in loosening the KMT dictatorship. Censorship, prohibitions on demonstrations, and restrictions on civic organizations proved ineffective in the face of passionate nationalism, which could not easily be suppressed precisely because of its patriotic support for the Chinese state.[4] Although it ultimately took the threat of a military coup in the Xi'an Incident of 1936 to force KMT leader Chiang Kaishek to respond to Japanese incursions, the National Salvation movement played a key role in mobilizing public opinion.

It was in this volatile period of a resurgent but vulnerable civil society that China's first national labor organization emerged. The Chinese Association of Labor (Zhongguo laodong xiehui) was established in 1935 in part to represent Chinese workers in the ILO, which required all member states to send independent labor and business representatives to the annual labor conference.[5] The new Chinese Association of Labor included both labor unions and individual workers as members, and it represented Chinese labor in the ILO from 1936 onward. But it was registered in China as a "cultural organization" rather than a labor union and given a limited mandate to research and publish about labor issues. As a result, the association mainly confined its activities to attending international meetings, holding press conferences, and publishing journals.[6] Since labor unions and workers were not required to join the Chinese Association of Labor but could voluntarily choose whether to support the organization, its status as a cultural organization ironically made the association the most democratic part of the official Chinese labor movement.

The first two men appointed to lead the new association, Lu Jingshi and Zhu Xuefan, were both prominent KMT party members whose careers had followed the rise of the official Nationalist labor movement. Their first introduction to labor politics came when they were young postal workers in the Shanghai Postal Workers Union during the massive general strike in the May Thirtieth Movement in 1925.[7] Led by Communist labor organizer Li Lisan, Shanghai's May Thirtieth Movement forged an alliance against imperialism that united labor, business, and students to shut down the city's economy, shatter warlord rule over the city, and eventually turn over the city to KMT control in 1927. As newly minted labor organizers, Lu and Zhu played relatively

---

4. Coble, *Facing Japan*, 293–95, 339–40; Fung, *In Search of Chinese Democracy*, 146.
5. Lu Xiangxian, ed., *Zhongguo laodong xiehui*, 21.
6. Ibid., 7–8.
7. Lu Xiangxian and Liu Songbin, *Zhu Xuefan*, 14–15.

minor roles in this high point of Shanghai's storied labor history. For example, Zhu Xuefan's only encounter with movement leader Li Lisan came when he was deputized to deliver a message to strike headquarters in 1925.

Their youth and inexperience helped Zhu Xuefan and Lu Jingshi to survive the bloody suppression of the CCP and leftist labor unions in 1927–28, when Li Lisan and other Shanghai labor leaders were forced to flee. Lu and Zhu joined the KMT in 1928 and then rose through the ranks in the party's "yellow" unions. One key to their rise was their membership in the Green Gang, the organized crime syndicate that dominated opium smuggling, gambling, and labor racketeering in Shanghai.[8] Although Lu and Zhu do not seem to have been labor racketeers themselves, they swore loyalty to Green Gang leader Du Yuesheng, who wielded the real power on the factory floor in Shanghai in the 1930s. By the time of their 1935 promotion to chairman and international liaison of the Chinese Association of Labor, Lu Jingshi led the national Postal Workers Union and his ally Zhu Xuefan led the Shanghai General Labor Union.

The leadership of Lu and Zhu demonstrated that every aspect of the association was ambiguous. A national labor organization that was not a labor union, the association was also officially independent of the Nationalist party-state but led by KMT cadres. Most ambiguous of all, the source of the two men's power in the labor movement was their role as disciples to Shanghai's most powerful gangster. This blurry overlap among state, society, and organized crime was no doubt not what ILO leaders had in mind when they pressed for liberalizing the Chinese labor movement, but the reform added new dynamism to labor politics in China.

Although both Zhu Xuefan and Lu Jingshi hoped to use the Chinese Association of Labor as a launching pad for achieving wider leadership roles in the Nationalist regime, they responded to the crises of the National Salvation movement and the 1937 Japanese invasion in very different ways. A National Salvation activist since the early 1930s, Zhu Xuefan worked to build on the popular mobilization of

---

8. Martin, *Shanghai Green Gang*, 82–85, 169; Lu Xiangxian and Liu Songbin, *Zhu Xuefan*, 27–29.

the movement to recruit new members and expand the labor association. After the war began, Zhu only accelerated his efforts, even as the conflict limited his scope of action. Forced out of Shanghai, Zhu traveled to the cities that remained under KMT control to rally workers behind the war effort. After the announcement of the Second United Front, an anti-Japanese alliance between the Nationalist and Communist parties, Zhu supported the application from the Communist base area unions to join the association in 1939.[9] In the face of strenuous objections from Lu Jingshi and other KMT labor leaders, however, Zhu was forced to stop the expansion of the association in Communist-held territories even after he took over leadership of the organization. Moreover, the friendship between Lu and Zhu never recovered from their fundamental disagreement over the role of the Communist base area unions in the Chinese Association of Labor.

Rather than try to build up the association, Lu Jingshi sought higher office in the central Nationalist government, requiring him to step down from his leadership position in the association in conformance with ILO regulations. In 1939, Lu succeeded in gaining an appointment to the central party Department of Social Affairs, which was upgraded to a central government ministry in 1940.[10] One key function of both the party and the government agencies was the regulation of civil society, with separate divisions to supervise business, labor, and all other civic organizations. Lu Jingshi's promotion to direct the Organization Division in the Ministry of Social Affairs meant that he gained the central power over labor unions that the labor association lacked as a cultural organization.

While this conflict within the KMT labor movement played out, the National Salvation movement also faced considerable uncertainty even as its popular support surged. On the one hand, the war gave new leverage to democracy activists inside and outside the KMT, pushing the party to establish political assemblies at every level of the political hierarchy from the local to the national level. The new assemblies were advisory organizations with no real power, but they represented the first significant step toward the "Tutelary Democracy" under one-party

9. Lu Xiangxian and Liu Songbin, *Zhu Xuefan*, 78.
10. Li Jiaqi, ed., *Shanghai gongyun*, 807.

KMT rule originally envisioned by party founder Sun Yat-sen.[11] On the other hand, the informal liberalization of civil society achieved by the National Salvation movement proved difficult to consolidate under wartime conditions. After the Japanese invasion, National Salvation groups were forced to retreat along with the KMT, dependent on its military protection for their survival.

In the temporary KMT capital of Wuhan in central China, the party and civil society groups reached a new accommodation of sorts. The groups were allowed to apply for registration with the Nationalist government, a process that held out the promise of gaining legal status. But the Nationalist government took no action to review the applications, leaving the organizations in a gray zone of being neither legal nor illegal.[12] When the Nationalists retreated again to the city of Chongqing in southwestern China in 1938, these groups were again forced to follow. The political and legal stand-off between state and society continued with no new efforts to return to the selective repression of the late 1920s, but also no initiatives to consolidate the liberalization of civil society of the mid-1930s.

Soon after Pearl Harbor widened the Second Sino-Japanese War into the Second World War in December 1941, the Nationalist government issued the 1942 Emergency National Mobilization Law.[13] The new wartime policy recast state-society relations in fundamental ways intended to mobilize key sectors of society proactively to support the state and the war effort. In the sectors of civil society deemed politically important, such as business, labor, and education, the KMT set up official associations which every business, industrial worker, and university student was required to join. Even though critics pointed out the marked similarities between the new Chinese regulations and the wartime labor policies of the fascist powers, the KMT portrayed the emergency regulations as an essential element of its renewed war effort.[14]

11. Fung, *In Search of Chinese Democracy*, 30, 144–65; Shyu, "China's Wartime Parliament," 276–78.
12. Israel and Klein, *Rebels and Bureaucrats*, 169; Epstein, *Notes on Labor Problems*, 81.
13. Epstein, *Notes on Labor Problems*, 62.
14. Wales, *Chinese Labor Movement*, 107.

A new Labor Union Law drafted by the Ministry of Social Affairs was issued the following year.[15] The 1943 law made the emergency expansion of the official labor movement permanent, consolidating the wartime shift to state corporatism. It also imposed numerous layers of state control over the new unions, including powers over leadership selection, prohibitions on holding meetings without the presence of KMT party members or government liaisons, and provisions for regular reports on their activities and finances to the Ministry of Social Affairs. Finally, emergency restrictions on labor politics were made permanent, including bans on all nonofficial labor organizations and all forms of collective labor protest, such as strikes and slow-downs. [16]

There were still limits on how comprehensive the Nationalists wanted this new union system to be. One important limitation was that many of the new enterprise unions were just paper organizations that existed in name only.[17] Another important limitation was that the new labor law did not authorize the creation of a national union organization, leaving the Chinese Association of Labor in its ambiguous role as a national cultural organization for labor.[18]

These political reforms in 1942–43 marked a decisive change in the KMT's approach to managing state-society relations. Rather than try to restrict and repress popular mobilization, the KMT sought to supplant it with top-down mobilization of key social forces in support of the state. In this swiftly changing context, Lu Jingshi seemed far more strategic than his former colleague Zhu Xuefan in making the jump from "society" to "state" in 1939. As a result, Lu was in a position to shape and control this new initiative to create a state corporatist regime, while Zhu was still struggling to sustain the labor association's operations in the rump territory still under Nationalist control.

But establishing state corporatism proved to be much more difficult than issuing new legislation. Taming unofficial organizations already in place was challenging, as was creating new organizations from scratch. Even more problematic was the surge of factional competition within

15. Li Jiaqi, *Shanghi gongyun*, 295; Shehui bu, *Laogong fagui*, 1–8.
16. Shehui bu, *Laogong fagui*, 5–6.
17. Epstein, *Notes on Labor Problems*, 89.
18. Shehui bu, *Laogong fagui*, 8.

the KMT to control these corporatist institutions and the new sources of power they promised to deliver.[19] The personal split between Lu Jingshi and Zhu Xuefan was magnified and institutionalized in the rapidly growing official labor movement mandated in the 1942–43 reforms. These forces for competition within the Nationalist regime set the stage for the welfare reforms of the 1940s.

## Wartime Welfare Policy Making

This major shift in state-society relations was soon followed by China's first major welfare legislation for workers: the Worker Welfare and Unemployment Relief programs. These new welfare initiatives fit the model of state corporatism, since they helped to build up the official labor movement by providing resources for organizational development and incentives for workers to join. But a closer examination of the politics of welfare in this period suggests that international influence and factional conflict played a more direct role in shaping policy than workers' incorporation into these new political institutions.[20]

For the Worker Welfare program, the international influence came from the American labor movement's effort to promote union solidarity among the Allied Powers. The U.S. Congress of Industrial Organizations (CIO) launched a war relief program for Allied labor unions, which expanded quickly, raising more than $22 million in donations

19. Wu T'ien-wei, "Contending Political Forces," 52–62; Perry, *Shanghai on Strike*, 120–23; Eastman, *Seeds of Destruction*, 91–96, 120–21.

20. Previous scholarship has traced the origins of the Worker Welfare program to the efforts by state-owned enterprises and private companies to expand their fringe benefits to cope with high personnel turnover during the Second World War. (See Frazier, *Making of the Chinese Industrial Workplace*; Howard, *Workers at War*; Bian, *Making of the State Enterprise System*.) The war accelerated the long-term trend toward company welfare that began in the 1920s, suggesting that political opposition to welfare from capitalists was declining. But this trend does not account for the introduction of unemployment relief in the same period, nor does it explain how and why reforms at the enterprise level translated into national policy. A broader view of welfare politics outside the workplace complements this earlier explanation.

from American workers.[21] The American union found a receptive partner in the Chinese Association of Labor. After Pearl Harbor, association director Zhu Xuefan was stranded in the middle of an international tour, due to the temporary suspension of commercial shipping in the Pacific. While staying with the sons of Green Gang leader Du Yuesheng in Massachusetts, Zhu was able to forge new contacts in the CIO, including Monroe Sweetland, director of the CIO War Relief Committee. Sweetland committed the American union to provide the Chinese Association of Labor more than $600,000 per year for the duration of the war.[22]

This new foreign aid allowed the Chinese association to set up welfare programs for workers based on American models, such as the CIO's own worker welfare program. In 1942, the association first established a free guesthouse for skilled workers who fled the occupied regions of China to come to the temporary Nationalist capital in Chongqing.[23] From that modest beginning, the association went on to establish worker welfare societies in every industrial district in Chongqing and every other major city under KMT control, including Chengdu, Guiyang, and Guilin. These worker welfare societies provided a wide range of services to their members, including medical care, subsidies for disabled and pregnant workers, day care, and schools for their children. The Chongqing Worker Welfare Society even had a large movie theater named the American Workers' Hall (Meigong tang) in honor of its donors.[24] The scale of the new resources transformed the Chinese Association of Labor overnight from a small public relations organization to a major player in the official KMT labor movement. In addition to expanding the association's mandate, the funding also helped it develop a cadre of young, well-educated labor activists and to recruit large numbers of workers to join as individuals.[25]

21. *CIO News,* Jan. 19, 1942, 5; *CIO News* Aug. 30, 1943, 7; Fones-Wolf, "Labor and Social Welfare," 617–18; Tone, *Business of Benevolence,* 52–53.
22. Lu Xiangxian and Liu Songbin, *Zhu Xuefan,* 79; *CIO News,* Jan. 19, 1942, 5.
23. Lu Xiangxian and Liu Songbin, *Zhu Xuefan,* 81; *CIO News,* Oct. 26, 1942, 8.
24. Lu Xiangxian and Liu Songbin, *Zhu Xuefan,* 83; Howard, *Workers at War,* 252.
25. Lu Xiangxian and Liu Songbin, *Zhu Xuefan,* 145, 149.

Lu Jingshi's initial attempt to secure direct control over the American aid flowing to the association failed because the CIO refused to provide funding to either government agencies or official government-sponsored labor unions. That failure led the KMT to imitate and institutionalize the association's program by issuing the Worker Welfare regulations in 1943,[26] which created worker welfare programs in large factories and government agencies with more than two hundred employees as well as in urban districts and entire cities, matching the hierarchy of the party-sponsored labor unions.[27] The government program was corporatist in design: managed by joint labor-management committees established at each level of the program and funded by taxes on both workers' wages and company profits. Each of these corporatist committees was designed to be dominated by the union, which received two-thirds of the seats by regulation. The program granted considerable discretion to these corporatist committees in deciding services and benefits, which could encompass anything from cafeterias to dormitories, health clinics, schools, public baths, laundries, libraries, and recreational facilities. Although the new KMT Worker Welfare program had the advantage of a more secure legal foundation, it was still hard-pressed to compete with the independent resources flowing to the Chinese Association of Labor's worker welfare programs.

The official KMT labor unions had more luck in controlling the new Unemployment Relief program, which was also adopted in 1943. In this case, international influence came from a different source: the United Nations Recovery and Rehabilitation Administration (UNRRA), which did not place any restrictions on the kinds of labor unions eligible for economic assistance. The new KMT Unemployment Relief program was shaped to meet UNRRA standards, which the Chinese government endorsed in 1943, when it signed the agreement for distributing foreign aid in the postwar period.[28] The program targeted union members in shut-down factories, offering them grain or cash from the union for a limited time period until the factory could be

---

26. Epstein, *Notes on Labor Problems*, 97; Shehui bu, *Shehui fagui*, 163–69; Howard, *Workers at War*, 251.
27. Shehui bu, *Shehui fagui*, 166.
28. *UNRRA in China*, 1, 43–44.

reopened, usually three to six months. In addition to this more passive form of relief to help workers survive temporary unemployment, the program also sought to provide proactive relief that offered more long-term assistance, such as vocational training, public works jobs, and worker-initiated projects known as "self-help production."[29]

In 1944, the Chinese National Recovery and Rehabilitation Administration (CNRRA) was established as a ministerial-level agency to receive and distribute more than $517 million in supplies and funding.[30] UNRRA's influence went even deeper than economic aid to include personnel, expert advice, and training. UNRRA placed 783 administrators from twenty-five countries in Chinese government agencies to provide advice and training on administering the aid program. The new CNRRA ministry even included an office staffed by five lawyers to draft any legislation needed by the agency for submission to the Legislative Yuan. In addition, UNRRA sent ninety-six Chinese government officials overseas for more specialized, long-term training in government agencies around the world.[31]

As the new CNRRA prepared its postwar relief programs, factional rivalry between the Chinese Association of Labor and the KMT official unions fueled the rapid expansion of the Worker Welfare program during the last two years of the war. For example, the Chongqing General Labor Union began organizing a separate municipal worker welfare society in 1944 to rival the association's existing Chongqing Worker Welfare Society. No attempt was made to coordinate much less merge the two organizations. Moreover, Zhu Xuefan was passed over when the board of directors for the new KMT Chongqing Worker Welfare Society was appointed.[32]

Zhu's response to this slight was to send more than two thousand individual association members to the founding meeting of the new organization, disrupting the rally with loud protests. Angry KMT labor leaders demanded that Zhu Xuefan sign a letter of regret on behalf of

29. Shehui bu, *Shehui fagui*, 201; Wu Li, "Jianguo chuqi," 72.
30. United Nations Relief and Rehabilitation Administration, *UNRRA in China*, 6, 14–15, 200.
31. Chinese National Relief and Rehabilitation Administration, *CNRRA: Purpose, Functions, Organization*, 20.
32. Epstein, *Notes on Labor Problems*, 99.

the Chinese Association of Labor, but he refused.[33] So even though the association could claim credit for having prompted the KMT to undertake its first significant welfare program for workers, it gained no role in the new program, which competed with the association's American-funded programs rather than complementing them.

This factional mobilization and countermobilization helped to spur the KMT's policy reversals after decades of pragmatic caution. Combined with direct foreign influence through economic assistance and policy advice, the new pressures produced China's first national welfare programs for workers. Even after the shift to authoritarian corporatism, however, the policy-making process was not a negotiation among competing factions, much less among the interest groups most affected by them. Instead, policy making was defined by mimicry, adopting foreign models and rival programs wholesale.

Although the KMT Worker Welfare and Unemployment Relief programs were significant welfare initiatives launched under difficult wartime conditions, they were never considered to be a possible alternative to social insurance. For example, at the KMT's Sixth National Congress in May 1945, the party passed a resolution calling for the expansion of the Worker Welfare program. But the KMT also adopted a resolution calling for a national social insurance program to insure citizens for disability, illness, maternity, old age, unemployment, and death.[34] Although the long-held goal of social insurance was not supplanted by these welfare programs, the KMT continued to show some measure of caution in the ambition of its welfare policies in the midst of the war.

## The KMT's Return to Shanghai, 1945

How did the political forces propelling the adoption of new welfare legislation shape its implementation in the postwar period? Top-down factional competition continued to be strong in the postwar period,

33. Pepper, *Civil War*, 103; Epstein, *Notes on Labor Problems*, 99–100.
34. *Zhongguo Guomindang di liuci quanguo daibiao dahui*, 35.

even after the Chinese Civil War broke out. Bottom-up political forces, however, became much more important at the local level. Capitalists and workers had more impact on local welfare politics because active cooperation was necessary to implement these new welfare programs and the new corporatist institutions created to administer them gave each group new sources of power as well.

After eight years of reform and planning, the Nationalist government had a comprehensive set of legislation ready to guide the takeover of Japanese-occupied territories when the Second World War came to an abrupt end on August 15, 1945. But the difficult political and economic conditions in these territories persisted. The Chinese economy was in shambles after eight years of war, with regional famine, millions of displaced refugees, and tens of millions of unemployed workers. Conditions for the outbreak of the Chinese Civil War were also in place, with the KMT ruling the Southwest, the CCP controlling the Northwest, and both sides eager to win the race to accept the Japanese surrender across the eastern half of the country.

There were two sources of hope, however, for the nascent Chinese welfare state in 1945. First, the colonial concessions had been eliminated during the Second World War, reunifying China's major ports for the first time in nearly a century. Second, UNRRA's offer of economic aid for relief and reconstruction promised new resources for the beleaguered Chinese government. Even with these gains, the economic and political obstacles to the implementation of the Worker Welfare and Unemployment Relief programs loomed large in 1945.

Shanghai was one of the biggest prizes in the race to take over Japanese-held territory. Initially, the CCP underground thought about exploiting its hard won advantage in wartime organizing by launching an armed workers' uprising to seize control of the city. But central CCP leaders called for caution instead in response to Soviet pressure.[35] As a result, the KMT's return to the city could proceed gradually over the weeks following the abrupt end of the war without facing any organized, armed political opposition.

Despite this respite, the KMT takeover of Shanghai was by all accounts a disaster. KMT officials were slow to assert their authority

35. Perry, *Shanghai on Strike*, 117.

and establish a new municipal government, but they rushed to seize control of surrendered Japanese assets—everything from factories, to villas, to cars—for personal gain as much as for the state.[36] In addition to this sudden surge in corruption, the Nationalist government turned the economic crisis at the end of the war into a full-fledged economic collapse. The breakdown of foreign trade, commodity shortages, and uncertainty over the ownership of Japanese and state-owned firms quickly led to the shutdown of most industrial production in Shanghai. The KMT's slow response to these problems only exacerbated them. Moreover, currency reform in September 1945 deepened the crisis, since it was marred by punishing exchange rates and extensive arbitrage by corrupt government officials.

In comparison to this economic disaster, the KMT had more success with its political reforms. Within months of the Japanese surrender, the KMT had established all the new political institutions that had been developed in southwestern China during the war. The official labor unions and business federations were first off the block. The prewar leaders of the Shanghai General Labor Union (Shanghai shi zong gonghui) and the Shanghai Chamber of Commerce (Shanghai shi zong shanghui) returned to the city within the first few days after the Japanese surrender and reclaimed their former offices from Japanese-sponsored wartime organizations that had taken their place.[37] Zhu Xuefan was still technically the chairman of the Shanghai General Labor Union since he had not resigned after the KMT retreat from Shanghai in 1937. But after the war, his ally Zhou Xuexiang took on the work of reviving and reforming the official union.

Lu Jingshi was also among the first KMT officials to return to Shanghai. Despite his position in the national KMT Ministry of Social Affairs, Lu avoided the former capital in Nanjing in favor of returning home to set up a special Shanghai office for the Ministry of Social Affairs. If this ad hoc government agency blurred the lines between the central and municipal governments, his Loyal Salvation Army blurred the lines between the official union and the Green Gang. Lu Jingshi recruited this paramilitary force from Shanghai's large reservoir

---

36. Pepper, *Civil War*, 17.
37. Shao Xinshi and Deng Ziba, eds., *Shanghai shi Laogong nianjian, 1948*, 82.

of gangsters and unemployed workers to break strikes and intimidate communist labor organizers in the chaotic period following the Japanese surrender.[38]

At the same time that Lu Jingshi was breaking strikes, the new postwar version of the Shanghai General Labor Union was mobilizing a much larger and more comprehensive organization than had ever existed before. In the first two and a half years after the KMT takeover, the general union established 453 enterprise unions with more than 500,000 members, making the postwar union more than four times larger than its prewar predecessor.[39] These postwar labor unions and business federations were also better integrated into the Nationalist regime, opening up new possibilities for corporatist bargaining and other forms of interest-group politics. For example, the new Shanghai Municipal Council (Shanghai shi canyi hui) included official delegates from both the Shanghai Chamber of Commerce and the Shanghai General Labor Union. Although the Shanghai Municipal Council lacked any defined power over the municipal government, it did provide a forum for discussing local issues and policies.

Since the leadership of all of these new political institutions was dominated by KMT members, the postwar political reforms seemed to give the KMT unprecedented reach and influence over two groups most important to its ambitious welfare agenda: business and labor. But both the unemployment relief and the worker welfare programs were implemented through a series of new ad hoc organizations that did not always have clear relationships to these corporatist institutions. These disjunctures within the Nationalist regime were not just transitional problems stemming from the KMT's sudden return to power in Shanghai. Instead, they only grew more numerous and more significant over time.

One reason for this contradictory outcome was that KMT factionalism in the official labor movement was much more complicated at the local level than at the national level. In place of the two-way struggle between the Chinese Association of Labor and the official labor unions

38. Perry, *Shanghai on Strike*, 20; Shen Yixing, et al., eds., *Shanghai gongren yundong shi*, 305–6.
39. Shanghai shi, *1946 Shanghai shi nianjian*, M2; Shanghai zonggonghui, *1948 laodong nianjian*, 83.

under the Ministry of Social Affairs in the wartime capital of Chong-qing, as many as six different KMT factions were competing to organize workers in Shanghai after 1945. In addition to Zhu Xuefan's and Lu Jingshi's factions, an underground KMT labor movement had been organized during the war. The KMT Youth League, the civilian secret police, and the military secret police were all trying to mobilize workers as well, despite lacking any organizational mandate or any previous connection to labor.[40] The Green Gang provided the final layer of complication, since it was still operating its labor rackets but no longer had the kind of exclusive control on the factory floor that the KMT had ceded to it before the war. The multiplication of factions provided more fuel for the mobilization of labor at the expense of its integration into the political regime.

## KMT Unemployment Relief

Unemployment relief was the first welfare program for workers established in Shanghai, an immediate response to the economic crisis that followed the Japanese surrender. The pressure to compete in this rough form of labor politics pushed KMT labor leaders to mobilize the urban poor far beyond the confines of the factory walls. Although the main purpose of the Loyal Salvation Army was to provide muscle for the KMT labor movement, Lu Jingshi also portrayed it as an emergency form of unemployment relief for the men who rallied to his cause.

Lu Jingshi soon followed up this informal unemployment relief with a more official effort based on the national regulations, establishing the Shanghai Unemployment Relief Commission on October 1, 1945. The Unemployment Commission was an interagency organization that included both central and local government officials. Central government officials included representatives from the military and the national Finance Ministry, Economics Ministry, and Ministry of Social Affairs. Local officials included staff from the municipal KMT party

---

40. Perry, *Shanghai on Strike*, 121–23; Pepper, *Civil War*, 105–6.

branch, the municipal police and social affairs bureaus, the Shanghai General Labor Union, and the Shanghai Chamber of Commerce.[41]

Since most of the resources for this emergency relief program came from the central government and UNRRA, it is not surprising that the Shanghai Chamber of Commerce supported the new initiative.[42] Indeed, business support extended beyond the official KMT business associations. For example, wealthy businessman Wen Yingchu submitted a report directly to the Nationalist government detailing the extent of the unemployment crisis in Shanghai and calling for comprehensive unemployment relief. Business support, however, only went so far, since plans to raise unemployment relief funds through voluntary donations from the official business associations under the Chamber of Commerce never materialized.[43]

Since the Shanghai General Labor Union was led by Zhu Xuefan's allies, Lu Jingshi's Unemployment Relief Commission did seem to promote factional cooperation in the early days of the program. In addition to the two general labor union representatives serving on the commission, the union was also directly involved in the administration of the new program in ways that created incentives for the unemployed to join. For example, the commission determined eligibility and distributed benefits by requiring group applications from each factory through the Chamber of Commerce and the official labor union. In addition to these group incentives to join the union, there were individual incentives as well. For example, workers who were union members were automatically eligible for benefits, whereas those who were not union members had to find at least three other workers to vouch for them in the application process.[44] Of the 393 factories that applied for relief in Shanghai, 323 were granted eligibility, an approval rate of more than 80 percent. The commission distributed grain cash benefits to the 90,640 workers from those factories over the last three months of 1945.[45]

41. Shanghai shi, *1946 Shanghai shi nianjian*, N18.
42. Li Jianhua, "Zhanhou Shanghai shi," 4; Shanghai shi, *1946 Shanghai shi nianjian*, N19.
43. SMA, Q201-2-31.
44. SMA, Q6-7-578.
45. Shanghai shi, *1946 Shanghai shi nianjian*, N19.

The unemployed workers laid off after the Japanese surrender were a small fraction of the urban poor in this period. Estimates of the total number of unemployed range as high as 250,000 to 300,000 in 1945–46.[46] The number of urban poor probably reached the millions. Although most of the urban poor continued to be ignored by the state in this period, several groups were targeted for government action. Probably the largest groups were "vagrants" (liumang), a vague category of working-age people without formal employment. In contrast to the recently unemployed, vagrants were detained in large "winter relief" camps and then evacuated from Shanghai by the city government and Chinese charities and native place associations. Both winter relief and evacuations of the poor were long-standing Chinese practices that the KMT expanded and institutionalized in the late 1940s.[47] The newly created identity of "unemployed worker" was infinitely preferable to being labeled a vagrant or even a refugee.

Although Lu Jingshi was actively involved in this interagency unemployment relief program, he was not above exploiting the unemployment crisis at the same time. In the early stage after the war, Lu Jingshi's most significant rival in the local KMT labor movement was Wu Shaoshu, who had led the KMT underground during the war. Wu was able to use his head start in Shanghai to secure the coveted positions of deputy mayor and director of the Shanghai Bureau of Social Affairs.[48] Lu Jingshi turned up the heat against Wu Shaoshu by sending his Loyal Salvation Army to lead street demonstrations in protest against the Bureau of Social Affairs. The most embarrassing protest mobilized more than two thousand unemployed workers to greet the arrival of U.S. troops in Shanghai on September 19, 1945, with noisy slogans and vivid banners demanding food and jobs.[49] But the most politically effective demonstration came a few months later, on January 22, 1946, when more than ten thousand unemployed workers broke through police barricades to march on the Bureau of Social Affairs, once again demanding relief and jobs. Within days, Wu Shaoshu was

46. Pepper, Civil War, 109; Li Jiaqi, ed., Shanghai gongyun, 282.
47. Janet Chen, Guilty of Indigence; Dillon, "Middlemen," 33–35
48. Shanghai shi, 1946 Shanghai shi nianjian, A1, A18.
49. Li Jiaqi, ed., Shanghai gongyun , 282.

*Figure 2.1.* Shanghai Soup Kitchen Providing Relief in the 1940s

forced to resign as director of the bureau, and Lu Jingshi's ally, Wu Kaixian, was appointed to replace him.[50]

After Lu Jingshi's allies took over the leadership of the Shanghai Bureau of Social Affairs, the Ministry of Social Affairs' Shanghai Unemployment Relief Commission was reconstituted under the municipal bureau of social a;ffairs. At the same time, the Shanghai Unemployment Relief Commission's three-month emergency relief program was extended for another three months. With a staff of nearly fifty employees, the emergency relief program distributed cash, food, and clothing to the unemployed in early 1946 (fig. 2.1).[51] But Lu Jingshi's political victory in Shanghai proved short-lived; a new crisis emerged at the national level that undermined this local accomplishment.

50. Ibid., 36; Perry, *Shanghai on Strike*, 123.
51. SMA, Q6-7-568.

## Labor Factionalism at the National Level

The source of the crisis was American-led peace negotiations between the KMT and the CCP in January 1946 in Chongqing. U.S. General George Marshall presided over the formation of a new Political Consultative Conference to negotiate a political settlement, and he did not allow the KMT to dominate its membership in the same way it had controlled all previous wartime political assemblies. With the KMT only holding eight out of the thirty-eight seats, the 1946 Political Consultative Conference was anything but a rubber-stamp for the Nationalist government. Independent delegates active in the nascent democracy movement formed a coalition with Communist delegates to set the agenda, passing a series of resolutions to end KMT one-party rule, establish a transitional multiparty coalition government, convene a constitutional convention, and unify the KMT and CCP armies under government control.[52]

In the face of this challenge to its authoritarian rule, the KMT turned to its new corporatist institutions for political support outside the Political Consultative Conference. The KMT launched a petition drive in favor of continued one-party rule and added the signatures of 170 civic organizations, including the Chinese Association of Labor, without their leaders' knowledge. Zhu Xuefan's response to this bit of political theater was to send letters to all the newspapers in Chongqing exposing the fraud.[53] After this open defiance of his own party, Zhu decided to seize the moment to throw the support of the Chinese Association of Labor behind the new peace movement. In consultation with his most trusted and progressive aides, Zhu crafted his own "Twenty-three Demands" for Chinese labor. In addition to calling for peace and democracy, he advocated nationalizing the military, separating the party and state, eliminating party supervision of labor unions, and turning the Chinese Association of Labor into a legal national labor union federation. Last but not least, Zhu's demands

52. Pepper, *Civil War*, 137–38; Chang, *Third Force*, 147–49.
53. Epstein, *Notes on Labor Problems*, 103–4.

also included a call for social insurance.[54] After being turned down by several KMT-controlled newspapers, Zhu used his Communist contacts to publish his demands in the CCP newspaper, *New China Daily (Xinhua ribao)*.

Zhu's public defiance of his own party revealed a weakness of the KMT strategy for maintaining control over the official labor movement: the elaborate institutional infrastructure of party supervision could simply be sidestepped by party members in leadership positions. Once Zhu Xuefan abandoned the principles of the KMT and embraced democracy, the party had no legal recourse to stop him. Moreover, the tactic of withholding clear legal status from the Chinese Association of Labor also proved to be an ineffective control mechanism. Despite its registration as a cultural organization, the more the association acted like a national union, the more people began to consider it to be one, both in China and abroad.

Even if most newspapers failed to publicize them, Zhu Xuefan's Twenty-three Demands provoked strong reactions from all sides. The Political Consultative Conference delegates were emboldened by their support from a national, KMT-sponsored organization. The Communists trumpeted Zhu's appeal as an honest critique coming from a KMT leader, exposing the hypocrisy of the party's brand of Tutelary Democracy. Zhu's fellow KMT members were furious. The KMT delegates to the Political Consultative Conference accused Zhu Xuefan of becoming a communist tool. Zhu's old friends and colleagues in the KMT labor movement criticized his views as naive. Wu Kaixian, an old friend despite his alliance with Lu Jingshi, wrote Zhu to tell him that the Twenty-three Demands had caused considerable unease among Shanghai's KMT labor officials. Even Zhu's mentor, Green Gang leader Du Yuesheng, sent him a letter warning him that he had made a serious political mistake with little impact to show for it.[55]

Zhu Xuefan may have exposed a weakness in the KMT's labor controls, but his failure to win any of his demands indicated the limits of the Chinese Association of Labor's power. Without any formal, institutionalized role in the policy-making process, the association could

54. Lu Xiangxian, ed. *Zhongguo laodong xiehui*, 198–99.
55. Lu Xiangxian and Liu Songbin, *Zhu Xuefan*, 208.

not advance new policies, particularly those that opposed the interests of the ruling party. Even expressing dissent was a risky undertaking.

The KMT stepped up the pressure on Zhu Xuefan to recant his views, at the same time searching for ways to discredit him. For example, when a coalition of twenty-four progressive organizations made plans for a peace rally in Chongqing in February 1946, KMT leaders Lu Jingshi and Chen Lifu ordered Zhu Xuefan to recant his Twenty-three Demands and denounce the rally. When Zhu ignored their orders and organized five hundred Chinese Association of Labor workers to participate, the KMT sent undercover agents to heckle the speakers and disrupt the event. The agents managed to turn the rally into a riot, and many of the scheduled speakers were beaten in the melee. Although Zhu Xuefan escaped injury, he and the other organizers did not escape blame. They were later indicted on criminal charges for inciting the riot that had been directed against them. Although this subterfuge undermined the momentum of the democracy movement, neither it nor the false charges dented Zhu's defiance.[56]

After Zhu Xuefan returned from his annual trip to Europe for the ILO labor conference in the summer of 1946, he was confronted with charges from the KMT Chongqing General Labor Union of instigating a strike wave in the city. The official union backed up these political charges with criminal charges. Chongqing labor leaders went to the police claiming that Zhu Xuefan had misused American donations to the Chinese Association of Labor for his own personal gain. Unlike the riot charges, the accusation of corruption provided enough leverage for the Chongqing labor union to arrest all the progressive Chinese Association of Labor activists in Chongqing and seize association property, including its coveted worker welfare societies. Zhu himself avoided arrest only by staying in Shanghai.[57]

This factional infighting hurt the reputation of the Chinese Association of Labor and the official labor unions alike, but at the same time it fueled the expansion of the nascent Nationalist welfare state. Instead of lying low in Shanghai, Zhu Xuefan plunged into local labor politics and renewed his challenge to Lu Jingshi. On May 31, 1946, the Chinese

56. Ibid., 210–12; Eastman, *Seeds of Destruction,* 114–15.
57. Lu Xiangxian and Liu Songbin, *Zhu Xuefan,* 216–17.

Association of Labor organized more than one thousand unemployed workers who had returned to Shanghai from wartime factory jobs in KMT-held territory to file a group petition seeking jobs and housing from the Bureau of Social Affairs. After bureau officials refused to meet with the petitioners, they staged a sit-in at bureau offices, threatening to occupy them until they gained the help they were seeking.

Zhu Xuefan personally intervened to resolve the stand-off, gaining promises of a new hostel to house and feed the returned workers and embarrassing Lu Jingshi's faction in the process.[58] Much like the Chinese Association of Labor's first welfare program in Chongqing, the new hostel for returned workers soon became the Shanghai Unemployment Relief Commission's largest program, housing more than 2,700 unemployed workers at its peak and providing them with food from UNRRA donations.[59] The commission also launched new active relief programs in 1946, including several public works projects. These active relief programs were small-scale, however; only 156 unemployed workers were hired on local construction projects in 1946, and their jobs lasted a mere twenty-nine days.[60]

## *The KMT Worker Welfare Program*

Rather than resist Zhu Xuefan's interference in the Unemployment Relief program, Lu Jingshi shifted his attention to the Worker Welfare program. The Shanghai Worker Welfare Committee was officially established in June 1946 with Wu Kaixian as secretary, Lu Jingshi as deputy secretary, and fifty-nine other KMT labor leaders as board members. In addition to running the worker welfare program, the committee was also secretly charged with directing the official labor movement and recruiting workers to join the KMT, ostensibly the main responsibilities of the Shanghai General Labor Union. With funding from the Shanghai

58. Li Jiaqi, ed., *Shanghai gongyun*, 283; Lu Xiangxian, ed., *Zhongguo laodong xiehui*, 78–82.
59. Shanghai shi, *Shehui xingzheng tongji*, 75.
60. Li Jianhua, "Zhanhou Shanghai shi," 6.

Bureau of Social Affairs, the Worker Welfare Committee quickly grew into a large organization with more than ten thousand paid cadres. [61]

In addition to its overall size, the structure of the Shanghai Worker Welfare Committee provided another indication that it was more than just a welfare program. The staff was organized into five divisions: Leadership, General Services, Inspections, Militia, and Welfare. The largest division by far was the Militia Division, with more than nine thousand members organized into workers' pickets.[62] The Shanghai Worker Welfare Committee was therefore much more than the welfare division of the Shanghai General Labor Union—in effect, it was an alternative municipal labor union under the direct control of Lu Jingshi. With the 1946 strike wave building in cities like Shanghai and Chongqing, the Worker Welfare Committee used both the militias and new welfare programs to try to gain control over the labor movement.

Although the paramilitary operations of the Shanghai Worker Welfare Committee were relatively centralized at the municipal level, its welfare program was highly decentralized, as mandated in the regulations. The workplace was the central focus of the program, with all enterprises with more than two hundred employees authorized (but not required) to establish corporatist committees to design and manage their own worker welfare programs.[63] Although the regulations stacked the deck in favor of labor by mandating that the union had a supermajority vote on these corporatist committees, it proved hard to relegate management to a secondary role. Because of the complexity of the program's funding formula, which included a tax on a company's capital stock, management had considerable discretion over the program's resources. In addition, management administered the program's welfare facilities and benefits, giving it considerable influence over the distribution of resources as well.

When enterprise managers supported the worker welfare program, this complicated corporatist structure was relatively effective. For example, the Jiangnan Shipyard, a state-owned enterprise under the control of the Nationalist navy, established an active worker welfare

61. Li Jiaqi, ed., *Shanghai gongyun*, 243–45.
62. Perry, *Patrolling the Revolution*, 127.
63. Shehui bu, *Shehui fagui*, 163–69.

program in 1946. Factory director Ma Deji was an outspoken advocate for company welfare, arguing that it promoted worker loyalty and boosted productivity. With his strong backing, the Jiangnan Shipyard's worker welfare committee launched a comprehensive program. Its biggest initiative was a proposal to build dormitories for nine hundred workers, but the program also included a consumer cooperative and special subsidies for food, clothing, and medicine.[64] Despite this close cooperation between management and the enterprise union, the Jiangnan Shipyard had difficulty overcoming budget restrictions imposed by the navy. As a result, the dormitory project was repeatedly delayed, and in the end no dormitory was built.

But even partial implementation was better than the situation in enterprises where management opposed the worker welfare program. The labor shortages and high turnover rates that made company managers proactive in expanding fringe benefits during the Second World War changed fundamentally in the postwar period, since high levels of unemployment rendered special incentives to retain employees largely superfluous. When managers opposed the program, labor's control over the enterprise worker welfare committees was no match for management's power over resources. For example, the worker welfare committee at the British Commercial Tramway Company (Ying shang dianche gongsi) set up a health clinic for tram workers in an empty warehouse in the company's main compound. The new clinic proved to be very popular—so much so that the more than one thousand employees who worked in warehouses and workshops located on the other side of the city petitioned the company's worker welfare committee to open a second satellite clinic for their use. The committee approved the request, noting that it would improve efficiency by saving those workers the half day to a full day of work required to travel to the clinic at company headquarters. Despite the committee's decision, managers repeatedly objected to the proposal, arguing that the company lacked sufficient resources to open a second clinic. Ultimately, the company's worker welfare committee had to appeal to the Bureau of Social Affairs, but the stand-off was never resolved.[65]

64. Frazier, *Making of the Chinese Industrial Workplace*, 78–80.
65. SMA, Q6-7-13.

*Table 2.1.* Shanghai Worker Welfare Implementation, December 1947

|  | Number of programs |
|---|---|
| Enterprise welfare programs | 53 |
| Primary schools | 46 |
| Consumer coops | 23 |
| Day care centers | 9 |
| Health clinics | 8 |
| Number of workers who received health care | 27,745 |

*Sources:* Shanghai zonggonghui, *1948 laodong nianjian*, 25–28.

This kind of effective veto power by management helps to explain why the worker welfare program made so little headway in Shanghai in the postwar period. By the end of 1947, the KMT had established fifty-three enterprise worker welfare programs in Shanghai, which represented only 12 percent of the total number of enterprise unions in the city (table 2.1).[66] The fifty-three programs operated forty-six primary schools for workers' children, twenty-three consumer cooperatives, nine child care centers, and eight health clinics. Although these services were clearly beneficial for workers in those fifty-three companies, it is difficult to determine how much should be credited to the worker welfare program itself, since a substantial number of these companies already had their own corporate welfare benefits and facilities in place long before the program began.[67]

It is even more difficult to gauge the political impact of the worker welfare program at the grassroots level. Obviously, the political gains from the program were limited by its narrow reach. But even in the minority of companies with active worker welfare programs, the impact of the program was largely dependent on the political skills of the labor leaders at the grass roots. Moreover, they faced plenty of competition. Managers and labor racketeers were often able to control the distribution of new benefits, obscuring the role that the union played in secur-

66. Shanghai zonggonghui, *1948 Laodong nianjian,* 28.
67. SMA, C1-2-331; Porter, *Industrial Reformers,* 23; Perry, *Shanghai on Strike,* 183; Cochran, *Big Business,* 137, 157.

ing these new gains. They also faced competition from underground Communist labor organizers.

An example that illustrates the complex politics of the worker welfare program at the enterprise level comes from the Shenxin No. 6 Cotton Mill. The Shanghai Worker Welfare Committee sent one of its cadres to Shenxin No. 6 in 1946 to organize an official labor union and an enterprise worker welfare committee. As a newcomer to the factory, he tried to build up a following among the skilled male machine operators by organizing sports teams that provided special benefits to the athletes, including wage subsidies and low-interest loans.[68] Although this approach may have helped to forge connections between the Shanghai Worker Welfare Committee and an influential group of workers in the mill, the KMT labor organizer failed to consider the electoral math in adopting such a gender-exclusive tactic in a factory dominated by women textile workers. When the new union held its first election for its enterprise supervisory council, the KMT-sponsored slate from the all-male sports teams lost decisively to a group of women suspected of being communist sympathizers. The KMT slate was only able to regain control over the official union by bribing the duly elected chairwoman to quit her job at the factory— and then attacking the rest of the winning slate with steel bars and pipes to intimidate them into stepping down from their union positions. Corruption and coercion proved to be more important in securing KMT control over the official union at Shenxin No. 6 than the subsidies and sports teams created by the worker welfare program.

It is difficult to know what this kind of anecdotal evidence about welfare politics at the enterprise level added up to in a city like Shanghai. The limited implementation of the Worker Welfare program certainly restricted its political impact. Moreover, the 1946 strike wave suggests that the problems in factories like the Shenxin No. 6 Cotton Mill were not unusual.

68. Frazier, *Making of the Chinese Industrial Workplace*, 88–90.

## *The 1947 Confrontation between the Nationalist State and Labor*

Even with these limitations, Lu Jingshi and his faction were proving to be more effective in the rough world of Shanghai labor politics than Zhu Xuefan and the Chinese Association of Labor. Although Zhu refused to back away from his Twenty-three Demands, it became increasingly clear over the course of 1946 that he had failed to achieve any of his objectives. Zhu Xuefan spent much of his time defending his reputation by holding press conferences and telegraphing union leaders across China and around the world to denounce the corruption charges against him as false and politically motivated. Zhu's credibility and the wide reach of his international contacts ensured that this intraparty conflict reached the highest levels of the KMT.[69] But even a meeting with General Chiang Kaishek failed to resolve the stand-off between the Chinese Association of Labor and the Chongqing General Labor Union.[70]

Furthermore, an international outcry was not going to save Zhu Xuefan from arrest as the court case against him proceeded. In this context, the only way Zhu could up the ante was to defect. With the support of his new allies in the Communist labor movement, Zhu secretly started planning his escape. In November 1946, Zhu and his top aides evacuated the Chinese Association of Labor headquarters to Hong Kong, beyond the legal reach of the Nationalist government.[71] Zhu immediately held a press conference with the international media to issue a bitter denunciation of KMT authoritarianism. The press coverage inflicted another blow to KMT legitimacy both at home and abroad. The KMT responded to this criticism with a clumsy assassination attempt. It only succeeded in injuring Zhu Xuefan, giving him another chance to hold a press conference to denounce his former party—this time from the more dramatic backdrop of a hospital bed.[72]

---

69. *CIO News*, Aug. 19, 1946, 6A.
70. Lu Xiangxian and Liu Songbin, *Zhu Xuefan*, 220.
71. Ibid., 226–27.
72. Ibid., 230; Epstein, *Notes on Labor Problems*, 107; *CIO News*, Dec. 23, 1946, 5; Chu, "Are the Workers in China Divided?" 38.

Zhu Xuefan's defiance again demonstrated the limits of the Chinese Association of Labor. The Twenty-three Demands and the association's defection to Hong Kong had no impact on the Nationalist regime beyond tarnishing its image. Within the KMT, most members remained committed to the party's efforts to maintain its political dominance and control the pace and direction of political reform. Indeed, a commitment to autocracy was one of the few things that the KMT's many factions seemed to agree upon. Zhu's clarion call for peace, democracy, and social reform was simply ignored in China, even as it brought him considerable attention and prestige abroad.

But even if Lu Jingshi and the powerful Shanghai Worker Welfare Committee were able to sideline Zhu Xuefan and his labor association, they had a much harder time gaining any measure of control over Shanghai's workers. In an ongoing effort to constrain runaway inflation, the Nationalist government issued emergency economic regulations in February 1947 to control wages and prices.[73] This was the first moment since the KMT's return to national power in 1945 that the interests of workers and the regime were directly opposed. In anticipation of this test of the regime's corporatist strategy, the emergency economic regulations also prohibited strikes, slowdowns, and other forms of worker protest, even though these forms of collective action were already illegal.[74] The double prohibition did not inhibit workers in Shanghai, however, and within days various enterprise and industrial unions were organizing delegations of petitioners and holding press conferences to press the regime to rescind the wage freeze. These protests were soon followed by slowdowns and short-term strikes.[75] Rather than suppress the growing protests, as the Worker Welfare Committee was struggling to do, the Shanghai General Labor Union endorsed them when it publicly petitioned the Bureau of Social Affairs and the municipal government to lift the wage freeze on February 22, 1947.[76] The public defiance of party policy proved to be temporary, but the damage had already been done.

73. Shanghai zonggonghui, *1948 Shanghai laodong nianjian*; Zhu Hua et al., *Shanghai yibai nian*, 273.
74. Xiong Yuezhi et al., *Shanghai tongshi*, vol. 7, 455.
75. Ibid., 456; Shen Yixing et al., *Shanghai gongren yundong shi*, 580–81.
76. Shen Yixing et al., *Shanghai gongren yundong shi*, 583.

As living standards rapidly eroded in the spring of 1947, rice riots broke out around the city.[77] The confrontation over the wage freeze policy came to a head at the May Day celebration that year. Underground Communist labor leaders helped to turn the KMT's carefully controlled rally at the race track in central Shanghai into a public embarrassment. The Worker Welfare Committee carefully screened all the participants at the rally, preapproved their banners and slogans, and mobilized workers' pickets to control the crowd. Even with all these precautions in place, the KMT was unable to pull off the event as planned. Minister of Social Affairs Gu Zhenggang gave the keynote speech at the rally, arguing that the wage freeze was the key to limiting unemployment in the long term. Despite the careful orchestration of the event, Gu was drowned out by shouts and chants from workers at the rally to lift the freeze. When Shanghai Mayor Wu Guozhen admonished the workers "not to kill the chicken in order to steal its eggs," underground Communist activists led the workers to abandon the rally in droves, forcing the KMT leadership to wind up the rally in an anticlimactic and embarrassing retreat.[78]

In the wake of the May Day protests, the ongoing strike wave escalated as tens of thousands of workers walked off the job to demand that their wages be indexed to inflation. With more than 280 factories involved, the 1946–47 strike wave surpassed the previous high point of the Shanghai labor movement, the May Thirtieth Movement that had introduced Lu Jingshi and Zhu Xuefan to labor politics more than twenty years earlier.[79] Just over a week after the chaotic 1947 May Day rally, the strikers began demonstrating in the streets. More than ten thousand silk weavers marched on the Bureau of Social Affairs and City Hall on May 8, even as police and undercover agents tried to block their progress. The next day tramcar workers took to the streets, and then telegraph workers declared a hunger strike. A few days later, department store clerks took their turn. In addition to demonstrating in front of City Hall, the department store workers took advantage of their window displays to post

77. Zhu Hua et al., *Shanghai yibai nian*, 273.
78. Shen Yixing, et al., eds., *Shanghai gongren yundong shi*, 583–85.
79. Perry, "Shanghai's Strike Wave," 1.

banners with dramatic slogans such as "Our wages were frozen, and our stomachs have shriveled."[80] The protests were effective. The next day, the Nationalist government caved to the pressure and lifted the wage freeze for all low-income workers. Soon after, the inflationary spiral escalated into hyperinflation.

The defeat of the KMT labor mobilization strategy was complete. The party was unable to hold the line during the struggle over the wage freeze in 1947. Moreover, even high levels of coercion proved inadequate for eliminating the Communist underground. With alternative factional and underground labor organizations in place, workers could organize protests and strikes, even if they had already benefited from the KMT's new welfare benefits. Their defections were not as dramatic as Zhu Xuefan's escape to Hong Kong, but they were ultimately much more powerful. The KMT's 1947 May Day rally in Shanghai is a vivid illustration of the risks that came with mobilizing labor—failing to control this new source of political power left the KMT much worse off than if they had never attempted it at all.

After this political setback, the Shanghai Worker Welfare Committee increasingly focused its resources and attention on the district and municipal levels of the organization, where it had more control over operations and faced less competition from rivals like the Communist Party than at the enterprise level. Initially, the Shanghai Worker Welfare Committee divided the city into six districts and set up seven district worker welfare offices as part of its effort to gain control over the enterprise unions from the Shanghai General Labor Union. But even in this restricted sphere, the municipal Worker Welfare Committee faced competition from other rival KMT labor leaders. To dislodge these rivals, the Shanghai Worker Welfare Committee moved to a new organizational structure based on twenty-four industrial unions.[81] Six of these industrial unions established worker welfare committees in 1947, each of which opened up a health clinic for workers.[82]

The expansion of the Unemployment Relief program also stalled in 1947. The new emphasis on active relief for the long-term unemployed

80. Zhu Hua et al., *Shanghai yibai nian*, 274; Perry, *Shanghai on Strike*, 210.
81. Li Jiaqi, ed., *Shanghai gongyun*, 244.
82. Shanghai zonggonghui, *1948 laodong nianjian*, 25.

was much more difficult to get off the ground than providing relief or shelter. The public works projects started in 1946 never grew into a significant program. Moreover, the new self-help production projects required authorization from the Ministry of Economic Affairs to take over shut-down factories and turn them over to workers.[83] Two self-help production factories were finally set up in 1947, but their production was severely limited. They could only operate at night when electricity was available, and even then they were able to employ only 110 workers. Moreover, the workers were paid in grain rather than wages, despite UNRRA's prohibitions on such arrangements.[84]

The Unemployment Relief program collapsed altogether before the year was out (table 2.2). When UNRRA rations ran out in October 1947, the Shanghai Unemployment Relief Commission shut down entirely, and the last of the grain was distributed to the residents of the hostel for returned workers before they were sent away.[85]

Even as the KMT's programs were disintegrating, the Worker Welfare Committee reorganized again in 1948 in another futile attempt to ensure factional control. Each new 1948 district had plans to establish large-scale worker welfare centers, but they never got past the planning stage.[86] Given the limited reach of the program at the enterprise level and the organizational chaos at the district level, it is not surprising that the Shanghai Worker Welfare Committee increasingly focused on the municipal level. The top priority at this level of the organization was on expanding health care for workers. The municipal committee set up a mobile health care clinic to provide free health care.[87] At the same time, the Shanghai Worker Welfare Committee worked with the local KMT party branch to provide free health care to workers on a much larger scale with a major expansion of the Shanghai Workers Hospital. Construction began in 1948, but it was never completed.

83. Li Jianhua, "Zhanhou Shanghai shi," 5–6.
84. Shanghai zonggonghui, *1948 Shanghai laodong nianjian*, 78; Shanghai shi, *1946 Shanghai shi nianjian*, N19.
85. Shanghai zonggonghui, *1948 Shanghai laodong nianjian*, 77.
86. Ibid., 27–28.
87. Ibid, 25.

Table 2.2. KMT Unemployment Relief, 1945–48

| Year | Unemployment relief handouts | Percent change |
| --- | --- | --- |
| 1945 | 90,640 | 100% |
| 1946 | 208,615 | 130% |
| 1947 | 27,612 | -87% |
| 1948 | 0 | -100% |

*Sources:* Shanghai shi, *1946 Shanghaishi nianjian*: N19; Li Jianhua, "Zhanhou Shanghai shi," 4-5; Shanghai zonggonghui, *1948 Laodong nianjian,* 78.

The collapse of the wage freeze policy in 1947 did not lead to labor peace in Shanghai. Another strike wave got under way in 1948–49 that soon proved to be even larger in scope than its predecessor.[88] The 1948–49 strike wave was primarily a response to inflation, but it also produced a wide range of welfare demands.[89] Workers were as likely to gain workplace welfare benefits through strikes as they were through the KMT official unions and the Workplace Welfare program.

## The Fall of the Nationalist Regime

As the KMT's new welfare initiatives in Shanghai gradually unraveled after the dramatic confrontation with labor in May 1947, its political losses in other arenas continued to mount. Labor defections continued, military defeats accumulated, and hyperinflation undermined the support of even the regime's strongest allies. Zhu Xuefan escalated his public relations battle with the KMT in international arenas by going over to the Communist side in 1947. His reasons for joining the Communist war effort were both principled and petty. The principles he touted included the relative freedom that labor unions enjoyed in the Communist base areas, since they were not subjected to any of the legal institutional controls that the KMT imposed on its unions. Zhu was also impressed with the evidence of good governance in the base

88. Perry, *Patrolling the Revolution,* 162.
89. SMA, C1-2-1118; Honig, *Sisters and Strangers,* 234–42.

areas, starting with relatively low levels of inflation. The petty reasons included the Chinese Association of Labor's funding crisis in Hong Kong, where it was safe from KMT interference but cut off from its membership.[90]

Even more pressing was the loss of the American funding that had transformed the organization in the first place. After corruption charges were leveled against Zhu Xuefan in Chongqing, the CIO received the backing of the U.S. State Department to conduct its own investigation. CIO vice president John Schulter went to China to review the evidence and inspect Chinese Association of Labor welfare facilities. He cleared Zhu Xuefan and the rest of the association's leaders of all charges, but the final outcome of the investigation was the CIO's decision to shut down the entire China war relief program. The rump Chinese Association of Labor organization in Chongqing was no longer deemed a suitable partner for American labor because it was clearly controlled by the KMT, whereas the association's headquarters in Hong Kong was no longer in a position to provide war relief.[91] Defecting to the CCP resolved these financial difficulties, even as it provided Zhu Xuefan with new opportunities to denounce the official KMT labor movement in international arenas.

The KMT's loss of political support was so widespread by mid-1948 that its last-ditch attempt to rein in inflation through another currency reform alienated even capitalists, its most favored class. In August 1948, the Nationalist government introduced a new currency and emergency regulations requiring people to divest their gold, silver, and foreign currency. As the financial center of the country, Shanghai received special attention. Indeed, it was the only place where these controls were strictly enforced.[92] Chiang Kaishek sent his son, Jiang Jingguo, to Shanghai to direct the emergency economic program personally. Faced with lackluster compliance, Jiang Jingguo organized paramilitary "tiger-beating teams" to arrest more than three thousand merchants and businessmen on vague charges of violating the new policies by currency speculation and hoarding.[93]

90. Lu Xiangxian and Liu Songbin, *Zhu Xuefan*, 274–75.
91. *CIO News*, March 10, 1947, 5.
92. Eastman, *Seeds of Destruction*, 180.
93. Pepper, *Civil War*, 121–23; Eastman, *Seeds of Destruction*, 186–88.

Even with this display of force, however, the entire effort collapsed in failure. Uneven enforcement of price controls, news of Communist victories on the battlefield, and distrust of the regime's fiscal discipline all contributed to widespread resistance to the new currency and price controls. Severe shortages shut down most industry and left consumers without food or fuel. Shanghai's economy ceased to function. The Executive Yuan was forced to abandon the emergency economic controls on October 31, and all imprisoned businessmen were released the following day.[94] Even this complete retreat was insufficient to mollify Shanghai's capitalists. The following day, the Shanghai Chamber of Commerce convened an assembly in which businessman after businessman condemned the Nationalist regime. Some speakers demanded the resignation of the minister of finance, a former mayor of Shanghai, while others went further and called for punishment of all the people responsible for the reform program up to Jiang Jingguo himself.[95]

Communist military victories were decisive in turning the tide against the Nationalists over the next six months. Manchuria fell to the People's Liberation Army (PLA) early in November 1948, and the Communists soon gained control of Beijing and Tianjin in January 1949. From that point on, the final chapter of KMT rule was defined by the Nationalist Army's retreat before the steady advance of the CCP's military. Among the many arenas of political competition between the KMT and the CCP during the Chinese Civil War, the battlefield was always the most important. The KMT held Shanghai for another four months after these decisive battles in the North China plain. By the time the Nationalist capital of Nanjing fell in April 1949, however, the KMT retreat from Shanghai was in full swing. Even the Nationalist officials who ran the city began to leave, abandoning their posts well before the arrival of the Communist military in May 1949.

94. Pepper, *Civil War*, 124–25; Eastman, *Seeds of Destruction*, 190–93.
95. Pepper, *Civil War*, 126.

## Evaluating the Nationalist Welfare State

Even at its high point in 1947, the reach of the Nationalist welfare state was limited. The Worker Welfare program was the larger of its two programs, covering nearly 12 percent of the total number of enterprise unions in Shanghai (table 2.1). If we assume that these enterprises were among the largest in the city, we can estimate that they may have covered as much as 20 percent of union members. If we make the generous assumption that the people who benefited from the enterprise Worker Welfare programs did not overlap with those who used the district and municipal Worker Welfare health facilities (or the unemployment relief program), all these programs together probably reached 3 percent of Shanghai's workforce, and perhaps 1 percent of the city's total population in 1947 (table 2.3). The challenging economic and political conditions of the Chinese Civil War clearly limited the scope of the KMT's flagship welfare programs for workers.

Turning to examine the implementation of unemployment relief at its high point in early 1947, we can see that it was significantly smaller in scope than the Worker Welfare program. The number of registered unemployed workers eligible for any of the Unemployment Relief program's benefits or services constituted a little more than 2 percent of the total union membership. The most important benefit that registered unemployed workers could receive was grain relief. This aspect of the unemployment program reached its peak in 1946, when more than 200,000 handouts were given to unemployed workers over the course of the year (see table 2.2).[96] The program's second largest service was the hostel for returned workers, which housed nearly 2,500 unemployed workers, established at the instigation of the Chinese Association of Labor in 1946.

The KMT experience showed that extending these welfare programs to more than a tiny minority of the workforce was extremely difficult under the chaotic conditions of the Chinese Civil War, even

96. No statistics on the average caseload for the relief program are given in the sources, and this total number of handouts adds up all the rations given to the same workers over the course of the year.

*Table 2.3.* Shanghai Welfare Coverage, 1945–49

| Year | Est. total beneficiaries | Workforce coverage | Population coverage |
|------|--------------------------|--------------------|--------------------|
| 1945 | 11,000 | 1.0% | 0.3% |
| 1946 | 56,000 | 3.0% | 1.0% |
| 1947 | 64,000 | 3.0% | 1.0% |
| 1948 | 50,000 | 2.5% | 1.0% |
| 1949 | n.a. | 0.0% | 0.0% |

*Note:* Worker welfare estimate based on assumption that average number of workers was 500 FTE.
*Sources:* Shanghai shi, *1946 Shanghai shi nianjian*, N19; Shanghai zonggonghui, *1948 Laodong nianjian*, 25–28; SMA, B31-1-12.

in a city far behind the battle lines. Hyperinflation undermined the economy and put severe constraints on the resources needed for new welfare programs. For unemployment relief in particular, budget problems were the fundamental factor limiting the scope and duration of the KMT program. The initial emergency funding from the central government was never supplemented by a regular source of revenue, so the program only survived as long as UN donations for postwar recovery lasted.

In contrast, the Shanghai Worker Welfare Committee was amply funded by the government. But it directed most of these resources to its paramililtary workers' militia program, the core of its alternate union organization. It left the funding of its enterprise-level welfare programs to enterprise committees, as the program was designed in 1943. This program structure gave management effective veto power over the program at the enterprise level, which helps to explain why its implementation was so limited. Similarly, by trying to fund the unemployment relief program with voluntary donations from the Chamber of Commerce, capitalists enjoyed veto power over that program as well. Given the institutional arrangements, resource constraints were more a reflection of the KMT's political priorities than a test of these companies' ability to finance new welfare programs.

The political obstacle to welfare state expansion posed by capitalists was significant. Although capitalists had no role in the policy-making process, their key role in providing resources for the welfare programs gave them considerable political leverage at the local level. Labor could not effectively counter this kind of power over unemployment relief and the worker welfare program, but workers managed to attain their own form of veto power by forcing the KMT to abandon its wage and price controls in 1947. This effective stand-off hurt both sides: workers failed to gain new welfare benefits, and capitalists failed to gain any limits on wages.

For both sides in this struggle, welfare politics primarily boiled down to the decision to resist or cooperate with state initiatives rather than negotiate over policies or institutional arrangements. The worker welfare committees were designed to be arenas for negotiation, but they did not feature much bargaining. For most workers, welfare politics consisted of rallies, counterdemonstrations, and strikes. This uninstitutionalized, sometimes violent form of welfare politics revolved around claiming credit for new welfare initiatives or assigning blame for failed welfare policies. Workers showed more independence in their strike demands, although these claims were often shaped by their underground Communist labor union organizers.

Ultimately, the central political problem that limited the KMT's welfare agenda did not stem from the Civil War or even the strike waves that rocked Chinese cities in the late 1940s. The KMT's own factionalism undermined its corporatist project. The KMT's early success in mobilizing capital and labor did not translate into more power, since the pattern of creating new ad hoc institutions made the mobilization drive rapid but centrifugal. Factionalism also limited the institutionalization and political impact of the KMT's new welfare programs, as different factions jumped from one initiative to the next in an effort to stay ahead of their rivals.

In this wartime context, top-down political pressure could produce new welfare policies, but these forces were insufficient to propel implementation on their own. The factional competition that spurred new welfare initiatives at the central level was the major obstacle to the implementation of these new welfare policies at the local level. With opposition from capitalists and only intermittent pressure from workers, there was insufficient bottom-up political pressure to widen the reach of the new Chinese welfare state beyond a small minority of the workforce.

In the long run, the Nationalist government's unemployment relief program and worker welfare program set important precedents because they were the first national welfare programs for workers in China. Even if these programs could not be considered very successful, their existence made it difficult for policy makers to return to the kind of caution toward welfare policy shown in the twenty years before the Second World War. Changed expectations about what the state should try to do for the welfare of ordinary people was probably the most important legacy of the Nationalist welfare state, even if expectations for the actual results were not high.

The institutional continuities from the Nationalist to the Communist welfare state were even more limited. The unemployment relief program did not survive until 1949, and the institutional continuities supplied by the Worker Welfare program were limited to the fifty-three firms that implemented it. Even in those firms, the demise of the Nationalist labor unions and the corporatist worker welfare committees scrambled many of the personnel and institutional arrangements responsible for administering these programs. As a result, any continuities depended on the support of company management to assume full responsibility for keeping the schools, housing, and other benefits of the Worker Welfare program going.

The strongest continuities between the Nationalist and Communist welfare states were the challenging economic and political conditions of the Chinese Civil War, which continued well after the May 1949 takeover of Shanghai. The problems of hyperinflation and trade disruptions stand out as significant constraints on the Chinese welfare state in the late 1940s, and these problems continued into the early 1950s. Moreover, the mobilization of both capital and labor ensured that their expectations vis-à-vis the welfare state were already primed. Although workers faced a much more difficult collective action problem than capitalists, stemming from their greater numbers and internal divisions, their extensive experience with strikes and street demonstrations in the late 1940s made collective action that much easier to spark and sustain in the 1950s.

# CHAPTER 3

# The Communist Foundations of the
# Chinese Welfare State, 1948–51

After their ill-fated experiment with unemployment relief in the early 1930s, the Communists proved to be more cautious with welfare policy than the Nationalists (see chapter 1). During and after the war with Japan, the CCP stayed on the sidelines, leaving welfare politics to the Nationalist regime. The CCP's strategy was simply to try to undermine KMT control over its official labor movement rather than do anything more proactive with welfare policy in the territories under its control.

The Communists, however, suddenly reversed course in 1948, at the height of the Civil War. By issuing the provisional Northeastern Labor Insurance Regulations, the CCP established the first social insurance program in Chinese history. After nearly twenty years of restraint, why did the Communists leap past the Nationalists' simpler, less expensive welfare programs to go for full social insurance? Moreover, why did they expand the program nationwide soon afterward? Since the Chinese Civil War merged into the Korean War that followed, did wartime conditions hamstring the CCP's efforts to implement its welfare initiatives? Was there a lasting legacy on the reach of the Chinese welfare state?

To understand how and why the CCP reversed course on welfare policy in the late 1940s, we need to examine the political forces behind welfare reform on the Communist side. The most important change came from within the CCP. The CCP's military victories in 1948–49 gave it control of northeastern China, including the first major cities and industries it had ever ruled. In this new context, the military competition between the two parties began to evolve into political competition as well: a contest over governance in the regions of China that each party controlled.

As partisan competition heated up, both parties completed their corporatist projects by establishing a national labor union. On the Communist side, labor was given a special role in welfare policy making, privileging labor over capital in an ostensibly cross-class "New Democratic" regime. Bottom-up pressure for welfare, however, was probably no stronger in 1948 than it had been earlier in the Civil War. Worker strikes and protests reached a new high in 1949–50, but the main demands of Chinese strikers continued to center on wages, especially demands to index wages to keep pace with inflation.

Partisan competition and the mobilization of labor help explain the CCP's policy reversal in 1948. These forces also shaped implementation of the welfare state in Shanghai after 1949. Comparison to the KMT experience in Shanghai shows that partisan competition proved to be more effective in advancing the welfare state than the factional competition that undermined KMT implementation. As a result, the CCP was better able to carry out its agenda in poor political and economic conditions. This chapter first focuses on policymaking at the national level and then shifts to implementation at the local level.

## Competitive Policy Making in the KMT and the CCP

The context for the CCP's first engagement in national welfare politics was the struggle between the two parties over the Chinese Association of Labor in their competition for international recognition, leading to the completion of the corporatist project begun by each political party during the Second World War. The emergence of rival national labor unions facilitated labor's incorporation into the policy-making process, at least on the Communist side. Workers themselves did not gain much input into policy decisions, but their self-appointed leaders played a central role in creating the Chinese welfare state.

The struggle over the Chinese Association of Labor heated up in 1947 after Zhu Xuefan's escape to Hong Kong. Each party sought control over the organization to gain access to international labor organizations and the legitimacy they could bestow. In addition to the ILO, the newly established World Federation of Trade Unions was another target for Chinese labor activists. Since Zhu Xuefan was a founding member of the WFTU and had been elected a vice president of the organization, the parties sought to capitalize on his position. CCP leaders provided funding to the Chinese Association of Labor in Hong Kong and encouraged Zhu and the rest of the association's cadres there to defect to the Communist side. In the meantime, the KMT turned to the remaining cadres left behind to rehabilitate the organization. In December 1946, the loyalists reorganized the rump association, expelled the Communist bases area unions, and selected An Futing as the new chairman. Although Zhu Xuefan denounced the move as illegal and declared An Futing illegitimate, there were then two Chinese Associations of Labor and two association chairmen vying for international recognition.[1]

The Nationalist government asked the World Federation of Trade Unions to recognize An Futing as the Chinese representative in February 1947, but the federation refused to unseat a duly elected officer of the organization and passed a formal resolution denouncing the KMT's "coup" against Zhu Xuefan.[2] The KMT's association had more luck with the ILO, which was reluctant to challenge the Nationalist government's sovereignty. The result was a stalemate: Zhu Xuefan represented China at the World Federation of Trade Unions, while An Futing represented China at the ILO.

At that point, the KMT had every reason to establish an official national labor union, since only an organization that fully met inter-

1. Lu Xiangxian and Liu Songbin, *Zhu Xuefan*, 232; Epstein, *Notes on Labor Problems*, 107.
2. Lu Xiangxian and Liu Songbin, *Zhu Xuefan*, 232–34; WFTU, *Information Bulletin*, July 1947, 26.

national standards could unseat Zhu Xuefan from the WFTU. In June 1947, the Nationalist government revised the Labor Union Law to authorize an official national labor union for the first time. KMT labor leaders began the organizing work immediately, issuing detailed regulations and establishing an official preparatory committee in August 1947.[3] The CCP also began laying the groundwork to create a rival national labor union at the same time, unwilling to cede the contest to the KMT.

Even as the KMT's Unemployment Relief and Worker Welfare programs were unraveling in 1947, the competition for international recognition led the KMT to continue pursuing new welfare initiatives. For example, a provision calling for social insurance was added to the Nationalists' new 1947 constitution. In addition, the Nationalist government established a new Social Insurance Commission to draft a social insurance bill and to set up a new Social Insurance Department in the Ministry of Social Affairs, all in preparation for the first Asian regional ILO meeting in New Delhi in October 1947.[4] The Social Insurance Commission drafted a bill defining the fundamental principles for a national social insurance program, but postponed further legislation until after the Civil War came to an end. The ILO regional conference prompted the KMT to take its planning for social insurance much further, but it continued to follow the same playbook that the KMT had been using since the 1930s: advocating the highest international standards, but postponing real action until conditions improved.

Several months later, the KMT won the race to establish a national union. It managed to complete the process of organizing a hierarchy of provincial union federations in the territories under its control and then established the national federation in time for the 1948 meetings of the ILO and the WFTU. The culmination of the process was the first national KMT labor union conference held in Nanjing in April 1948, when delegates from twenty-nine new provincial union federations, which constituted two-thirds of the total number of provinces, voted

3. Lu Xiangxian and Liu Songbin, *Zhu Xuefan*, 302–3.
4. Guoji laodong ju, *Yazhou laogong*, 25–26; Ma, "China's Beveridge Plan," 344; Shanghai zonggonghui, *1948 laodong nianjian*, 88.

to establish the national labor union.[5] Immediately afterward, the new union demanded recognition from the ILO and the World Federation of Trade Unions. Although the KMT trumpeted the legal procedures followed in creating its new national union federation, critics dismissed the process as "fascist streamlining" rather than a democratic convention of union delegations.[6] As a result, the new union federation still failed to secure WFTU membership, giving an opening to the lagging CCP effort to win international support for its official labor movement.

To create the Communist version of a national labor union, the CCP brought back their best-known labor leader, Li Lisan, from exile to the Soviet Union. Li Lisan had made his reputation as leader of the May Thirtieth Movement in Shanghai, the massive general strike against imperialism and warlord rule (see chapter 1). Li went on from that political triumph in 1925 to become chairman of the CCP in 1927, only to resign in disgrace a few years later after a series of failed armed uprisings nearly destroyed the party. His recent return to a leadership position in the CCP was a long-awaited political comeback after nearly twenty years of exile in the Soviet Union. Fluent in Russian and married to a woman from the Soviet Union, Li Lisan drew on his foreign expertise to build the official Communist union movement.

The CCP's efforts to establish its own national union federation in time for the June 1948 international meetings were delayed by the difficulty of moving across enemy lines at a point when the Nationalist armies occupied most of the North China plain.[7] But after hearing about the KMT's failure in the WFTU, the Communists renewed their efforts to ensure their version of a national labor union met international standards. This incentive was a major factor in the CCP's efforts to lure Zhu Xuefan from Hong Kong, since he was still a WFTU vice president. Zhu Xuefan's participation in the planning process, along with nine other Chinese Association of Labor officials, helped to provide symbolic representation of all Chinese labor unions. In addition, the CCP smuggled seventeen union representatives from KMT-controlled areas across the front lines for the founding assembly

5. Liang, *Kuomintang and the Chinese Worker*, 24.
6. WFTU, *Information Bulletin*, Aug. 1948, 13.
7. Ibid., 12.

of the new national union. Even after all these efforts, the Chinese Association of Labor and KMT-area representatives comprised only one-twentieth of the total number of union delegates. To compensate, Li Lisan constructed an elaborate voting system to weigh each delegate's vote by the number of union members he or she represented, regardless of whether the unions were in KMT or CCP territory. Thus, Shanghai's seventeen delegates had 289 votes among them, since they represented the largest number of union workers in the country.[8]

The elaborate electoral system not only tried to make the new labor union more national in scope, it also fit with Li Lisan's efforts to make the Communist-sponsored labor federation seem more democratic than its KMT counterpart. In drafting the union charter, Li Lisan left out all mention of party supervision—no power of appointment, no control over financing, no supervision of meetings or activities. Instead, the charter established an election system for union leaders and provided for a wide range of individual rights for members. The political right highlighted most prominently in the charter was the right to freely join or quit the union.[9] Although its informal powers were not institutionalized, the CCP exerted just as much control over its unions as the KMT. Li Lisan's emphasis on democracy within the union movement fit in with the CCP's larger "New Democracy" agenda of making the people's congresses in its territory seem more democratic than their counterparts under the KMT while maintaining party dominance through informal means.[10]

The CCP's Sixth National Labor Congress was held in Harbin in August 1948.[11] The main purpose of the meeting was to found the new CCP-sponsored national labor union, the All-China Federation of Trade Unions. Both Zhu Xuefan and Li Lisan gave speeches to the assembly and were selected as vice chairmen of the new organization. Despite the similarities in their titles, their roles were completely different: Li

8. Lu Xiangxian and Liu Songbin, *Zhu Xuefan*, 294; Tang Chunliang, *Li Lisan*, 34.
9. Huabei zonggonghui, *Di liuci quanguo laodong dahui*, 32–36; Lin Ping, ed., *Quanguo diliuci laodong dahui*.
10. O'Brien, *Reform without Liberalization*, 22; Van Slyke, *Enemies and Friends*, 143-46
11. To emphasize the CCP's early history of labor organizing, the 1948 conference was described as the successor to the Fifth Labor Conference, held in secret in Shanghai in 1929.

Lisan was put in charge of the day-to-day management of the new labor union movement, whereas Zhu Xuefan's main role was to represent the organization outside of China. In the midst of this organizing work, the 518 delegates also debated the policy agenda for the new union. Several alternative social insurance policies were considered, in keeping with the long-held Chinese consensus on social insurance as the preferred program design. Their final decision, however, was simply to call for establishing social insurance for workers in cities where conditions were suitable. Both the policy and the conditions were left unspecified.[12]

Li Lisan's efforts to make the CCP's national labor union meet international standards did not succeed in unseating the KMT union from the ILO, even if the communist union was more national in scope and more democratic on paper. By that point the Cold War was heating up in Europe, and the KMT solidified its hold on the UN. Once the Chinese political competition in the international arena stalled, the rival national labor unions shifted their focus to domestic politics. The People's Liberation Army (PLA) seizure of major industrial centers in the Northeast in the winter of 1948–49 turned China's cities into an important new arena for political competition.[13] The Communists pursued a deliberate strategy to heighten the contrast in governance on the two sides, with the Communist underground in Nationalist territory actively trying to subvert KMT rule, while the new Communist city governments sought to restore order and improve living conditions as rapidly as possible. In addition to trying to win over public opinion in its territories, the CCP relied on both Chinese and international journalists to help spread the message more widely.

This new form of competition between the parties at the height of the Civil War pushed the CCP to engage in the kind of welfare politics that the KMT had been pursuing since the early 1940s. It was no longer sufficient to subvert the KMT's mobilization efforts— in the cities under its control the CCP also faced the task of rallying the working class to its side. Keeping pace with the KMT in social policy became another aspect of the competition over governance

The CCP launched a provisional social insurance program for work-

12. Pepper, *Civil War*, 364; Li Guicai, ed., *Zhongguo gonghui sishinian*, 42.
13. Lieberthal, "Mao versus Liu?" 509; Yu Jianting, *Chen Yun*, 209–12.

ers in the Northeast in December 1948. Rather than start small with something like a worker welfare program, the Communists jumped straight to the policy goal both parties had been advocating for more than twenty years: social insurance. Under Li Lisan's leadership, the new national labor union played the central role in drafting the regulations.[14] Although the union's participation was unprecedented, Li's role suggests that the policy-making process was no less top-down than in the Nationalist regime. Since Li was both the head of the national labor union and a top-level party official, his leadership blurred the distinction between an internal party policy-making process and a more inclusive process incorporating elements of the broader political regime.[15] (Later in 1949, Li Lisan was also appointed labor minister in the new central government, further blurring the distinctions.) Workers may not have gained more voice in the policy process, but for the first time there was an institutional link between ordinary workers on the factory floor and policy makers in Beijing.

Although the 1948 labor insurance program was provisional, the CCP's goals were ambitious. The regulations for the program were prefaced with an explanation that the program's benefits and coverage were limited by difficult wartime conditions but would be improved in the future. Labor union cadres charged with implementation were also instructed to tell workers that their ultimate goal was to establish a program as comprehensive as the Soviet Union's welfare state.[16] The domestic comparison was implicit: the KMT had promised a full-scale social insurance program in a better future that might never come, whereas the CCP was delivering social insurance to workers as soon as it could, even if it had to start on a small scale.

The provisional program was limited in several ways. Beyond its regional scope, another restriction of the CCP's first labor insurance program was that it was only mandatory for state-owned enterprises in seven industries considered vital to the military effort, such as the railways and the arms industry.[17] Moreover, the new program was less

14. Pepper, *Civil War*, 364–365; Lin Ping, ed., *Quanguo diliuci laodong dahui*, 72–75.
15. Tang Chunliang, *Li Lisan*, 254.
16. Pepper, *Civil War*, 365.
17. Dongbei xingzheng weiyuanhui, "Dongbei gongying qiye," 1.

of an innovation than the propaganda claimed, since most of the enterprises had been taken over from the Japanese at the end of the Second World War and already had Japanese-established company welfare programs in place.

But Communist labor insurance made several significant improvements over company welfare programs. It provided workers with comprehensive protection from risk, including retirement, disability, health care, and maternity programs. In addition, its benefits were generous, and its eligibility requirements were easy to meet, such as qualifying for a retirement pension after only one year of service. The new program also provided tools for labor mobilization and union development. For example, the regulations created an incentive for recruitment, since only union members qualified for full benefits.[18] The program gave union cadres control over the labor insurance funds and made them responsible for all spending and eligibility decisions. Union cadres therefore had new resources and new sources of power at their disposal. As the first social insurance program ever adopted in China, the most significant legacy of the Northeast provisional labor insurance program did not lie in any of the details of its benefits or coverage—instead it was the creation of an entitlement to welfare, committing the government to providing individual workers with benefits for the rest of their lives.

Soon after the adoption of the Northeast provisional labor insurance program, the tide in the Chinese Civil War turned. In January 1949, the PLA seized control of Beijing and Tianjin during the decisive Huaihai battle for control of the North China plain. The Communist victory at Huaihai led to a new phase in the Civil War in 1949–50, when the Nationalists retreated rapidly in the face of steady PLA progress in securing control of mainland China.

The KMT's rapidly accumulating military defeats did not end the welfare competition between the two parties. After the Nationalist government was forced to retreat from the mainland to Taiwan in December 1949, Lu Jingshi was able to counter the CCP's regional labor insurance program with a new KMT "national" labor insurance initiative in March 1950.[19] Although the KMT could in fact only

18. Nonunion members qualified for half the benefits of union members. Ibid., 2.
19. Lu Jingshi, *Zhongguo laodong zhengce*, 57; Wong, *Healthy Democracies*, 48–49.

implement the program in the one province left under its control, the national scope of the regulations was designed to appeal to workers on the mainland. The KMT also sought to improve on the CCP provisional labor insurance program in other ways. For example, the KMT program extended coverage to all publicly owned enterprises, without making any distinctions between military and nonmilitary industries.

The KMT labor insurance program was launched in the midst of a series of air raids on China's major coastal cities. In addition to bombs, the Nationalist air force dropped propaganda leaflets reassuring workers that the KMT would soon return. Lu Jingshi made sure the program was publicized in English-language pamphlets as well, suggesting that the KMT was targeting an international audience as well as Chinese workers with its new welfare state legislation.[20]

Lu Jingshi's bid to keep the political competition going after the military competition had tilted decisively in favor of the Communists had an air of desperation. In contrast, Zhu Xuefan seemed to have finally outsmarted his rival by defecting to the winning side. Zhu, however, did not gain much power in the official Communist labor movement. The Chinese Association of Labor was disbanded in 1949 after the All-China Federation of Trade Unions was formally accepted by the WFTU as the official representative of Chinese labor.[21] Zhu Xuefan continued to play an ad hoc role in international labor politics, but his new position as central government minister of post and communications occupied most of his time. In this role he served as a symbol of proletarian revolution: a postal worker turned union leader and then promoted to direct the entire postal system. His achievement also effectively sidelined Zhu Xuefan from the mobilizational politics he had honed through twenty-five years of labor organizing. The men who transformed KMT labor politics in China in the 1940s were obsolescent by the early 1950s.

Before Li Lisan and the remaining leaders of the CCP union movement could respond to the new KMT social insurance initiative, the

---

20. Liang, *Kuomintang and the Chinese Worker*; Lu Jingshi, *Zhongguo laodong zhengce*; Perry, Patrolling the Revolution, 179.
21. Lu Xiangxian and Liu Songbin, *Zhu Xuefan*, 306; Lu Xiangxian, ed., *Zhongguo laodong xiehui*, 140.

CCP faced a more immediate economic crisis in 1950: urban unemployment. The CCP responded by adopting a comprehensive unemployment relief program in June 1950. [22] Li Lisan and the national labor union in Beijing again played a central role in formulating the Communist unemployment relief policy. The union drafted regulations for a comprehensive unemployment relief program very similar in design to the program that the KMT had tried to implement several years earlier. The biggest innovation in the Communist program was in the financing mechanism, since it was funded by a dedicated 1 percent payroll tax on all employers rather than adopting the Nationalist approach of relying on foreign aid and voluntary donations. [23] The revenue raised by the new tax gave the CCP program resources that the KMT counterpart never had.

Every other aspect of the program followed the precedent set by the Nationalist program. Eligibility for the program was restricted to workers who had been laid off since the 1949 takeover. Another similarity was that the new unemployment relief program was envisioned as a temporary measure until the economy recovered from the dislocations of war. [24] The final similarity between the programs was the combination of "passive" and "active" relief, with passive relief being the distribution of grain rations or cash grants, and active relief including employment programs such as public works jobs and worker cooperatives. The Communist program also added vocational education and job placement services to the active forms of unemployment relief.

The unemployment initiative came at a moment when the People's Liberation Army was mobilizing for the invasion of Taiwan. Before what promised to be the final military campaign of the Chinese Civil War, the Korean War intervened. When the U.S. enforced its new containment policy and came to the defense of Taiwan, the KMT avoided complete defeat in the Chinese Civil War. The CCP halted its planned invasion of Taiwan and instead sent its troops to Korea, committing the country to its third major war. Although the conflict with the U.S. provoked widespread fear in China that a third world

22. *Laodong gongbao* June 1950:9; Wu Li, "Jianguo chuqi," 70–71.
23. *Laodong gongbao* June 1950:10.
24. Ibid, 10–11.

war was on the horizon, it did not slow the CCP's social policy agenda.

At that point, the All-China Federation of Trade Unions began drafting its own national labor insurance policies. In addition to ordering union officials to research the new KMT policy and existing private company benefits, Li Lisan also led the translation of Soviet labor insurance legislation and union program manuals from Russian into Chinese.[25] These efforts contributed to the national union's draft version of a national labor insurance program issued in October 1950.

Although the policy matched the broad contours of the Soviet program, the new draft regulations also showed the influence of both the KMT initiative and the CCP's own experience with its provisional program in the Northeast. The impact of the rivalry with the KMT could be seen in the benefit changes, which were increased to match KMT standards. The impact of the Northeast experience could be seen in tighter eligibility requirements, such as increasing the number of years of work to qualify for a retirement pension from one to ten years. Union cadres in the Northeast complained that early retirements had surged in their enterprises, undermining the effort to recruit and retain skilled workers rather than enhancing it.[26]

One purpose of issuing draft regulations was to give local governments and lower levels of the union hierarchy an opportunity to provide feedback and suggestions for improvement. As part of the new consultative policy-making process, workers were given a small measure of participation. For example, the Shanghai Municipal Labor Union convened meetings and small-group discussions with more than 50,000 grassroots union cadres and workers to solicit their opinions on the program.

One goal in these discussions was to gauge workers' political response to the policy, a critical part of a sophisticated political planning process that was not matched by any significant administrative or budget planning. The union's small-group discussions on the draft policy in 1950 showed that many workers were positive about the proposal, but skeptical that it could ever be implemented because of the power of the capitalists to forestall social reform. Some workers with

25. Tang Chunliang, *Li Lisan*, 325.
26. Zhongqong zhongyang wenxian yanjiu shi, *Jianquo yilai*, vol. 2, 55–56..

private welfare benefits from their companies expressed hostile opposition. For example, seventeen workers from Huifeng Bank threatened to retire en masse to avoid taking a cut in their expected pension benefits. More dramatically, a worker at Shanghai Electric Power Company threatened: "If I lose my retirement pension because labor insurance is implemented, I will take arsenic to kill myself."[27]

In addition to giving the union a sense of the policy's potential political impact, the consultative process also provided workers with a chance to make policy suggestions of their own. The Shanghai labor union incorporated some of the workers' demands into its own recommendations, including a provision to guarantee workers with better corporate benefits than the amounts originally promised to them. Similarly, the Shanghai union advocated improving sick-pay benefits because many workers already had better sick-pay provisions.[28] Although this consultative process was probably the first time that ordinary workers were given a role in policymaking in China, their only recommendation to be incorporated into the final regulations was the extension of sick-pay benefits. The information about workers' political attitudes was more highly valued than their policy proposals.

The final CCP national labor insurance regulations issued in February 1951 laid the foundation for the Chinese Communist welfare state. Like its predecessors, the new program provided comprehensive protection from risk with retirement, disability, work injury, health, and maternity programs. It provided broader coverage than its predecessors by mandating implementation in all large firms with more than one hundred employees, regardless of industry and regardless of whether they were private or state-owned enterprises. Finally, many of its benefits were better than those in the KMT program. In the long run, the most significant improvement in the Communist policy was that the retirement benefits were paid out as a monthly pension for the rest of a worker's life rather than as the lump-sum payment that the Nationalist program provided. Although workers in the early 1950s did not expect to live much longer than retirement age and therefore often preferred the lump-sum payment, the unlimited entitlement provided

27. SMA, C1-2-332.
28. Ibid.; SMA, C1-2-328.

for in the CCP program was ultimately much more valuable as life spans increased.

The enactment of two national social insurance programs for Chinese workers in 1950–51 was the culmination of the back-and-forth competition between the two parties over governance. The strong consensus among Chinese intellectuals and political activists on the broad principles of social insurance facilitated this convergence in agendas, but both the timing and the content of the programs were shaped by the process of competitive adaptation between the two parties. The parallels in their unemployment relief policies only accentuate how closely the social policy agendas of these two bitter enemies converged with each other over the course of their violent struggle.

Although the new national labor unions were both catalysts in producing parallel welfare policies across the Taiwan Strait, their role in the policy-making process differed. KMT labor union leaders remained on the outside of a policy process anchored in the party-state, whereas the CCP's labor union carved out a central role in formulating welfare policy. The role was not well institutionalized, especially at the top of the organization where Li Lisan's personal credibility and overlapping positions were as important as his role as vicechairman of the All-China Federation of Trade Unions. But for the first time, workers were incorporated into the policy process by a union hierarchy that reached from the factory floor to central policy makers in Beijing. Their participation may have been marginal, but it marked a significant step in completing the corporatist project initiated by the KMT in 1943.

The disconnect between policy makers and the targets of social policy was most visible in the informal effort by the Communist unions in 1949 to poll workers in the newly occupied regions of China about their policy priorities. Not surprisingly, workers asked for what they knew: the kinds of services and benefits provided by the KMT Worker Welfare program.[29] Furthermore, those demands were only expressed in response to direct questions about welfare. Wages, not welfare, continued to be the main concerns workers expressed in strikes and demonstrations. Even if workers were the beneficiaries of labor insurance, it cannot be construed as a response to their political demands.

29. SMA, C1-2-331.

National and international organizations had a larger impact on policy than the people whom they claimed to represent.

## *The Politics of Implementation in Shanghai, 1949–51*

How did the political forces pushing for the adoption of new welfare regulations at the national level shape implementation at the local level? Implementation was driven by top-down pressure from the competition between the two parties and bottom-up pressure from the mobilization of workers and the unemployed by the new official Communist labor unions. In contrast with the KMT, capitalists were largely sidelined in implementation in favor of giving workers a central role.

Since the policy-making and implementation processes overlapped in the period between 1949 and 1951, we need to go back to 1949 to examine welfare politics at the local level. The Communist takeover of Shanghai took place in May 1949. Where the KMT takeover of Shanghai four years earlier had been marked by a chaotic scramble to seize anything of value, the CCP takeover was a relatively well-disciplined operation designed to heighten the contrast between the two parties. Soldiers were instructed to sleep on the streets and to pay for anything they requisitioned in a well-publicized display of respect for property rights. More than eight thousand party cadres followed the PLA into the city, armed with experience in the takeover of Nanjing and a month of specialized training in the operations of the Shanghai municipal government and key local industries. The training course was taught by members of the Shanghai underground who had infiltrated these institutions.[30]

In addition to moving quickly to prevent chaos, the entire takeover operation was designed to minimize any incipient factionalism between the outside cadres from North China and the underground operatives from Shanghai. After the newly arrived cadres met with thousands of underground party members, they formed joint teams

---

30. Wakeman, "Cleanup," 23–24, 32; Wang Yaoshan, "Huiyi jieguan Shanghai," 9–11.

to quickly seize control of every government agency, public utility, and state-owned enterprise.[31] Once order was established, the CCP moved quickly to revive the economy, moribund from hyperinflation and the uncertainty of the transition. In addition to restoring public utilities as fast as possible, the new military government also brought in supplies of food and fuel in order to avert the kind of shortages and disruptions that had followed the KMT takeover four years earlier.

The next priority was to establish new political institutions. Organizing official labor unions and business federations began immediately, building on the work of the Shanghai underground. Liu Changsheng, head of the underground labor movement, was appointed chairman of the new, above-ground labor union. In contrast to the blurry division of responsibility among KMT labor leaders, central CCP labor leaders with strong ties to Shanghai like Li Lisan and Zhu Xuefan remained in Beijing and resisted the temptation to become personally involved in Shanghai labor politics. This discipline ensured that the personalistic factionalism of the KMT could not develop in the same way. In addition, it meant that mobilization efforts contributed to building the new regime rather than undermining it. With its head start in underground organizing, the CCP was able to expand its new official labor union more rapidly than the KMT had, organizing more than one million workers in its first two years.[32]

The CCP also reorganized the KMT chamber of commerce system in 1949–50, consolidating the number of trade and industrial associations and at the same time nearly doubling their membership.[33] The new chairman of the CCP-sponsored Shanghai Business Federation (Shanghai shi gongshang lianhehui), Sheng Pihua, was a businessman who had been active in the peace movement during the Chinese Civil War and a critic of the Nationalist regime. But the CCP also went to considerable effort to recruit the former KMT chairman of the Shanghai Chamber of Commerce to return to Shanghai from Hong Kong in 1950 and endorse the new organization and the new regime.[34]

---

31. Wang Yaoshan, "Huiyi jieguan Shanghai," 12–13; Zhu Hua, et. al., *Shanghai yibai nian*, 294–97.

32. Shanghai zonggonghui, *Liangnian laide gongren yundong*, 23–24.

33. Zhonggong Shanghai shi zuzhi bu, *Shanghai shi zhengquan xitong*, 505.

34. Gardner, "Wu-fan Campaign," 504; Xiong, *Lao Shanghai*, 13.

Both the official labor union and the business federation were incorporated into the Shanghai People's Congress with reserved seats. Like its
KMT predecessor, the new political assembly had no power, so this form
of corporatist representation did not do much more than provide these
organizations with a forum to voice their concerns. But capitalists were
also incorporated into the new welfare and winter relief commissions,
where philanthropists in particular were given substantive roles in their
operation.[35] In addition to the kind of fund-raising they did for KMT
relief commissions, philanthropists gained key administrative roles in the
new Communist committees. In many respects, the CCP's New Democracy was a subtle variation on the KMT's brand of state corporatism.

The rapid success of the CCP's takeover and construction of new
political institutions in Shanghai was not matched in its efforts to revive
the local economy. Limiting chaos and corruption was not enough to
tame inflation or avert a sharp economic recession in 1949–50. The
KMT naval blockade and the ongoing fighting in the Chinese Civil
War created problems for Shanghai's economy. As supply routes were
cut off, factories were forced to shut down and unemployment surged.
The conversion to the new Communist "people's currency" (*renminbi*)
on June 1, 1949, sparked a new inflationary spiral almost immediately.[36]
Efforts to crack down on currency speculators with raids and arrests
over the summer failed to rein in the problem. KMT bombing raids in
the summer and fall of 1949 further undermined Shanghai's economy.

By the end of 1949, Shanghai was experiencing severe rice shortages, which led to riots and other protests. At the same time, the strike
wave that began in 1948 reached a new peak of intensity in 1949–50.[37]
Wage demands were the key issue in the strike wave, as workers sought
to return to the KMT practice of indexing their wages to inflation. The
economic and political crisis came to a head in the spring of 1950. The
biggest KMT bombing raid on Shanghai took place in February 1950,
killing and wounding more than 1,600 people and making another
50,000 people homeless.[38] Most dramatically, the founding workers'

35. Dillon, "New Democracy, 85–87"
36. Zhu Hua et. al., *Shanghai yibai nian*, 302.
37. Perry, "Shanghai's Strike Wave," 1.
38. Zhu Hua et al., *Shanghai yibai nian*, 305.

congress to establish the new Shanghai Federation of Trade Unions was disrupted with a direct hit to the hall where the communist labor delegates had been meeting. In the wake of the military attack, shortages of many daily necessities set in, just as people were preparing for the lunar New Year holiday.

Rather than follow the KMT's direct approach of mandating wage and price controls, the CCP pursued a more indirect approach to resolving the crisis. Although no announcement of a wage freeze was ever made, negotiators from the Shanghai Labor Bureau and the Shanghai Municipal Labor Union quietly held the line on wage demands in their effort to end the strike wave.[39] At the same time, the CCP sought to bring down the price of grain and other commodities by shipping in supplies to flood the market just before the holiday began. Finally, the CCP slashed government budgets and sharply reduced the currency in circulation in March 1950. This combination of measures brought inflation under control but at the cost of a sharp economic recession. Economic production only began to recover in late 1950 and slowly returned to prewar levels over the course of 1951–52.[40]

The CCP's less confrontational approach to resolving the inflation crisis showed that the communist unions were not yet able to command workers' compliance. More important, it did not produce any crippling displays of public defiance in the first direct conflict between the interests of the party and its key urban constituency. Rather than demanding workers' obedience or buying off their acquiescence, the CCP tried to depoliticize its sharpest conflict with labor as much as it could.

## UNEMPLOYMENT RELIEF

The Unemployment Relief program was implemented in the midst of this economic crisis, when austerity policies led to a surge in unemployment in the city. The Shanghai Federation of Trade Unions and the municipal government had been providing unemployment relief on an emergency basis since August 1949, before the national policy

---

39. Frazier, *Making of the Chinese Industrial Workplace*, 99–103.
40. Riskin, *China's Political Economy*, 43; Xiong Yuezhi et al., *Shanghai tongshi*, vol. 12, 44–45.

*Table 3.1.* Shanghai Unemployment Relief, 1947 versus 1951

| Measure of implementation | KMT 1947 | CCP 1951 |
| --- | --- | --- |
| Registered unemployed | 11,306 | 74,979 |
| Total relief handouts | 27,612 | 309,353 |
| Public works jobs | 156 | 3,181 |
| Self-help production jobs | 110 | 3,219 |
| Vocational training | 0 | 3,190 |
| Political education | 0 | 16,565 |
| Shelter residents | 2,453 | 0 |

*Sources:* Shanghai shi, *Shehui xingzheng tongji*, 75; Shanghai zonggonghui, *1948 Shanghai laodong nianjian*, 78; SMA, B127-1-53; SMA, B127-1-15.

had been adopted.[41] When the CCP issued the national unemployment relief regulations almost a year later in July 1950, it was able to build on the provisional relief distribution program to implement the new comprehensive program (table 3.1).

The first step was to create the Shanghai Unemployment Relief Commission, chaired by Shanghai Mayor Chen Yi and under the day-to-day leadership of Shanghai labor union chairman Liu Changsheng. The CCP unemployment committee was not just an interagency group of government officials, as the KMT committee had been, but also included more than a dozen businessmen and other prominent local citizens as well as representatives from all the local CCP mass organizations, including the Youth League and the Women's Federation.[42]

The new program expanded the emergency relief program significantly, distributing cash and rice to more than 75,000 unemployed workers in 1950. In addition to expanding the relief program, the commission started public works projects in conjunction with the municipal Public Works Bureau, employing more than 13,700 unemployed workers to repair roads, parks, and public buildings. Self-help production factories were also set up with funding from the unemployment relief commission as well as supply contracts for the PLA. More than 9,100 unemployed workers were hired to produce military

41. Shen Zhi and Li Tao, eds., *Shanghai laodong zhi*, 100–102.
42. Ibid., 562.

*Figure 3.1* Shanghai Unemployment Relief in the Early 1950s

uniforms, shoes, and gloves.[43] Just six months into the new program, the CCP's unemployment relief program was already more than ten times as large as the KMT program had been at its peak. With a dedicated tax and more effective interagency cooperation, the CCP program was able to overcome many of the obstacles that had frustrated its predecessor (fig. 3.1).

Although the Communist unemployment relief program was much bigger than the KMT program had been, it still only served a fraction of Shanghai's poor residents. Like the Nationalists, the Communists continued the policy of detaining and evacuating vagrants and refugees from the city. The winter relief commissions continued to operate, and they moved more than 180,000 people from the city over the course of

43. Ibid, 109.

1949–50.[44] As in the past, the distinctions between the unemployed and vagrants were often arbitrary.

## LABOR INSURANCE

Even if the CCP had the capacity to implement a comprehensive unemployment relief program in the midst of war and recession, labor insurance was a much more expensive and complex program. Each program and benefit was defined by the central government in the regulations, leaving no scope for local policy discretion as in the KMT Worker Welfare program. Moreover, determining eligibility, managing reserve funds, and providing benefits were much more complicated tasks than distributing unemployment relief rice, requiring a more sophisticated bureaucracy. Implementing a social insurance program was a task of a different order.

Planning for the implementation of labor insurance began in Shanghai as soon as the draft regulations were issued in October 1950. Despite the complexity of the program, the main focus of the planning process continued to be political rather than administrative. The Shanghai Federation of Trade Unions launched a major educational effort to train its cadres, distributing more than 20,000 copies of the draft regulations and holding training meetings to discuss them.[45] One of the cadres' main tasks to prepare for implementation was to gather information about other labor organizations that had been active in their factories, especially their membership lists, organizational structure, and leaders.[46] Political information about the CCP's rivals on the factory floor, rather than bureaucratic planning or budget forecasting, was the focus of union planning efforts.

The Shanghai Federation of Trade Unions and the Shanghai Labor Bureau began implementation in February 1951, immediately after the final regulations were issued. The CCP attacked the most politically difficult step in the process first: screening employers for eligibility. Because determining an enterprise's eligibility for the program was

44. SMA, B168-1-510.
45. SMA, C1-2-332.
46. SMA, C1-2-606.

in effect a decision of whether to impose a new, permanent 6 percent payroll tax, this stage in the process was inherently controversial.[47] The review of each company's size and financial condition represented the best opportunity for employers to resist the new program. Although some companies did fire employees to escape the hundred-employee threshold for eligibility, the most common strategy to resist the program was to argue that the company could not afford the new tax.[48]

In contrast to the corporatist model of the KMT Worker Welfare program, employers were given little scope to participate in this decision-making process. Rather than negotiate with employers, much less set up a corporatist framework to institutionalize their participation, the city government determined their eligibility largely on its own initiative. The Shanghai Labor Bureau identified the enterprises large enough to qualify for the program and reviewed their finances to determine whether they could afford it. The companies that claimed financial hardship were subject to an additional review by the Shanghai Tax Bureau.[49] When the Labor Bureau did exempt a company for financial hardship, the exemption only represented a temporary delay until conditions improved. Out of the 726 enterprises that the Labor Bureau targeted for labor insurance in the initial phase of implementation, 177 sought exemptions, and 115 were granted temporary delays. In this group of laggards, 70 percent postponed labor insurance owing to financial problems, whereas another 20 percent were delayed because their workers objected to having their preexisting private benefits cut.[50] The entire process was carried out quietly, with little publicity in a few weeks in late February and early March of 1951.

The main task in the next phase of implementation was to determine the eligibility of individual workers for labor insurance. In contrast to the top-down, bureaucratic process for determining the eligibility of employers, workers' eligibility was determined by the

---

47. This effective tax rate included a 3 percent payroll tax plus the mandate to pay for work injury and health care benefits directly. In the first few years of the program, these direct costs averaged another 3 to 4 percent of the payroll. SMA C1-2-591b.
48. SMA, C1-2-591b; SMA, B127-1-15.
49. SMA, B127-1-1186.
50. SMA, C1-2-591a.

workers themselves during the course of a mass struggle campaign: the Campaign to Suppress Counterrevolutionaries (*zhenya fangeming yundong*). The process was not only participatory, but the charged political atmosphere of the campaign made implementing labor insurance in the factory anything but a boring clerical task.

The goal of the larger campaign was to identify the people deemed enemies of the revolution and eliminate the threat they posed to the new regime. In late March, when the union phase of the campaign was getting under way, the Shanghai Party Committee turned up the heat by staging public trials and executions of ninety-one people considered to be high-ranking counterrevolutionaries.[51] This very public display of power and intimidation set the tone for the rest of the campaign.[52] In April, campaign work teams sought to extend the political battle to the factory floor, portraying labor insurance as the culmination of a bloody, thirty-year revolutionary struggle to make workers the masters of a new society.[53] But the counterrevolutionaries were not the bourgeois owners and managers of their companies, as many workers anticipated. Earlier struggle campaigns in factories in the Northeast showed how dangerous mobilizing workers against their bosses could be, since some workers carried their enthusiasm for redistribution as far as dismantling factory machinery and crippling production.[54]

Instead, the targets of the Campaign to Suppress Counterrevolutionaries were the CCP's rivals on the factory floor: labor racketeers who were part of organized crime outfits like the Green Gang as well as underground KMT labor union activists, especially cadres from the former Shanghai Worker Welfare Committee. It was the leaders of the underground rivals to the CCP labor unions who were defined as threats to the regime, not the capitalists who paid for the welfare state.

The process laid out for the factory-level campaign started with an emotional mass meeting of the entire firm to introduce labor insur-

51. Qian Lijun, "Shanghai jiefang chuqi," 74.
52. Ibid, 75–76. Yang, "Reconsidering the Campaign," 105–6.
53. SMA, C1-2-591a.
54. Levine, *Anvil of Victory*, 184; Pepper, *Civil War*, 351–52.

ance and place it in the context of the larger revolution. Then workers split up into small groups in their workshops, where union activists helped guide workers in the new practice of "speaking bitterness" about the hardships they experienced before 1949. In the process, the groups determined each other's eligibility for labor insurance by reviewing each other's work history and political history. KMT and Green Gang "spies" were denounced, reported to union authorities, and denied labor insurance. The last stage in the process featured a loyalty oath to the new regime by all the workers deemed to be politically reliable, followed by the distribution of the new labor insurance cards.[55]

Union cadres were instructed that the key to carrying out a successful factory campaign was to inspire an "accusatory mood" among the workers in order to encourage them to "draw a clear line between us and the enemy."[56] As the campaign played out across the city, factories responded in very different ways. Some workers were so zealous about eligibility determination that they only managed to complete one or two reviews a day because the group discussions delved into every detail of the workers' employment history and political views. Other factories skipped the group process entirely, assigning a few literate workers to the task of interviewing coworkers and filling out the forms.

During the Shanghai campaign, more than 5 percent of the labor force in these enterprises were identified as counterrevolutionaries and denied labor insurance.[57] All the concern about promoting vigilance and overcoming sympathy in small-group meetings turned out to be unnecessary, since Shanghai workers ended up denying labor insurance to far more people than the union had intended, excluding even low-level KMT union cadres and Green Gang members. After provoking anger and outrage among the workers by overturning some of their eligibility decisions, union officials chose to let them stand indefinitely until feelings had cooled off.[58]

The high point of the citywide campaign came in time for May Day and featured the same combination of fear and triumph that launched

55. SMA, C1-2-591a.
56. Ibid.
57. SMA, C1-2-5-591b.
58. Ibid.

the campaign two months earlier. A midnight raid on April 27, 1951, led to mass arrests of more than 8,300 counterrevolutionaries. After a public trial that was broadcast across the city, 285 political enemies were publicly executed on April 30.[59] The violent crackdown was followed by a rally convened by the Shanghai Federation of Trade Unions to celebrate the beginning of labor insurance on May 1. With great fanfare, union leaders handed out the first pension checks for retiring workers and sent off the first contingent of sick workers to the new workers sanatorium in the resort town of Hangzhou, where emperors and the wealthy had vacationed for thousands of years.[60] The symbolism was not subtle: the enemies of the revolution had been vanquished, while the proletarian heroes were rewarded with the best benefits the welfare state could provide.

The citywide Campaign to Suppress Counterrevolutionaries officially came to an end in October 1951, after several months of review of all the accusations levied since the beginning of the year. More than 25,100 people had been arrested in the campaign, the vast majority of whom were sentenced to labor reform. About 10 percent, or 2,456 people, were executed, making it the most violent mass campaign in Shanghai's history.[61]

The campaign was an effective tool for program implementation. By the end of 1951, more than 300,000 workers in 611 enterprises had been enrolled in labor insurance, surpassing the Shanghai Federation of Trade Union's target for the initial stage of implementation (table 3.2). It was only after the program was up and running that the labor union began building up a labor insurance bureaucracy to administer it.[62] Activists from the Campaign to Suppress Counterrevolutionaries were recruited to staff the new enterprise labor insurance committees, responsible for determining benefits and enrolling new workers on an ongoing basis. Company management was given responsibility for collecting payroll taxes and paying the benefits authorized by the labor insurance committee. At the district and municipal levels of the

59. Qian Lijun, "Shanghai jiefang chuqi," 74–76.
60. SMA, C1-2-591b.
61. Qian Lijun, "Shanghai jiefang chuqi," 77; Yang Kuisong "Reconsidering," 120.
62. SMA, C1-2-609.

*Table 3.2.* Shanghai Worker Welfare and Labor Insurance Implementation, 1947 versus 1951

| Measure of implementation | KMT worker welfare, 1947 | CCP labor insurance, 1951 |
| --- | --- | --- |
| Number of enterprises | 53 | 611 |
| Number of workers covered | 25,000* | 306,823 |
| Number of workers receiving health care | 27,745 | 157,570 |

*Estimate based on assumption that worker welfare enterprises averaged five hundred employees.
*Sources:* Shanghai zonggonghui, *1948 laodong nianjian*, 25–28; SMA, C1-2-601.

union, labor insurance divisions were created to oversee the enterprise committees, manage the labor insurance reserve funds, and provide specialized welfare services and programs such as the sanatorium in Hangzhou.

Early inspections of the union's new enterprise labor insurance committees judged them to be enthusiastic but disorganized, with no division of labor in place and staffed by cadres with only a dim understanding of their duties.[63] The recommended solution to the problem was to conduct more training classes and to publish labor insurance handbooks. The inspections also discovered enterprise unions that were intentionally flouting the regulations. For example, one factory investigated by the municipal labor union was paying higher benefits to male workers than female workers, and several transportation companies were continuing to pay higher benefits based on their previous private programs.[64] In these cases, the municipal labor union quietly intervened to convince the enterprise unions to comply with the new policy.

Even if union cadres were not well versed in the labor insurance regulations, workers quickly began to figure out how the program operated. Within months of implementing labor insurance, union cadres were complaining that the program was too popular among workers, who were taking paid sick leave to go window shopping and gamble in local parks. But the biggest problem that the labor insurance program faced after implementation was the severe shortage of health

63. SMA, C1-2-591b.
64. Ibid.

care services for the more than 300,000 workers who now qualified for free care. Shanghai did not have enough doctors or hospital beds to meet the surge in demand, although the city boasted some of the largest and best hospitals in the country. In addition, many doctors resisted treating workers. Yet another problem was that most workers preferred Chinese medicine to the Western medicine hospitals and doctors provided. Despite these shortcomings, health care was by far the most popular labor insurance benefit among Shanghai's relatively young workforce, with more than 150,000 seeking care in the first few months of the program.[65]

The economic constraints that loomed so large for the KMT a few years earlier seemingly disappeared. No doubt it helped that by 1951 the economy was improved in comparison to almost any time since the end of the Second World War. But better economic conditions alone cannot explain the CCP's relative success in implementation. Nor do they explain how and why companies paid significant new payroll taxes with little resistance. One reason for the very different economic constraints faced by the new regime is simply that the CCP dared to impose new taxes on business for its welfare programs rather than relying on voluntary contributions.

By giving labor an important role in the implementation of labor insurance, the Communists were able to harness worker enthusiasm to help create the new program. At the same time, they gained valuable political information that helped them demobilize KMT labor organizations and labor racketeers who had gone underground with the transfer of power in 1949. Finally, by denying capitalists any real role in either program, the CCP was able to sidestep the kind of grassroots political opposition that had held back the KMT's welfare programs just a few years before. The differences in the state corporatist regimes the two parties were trying to construct were subtle and largely uninstitutionalized. Even transitory differences in political processes at the local level had a profound impact on the welfare programs of the two regimes.

65. Ibid.

UNEMPLOYED WORKERS CONGRESSES

Although the beneficiaries in the unemployment relief program did not participate in the Campaign to Suppress Counterrevolutionaries in the same way as their employed counterparts, the drive to mobilize workers outside the workplace was evident in other ways. The Shanghai Unemployment Relief Commission took the innovative step of convening an Unemployed Workers Congress in the spring of 1951. At that point Shanghai's unemployment problem was still serious, even after the 1950 recession was beginning to ease. In fact, the unemployment rolls surged in the spring of 1951 to a new high of more than 82,730 people.[66]

The Unemployed Workers Congress was modeled on the workers congresses convened by the Shanghai Federation of Trade Unions the year before. More than 700 delegates were chosen for the Unemployed Workers Congress, including 300 cadres and 400 unemployed workers. The 400 unemployed workers were split evenly: 200 delegates represented the various relief programs operated by the commission, and the other 200 represented unemployed workers from various industries.

The stated goal of the Unemployed Workers Congress was to solicit feedback about the unemployment relief program from both the beneficiaries and cadres who ran it.[67] Although the Unemployed Workers Congress was no more democratic than the union's workers congresses or the city's people's congress, it was unusual for bringing together welfare providers and recipients in a common forum to discuss a welfare program. In addition, the congress dramatically symbolized unemployed workers' inclusion among the "people" valued by the Communist regime.

The unemployed delegates seized the opportunity to push for greater inclusion. More than two hundred proposals were submitted to the congress, including everything from denunciations of American imperialism to suggestions for improving the collection of unemployment statistics.[68] Beyond calling for jobs, the delegates also advocated

66. SMA, B129-2-16d.
67. SMA, B129-2-6.
68. Ibid.

giving unemployed workers equal status with employed union members and expanding unemployment programs to all the unemployed people who needed them.

Proposals to expand access to the commission's job training, literacy, and political education classes were especially common, amounting to nearly one-third of the total number. In addition to advocating for easing eligibility restrictions based on education, physical health, and political background, the delegates also called for expanding access to unemployed workers laid off before 1949. There were even proposals to facilitate women's participation in education programs by providing free child care.[69]

Whether the demands for greater inclusion truly reflected the concerns of the unemployed or in fact reflected the agenda of the Shanghai Unemployment Relief Commission, they lent support to several initiatives undertaken in 1951. The definition of unemployment became more inclusive when the Commission loosened its eligibility requirements to include industrial workers who had been laid off before 1949.[70] In addition, the commission's educational programs expanded until they became the most popular unemployment programs, larger than the distribution of relief grain. In addition to new vocational training classes for the machinery, electronics, construction, and health care industries, the largest education program the commission operated in 1951 was the political education classes taught by the Shanghai labor union.[71] Enrolling 16,565 unemployed workers, these three-month study courses combined literacy and political education. The goal of the classes was to raise the class consciousness of the unemployed, and more particularly to convince them that the KMT and American imperialism were the sources of Shanghai's ongoing unemployment problems rather than the Communist regime, where many unemployed workers were placing the blame.[72]

Finally, the Unemployment Relief Commission undertook a major reorganization of the unemployed in 1951 to better integrate them into

69. Ibid.
70. SMA, B129-2-16b.
71. SMA, B127-1-15.
72. SMA, B129-2-16c.

the Shanghai Federation of Trade Unions. The program had originally been set up using factories as the basic unit of organization, much like the KMT program before it. But as time went on and many factories remained closed, this organizational structure grew problematic. For example, it was becoming increasingly clear that many companies would never reopen or return to their former levels of production. Furthermore, as unemployed workers moved away from the factory and participated in unemployment programs like public works projects, they lost touch with their former coworkers and meetings were increasingly difficult to organize. As part of the 1951 reorganization, factory units were abolished, and unemployed workers were assigned to new groups based on their current residence and former industry. When district and industrial groups were too large, they were further subdivided by gender. The new grassroots union organizations were called unemployed workers liaison stations (*lianluozhan*) and were given the same rank as enterprise unions in the union hierarchy. Moreover, the stations were led by union cadres drawn from the unemployed and were often housed in the district union office, local temples, or the cadres' own homes.[73]

Union work teams led a thorough review of unemployment registration rolls in the course of the reorganization. They delegated much of the task to the unemployed workers themselves, mobilizing them to determine each other's eligibility in small-group meetings in the new liaison stations, in a manner very similar to the implementation of labor insurance. The outcomes of the small-group reviews by the unemployed, however, were more unpredictable. Many of the unemployed complained about the eligibility requirements for unemployment relief, so cadres had considerable difficulty in convincing them to enforce those rules on each other. For example, they criticized the limits on the distribution of relief rice, arguing that too few people qualified for the benefit, and even when they did, the rations were too small to keep them from going hungry. Others argued that unemployed workers with working family members (most of whom were married women) should not be purged from the program, since their families were still

73. SMA, B129-2-16d; SMA, B129-2-16d.

poor and needed two incomes to get by.[74] Despite resistance, however, the reviews did gradually reduce the unemployment registration rolls to 74,979 by the end of the year.[75]

But, in the long run, the most significant outcome of the reorganization was that the unemployed had been integrated into the official union as unemployed workers. No longer loosely connected to the union through shadow enterprise unions with no resources and haphazard leadership, they now had their own small groups, activists, and grassroots unions. The symbolic representation of their inclusion in the Unemployed Workers Congress was now matched by their organizational inclusion in the labor union as unemployed workers.

TEST OF CORPORATISM

The CCP's political acumen may have been sufficient to implement its welfare state agenda and begin to incorporate both workers and an important segment of the urban poor into the regime. But as the Nationalists showed four years earlier, union membership and new welfare programs did not necessarily translate into political support. Just as it had done in the 1949–50 strike wave, the CCP continued to avoid testing the loyalty of its official labor movement.

The CCP also took a different approach from the Nationalists with broader political issues, such as war and peace. Where the KMT literally put words in the mouths of its labor leaders to declare working-class support for the Chinese Civil War, the CCP was more cautious. For example, during the Korean War, union cadres carefully reported complaints from unemployed workers that there was no difference between American and Soviet imperialism, as well as their fears that China would lose the third world war that many anticipated would begin soon. But the response to politically incorrect views was quiet political education rather than public punishment.[76] Similarly, the party launched a fund-raising drive for the Korean War effort, soliciting donations from workers. Externally, all donations were trumpeted

74. SMA, B129-2-16a.
75. SMA, B127-1-53.
76. SMA, B129-2-16c.

as evidence of enthusiastic working-class support for the war. Internally, the union carefully tracked the rate of participation and amount of donations as a gauge of workers' political attitudes.[77] The fact that there was so much institutional and peer pressure to donate meant that the fund-raising drive was not a very accurate measure of labor support for the war. But the difference with the KMT's approach suggests the CCP's reluctance to test its success in building a working-class political constituency for the regime.

The most important indication of the fragility of the CCP's victory in the competition to mobilize and incorporate labor came in late 1951, when a debate among the top party leadership over the role of the official labor union emerged.[78] One side in the debate favored a measure of autonomy for the labor union within the regime—especially in state-owned enterprises, where the interests of management and workers sometimes came into conflict. Li Lisan, as the day-to-day leader of the All-China Federation of Trade Unions, advocated allowing the union to represent the workers in conflicts with the enterprise party committee. Liu Shaoqi, the second highest ranking leader in the CCP and leader of the underground labor movement before 1949, also backed this view. The other side in the debate pointed to the Soviet experience in the 1920s to argue that the party had to maintain tight control over the union or risk having its own role in representing the working class come into question.

Mao Zedong settled the debate by backing the side advocating party control. To carry out the new policy, the party held a secret meeting of the top party leadership at the end of December 1951. The main agenda at the meeting was to place blame: Li Lisan was forced to perform self-criticism and resign from his leadership position in the All-China Federation of Trade Unions. The other leading advocate for giving unions a more clearly defined role in state-owned enterprises, Liu Shaoqi, skipped the meeting altogether rather than share in this political setback.

Li Fuchun, the man put in charge of creating a new economic planning system, led the criticism of Li Lisan's leadership of the union.

77. SMA, C1-2-591b.
78. Teiwes, *Politics at Mao's Court*, 39–40.

In the course of the meeting, Li Lisan was attacked for almost every policy decision he made, going far beyond his advocacy for more union autonomy in state-owned enterprises. For example, Li Lisan's critics accused him of promoting "economism," arguing that labor insurance and unemployment relief only made workers more concerned with their own economic interests over the larger political goals of the revolution.[79] In a confusing turnaround, he was also accused of promoting redistribution, ostensibly the goal of the revolution, over economic production. But most devastating was the charge of promoting "syndicalism," an accusation that Li Lisan was building up the official labor union to be an alternative to the CCP rather than a subsidiary. Indeed, concern about the extent of Li Lisan's influence in the official labor union was so high that the party leadership decided to keep his purge secret to prevent the open opposition that it was seeking to contain.[80] Both Li Lisan and Zhu Xuefan had been used to build up the Communist labor movement precisely because they had their own national and international legitimacy. But because their power was personal and therefore independent of the institutions they led, they were also quickly shunted aside into administrative roles that cut them off from their grassroots supporters.

Although the CCP's victory in the race to mobilize Shanghai's workers was impressive, it is also striking that the Communist leadership was tentative rather than triumphant about its achievement. Carefully monitoring workers' responses to its new programs and policies, avoiding any direct confrontation between the party and the working class, and purging union leaders with its own political constituencies were all signs of the vulnerability of the new Communist regime. Caution was one reason the CCP "won" its competition with the KMT.

79. This criticism fits with the term's general meaning. In the Chinese Communist lexicon, "economism" was used to describe the practice of placing economic interests ahead of political interests.

80. Harper, "Party and Unions," 95–96; SMA, C1-2-2255.

## Evaluating the Communist Welfare State

When it comes to judging the outcome of the competition to implement new welfare programs for workers, there is no doubt which party won. But the scale of the CCP's victory is worth noting. Comparing the two parties' implementation of their welfare programs two and a half years after their respective takeovers of Shanghai, it is clear that the CCP was able to break through the economic, administrative, and political constraints that held back the KMT.[81] Although the CCP's labor insurance program had only been operating for eight months by the end of 1951, it reached eleven times as many enterprises as the KMT's worker welfare program and probably covered ten to eleven times the number of workers as well (see table 3.2). In addition, the CCP's labor insurance program provided free health care to more than five times the number of workers that the KMT had been able to reach four years earlier, even though health care had been one of the top priorities of the municipal Worker Welfare program. The difference in the scale of the two programs is all the more striking considering that the labor insurance program was a much more comprehensive and complicated program.

The differences are just as stark between the two parties' unemployment relief programs, which were much more similar in their structure and services. Although neither program served more than a fraction of the total number of unemployed and underemployed urban poor in Shanghai, the CCP's unemployment registration rolls were about seven times larger than those of the KMT program at comparable points in their development (see table 3.1). Similarly, the CCP's program for distributing relief, which included both cash benefits and grain rations, was eleven times larger.

The differences are especially clear in the "active" unemployment relief programs that both parties preferred, such as public works projects, self-help production, and vocational training. The CCP's active relief programs were more than twenty times as large as the KMT's (and

---

81. This time period marks the high point of KMT implementation before its program began to unravel.

*Table 3.3.* Shanghai Welfare Coverage, 1949–51

| Year | Total beneficiaries | Percent increase | Workforce coverage | Population coverage |
|------|---------------------|------------------|--------------------|---------------------|
| 1949 | 9,011 | | 0% | 0% |
| 1950 | 94,309 | 947% | 4% | 2% |
| 1951 | 381,302 | 304% | 14% | 7% |

Sources: Shanghaishi tongji ju, *Shanghai shi guomin jingji* 22, 46; SMA, C1-2-601; SMA, B127-1-53; SMA, B127-1-15.

lasted significantly longer). The only KMT unemployment program that stands out favorably in the comparison was its shelter for returned workers, since the CCP never set up anything similar to it.

When we look at how far the new Communist welfare state reached into Shanghai society, the major new programs covered only a small fraction of the people who needed protection (table 3.3). By the end of 1951, labor insurance and unemployment relief combined to cover 14 percent of the workforce and just 7 percent of the city's population. The CCP's victory over the Nationalist regime in implementing its welfare agenda was only the beginning of the effort to resolve the problem of urban poverty.

How did the CCP overcome the obstacles that constrained the KMT? Two differences stand out as important in the top-down and bottom-up forces shaping implementation of the Chinese welfare state. First, in comparing top-down pressure, the internal discipline of the CCP was a distinct advantage over the factionalism and disorganization of the KMT. Factional and partisan competition both produced new welfare initiatives at the central level. Their competition also produced mobilization drives at the local level that opened up new opportunities for political participation for ordinary people. But the KMT's mobilization efforts were centrifugal, creating disjunctures that undermined control over its new labor organizations and opened up opportunities for its rivals on the factory floor and in the streets. In contrast, the CCP was able to build its underground labor organization into a single official labor organization that reached from the factory floor and the homes of the unemployed up to the national union in Beijing. As a result, Communist leaders could target the KMT underground and the Green Gang in the Campaign to Suppress Counterrevolutionaries, striking a major blow against its two main rivals in the ongoing competition to mobilize Shanghai's workers.

The second key difference lay in the bottom-up pressure for welfare. Small differences in the kinds of corporatist regimes the two parties were trying to construct, with the KMT favoring capitalists and the CCP favoring workers, had an impact on implementation. In its reluctance to tax employers and the discretion given to them in the Worker Welfare program, the KMT favored capital in both formal and informal ways. In contrast, CCP favoritism for labor was selective, but effective. Sidelining capitalists in the implementation of labor insurance limited their opportunities to resist the new program. In addition, labor was incorporated into the implementation of labor insurance through the Campaign to Suppress Counterrevolutionaries, helping to propel implementation of the program before any semblance of a labor union bureaucracy could be constructed.

Differences in the kind of corporatism the parties established at the grass roots had a significant impact on the implementation of labor insurance and unemployment relief, but it is hard to assess whether the transient political gains for labor could be consolidated. The secret purge of Li Lisan after he had led the successful construction of a national union organization and creation of the welfare state was an indicator of how fragile labor's gains under the new political regime really were.

The fact that the Communists tried to avoid redistributive bargaining at the very moment that the redistribution of income was actually taking place shows how different this form of welfare politics was from the grassroots corporatism of the KMT as well as the democratic politics of the advanced industrial countries. The Communists' political acumen led them to identify a more significant threat in this brand of mobilizational welfare politics than capitalists: their rival labor organizers on the factory floor. To claim credit for the welfare state (and avoid blame for the economic problems of the day), the CCP sought to eliminate underground KMT labor organizations and Green Gang labor rackets. Only then could they use the new benefits of the welfare state to bolster their own political support. Through a carefully targeted struggle campaign, the Communists were able to gain control over the politics of mobilization and countermobilization in a way that the factionalized KMT never could.

The Communists' relative success in founding a welfare state showed that the challenging economic and political conditions posed by war could be overcome. The shortcut of establishing a labor insurance bureaucracy after implementation meant that the program was only weakly institutionalized. But the economic constraints posed by years of trade disruptions and hyperinflation proved more elastic than many had feared, at least for the largest and best-financed companies in Shanghai.

The only lasting legacy of the difficulties in founding the Chinese welfare state stems from the CCP's achievements rather than from the KMT's failures. The choice of social insurance was a foregone conclusion by 1950–51, when the rival parties issued their parallel labor insurance programs. The high costs and administrative hurdles involved in expanding the reach of social insurance were inherent in the program's design. By starting the process when China was one of the poorest countries in the world, both regimes ensured that the path to a broad welfare state would be daunting.

## PART II

*The Politics of Expanding China's Welfare State*

# CHAPTER 4

# *The Soviet Model: Transitional Welfare in the First Five-Year Plan, 1952–54*

The Soviet Union helped set a clear agenda for Chinese welfare reformers in the early 1950s. Paradoxically, the effort to follow the precedents established by the Soviet Union and the more recent Eastern European revolutions in fact sent China down a different path in its welfare state development. Rather than having decades separate the adoption and the expansion of the welfare state, Chinese policy makers started expanding their welfare state immediately. The timing posed challenges that most other communist countries did not experience. With only very narrow welfare coverage in place, Chinese faced the problem of incorporating the vast majority of the population rather than the smaller minorities that remained uncovered in countries like Czechoslovakia and Hungary. Furthermore, the CCP could not fall back on decades of administrative experience to help meet its goals. The task facing Chinese policy makers was far bigger and the foundations of the welfare state significantly weaker.

There were significant changes in the top-down pressure for welfare reform coming from within the Communist party-state in the early 1950s. The new concern about controlling labor mobilization evident in the December 1951 ouster of Li Lisan from the leadership of the national union was accompanied by larger political shifts. The competition between the Nationalist and Communist parties waned over the course of the Korean War (1950–53). As the limits of the Korean War and U.S. containment policy gradually became clear, the Chinese Civil War settled into a stalemate. The political competition between the Communists and the Nationalists faded along with the military competition, putting less pressure on the Communist regime to mobilize labor.

As the political competition eased, economic development policy provided a new impetus for welfare reform. The cadres who led the construction of the new economic planning bureaucracies in the central government also began formulating welfare policies that fit with the larger Soviet economic development strategy. Economic planners were less attuned to workers' economic needs and political concerns than labor leaders like Li Lisan had been, but the scope of their ambitions were far larger. As a result, the CCP's top-down pressure for welfare reform remained strong throughout this period.

Bottom-up demand for welfare reform was also increasing in the early 1950s. As workers and other urban residents learned more about China's new welfare state, they began to realize how valuable its benefits could be. The workers who discovered the guilty pleasures of sick pay and the unemployed who clamored for more vocational training are just two examples of how quickly exposure to new welfare programs began to reshape people's expectations. Moreover, Li Lisan's 1951 reforms to more fully incorporate the unemployed into the labor union ensured that at least one group among the urban poor was organized into an equal alliance with workers and incorporated into the regime.

These were good political conditions for the expansion of coverage, with only capitalists as a potential source of opposition. Indeed, significant expansion was achieved very quickly in the first few years of China's welfare state, but proved to be unsustainable. The scale of the challenge forced Chinese welfare reformers to confront the limits of their new welfare state almost immediately. No matter how widely shared, political enthusiasm for the welfare state could not overcome China's economic constraints.

## *The Soviet Economic Development Strategy*

The Chinese Communist leadership made the decision to follow the Stalinist development strategy in February 1951 and committed to beginning the First Five-Year Plan less than two years later, in January 1953. In 1952, the first national economic planning agencies were created under the State Council.[1] Premier Zhou Enlai, the third highest ranking leader in the CCP and the man with the most administrative experience, led the initiative. Li Fuchun, who had spearheaded the criticism of Li Lisan, was put in charge of creating the new central planning system. In addition to his experience in managing the takeover of the industrial centers in Northeast China, Li Fuchun had studied in both France and the Soviet Union as a young man. In the early 1950s, he was sent to the Soviet Union for advanced training in economic planning. The new bureaucracy that Zhou Enlai and Li Fuchun helped to create became the center of the policy-making process within the regime for most issues touching on political economy.

The economic development strategy the Chinese imported from the Soviet Union was sweeping in scope. The Stalinist development strategy focused on engineering massive structural economic change to achieve rapid, sustained industrialization. The institutions of the command economy were designed to give policy makers in Moscow or Beijing the tools to direct this kind of structural change. Among the most important were central planning agencies to replace banks and capital markets, state ownership of industry to replace private corporations, and government bureaucracies to allocate goods and labor in place of market coordination. Once the new institutions were in place, central planners could invest heavily in industry, especially producer industries. Labor insurance and other new welfare programs were just one piece of a much larger agenda, serving as pillars for the new bureaucracies designed to replace private labor markets.

Pursuing the Stalinist development strategy was extremely difficult for any regime and particularly difficult for a newly consolidated one

---

1. Riskin, *China's Political Economy*, 53; Li, *Mao and the Economic Stalinization*, 69, 110, 112.

with a poor, agricultural economy. The Chinese sought to implement the new development strategy gradually, building on their early achievements in economic recovery after the war. The initial phase of China's First Five-Year Plan focused on the elements of the Soviet investment strategy that could be carried out while the rest of the command economy was still being built. With a state-controlled banking sector inherited from the Nationalist regime and new assistance from the Soviet Union, the Chinese started the First Five-Year Plan with an investment drive. Announcing a list of 156 major industrial projects in 1953, the planners increased total investment in China more than 20 percent.[2]

As the initial investment drive got under way, the planning agencies were also tasked with formulating the content of the rest of the First Five-Year Plan. Only after the new economic bureaucracy was built could the investment phase of the First Five-Year Plan give way to the kind of central planning the Soviets employed. To make the Stalinist development strategy self-sustaining in the long run, planners needed systemic control over the economy to restrain consumption (including welfare) below the level of productivity growth, allowing them to generate the capital necessary for investment.

The most important policy decisions to be made during the plan were the timing of the two key structural transformations for a command economy: the nationalization of industry and the replacement of private markets with bureaucratic allocation of labor, goods, and services. Some CCP leaders envisioned ten to fifteen years of economic recovery and growth under a partial planning system, much like the Soviet experience under the New Economic policies of the 1920s. Others anticipated a much more rapid process of simultaneous restructuring and development during the First Five-Year Plan, more similar to the Eastern European pattern.[3]

---

2. Naughton, *Chinese Economy*, 63, 66.
3. Hua-yu Li, *Mao and the Economic Stalinization*, 46, 84.

## *The Soviet Model of Welfare State Expansion*

The Soviet model of welfare state development fit closely with this economic reform agenda. Soviet advisers warned the CCP leadership that the Stalinist development strategy and the transition to a command economy would be disruptive. Even if employment could be expected to grow significantly over the long term, in the short run many workers in low priority industries or in capitalist institutions such as trading companies would lose their jobs and whatever benefits had come with them. Temporary welfare programs would be required to ease people through the dislocations of economic restructuring until they could find a permanent place in the command economy and the communist welfare state.

When the CCP committed itself to transitional programs, great care was taken to tailor welfare programs to the new demands of economic planning. Creating consistent work incentives became an important principle of program design. To achieve this goal, the new economic planners sought to create a hierarchy of transitional welfare programs to encourage work as the labor market was gradually eliminated. They sought to revise the labor insurance program to provide stronger work incentives, especially to crack down on sick pay abuse and lax disability requirements.[4] At the same time, they also sought to increase other labor insurance benefits to ensure the program remained at the top of the newly forming ladder of welfare programs.

Second in the hierarchy after labor insurance was labor insurance contracts. These transitional programs were designed for medium and small enterprises that fell below the hundred-worker size limit for labor insurance as a way of preparing them for the full labor insurance program.[5] In negotiations between the labor union and enterprise management, the labor insurance contract program created benefit programs tailored to each firm's financial resources and working conditions. Labor contract programs usually started with modest health benefits, such as securing access to free or subsidized health clinics. As

4. Zhonggong zhongyang wenxian yanjiu shi, *Jianguo yilai*, vol. 2, 68–74.
5. Ibid. 55; SMA, B127-1-19.

the economy expanded and these firms grew more stable and profitable, new benefits could be added to the contract, until the point when the enterprise was ready for the full labor insurance program.

Third in the welfare hierarchy was unemployment relief. Broadening eligibility to all of the unemployed, the new program prioritized vocational training and job placement services to find a permanent solution to unemployment. As a transitional program, this new form of unemployment relief would be rendered unnecessary by industrialization and rapid expansion of formal sector employment.

At the bottom of the hierarchy came a long-term welfare program: social relief (*shehui jiuji*)[6] Social relief was designed for elderly and disabled people who were physically incapable of working and who had no families to take care of them. Social relief provided modest handouts of grain or cash to allow them to continue living in their own homes. The program operated in conjunction with the welfare institutes for the elderly, disabled, and orphaned children that housed and cared for people who could not live on their own.[7]

According to the roadmap laid out in Soviet manuals on labor insurance, the end of the First Five-Five Year Plan marked the end of transitional welfare programs. Once labor insurance expanded into social insurance and covered the majority of the population, labor insurance contracts and unemployment relief could be eliminated. At that point, social insurance would protect the working population, and social relief would provide for those few incapable of productive labor. Since the Chinese leadership had not yet decided whether the economic reforms could be carried out within five years or within fifteen years, the timetable for welfare reform was not clear. But the route and the final destination had been identified. The political and administrative difficulties of carrying out such an ambitious welfare reform agenda while constructing a new command economy may have been daunting, but reports of rapid and successful revolutions in Eastern Europe and the CCP's own record of achievement no doubt gave Chinese leaders an important measure of confidence.

6. SMA, B168-1-510; Fan Jingsi, *Shanghai minzheng*, 385-86.
7. Chen, *Guilty of Indigence*, 216.

## *The Three Antis and Five Antis*
## *Campaigns against Corruption*

Before the new leaders of the command economy could begin to carry out their vision of reform, workers in Shanghai and other major cities seized the opportunities provided by the Three Antis and Five Antis campaigns against corruption (*sanfan wufan yundong*) to take political action on their own. For many workers, the new anticorruption campaigns seemed to be the social revolution that they had been eagerly anticipating since 1949.

The Three Antis movement originally began in the fall of 1951 as an internal party rectification campaign against cadres and government officials. A response to corruption in government procurement for the Korean War, the campaign began in the Northeast, which was the staging ground for the Chinese war effort. As the campaign went national in the winter of 1951–52, it expanded to include the Five Antis mass campaign against capitalists, targeting the other side of the corruption problem in government procurement.[8] The CCP leadership portrayed corruption as more than the moral failures of individuals—corruption was instead described as a capitalist conspiracy to subvert the regime from within by inculcating bourgeois values in the party itself.[9]

In Shanghai, the Three Antis phase of the anticorruption campaign started in January 1952. It was a tepid affair, with internal party investigations of cadres and government officials that were only publicized when punishments of high-level officials were announced.[10] For investigations of people outside the party-state, the city established a campaign committee that included a broad swathe of Shanghai society, including leading capitalists and labor union leaders. The Shanghai Business Federation's effort to solicit confessions from its members was emblematic of the early phase of the campaign. China's richest capitalist, Rong

---

8. The Three Antis was a campaign against corruption, waste, and bureaucratic abuses of power. The Five Antis campaign countered bribery, tax evasion, theft of state property, cheating on government contracts, and stealing of state economic information.
9. Bo Yibo, *Ruogan zhongda juece*, 164.
10. Zhu Hua, et al., *Shanghai yibai nian*, 321.

Yiren, led the way with his confession of a minor infraction, revealing that one of his textile mills had delayed fulfilling a government procurement contract for almost ten months. The cause of the delay was supply problems rather than any underhanded attempt to wring extra profits from the deal, and Rong Yiren simply apologized and offered to refund the contract.[11]

As the anticorruption movement broadened to include the Five Antis campaign in industry in late January 1952, the CCP took leadership of the campaign from the cross-class campaign committee that it had just established and turned it over to the Shanghai Federation of Trade Unions. Even with the change in the leadership of the campaign, its scope remained narrow. The campaign's targets initially focused on the most serious forms of corruption, and the mobilization of workers was supposed to be limited to helping with investigations of their employers. Campaign rules prohibited companies from shutting down, laying off employees, withholding wages, or penalizing workers in any way for time spent on the campaign.[12]

The union kicked off the new phase of the movement by convening a rally for more than 3,600 union activists on February 7, 1952, that was broadcast all over the city. Union leaders anticipated that it would be difficult to mobilize workers to investigate their employers, whether out of sympathy or out of fear. Shanghai union chairman Liu Changsheng exhorted Shanghai's workers to protect the revolution from their employers' attempts to undermine the regime from within. With drummers beating in the background to make his speech more stirring, Liu sought to inspire a militant tone for the campaign.

It is not clear that the drums were necessary, since Shanghai's workers responded with alacrity. As the union organized investigations, solicited accusations, and carried out its propaganda "battle," tens of thousands of workers abandoned their regular work to join the investigations. In addition to organizing tiger-beating teams to arrest capitalists, the union also set up blackboards, posters, and loudspeakers on street corners to spread news and gather accusations and evidence. In less than two weeks, the union managed to solicit 210,000 accusations

11. Gardner, "Wu-fan Campaign," 507.
12. Ibid., 508.

of corruption from workers as well as repeated rounds of confessions from employers.[13]

One textile mill manager's description of the investigation in his factory provides some sense of the tenor of the second phase of the anti-corruption campaign. His ordeal started with being held in his office for five days and nights to write and rewrite his confession, forced to respond to each new accusation from his workers. Finally his investigation culminated in a factory-wide struggle meeting, where his accusers confronted him face to face. After his confession was finally accepted and he agreed to pay a large fine, he was allowed to go home.[14] His experience was relatively mild; at the other end of the spectrum, forty-eight company owners and managers attempted suicide, and thirty-four of them succeeded.[15]

The scale and intensity of the campaign provoked concern at the top levels of the CCP. Industrial production had already plummeted in just a few weeks, and shortages of food and other goods were developing in most major cities, including Shanghai. Finance Minister Bo Yibo was sent to Shanghai on February 25 to reassert central control over the campaign. By that point, the movement was at a fever pitch, with more than two hundred capitalists being held in their offices as their investigations continued. Bo Yibo reported back to Beijing that the Shanghai Federation of Trade Unions was in disarray and unable to rein in Shanghai's workers. Some workers had declared profit itself as a form of corruption and were pressing for the immediate socialization of industry.[16]

By March, the economic recession caused by the Three Antis and Five Antis campaigns was severe, with factory shutdowns and slowdowns all over the city. To regain control over the movement, Bo Yibo and the Shanghai Party Committee took control over the campaign from Liu Changsheng and the labor union. In place of union cadres, more than 12,000 government and military cadres were brought in to finish the campaign. In addition, new limits were imposed on the kind

13. Ibid., 515.
14. Loh and Evans, *Escape*, 86–94.
15. Bo Yibo, *Ruogan zhongda juece*, 168–70.
16. Ibid., 170–71.

of infractions that could be investigated as well as the severity of the punishments that could be imposed. Prominent capitalists like Rong Yiren received personal guarantees that their treatment during the new phase of the campaign would be lenient.[17] When the third phase of the campaign finally concluded, the punishment for corruption was limited to fines, and only 27 percent of the companies in Shanghai were forced to pay them.[18]

The urban revolution had been postponed yet again. But although workers were held back, the campaign permanently undermined the status of the capitalist class. The experience of class struggle transformed the relationship between labor and capital, despite the fact that the institutional structure of New Democracy corporatism remained intact. Increasingly, party cadres and union activists on the labor-management committees of private firms made most of the important management decisions.[19] Furthermore, as government procurement contracts increasingly replaced production for the market, budget constraints for many firms seem to have softened considerably.[20]

Postponing the urban revolution did not mean that workers failed to make significant gains in welfare during and after the 1952 anticorruption campaigns. The sudden surge in unemployment was much harder to turn around than the violence. According to incomplete Shanghai Labor Bureau statistics, more than 250,000 workers were laid off in the spring and summer of 1952 despite the campaign prohibition on layoffs.[21] In response, the Shanghai Federation of Trade Unions and the municipal labor bureau worked together to set up an emergency relief program in May 1952. In addition to providing relief to newly registered unemployed workers, the program provided relief to entire factories while they were out of operation. The union also set up a new political study program for unemployed activists that combined political education with room and board for three to six months of intensive training.

17. Ibid., 173–74.
18. Zhu Hue et al., *Shanghai yibai nian*, 323.
19. Loh and Evans, *Escape*, 113; Frazier, *Making of the Chinese Industrial Workplace*, 129; Gardner, "Wu-fan Campaign," 526.
20. So, "Policy-Making and Political Economy," 695–96.
21. SMA, B127-1-19.

The new initiatives increased the scale of Shanghai's unemployment relief program significantly. Relief distributions to individual workers and their families ballooned to more than four times the precampaign caseload, reaching an average of nearly 45,000 families per month. The factory relief program provided food to an additional 307,076 workers and their families.[22]

In the same period, the Shanghai Bureau of Civil Affairs also launched the social relief program, providing more than 217,000 handouts of rice and other grains to help the urban poor survive the economic crisis.[23] Only six months after Li Lisan was forced out of union leadership for putting too much emphasis on unemployment relief, the program had nearly quadrupled in size.

Emergency unemployment relief was not enough to quiet Shanghai's restive unemployed workers. Over the summer of 1952, the Shanghai Labor Bureau and labor union struggled to respond to more than a thousand collective labor disputes, most of which centered on layoffs and unpaid wages during the campaign. Ironically, the new comprehensive political education programs set up as a form of emergency unemployment relief were almost too successful in raising the class consciousness of unemployed workers. Participants in more than half of the twenty new political study programs took to the streets in protest, going as far as attacking trade union and party cadres.[24] As many as twenty-two unemployed workers attempted to commit suicide, a long-standing form of Chinese remonstrance. The protests extended beyond Shanghai: Chairman Mao received more than six hundred letters from the unemployed around the country during the course of the anticorruption campaign, pleading for his personal intervention.[25]

Some of the most persistent protesters were former workers at Shanghai's Dadong Tobacco Factory, which had been closed down for two years. In the excitement of the Five Antis campaign, several former Dadong workers petitioned the municipal labor bureau and

22. Shen Zhi and Li Tao, eds., *Shanghai laodong zhi*, 103; SMA, B127-1-19.
23. SMA, B168-1-510.
24. SMA, B127-1-19.
25. Zhongguo shehui kexue yuan, *Zhonghua renmin gongheguo jingji dang'an 1949–1952*, 176.

the Shanghai labor union to reopen the factory. After failing to get a favorable response in Shanghai, eighteen of the Dadong petitioners took their cause to Beijing in late July 1952. The protesters dressed the part for their trip to the capital, wearing old, torn clothes and making sure that their hair was disheveled by the time they arrived.

Parading through the streets of Beijing with their petition and pictures of Chairman Mao, they threatened to commit suicide by drowning themselves in Beihai Lake, just north of the CCP's leadership compound. The melodramatic protest tactics were effective. The Dadong workers succeeded in getting cadres from the All-China Federation of Trade Unions to meet with them and accept their petition over the objections of a harried cadre who rushed up from the Shanghai Federation of Trade Unions to forestall them. When national labor union officials reported the protest to Mao, he furiously ordered that the factory be reopened immediately—and that all the officials who had originally approved the factory closure in 1950 be fired.[26] The Shanghai city government had to provide substantial subsidies to Dadong's owners to comply with Mao's orders, while the rest of the tobacco industry in the city struggled to stay in business.

The welfare gains made by workers in the wake of the anticorruption campaigns went much further than Mao's personal intervention or emergency relief. The anticorruption campaigns also helped the implementation of the new labor insurance contract policy. With little or no resistance from management, contracts were negotiated rapidly in the last half of 1952. The Shanghai Federation of Trade Unions initially targeted the firms that had just missed the cut for the full labor insurance program: medium-sized firms with more than eighty employees. The union focused on the metalworking industry in particular, since it typically had high revenues and therefore could more easily afford significant benefits. By the end of the year, the union had negotiated separate contracts with 154 firms in these sectors, providing approximately 10,653 workers with a wide range of benefits. In addition, three industrywide contracts were negotiated with the steel, copper, and nail trade associations, covering another 187 factories with 6,659 workers.[27]

26. Zhang Jinping, "Dadong yanchang," 32–33.
27. SMA, C1-2-846.

In many private firms, workers also wielded their new clout to exact their own wage and benefit gains. Although there are no systematic data available, anecdotal evidence suggests that the expansion of welfare provisions and other fringe benefits in private firms was much larger in scale than the labor insurance contracts, both in terms of the benefits provided and the number of workers who enjoyed them. For example, workers at the Shenxin No. 6 Cotton Mill managed to exact an agreement from their managers to invest more than one billion yuan in dormitories, a new cafeteria, and a barbershop for workers. The company even began to distribute free umbrellas as a fringe benefit.[28] Workers in other firms concentrated on welfare benefits that could be converted more directly into income, such as food, housing, and clothing subsidies. In one of the most egregious examples, a company in the dying industry gave its workers welfare subsidies worth forty-two times the value of their wages. More typically, new welfare benefits reached 40 percent to 60 percent of workers' wages.[29] Because of data limitations, the gains cannot be easily quantified and compared, but the contrast with the limited gains workers made in the corporatist worker welfare committees under Nationalist rule suggests that the changes in labor-management relations wrought by the 1952 struggle campaign were profound.

## Unemployment Relief Policy

The unplanned expansion of welfare programs during and after the 1952 anticorruption campaigns did not delay a new round of welfare reform in preparation for the First Five-Year Plan. Premier Zhou Enlai convened a policy conference under the State Administrative Council in Beijing in July 1952 to draft the new unemployment policy.[30] The policy conference brought together more than 130 officials from all the

28. Frazier, *Making of the Chinese Industrial Workplace,* 126.
29. SMA, C1-2-2322.
30. Zhongguo shehui kexue yuan, *Zhonghua renmin gongheguo jingji dang'an 1949–1952,* 176.

relevant central, provincial, and municipal government agencies. In preparation for the conference, each of the six administrative regions prepared a report on the unemployment situation in that region as well as the political attitudes of both unemployed and employed workers. On the basis of this review, policy makers criticized the union unemployment relief program for focusing too much on relief provision at the expense of job training and placement. Looking forward, the policy conference organized five working groups to address specific groups and issues in more detail: unemployed workers, unemployed intellectuals, unemployed former KMT soldiers and officials, relief provision, and general rural-urban issues.[31]

In reformulating the CCP's unemployment policy, the conference drew heavily on Soviet ideas and models. The influence can be seen in the reconceptualization of unemployment as surplus labor rather than as the result of economic dislocations such as the Civil War or the American naval blockade.[32] In this new view, surplus labor was a structural characteristic of China's backward agricultural economy, not a temporary crisis. Zhou Enlai and the other conferees cast unemployment as a specifically urban manifestation of surplus labor. They argued that urban unemployment was a more pressing problem than rural surplus labor, since unemployed urbanites lacked alternative means of survival. As the conference report put it, surplus laborers in the countryside had land to plant and food to eat.[33] Thanks to land reform, they could wait.

Just as this view of the unemployment problem bore the mark of Soviet influence, the new solution also drew on Soviet models. In place of the rice distributions and political mobilization that Li Lisan's program provided in order to help the unemployed survive a temporary economic downturn, the new Universal Job Placement program (*quanmiande laodong jiuye*) sought to eliminate unemployment altogether. The ultimate solution to the problem of surplus labor was rapid industrialization, which would turn surplus labor to new, more productive uses. By regulating employment and replacing the job market with

---

31. Wu Li, "Jianguo chuqi," 74–75.
32. Zhonggong zhongyang wenxian yanjiu shi, *Jianguo yilai*, vol. 3, 287.
33. Ibid., 292.

centralized, bureaucratic job allocation, the new policy was designed to create one of first pillars of a Soviet-style command economy.

The new job placement program was scheduled to start as the First Five-Year Plan was put into action in January 1953.[34] Although the goal of full employment was clearly Soviet in inspiration, Chinese policy makers recognized that at first they would not face the same labor shortages that the Soviets had struggled with during their own industrialization drive. Instead, the problem would be to temper the strong demand for factory jobs and impose some order on the recruitment process until the plan picked up speed and began expanding employment more rapidly.

In his speech to the unemployment policy conference, Zhou Enlai envisioned a gradual process of placing the unemployed and then the underemployed in permanent jobs, eventually leading to full employment. He predicted that the first step in tackling the problem of urban unemployment would take three to five years to resolve. During that first stage, Zhou pressed for propaganda and programs to encourage other surplus laborers to wait their turn by spreading the message that the job placement process would be gradual, defined by the production demands of the First Five-Year Plan. Access to new jobs would be determined by production needs first and welfare concerns second. Thus, skilled workers needed for the industrialization drive would receive top priority, and unskilled workers would receive priority based on their need for income. In this vision, the First Five-Year Plan and the new job placement bureaucracy opened up new ladders of advancement for Chinese workers based on their education and technical skills. To deal with surplus labor in the countryside, Zhou called for expanding production by planting export crops, building new roads and irrigation systems, and establishing sideline processing and handicraft industries. These new opportunities, combined with political persuasion, were intended to encourage peasants to wait to be recruited rather than move to the cities to seek jobs on their own.[35]

The ambitious new policy was promulgated in July and August 1952 in a series of State Administrative Council reports, regulations,

34. SMA B131-1-7.
35. Zhonggong zhongyang wenxian yanjiu shi, *Zhou Enlai,* 109–10.

and orders. The most important policy change was that registration for the program was opened to all of the urban unemployed, regardless of when or how they lost their jobs, or whether they had ever worked.[36] In addition, the program targeted for special attention people whose occupations were disappearing, such as street peddlers, small business owners, priests, nuns, and former KMT soldiers.[37] Envisioning a three- to five-year transition, the new program would end before the end of the First Five-Year Plan, once structural unemployment had been eliminated. Even with these major changes, the new 1952 Universal Job Placement program was similar to the 1950 unemployment relief program in two ways. They were both funded by the same unemployment relief tax on employers, and they both used those funds to provide vocational training and relief grain to the unemployed until they received their new job assignments.

However, the administration of the program was designed to be more bureaucratic and less political than that of its predecessor. For example, the new policy explicitly called for more vocational training and less political education. In addition, the union's role in the new program was drastically curtailed. It was supposed to continue to provide unemployment relief to its members, but most of the new enrollees in the program were supervised by the municipal government rather than the union. The city government's district offices and the fledgling system of street and lane residents committees assumed the key tasks of registering the unemployed. A new network of job placement committees was established at the national, regional, and municipal levels to replace the existing unemployed workers' relief committees and oversee the new program.[38] In addition, the Labor Ministry's factory inspection program was expanded to broaden the scope of labor regulation to hiring, firing, and work hours, and the existing job placement program was expanded significantly.[39]

36. Zhonggong zhongyang wenxian yanjiu shi, *Jianguo yilai*, vol. 3, 287; Zhonggong zhongyang wenxian yanjiu shi, *Zhou Enlai*, 108.
37. SMA, B131-1-4.
38. SMA, B131-1-2.
39. SMA, B127-1-29.

## Labor Insurance Policy

While preparations were under way for implementing the new unemployment program, policy-making work proceeded in the fall of 1952 to revise the labor insurance regulations in preparation for the First Five-Year Plan. Although the economic planners had completely taken over unemployment relief policy, the union was still involved in the policy-making process for the labor insurance revisions. Party committees, however, were involved at every step in the process.

The Shanghai municipal union forwarded its own proposals for revising the labor insurance program and commented on the draft regulations issued in Beijing. As it had done before, the union convened small-group meetings and roundtable discussions with union cadres and workers to gauge their responses to the proposed revisions. One of the Shanghai Federation of Trade Unions' main proposals in 1952 was to seek more flexibility in the use of the large labor insurance reserve funds that were already being generated by the program. Rather than save all the funds to finance retirement pensions in the decades ahead, the Shanghai labor union sought to use them immediately to create health clinics and child care centers for union members in small factories excluded from the labor insurance program. Consistent with this proposal to redistribute resources from welfare state insiders to outsiders, the Shanghai labor union also called for expanding coverage rather than increasing benefits.[40]

It was not just the labor union that was concerned about the people excluded from the welfare state. The Shanghai Party Committee agreed with the Shanghai labor union in calling for a more egalitarian approach to expanding the welfare state. Led by First Party Secretary and Mayor Chen Yi, the Shanghai Party Committee argued that the original labor insurance program's benefits were already too generous relative to the general standard of living. They criticized the proposed revisions for making the problem worse. In its report to the central CCP, the Shanghai Party Committee quoted a Shanghai worker's description of the impact of the proposed revisions: "In large factories, flowers have been

40. SMA, C1-2-1114.

added to the brocade, while for small factories and the unemployed, frost has been heaped on top of the snow."[41] Another worker's description of the working class's new inequalities was also quoted without any acknowledgment that it actually reflected the priorities of the First Five-Year Plan: "The workers in state-owned factories are first class, those in large private factories are second class, while those in small factories are only third-class workers. Shop clerks are fourth-class workers, and the unemployed are fifth-class workers."[42]

Like the union, the Shanghai Party Committee advocated putting a priority on expanding coverage rather than improving benefits. As a start, it called for freezing labor insurance benefits until the general standard of living had improved. In addition, the committee revived the union's proposal to redistribute some of its large labor insurance reserve funds to workers excluded from the program, especially to broaden access to health care. This more egalitarian approach to welfare reform found backing in the East China Party Committee as well, which also characterized Shanghai's workers as being more open to redistribution than central policy makers had assumed. In its report on the labor insurance revisions, it quoted a Shanghai construction worker who was building a new housing development for workers as saying: "Employed workers have already made it, so why don't we take this money and spend it on building factories to make sure the unemployed have jobs too?"[43]

The All-China Federation of Trade Unions in Beijing rejected the proposals from Shanghai, claiming that they would only create dissatisfaction among the workers already enrolled in the labor insurance program.[44] The final policy issued in January 1953 kept to the same framework as the original draft, and most of the changes improved benefits. For example, time limits imposed on health care for work accidents were removed, and a new subsidy for imported medications was created. The preamble to the new regulations described their improve-

41. Ibid.
42. Ibid.
43. Zhongguo shehui kexue yuan, *Zhonghua renmin gongheguo jingji dang'an 1949–1952*, 235.
44. SMA, C1-2-849.

ments as a modest step forward, constrained by the demands of the Korean War and the need to accumulate investment capital.[45]

## Reforming the Labor Union

Both the labor insurance revisions and the new unemployment program were launched in January 1953 at the beginning of the First Five-Year Plan. Not surprisingly, the labor insurance revisions were much easier to implement than the unemployment program, but they both ran into difficulties.

The labor insurance revisions were implemented in the context of political reform of the official labor unions. The new role for the labor unions in the command economy was to promote economic development rather than mobilize political support for the regime. But the electric atmosphere of the anticorruption campaigns proved that transforming the official labor unions into a bureaucratic cog in the command economy was not going to be easy. To carry out its new agenda, the CCP quietly appointed Lai Ruoyu as acting chairman of the All-China Federation of Trade Unions in 1952, while continuing to keep the purge of Li Lisan from the union leadership a secret outside of Beijing. Lai Ruoyu was a party man with absolutely no experience in the labor movement. He had joined the CCP as a teenager in 1929 and had performed a wide variety of administrative and political work under Deng Xiaoping's leadership. His rapid rise in the party made him governor and first party secretary of Shanxi province when he was just forty years old.[46] Replacing a popular revolutionary labor leader like Li Lisan with a young party secretary known for his administrative expertise accomplished two goals: asserting clear party control over the union leadership and carving out a new role for the union in the command economy.

The purge of the union leadership continued down the hierarchy.[47] The most prominent victim in Shanghai was Liu Changsheng,

45. Zhonggong zhongyang wenxian yanjiu shi, *Jianguo yilai,* vol. 2, 68.
46. Harper, "Party and Unions," 97.
47. Ibid., 96.

chairman of the Shanghai Federation of Trade Unions. He was immediately suspended by Bo Yibo in March 1952 for letting the Five Antis
movement get out of control. After a four-month investigation of his
leadership, he was exonerated but also transferred to Beijing, where he
was appointed vice chairman of the national union and China's liaison
to the World Federation of Trade Unions in 1953.[48] The promotion
restored his reputation, but it also cut Liu Changsheng off from his
newly mobilized supporters in Shanghai and ensured that he would
never be able to use that clout again. In March 1953, he was replaced
in Shanghai by Zhong Min, as acting chairman.[49] Like Lai Ruoyu,
Zhong Min did not come from the labor union. Before his promotion,
he was party secretary in the city of Wuxi, north of Shanghai. Only
four years after the Communists seized power, all the labor leaders
with experience in mobilizing strikes and protests were pushed out of
union leadership, replaced by party officials known for their administrative skills.

The labor insurance revisions were issued in the midst of these
personnel changes with no fanfare and without worker mobilization
to implement them. Instead, the improvements in welfare benefits
were immediately followed by a propaganda campaign that criticized
welfare: the 1953 campaign against economism. Confusingly, the movement was designed to redirect the unions away from welfare work and
toward the kind of labor discipline required by the First Five-Year Plan.

The campaign finally revealed that Li Lisan had been purged from
the national union more than a year after the fact. In criticizing Li's
leadership, the campaign highlighted "syndicalism" and "economism"
as serious errors that needed to be weeded out of the official labor movement.[50] Combating syndicalism meant ensuring strong party control
over the union, whereas overcoming economism entailed convincing
workers that production, rather than redistribution, was their core
revolutionary task. The campaign tried to eradicate the commonplace
idea among union cadres that production was management's responsibility rather than their own and harshly criticized the notion that

48. Li Jiaqi, ed., *Shanghai gongyun*, 792.
49. Ibid., 385.
50. SMA, C1-2-2322.

efforts to expand production in state-owned enterprises amounted to a form of government exploitation of workers. The campaign also explicitly criticized the idea that welfare work was the key to the union's popularity and prestige.[51]

In Shanghai, the campaign began in March 1953, when Mayor Chen Yi convened an enlarged party meeting of the Shanghai Federation of Trade Unions. The party meeting was followed by a citywide workers congress on April 20 and then several rounds of industrial and district union meetings and training sessions. Over the next six months, the new union leadership tried to indoctrinate the union's rank and file in the new production-oriented ideology of the First Five-Year Plan.

Three industries critical for the First Five-Year Plan were targeted for special treatment in the campaign: the steel, machinery, and electronics sectors. More than three hundred cadres from 158 private companies in those three industries went through a month of intensive political education before they were sent back to their enterprises with work teams. While the work teams investigated each firm's wages and benefits, union cadres held roundtable discussions with various influential groups of workers, such as older workers and skilled workers, in order to educate them about the new policies. More than 300,000 workers in these industries went through the political education program. The campaign concluded with the negotiation of new labor insurance contracts that limited welfare benefits to the standards set in the labor insurance program. Later investigations revealed, however, that the effort to roll back the wage and welfare gains in private industry only scratched the surface of the problem, and many benefit reductions were soon reversed again.[52]

Although the impact of the campaign against economism seemed limited at the grass roots, the union's new leadership considered it a success. When Shanghai's campaign was wrapped up in October 1953, the reorientation of the union toward its new role in the Communist regime was judged complete. The campaign was followed by institutional changes to reinforce the new relationship between the party and the union. At the Seventh National Labor Congress in November 1953,

51. Ibid.
52. SMA, B54-1-5a.

the labor union's charter was amended to assert party leadership over the organization. In addition, the provisions in the union charter for democratic elections of union leaders were revised to emphasize the Leninist principles of democratic centralism.[53] The repudiation of the 1948 labor union charter's freedom from party control was explained as a sign of progress. Labor freedom was deemed unnecessary in a proletarian state.

Two years after Li Lisan's sudden ouster from the leadership of the national union, the purge down the union hierarchy had been completed, a national campaign carried out to reorient both cadres and members toward economic development as their top priority, and the institutional structure of the union had been changed to reinforce party control. Taken together, the union reforms marked the end of New Democracy state corporatism for workers and the beginning of a more classic style of Leninist state-society relations. Ironically, the official business federations were not reformed, even if their members' political position had been utterly transformed by the 1952 anticorruption campaigns.

## Implementation of the Universal Job Placement Program

Although the campaign against economism and labor union reforms may have had mixed success in inculcating the new priority placed on production, they were sidelights in the transition to the First Five-Year Plan. The new Universal Job Placement program was the centerpiece of the welfare reform agenda in 1953. The Shanghai municipal government led the implementation of the new program, carrying out registration of all urban unemployed people over three months from November 1952 to January 1953. With the help of more than five thousand cadres sent out in work teams from the new Shanghai Job Placement Committee, the city's lane and alley committees collected applications for the program as they conducted the China's first national census.

---

53. Wang Yongxi, et al, eds., *Zhongguo gonghui shi*, 350–351.

*Table 4.1.* Shanghai Transitional Welfare Program Enrollees, 1951–54

| Year | Labor insurance contracts | Increase | Unemployment registration | Increase |
|------|---------------------------|----------|---------------------------|----------|
| 1951 | 0 | | 74,979 | |
| 1952 | 51,321 | 100% | 216,459 | 189% |
| 1953 | 72,063 | 40% | 336,380 | 55% |
| 1954 | 87,583 | 22% | 301,640 | -10% |

*Sources:* SMA, C1-2-1764; SMA, B127-1-53.

Each applicant's education, employment history, political background, family situation, and finances were reviewed by the residents committees and work teams, sometimes requiring the applicants to undergo criticism and self-criticism in the process.[54]

Such an intrusive evaluation by their neighbors may have been intimidating to applicants, but the response to the campaign was enthusiastic. The new Universal Job Placement program promised to open up a major new avenue to permanent jobs and full inclusion in the welfare state for some of the most marginal members of the new society. The campaign registered another 199,217 people in addition to the 175,861 that were still registered in the union program. With a total of 375,078 people registered as unemployed in January 1953, Shanghai's new Job Placement program more than doubled the size of the earlier unemployment program (table 4.1).[55] The response from housewives was so strong that a new registration status was created to give those with little or no work history second priority for job placement and vocational training after unemployed workers had been served.[56] Officials were especially surprised at how far and wide news of the registration campaign had spread. Skilled workers who had taken jobs with economic reconstruction projects in the interior quit to go home to Shanghai and register as unemployed. More remarkably, Chinese workers in Hong Kong, Southeast Asia, and India returned home to register for job placement, prompting labor officials to consult with

54. Shen Zhi and Li Tao, eds., *Shanghai laodongzhi*, 101.
55. SMA, B127-1-29.
56. SMA, B131-1-7.

the Foreign Ministry about how to stop the flow of returnees.[57] The unemployed may have been given no role in the implementation of the new program, but their enthusiastic embrace of the policy had a decisive impact on the urban welfare state. Universal unemployment registration was a runaway success.

Their enthusiasm did not prevent the program from turning into a disaster. Zhou Enlai's vision of gradual, orderly job placement according to the dictates of the First Five-Year Plan was not shared by the unemployed: many thought that unemployment registration would automatically lead to job placement. More problematic than the gap in expectations, the Shanghai Labor Bureau's Job Placement Office was not up to the task of even gradual job placement. Well before the scope of the program expanded so dramatically, the Job Placement Office had a serious backlog. In 1952, the office had filled fewer than 40 percent of the hiring requests it had received, and high priority cases like demobilized Korean War soldiers had been waiting for more than a year to be assigned to a factory job.[58]

The labor bureau did add new staff in the transition to the First Five-Year Plan, but the expanded Job Placement Office quickly descended into chaos after the new Universal Job Placement program was launched. Most of the new staff had been added to the municipal level of the program rather than the district offices that reviewed most hiring requests from employers and referred unemployed workers to fill them. In addition, the new placement procedures put in place in January 1953 were complex, requiring multiple layers of review and provoking strong complaints from employers about the hassle and delay. Once the requests were finally approved, the Job Placement Office often referred unemployed workers with little regard to the skills or experience required for the job.[59] As the official hiring process bogged down, the labor bureau tried to crack down on independent hiring, imposing fines on firms that hired workers on their own even if the new workers were registered as unemployed. For the most part, however, the sanctions were ineffective.

57. SMA, B131-1-8.
58. SMA, B127-1-19.
59. SMA, B127-1-29.

With the Three Antis and Five Antis anticorruption campaigns in such recent memory, factory owners and managers did not go further than complaining or quietly avoiding the new bureaucracy. For example, some factories started hiring only temporary workers, since they were not subject to the new regulations. Frustrated labor officials blamed the job placement mess on resistance from capitalists, but it is far from clear that perfect compliance could have rescued the program.

The failures of the new job placement bureaucracy quickly turned the eager reception of the registration campaign, with all of the hopes it inspired for people's futures, into bitter disappointment. Unemployed workers responded to the labor bureau's problems more directly than capitalists, taking to the streets in a new surge of collective protest in the spring of 1953 that reached a peak over the lunar New Year's holiday. As they had done during the anticorruption campaign, the unemployed gathered in groups to petition the Shanghai Job Placement Committee and the Shanghai Labor Bureau for jobs. Many petitions turned into violent protests, with the unemployed storming into the organizations' offices, where they overturned the furniture, stole cadres' rice bowls, and sometimes went as far as beating the cadres into submission. Cadres responded to the protesters by handing out extra relief grain and making empty promises about future jobs.[60]

In the midst of the growing protest movement, Li Weihan, head of the central CCP's United Front Department, led an investigation tour to study the state of the private sector. Although published documents on the two-month investigation focus on economic production and the issue of ownership, it is highly likely that the investigation would also have touched on the unemployment problem. Li Weihan was concurrently chairman of the national Job Placement Committee, and his itinerary focused on the two cities that suffered the most severe protests by the unemployed—Shanghai and Wuhan.[61]

Following Li's return to Beijing, in May 1953, another unemployment policy conference was convened, which ordered an immediate reduction in the scope of the new job placement program. Firms were once again allowed to do their own hiring, and the unemployed were

60. Ibid.
61. SMA, B131-1-2; Li Weihan, Huiyi, 739.

encouraged to look for jobs on their own as well.[62] After a thorough review of the Universal Job Placement program was completed in August 1953, the national Job Placement Committee, Labor Ministry, and Interior Ministry concluded that the program had failed to reduce the number of registered unemployed during the first year of the program. Despite the new policy of combining bureaucratic job allocation with the private labor market adopted in May, officials predicted that they would not be able to reduce the number of unemployed in the program's second year. Based on this sober assessment, they recommended shutting the program down altogether: halting registration of the unemployed, abolishing the entire network of job placement committees, and then merging their staff into the Labor Ministry.

To deal with the millions already registered as unemployed, the report called for reexamining the eligibility of the entire caseload to winnow it down and then splitting responsibility for the remaining people on the rolls between the Labor and Civil Affairs bureaus based on their ability to work. The policy review did not reject comprehensive job allocation entirely—instead it was judged premature for China's economic conditions.[63] Without any public announcement to herald the policy change, Shanghai's Job Placement Committee stopped new registrations in August 1953.[64]

Then the Job Placement Committee launched a "democratic reform" (*minzhu gaige*) campaign to review the entire caseload.[65] In addition to reducing their numbers, the campaign also sought to educate the registered unemployed about the long-term nature of unemployment and encourage them to find jobs on their own. The individual reviews categorized the unemployed for differential treatment. At one extreme, "counterrevolutionaries" were supposed to be purged immediately from the program, although the original policy had specifically targeted groups such as former KMT officials for inclusion. At the other extreme, workers who lost their jobs because of the Five Antis anticorruption campaign were given first priority for job

62. SMA, B131-2-4.
63. SMA, B131-1-2.
64. SMA, B131-1-8.
65. Ibid.

*Table 4.2* Shanghai Relief Handouts, 1951–54

| Year | Unemployment relief handouts | Social Relief Handouts | Total | Percent Change |
|------|------------------------------|------------------------|-------|----------------|
| 1951 | 315,617 | 0 | 315,617 | -31% |
| 1952 | 425,067 | 217,213 | 642,280 | 103% |
| 1953 | 917,393 | 294,296 | 1,211,689 | 89% |
| 1954 | 503,841 | 362,287 | 866,128 | -29% |

Sources: SMA, B127-1-53; SMA, B168-1-512.

placement, and they also received supplemental relief payments until they did get a job.

The democratic reform campaign was conducted in the summer and fall of 1953, followed by an effort to convince housewives and other unemployed people unlikely to find jobs to give up on the program. Even so, cadres were instructed not to take away people's unemployment registration cards in order to avoid inciting more protests.[66] By the end of the eligibility review, 336,380 people remained on the registration rolls in December 1953, more than triple the caseload of Li Lisan's unemployment program. The combination of reviving the job market and democratic reform reduced the number of registered unemployed workers by a modest 10 percent from 1953 to 1954 (see table 4.1).

Far more effective than these reviews in reducing the caseload were benefit cuts in the relief program. Relief rations were cut, and the cadres in charge of distributing relief were pressured to restrict eligibility to only those in dire need.[67] As a result, the number of people receiving relief dropped a dramatic 45 percent from 1953 to 1954. After those reductions, the level of relief was still higher than the previous peak of the relief program in 1950.[68] In the end, the effort to replace relief with a more fundamental solution had only expanded the relief program to new heights (table 4.2).

The job placement committees were quietly dismantled in February 1954 and their staff transferred to labor bureaus and district

66. SMA, B131-1-2; SMA, B131-2-4.
67. SMA, B127-1-29.
68. SMA, B127-1-53.

governments. Once again, there was no public announcement in order to avoid sparking controversy. After inheriting the remaining pieces of the failed program, the Shanghai Labor Bureau carried out its own investigation of the unrest among the unemployed, going back to review the protests during the 1952 anticorruption campaigns as well as the 1953 demonstrations. The bureau came to the conclusion that this collective action was a legacy of the union organization established under Li Lisan's original unemployment relief program in 1951. Although the new people who registered as unemployed with the Universal Job Placement program were not incorporated into the union, the original unemployed workers maintained their labor union liaison stations after the unemployment relief program was shifted out of the union and into the municipal government. The Shanghai Labor Bureau concluded that these grassroots organizations were the key to sparking and sustaining the protests during both the 1952 Five Antis campaign and the 1953 Universal Job Placement program.

Since the CCP feared that any direct attempt to eliminate the unemployed liaison stations and dismantle the remnants of the union organization would only provoke more protest, it pursued an indirect approach of demobilizing them through reorganization and reform. In yet another democratic reform campaign that began in 1954, the most difficult liaison station leaders were quietly replaced by party cadres, and then all the liaison stations were reorganized in the name of formally combining the union and municipal government programs.[69] The reforms scrambled the original labor union networks that had sustained the protests and diluted the trained activists with an influx of educated youth and housewives with no prior experience in the rough world of Shanghai's labor politics. Although the unemployed union members were allowed to keep their union cards and the political status membership conveyed, the new registrants under the Universal Job Placement program were not given union membership, although they were now supposedly equal members of the same streamlined program.

69. SMA, B131-1-11; SMA, B127-1-29.

## Political Consolidation

As the unemployed were being quietly pushed out of the labor union at the grass roots, the Chinese Communist regime was also going through a process of consolidation at the top. Two major changes were carried out simultaneously. First was the transition to civilian rule as the new constitution was put in place in 1954. Second was the push to centralize control over the economy as the First Five-Year Plan was finalized. The six regional governments that had ruled China since the takeover in 1949 were dismantled, and many of their leaders were transferred to Beijing to staff the new economic planning system.[70] In addition, the First Five-Year Plan put new restrictions on the growth of China's two industrial centers in Shanghai and the Northeast so their revenues could be redirected to new development projects in the interior.

Secretive purges of the top political leaders in both Shanghai and the Northeast accompanied these changes. Three of the top leaders in the Shanghai and East China party committees were denounced as traitors: East China Party Secretary Rao Shushi; the Shanghai deputy mayor who was in charge of economic policy, Pan Hannian; and Shanghai Public Security Bureau Director Yang Fan. All three were purged from the party and imprisoned with no public explanation of how or why they had betrayed their country. The one survivor of this high-level purge in Shanghai, Mayor and Party Secretary Chen Yi, was promoted to high-ranking government and military positions in the central government in Beijing. Jiangsu Party Secretary Ke Qingshi, a member of Mao's faction who had led the attacks on Rao, Pan, and Yang in 1954, was promoted to replace Chen Yi as mayor and first party secretary of Shanghai. Whether through punishment or by promotion, all of Shanghai's revolutionary leaders—in the military, police, party, and labor unions—were gone.

It is striking that, in the midst of these mysterious purges, the men who had failed so badly with the Universal Job Placement program did not seem to suffer more political setbacks. Although we know Zhou Enlai was criticized for his part in a controversial tax policy in this

70. Teiwes, *Politics at Mao's Court*, 20–21.

period, there is no mention in available sources about his failure with job placement. But these purges of lower-ranking officials may have had a policy dimension. In addition to the conflict over Shanghai's role in the First Five-Year Plan, the job placement program may have also been a factor. Rao Shushi had been in charge of labor planning in 1953. In addition, the 1955 Sufan campaign, conducted in secrecy, was an internal party rectification campaign that targeted Rao Shushi's supporters in Shanghai as well as planners considered too closely wed to Soviet economic planning principles.[71] The reputation of China's top economic officials seemed to be invulnerable, but the early failures of the First Five-Year Plan were casting doubt on the value of Soviet advice.

## The Gains Made with the Soviet Model

China's new welfare state expanded in every possible direction in the early 1950s: better benefits, wider coverage, and new programs. The biggest gains in coverage came in the new Universal Job Placement program, with the number of registered unemployed eligible for benefits and services more than tripling in 1953. Despite all the efforts to whittle down the caseload in 1954, it only dropped 10 percent. In addition, the total number of handouts of unemployment relief received in 1953 nearly quadrupled over the earlier program after universal unemployment registration was carried out (see table 4.2). Although the democratic reform campaigns carried out in 1954 reduced both unemployment registration and relief handouts, steady growth in the social relief program ensured that the total number of handouts in 1954 was more than double the number in 1951, when Li Lisan was criticized for emphasizing relief at the expense of production.

The gains in the new labor insurance contract program were also significant. Although the program was less than one-third the size of the Universal Job Placement program, its benefits promised to be longer lasting. After the initial burst of contracts negotiated in the wake of the

71. Teiwes, *Politics and Purges*, 29; Meisner, *Mao's China*, 123.

*Table 4.3.* Shanghai Permanent Welfare Program Enrollees, 1952–54

| Year | Labor insurance | Increase | Social relief | Increase |
|------|-----------------|----------|---------------|----------|
| 1952 | 364,087 | 19% | 18,101 | 100% |
| 1953 | 421,577 | 16% | 24,525 | 35% |
| 1954 | 430,456 | 2% | 30,191 | 23% |

Sources: SMA, B127-1-19; SMA, C1-2-1117; SMA, C1-2-1431; SMA, B168-1-510; SMA, B168-1-511.

anticorruption campaign, the labor insurance contract program was gradually extended to more industries and progressively smaller firms. By the end of 1954, more than five hundred contracts were in place, providing varying benefits to more than 87,000 workers (see table 4.1).[72] Although we have no way to measure the coverage or the comparability of the new benefits in the private sector, we can guess that they made a significant contribution as well.

The labor insurance program expanded within its existing framework through the addition of new jobs in labor insurance firms. Employment in Shanghai increased a brisk 16 percent in 1952 despite the disruptions of the Five Antis campaign. After that point, most of the new investment in the First Five-Year Plan went to other regions, bypassing Shanghai.[73] As a result, the city's labor force increased by a more modest rate of 7 percent in 1953 and only 3 percent in 1954, as the lack of capital and inflation sparked by the First Five-Year Plan's investment drive slowed Shanghai's growth. Labor insurance coverage largely followed the growth in employment, increasing 19 percent in 1952 and 16 percent in 1953 (table 4.3). After the 1954 anti-inflationary measures took effect, coverage grew at a much slower pace of 2 percent. Even with this plateau, the overall growth in coverage in this four-year period was significant, increasing by more than one-third to a new high of more than 430,000 workers covered.

Stepping back to assess China's first effort to expand the welfare state shows that the expansion of coverage was significant in 1952–54. The reforms more than doubled the reach of the urban welfare state in three short years. Since Shanghai's urban population grew at the rapid

72. SMA, C1-2-1764.
73. Naughton, *Chinese Economy*, 66; Howe, "Industrialization," 168–69.

*Table 4.4.* Shanghai Welfare Coverage, 1952–54

| Year | Total beneficiaries | Increase | Workforce coverage | Population coverage |
|------|--------------------|----------|--------------------|--------------------|
| 1952 | 649,968 | 70% | 21% | 11% |
| 1953 | 854,545 | 31% | 27% | 14% |
| 1954 | 849,870 | -1% | 26% | 13% |

*Sources:* SMA, B127-1-19; SMA, C1-2-1117; SMA, C1-2-1431; SMA, B168-1-510; SMA, B168-1-511; SMA, C1-2-1764; SMA, B127-1-53; Shanghaishi tongji ju, ed., *Shanghai shi guomin jingji.*

pace of 20 percent during this same period, rapid expansion of the welfare state contributed to real, but small, net gains in workforce and population coverage. Taken together, the population coverage of labor insurance, labor insurance contracts, and unemployment relief jumped from 11 percent in 1952 to 14 percent in 1953, after the increase in population is taken into account (table 4.4).

China's first attempt at expanding the reach of the welfare state showed that the task was not difficult politically. Top-down pressure stemming from China's new economic development strategy and a sudden surge of bottom-up demand for welfare quickly produced results. Furthermore, with no opposition to expansion, welfare reform was deceptively easy. Economic development policy turned out to be a stronger top-down pressure for welfare reform than partisan competition. Moreover, workers and the unemployed were incorporated into the regime and given more leverage than capitalists. In a period of high income inequality, workers in particular were eager to redistribute wealth and both groups embraced their new welfare programs with enthusiasm. Considering that there had been so little demand for welfare among Shanghai's workers in 1950 before the labor insurance program was implemented, it is striking how rapidly the new rhetoric about welfare state expansion was embraced by Shanghai's workers and the unemployed. Within a few short years, welfare had gone from an abstraction that most people knew nothing about to a concrete set of benefits that they wanted and came to expect as their due.

There were also multiple avenues for the expansion of the welfare state. Policy makers in Beijing created the universal job placement, labor insurance contract, and social relief programs. Protesters and political activists in Shanghai pushed the expansion of the welfare state further than policy makers had ever intended. Whether it was the unemployed Dadong workers pleading to Chairman Mao or the private sector textile workers demanding free umbrellas from their capitalist employers, the people of Shanghai were not shy when it came to pursuing their interests and they faced little or no political opposition at the local level. As a result, welfare state outsiders were able to change the contours of the welfare state.

At the grass roots, the more difficult political task was to shift welfare politics away from mobilization toward a more disciplined, development-oriented style of politics. Even without the pressure of countermobilization from underground KMT labor organizations, sustaining political mobilization turned out to be much easier than shutting it down. The CCP could eliminate institutions for political participation, such as the unemployed workers congresses. But Shanghai's workers and the unemployed showed that they did not need formal institutions to engage in politics. After the labor unrest in 1952–53, the CCP imposed leadership purges, the 1953 campaign against economism, and new institutional controls on the official labor union in an effort to transform the organization into a more bureaucratic element of the Chinese Communist regime. After all these political reforms, the CCP was still cautious when it demobilized the unemployed workers in the labor union in 1954. The streets turned out to be just as useful a political arena as an unemployed workers congress, and they could not so easily be shut down or controlled.

In contrast, the official business federation was not subjected to the kinds of reforms imposed on the labor unions. The reason was not that the CCP suddenly favored capital over labor—the reason was much more likely to have been that political reform was unnecessary to get capitalists to comply with party policy after the 1952 anticorruption campaigns. Not only did capitalists cooperate with government procurement and investment policies, but, after their first taste of class struggle, capitalists posed no obstacle whatsoever to the expansion of welfare in their own companies. Although their property rights were ostensibly protected by the central CCP and their official business federations continued to function after the campaign, capitalists lost the power and prestige in the workplace to oppose the union. As a result, the private sector provided one of the fastest routes to welfare state expansion rather than posing an obstacle to it.

The Universal Job Placement program turned out to be the Communists' first major failure in welfare politics. The complete disarray in the labor bureau's job placement division was one reason for the program's failure. But even if the Shanghai Labor Bureau had set up a bureaucracy that could match job seekers with new positions, it could not have met the broader goal of eliminating unemployment. There simply were not enough jobs to go around. After the CCP allowed the labor market to revive without interference in 1954, unemployment registration only fell 10 percent to just over 300,000 people (see table 4.1).

The real source of the problem lay in the limits of the Chinese economy and the Stalinist development strategy. The inability of Chinese planners or their Soviet advisers to recognize those limits before the program was adopted reveals how rudimentary the planning process was in this period. The labor shortages that Soviet planners led the Chinese leadership to expect were nowhere on the horizon in the early 1950s, and gradual implementation of the First Five-Year Plan only postponed them further. The CCP's success in rapidly implementing the welfare aspects of the Universal Job Placement program highlighted the failure of its larger development strategy. Furthermore, Soviet economic planners could provide no guidance in resolving the political and administrative problems involved in rationing scarce resources, since the Soviet Union faced different problems, with labor shortages during its own First Five-Year Plan. As a result, Chinese policy makers were facing a new problem: regulating the expansion of the welfare state to ensure that it did not outstrip the resources necessary to sustain it.

The premature attempt to replace the labor market with bureaucratic job allocation ended up making the rationing inherent in the labor insurance program visible to everyone who wanted a job and the income and benefits that came with it. A single government agency rather than impersonal market forces could be blamed for failing to provide enough jobs for everyone who wanted one. Moreover, this single agency became a target for protest. The CCP had gone to great lengths to downplay and depoliticize its conflicts with labor, its key urban constituency. But with the Universal Job Placement program, the CCP inadvertently politicized the job shortage. The hierarchy of jobs and welfare programs that central planners thought would provide a ladder of opportunity turned out instead to be a new source of inequality and injustice for the frustrated people searching for their place in New China. The benefits offered by unemployment relief may have been a step forward for people who had no welfare benefits to rely on, but their new standard of reference was set by the pay and benefits of permanent employment.

The combination of high expectations and scarce resources was a recipe for political discontent. Though the CCP was successful in doubling the reach of the urban welfare state in its first three years, the failure of unemployment relief overshadowed its other accomplishments. As a result, efforts to expand the welfare state inspired as much or more criticism than political loyalty. The Communists quickly learned that it was not sufficient to be capable of implementing new welfare programs. It was just as important to be able to sustain them. The achievements of the first few years of Communist rule were already becoming tarnished, not because the CCP's power or competence had dimmed, but because its ambitions had soared so quickly.

CHAPTER 5

*Chinese Austerity: Transitional Restraint*
*in the Urban Revolution, 1955–58*

In 1955, even after China had doubled the reach of its new welfare state, the task of achieving broad coverage remained huge. Most of the urban population remained unprotected. Moreover, there were many competing priorities for China's scarce resources as its economic development strategy was being fully implemented. Although the Universal Job Placement program was a significant failure, it at least provided a useful lesson to Chinese policy makers. Without experiencing the labor shortages that developed in the Soviet Union and Eastern Europe during their First Five-Year Plans, China was forced into the realization that its economic conditions in the 1950s were vastly different from those of Eastern Europe in the late 1940s and the Soviet Union in the 1920s. With a much larger population and a much smaller industrial sector, China had no easy way to follow the Soviet economic development strategy.[1] Recognizing the problem was a step toward more realistic and more effective welfare reforms.

Growing recognition of China's tight economic constraints began to temper the influence of the Soviet Union and its economic development and welfare policies. The difficulties in following the Soviet model, however, did not dissuade Chinese policy makers from trying

---

1. Howe, *Employment and Economic Growth*, 103–4, 108.

to achieve the goals of the First Five-Year Plan, including the goal of a broad welfare state. Instead, they changed the means by which they sought to achieve those goals. A new policy of eliminating transitional welfare programs in favor of increasing investment in industry sought to turn short-term sacrifices into long-term solutions to China's welfare problems. Beyond the new austerity, there was considerable disagreement among policy makers and policy factions began to form among the central CCP leaders. The breakdown of the early, easy consensus around the Soviet model created a new dynamic in the top-down pressure for welfare reform. Economic development policy was still a major force shaping welfare policy, but its impact fluctuated as different factions vied for power.

Bottom-up pressure for welfare reform also changed. Workers and the unemployed alike continued to seek expansion of the welfare state, but their ability to voice their demands changed. The unemployed were still ostensibly union members, but they were no longer integrated into the organization. Although the union was no longer centrally involved in all aspects of welfare reform, it gave workers some access to the policy-making process in Beijing. As a result, workers continued to be preferentially incorporated into the regime, while the unemployed increasingly found themselves on the outside with the rest of the urban poor. This combination of wavering top-down pressure and unequal bottom-up demand for welfare reform was a volatile mix. New temporary constraints on the welfare state initially held back its growth but then disappeared in a sudden surge of welfare state expansion that policy makers had not foreseen, much less planned.

## Adapting the Soviet Development Strategy

The difficulties of matching the economic performance of other communist countries was driven home by China's recession in 1954–55, as the First Five-Year Plan was being finalized. A poor harvest in 1954 led to a sharp recession in consumer industries that relied on agricultural inputs. The central Chinese government quickly responded to the economic setback with a return to its earlier policy of fiscal austerity, imposing sharp cuts in government spending in order to avoid budget deficits and to prevent inflation.

At the same time that they coped with the short-term recession, the long-term problem of reformulating China's economic development strategy preoccupied most of the CCP leadership. Two broad factions eventually emerged among party leaders, each supporting a different alternative.[2] Mao and many provincial officials argued for sticking with the basic strategy borrowed from the Soviet Union, but accelerating structural reform to overcome the constraints on the Chinese economy. Acceleration meant higher investment rates in producer industries as well as carrying out the urban revolution: the elimination of private ownership and the state takeover of industry.

Zhou Enlai and other central leaders who had shaped the post-1949 economic recovery advocated for slowing the transition to a command economy. To build on China's existing strengths, they proposed a more balanced investment strategy that included agriculture and consumer industries, which had provided much of the growth in the early 1950s and also had a greater impact on employment. They also called for temporarily limiting the scope of economic planning and state owner-ship of industry. Only after China had achieved more growth and greater industrialization within its mixed economy did they advocate for carrying out the urban revolution and completing the transition to a command economy.

The one policy change that both factions could agree on immedi-ately was adopting a more conservative fiscal policy, already evident in the response to the 1954–55 recession. Mao and the faction promoting an accelerated version of the Soviet development strategy saw budget cuts as a means to free up more capital for a big-push investment drive. The go-slow faction that wanted to build on the strengths of the mixed

2. Although scholars disagree about the identity of these factions and Mao's role in the policy-making process, there is more consensus about the policies each side was advocating. MacFarquhar argues that the split was among the top leadership, Teiwes and Sun draw the line between central planners and provincial officials, whereas Bachman argues it was a struggle between planning and finance officials. See MacFar-quhar, *Origins of the Cultural Revolution*, vol. 1, 57–80; Teiwes and Sun, *China's Road*, 59; Bachman, *Bureaucracy, Economy, and Leadership in China*, 2–7.

economy saw the budget cuts as a means of keeping inflation low, their greatest economic policy success in the first few years of the regime.[3] For different reasons, both sides agreed that short-term restraint was the key to long-term economic gain.

After the First Five-Year Plan was finalized in 1955, the debate between the two factions over the pace and scope of structural reform continued. As a result, the most basic policies underpinning the plan were still in flux after it was publicly announced, as different factions contended for control. Schedules for major reforms were constantly being updated, and sudden surges in investment were followed by equally sudden austerity measures. The instability in economic policy was no doubt a reflection of the daunting challenges that policy makers faced, but it in turn posed its own difficulties.

## *The New Unemployment Policy*

The shifting uncertainties in economic development policy had a major impact on welfare reform. Although we know little about the policy process in the economic planning system that produced the new approach to welfare reform, the propaganda that accompanied it provides some insight into the logic behind it. The short-lived consensus behind fiscal austerity in 1955 seems to have contributed to a shift in policy makers' views of welfare spending. Rather than short-term transitional costs necessary in the shift to a command economy, Chinese policy makers began to emphasize the trade-off between welfare spending as consumption and capital spending as investment. Building on the lessons learned from the Universal Job Placement program, the new approach went beyond making rationing of employment and welfare benefits explicit—the goal was to carry out rationing intentionally and openly in order to reach China's long-term development goals.

The trade-off between consumption and investment was not an abstraction to Chinese policy makers. In one propaganda piece developed

3. Bachman, *Bureaucracy, Economy, and Leadership,* 61–62, 100–101; Teiwes and Sun, *China's Road,* 22.

to explain the new welfare policies, a direct comparison between welfare spending and investment was drawn, calculating that the amount spent on unemployment relief since 1950 could have financed a new, large-scale modern textile factory employing more than four thousand workers in permanent jobs.[4] Although the investment would have helped only a tiny fraction of the hundreds of thousands of people that unemployment relief served, the hypothetical factory was portrayed as a permanent rather than a temporary solution to their problems. The goal of such propaganda was to convince the Chinese public that it was in their interest to embrace temporary sacrifice.

This kind of propaganda set the stage for a dramatic new change in welfare policy: elimination of the unemployment relief program in favor of a new mass ruralization (*xiafang*) campaign.[5] Ruralization drew on the long-standing practice in China of evacuating refugees and other poor rural migrants from the cities after the countryside had recovered from the natural disasters or famines that had driven them off the land. Escaping to the cities provided a safety net of last resort for peasants, since Chinese charities and municipal governments cooperated to provide soup kitchens and emergency shelter during crises.[6] Charities often also subsidized the return trip home after the emergency was over, including organizing large-scale evacuations of refugees.[7]

The new ruralization policy sought to place unemployed urbanites in jobs working on development projects in the interior. But since there were more unemployed workers than jobs, many were simply given land to farm in an effort to make them self-sufficient. The budget funds spent on unemployment relief could then be redirected to turn the hypothetical new modern factory from propaganda into reality.

Although it drew on old practices, the ruralization policy was premised on a new conception of China's unemployment problem.

4. SMA, B25-1-1.
5. *Xiafang* is usually translated literally as "sending down" or more meaningfully as "rustification." But I will use "ruralization" because this term makes it clear that the goal was to limit or reverse urbanization as well as to make urbanites more rural in their outlooks and values.
6. Li, *Fighting Famine*, 228–33.
7. Dillon, "Middlemen in the Chinese Welfare State," 28–40; Dillon, "The Politics of Philanthropy," 181–83, 186–89.

Rather than attribute unemployment to the old regime or to the transition to a command economy as was done in the early 1950s, the CCP now blamed rural-urban migration for the problem. Indeed, rural-urban migration was now described as blind, irrational, and even as an escape route from labor reform for counterrevolutionaries. From this new perspective, the unemployed were no longer victims of imperialism and capitalism, but burdens obstructing China's economic development.[8]

To limit migration, the central government established a national household registration policy in 1955.[9] The new policy extended the existing urban household registration system to the countryside and imposed a new requirement that migrants obtain official approval to move their residence legally. The third pillar of the population control policy was a new grain-rationing system for urban residents established in 1955, making it harder for people without official urban residency permits to obtain food.[10]

In addition to limiting rural-urban migration, large industrial cities like Shanghai were ordered to reduce their overall size. Although Soviet economic policies were being questioned by Chinese policy makers, Soviet urban planning was still embraced. A long-term goal of the new policy was to decrease Shanghai to Moscow's size, considered the optimal standard of efficiency for socialist cities worldwide.[11] Another motivation for the new urban planning policies was the precedent set by Japan's rapid invasion of the cities on China's coast in the 1930s. Strategic concerns about protecting military industries reinforced the new policies on urbanization.

Evacuating the urban unemployed was one element of the new policy of population control. The key issue in question was the length of the transitional period of austerity: how long would the unemployed have to wait for a permanent solution to their problems? The big-push faction argued they only had to wait for the end of the First Five-Year Plan, whereas the go-slow faction predicted a ten- to fifteen-year wait.

8. SMA, B25-1-1.
9. Cheng and Selden, "Origins and Social Consequences," 655.
10. Ibid., 657.
11. SMA, B25-1-1.

Either way, short-term sacrifices were seen as the key to reaching the same goal of mass employment and a broad welfare state.

## The 1955 Ruralization Campaign

It was only in the summer of 1955 that the content of the First Five-Year Plan was announced. Until that point, the only public disclosures about the plan were the major new investment projects that received Soviet technical and economic assistance. The investment projects were the good news in the First Five-Year Plan; full disclosure in 1955 revealed for the first time the bad news of who was going to pay for it. Shanghai turned out to be the biggest loser, providing the bulk of the revenue for the new development plan and getting very little investment in return.[12]

At the same time that the bad news about the economy was delivered, the Shanghai Party Committee announced the goal of decreasing the urban population by half a million to one million people through a ruralization campaign to meet the newly imposed size limit on the city. Although the policy-making process had been secretive up to that point, considerable effort was exerted to convince urbanites to support the new population control policy once it was issued. The first groups the CCP sought to win over were local officials and cadres who were tasked with implementing it. Many cadres were negative about the new limits on Shanghai's size, and much of the initial propaganda was directed toward changing their views.[13]

Shanghai's business leaders were more supportive of the ruralization policy, perhaps because it fit with long-standing philanthropic practices for coping with refugees and seasonal migration. They were also still chastened by their treatment in the Three Antis and Five Antis anticorruption campaigns, and reluctant to take any further political risks by opposing a major new policy initiative. Still, they expressed concerns that they themselves would be targets for ruralization. One man who

12. Howe, "Industrialization," 166–68.
13. Zhongguo shehui kexue yuan, *Zhonghua renmin gongheguo jingji dang'an 1953–57*, 62–63; SMA, B127-1-54.

owned a textile factory reported that he was very nervous when the police came to interview him about his household registration, but once he passed that three-hour ordeal, he strongly endorsed the policy for others. Capitalists whose factories were designated to be moved into the interior raised many practical concerns, such as the difficulties of moving machinery and securing new sources of supplies. But they did not pose more fundamental objections to the policy. Indeed, the most vocal opposition that businessmen expressed was concern over the fate of their nannies and other household servants from the countryside.[14]

Ordinary Shanghai citizens were much more critical of the policy change. Delegates to the Shanghai Political Consultative Conference from Shanghai's residential neighborhoods complained that the ruralization policy was not voluntary, as described by the party and the press, but compulsory because the new rationing system ensured that the unemployed would not have access to food even if they could find some alternate source of support. Other delegates argued that the policy violated the new constitution's guarantee of freedom of movement. Still others worried that the policy encouraged divorce. The most pointed criticism was political. One delegate claimed that, "in the past, the KMT never did anything this [bad]."[15] But political opposition to ruralization never went beyond individual complaints and criticisms.

Logistical planning for the ruralization campaign began in the spring of 1955 before the new policy was publicly announced. Cadres were sent to Jiangsu, Jiangxi, Shaanxi, and Gansu to make arrangements for placing the unemployed in jobs or giving them land to farm. Jiangxi province turned out to be the most welcoming, agreeing to accept 390,000 Shanghainese over the course of the First Five-Year Plan to reclaim land for farming, starting with a more modest target of six thousand people in 1955.[16] Jiangxi's decision to accept the majority of Shanghai's quota for the ruralization campaign indicates that most of the city's surplus labor would be redirected to farming rather than construction or industrial projects in more remote provinces.

---

14. SMA, B168-1-862.

15. Ibid.

16. Zhongguo shehui kexue yuan, *Zhonghua renmin gongheguo jingji dang'an 1953–57*, 71.

Once the ruralization campaign began in the summer and fall of 1955, however, it proved difficult to recruit people to move to the interior, just as the critics had predicted. City officials organized rallies for "unemployed activists" to urge them to sign on, portraying farming as a way to contribute to the country's socialist construction and making the argument that staying in Shanghai by relying on social relief or support from relatives was a life with no future.[17] Cadres charged with the task of trying to recruit volunteers reported that the message was a hard sell. Some recruiters complained that the unemployed said that farming would demean their class status as workers; others complained that the unemployed were proud of their unemployment registration cards, acting as if they were "signs of royalty" (wang pai).[18]

Despite the difficulty in recruiting the able-bodied, the officials in charge of the campaign did not shrink from the task of mobilizing people with special needs. Elderly unemployed workers without families to rely on were encouraged to go to the countryside if they could work, with the suggestion that they take jobs in rest homes to care for even more elderly people. Although unemployed workers with tuberculosis were reported to be pleading for health care benefits, they were given subsidies to go to the countryside to rest instead.[19]

For both the able-bodied and the weak alike, incentives were more important than persuasion. The threats of losing social relief and access to rations were decisive, and the offer of subsidies for transportation and start-up costs helped mitigate the financial obstacles. People with alternatives to relief, such as skilled workers, intellectuals, and youth, generally succeeded in evading evacuation. It was rural migrants without urban registration and unskilled, poorly educated unemployed workers who had difficulty staying in the city.

The contrast between the union's treatment of workers and of the unemployed after the 1954 democratic reform campaign was vividly displayed during the ruralization campaign. Workers whose factories were slated to be moved into the interior were singled out for gentle

17. SMA, B127-1-1432; SMA, B25-1-1.
18. Zhongguo shehui kexue yuan, Zhonghua renmin gongheguo jingji dang'an 1953–57, 64.
19. SMA, A36-1-102a.

*Table 5.1.* Shanghai Unemployment Programs, 1954–57

| Year | People registered unemployed | People evacuated | Social relief recipients |
|------|------|------|------|
| 1954 | 301,640 | 12,038 | 30,191 |
| 1955 | 0 | 674,169 | 90,852 |
| 1956 | 0 | 10,303 | 114,280 |
| 1957 | 0 | 35,425 | 91,744 |

Sources: SMA, B127-1-53; SMA, B168-1-512; SMA, B168-1-521; SMA, B168-1-712; SMA, B168-1-880.

treatment. Cadres were instructed to emphasize the positive gains from the move and to downplay the possible hardships in order to gain their compliance.[20] Moreover, many workers were allowed to leave their families behind, so their children could stay in Shanghai schools and maintain their urban household registration. Higher wages and especially the lower cost of living in the interior were emphasized as an opportunity to get ahead and provide a better future for their children.[21]

The ruralization campaign met its targets despite its ambitious goals and reluctant participants. A total of 684,472 people were evacuated from Shanghai in 1955–56, the vast majority of whom were rural migrants who could not prove they had urban household registrations (table 5.1). The number of unemployed with Shanghai registrations shipped out of the city was much smaller, but not insignificant. More than 2,800 unemployed workers with Shanghai household registrations went to work on new construction and industrial projects in Gansu and Shaanxi, while another 29,688 went to Jiangxi to reclaim land.[22] All of this was accomplished without any of the street protests that had plagued Shanghai's unemployment relief programs over the last decade, suggesting that the 1954 democratic reform campaign had been effective in demobilizing the unemployed.

Despite the scale of the ruralization campaign, it did not manage to eliminate unemployment relief, much less unemployment itself. All of the "active" relief programs, such as self-help production and educational programs, were cut, but the "passive" relief of distributing grain

20. SMA, B25-1-1.
21. SMA, A36-1-102b.
22. SMA, B168-1-512; SMA, B127-1-54.

*Table 5.2.* Shanghai Relief Handouts, 1954–57

| Year | Unemployment relief handouts | Social relief handouts | Total | Percent change |
|------|------------------------------|------------------------|-------|----------------|
| 1954 | 503,841 | 362,287 | 866,128 | |
| 1955 | 208,605 | 1,090,220 | 1,298,825 | 50% |
| 1956 | 0 | 1,371,360 | 1,371,360 | 6% |
| 1957 | 0 | 1,100,922 | 1,100,922 | -20% |

*Sources:* SMA, B127-1-53; SMA, B168-1-712.

and relief payments proved to be a more difficult target. In fact, social relief distributions more than tripled in 1955 (table 5.2).

Part of the problem was that the 1955 recession was increasing the ranks of the unemployed at the same time the evacuations were getting under way.[23] The situation did not improve much the following year, when the evacuations escalated and the new investment drive revived the urban economy. (Because unemployment relief was transferred from the Labor Ministry to the Civil Affairs Ministry and consolidated into the social relief program, the two programs need to be examined together to understand the impact of the new unemployment policy on welfare spending.)[24] In Shanghai, both programs provided more than one million relief handouts in 1955, an increase of 50 percent over the previous year. Unemployment relief had not been eliminated, but renamed.

## *The Urban Revolution*

As the ruralization campaign proceeded in the winter of 1955–56, Mao and the faction that favored accelerating structural reform of the economy gained dominance. In December 1955, Mao made the triumphant pronouncement that the campaign to collectivize agriculture was at its peak, with 60 percent of the countryside collectivized nearly a year

23. SMA, B127-1-54.
24. SMA, B127-1-1930; Zhongguo shehui kexue yuan, *Zhonghua renmin gongheguo jingji dang'an 1953–57*, 31–33.

ahead of schedule.[25] He called for a new big-push investment drive in 1956, and Zhou Enlai apparently went through self-criticism for pushing austerity too far. Convening a meeting with Shanghai's leading capitalists, Mao announced his new goal of socializing industry in two years, before the end of the First Five-Year Plan.[26] The urban revolution that Shanghai's workers had wanted since 1949 now had the backing of the top CCP leadership. Immediately after this sudden decision, a new big-push investment drive began in January 1956.

Before the union began its preparations for the socialization campaign, the official business federations in both Beijing and Shanghai seized the initiative. Over the course of a few weeks in January 1956, they organized their own version of a socialization campaign, hastily seeking to preempt another round of class struggle similar to the Five Antis anticorruption campaign. Rather than face struggle meetings and public trials, the capitalists organized parades and political rallies with their factory managers and family members in a festive and very public display of loyalty to the communist regime. Posting new signs over their factory gates and ostentatiously turning over the titles to their factories to representatives of the party-state were all part of an effort to transform property titles and ledger books into more dramatic symbols of the revolution.

By January 18, both Beijing and Shanghai had completed the socialization of all private industry. Within a few weeks, capitalists across the country followed their example, turning over the titles to their property in hastily completed negotiations over compensation.[27] Just the threat of another struggle campaign was sufficient to scare China's remaining business leaders into sudden and complete compliance with Mao's call to socialize industry. The capitalists' enthusiasm for the state takeover of their companies may have been manufactured for the occasion, but no doubt their relief at avoiding another struggle campaign was genuine.

For the CCP, the campaign to socialize industry was a surprising and spectacular success, and press coverage of the capitalists' rallies was triumphant. For workers, the sudden conclusion of the "campaign to

25. MacFarquhar, *Origins of the Cultural Revolution*, vol. 1, 15.
26. Ibid., 315–22.
27. Xiong, *Shanghai Tongshi*, vol. 11, 118–20.

end all struggle campaigns" that they had been anticipating for years was anticlimactic and confusing. Capitalists and managers were now reporting to work without any clearly defined role in the operation of their former factories, and many of them applied for union membership as well. The party and the union were ostensibly in charge of the new joint-owned enterprises, but none of the practicalities of how they were supposed to function had been worked out.[28] Moreover, without any rallies or parades for workers to join in, let alone struggle meetings, the union lost a key opportunity to renew the bond between its cadres and members.

It was only at that point that the party committees and union branches in the new joint-owned enterprises began the process of working out mergers, new management structures, and the standardization of wages and benefits across industries. Turning over the titles to their factories was only the beginning of the process, but at the very least it clarified the basic fact that capitalists were not going to bargain over any aspect of the socialization of industry. But even if capitalists took themselves out of the equation, the management problems involved in the state takeover of industry still loomed large.

## Labor Union Reforms

Although workers were denied their long-anticipated struggle campaign by the peaceful socialization of industry, a new round of political reform in the official labor movement sought to meet their needs in other ways. The new leaders who were brought in to exert party control over the union were worried that the pendulum had swung too far in the direction of top-down control, alienating workers when the critical tasks of economic development required their enthusiastic participation. All-China Federation of Trade Unions chairman Lai Ruoyu issued a report criticizing union cadres for ignoring workers' standard of living out of misplaced fear that any attention to economic issues

28. Frazier, *Making of the Chinese Industrial Workplace*, 159–60, 177–82; MacFarquhar, ed., *Hundred Flowers*, 202.

would be construed as a political error. Likewise, he accused the party of overstepping its role in supervising the union, monopolizing its day-to-day management rather than concentrating on providing political and policy leadership.[29] The ambitious administrator was turning into a labor advocate.

With backing from the CCP Central Committee, Lai Ruoyu led the effort to renew the bond between the union leadership and its members. In addition to urging union cadres to focus on the economic needs of the workers, especially "backward" workers, Lai also criticized cadres for relying too much on issuing orders and using coercion in their efforts to mobilize their members. Attempts to change union cadres' attitudes and leadership styles were combined with structural reforms designed to facilitate a new, more positive relationship between cadres and workers. The goal was to inspire the hard work and discipline necessary to achieve the production targets in the First Five-Year Plan.

In January 1956, the All-China Federation of Trade Unions decided to create a new line of authority in its national hierarchy by establishing industrial unions for all industries (and not just for industries that crossed multiple political jurisdictions, such as the railroad industry).[30] In the new structure, the provincial and municipal unions had two supervisors: the party committee at their same level in the political hierarchy as well as the national industrial unions operating outside of it. This cross-cutting organizational structure was seen as a way of clarifying the distinct roles of the party and the union in the new command economy and therefore providing a bureaucratic solution to the problem of union autonomy.

## The Move to Social Insurance

The labor union also began its policy-making process to develop a social insurance program in 1956. After Mao announced the push to socialize industry by the end of the First Five-Year Plan, the All-China Federation

29. Wang Yu et al., *Dangdai Zhongguo*, 116–17.
30. Ibid., 125.

of Trade Unions issued a new twelve-year plan in February 1956 to meet Mao's preferred timetable for structural reform. (The twelve-year plan included the remaining two years of the First Five-Year Plan plus the following two five-year plans, by which point Mao hoped to complete the industrialization of the Chinese economy.) The national labor union's twelve-year plan committed the union to implementing a unified social insurance system in all industrial, administrative, cultural, and cooperative organizations by the end of the First Five-Year Plan in 1957.[31] In addition to completing the core program of the Chinese welfare state, the twelve-year plan also proposed a long-term agenda of expanding health care services, improving housing, expanding child care, and offering more benefits for workers' dependents over the next decade.

The All-China Federation of Trade Unions quickly followed up its ambitious long-term plan by issuing draft regulations for the new social insurance program in March 1956. The draft regulations proposed expanding coverage to include the entire urban workforce by incorporating all kinds of employers into the program and eliminating the hundred-employee size restriction.[32] The report accompanying the draft regulations described the existing labor insurance program as successful in many ways but singled out limited population coverage as the program's most significant shortcoming. Arguing that the gradual approach to expanding labor insurance coverage taken so far was unable to keep pace with China's growing workforce, the national labor union maintained that a command economy required a comprehensive, unified approach to broadening coverage.

The new social insurance policy also sought to standardize benefits. By incorporating the government and party agencies that had been part of the free supply system up until this point, the draft social insurance regulations eliminated the special benefits reserved for party and government employees. In addition, lifting the size restriction on employers entailed upgrading all the labor insurance contract programs with limited benefits. Finally, the distinction between permanent and temporary employees made in the labor insurance regulations was eliminated. An integrated approach to welfare state expansion prom-

31. SMA, C1-2-1840.
32. SMA, C1-2-2159.

ised a broader, more egalitarian urban welfare state, excluding only the urbanites who had been deprived of their political rights.

The national labor union report on the new social insurance policy repeatedly referenced Soviet models as a rationale for its recommendations. For example, the draft regulations unified program administration under union management as was the practice in the Soviet Union, eliminating the distinction between benefits paid directly by enterprise management from its revenues (such as work injury benefits) and benefits paid for by the union from its labor insurance funds (such as pensions).[33] The regulations also drew on the Soviet example in calling for program taxes that varied by industry rather than the uniform payroll tax levied by the Chinese labor insurance regulations.

As in the case of the previous labor insurance initiatives, municipal and provincial unions were asked to gauge workers' opinions and provide feedback on the draft social insurance regulations. The Shanghai Federation of Trade Unions organized 220 roundtable discussions in the spring of 1956 in order to solicit opinions and ideas on the proposal from union cadres and ordinary workers.[34] Overall, the feedback was positive. Workers praised the new regulations for expanding coverage and improving benefits, describing the proposal as evidence of the CCP's concern for the working class. Among the nearly three hundred opinions and suggestions that came out of these roundtable discussions, most addressed specific benefits, usually pushing for yet more improvements. The one query about population coverage sought more detail on how independent workers, such as dock workers and rickshaw pullers, were going to be incorporated into the social insurance program.

When the Shanghai labor union reported back to Beijing on the results of its consultative process, the Shanghai Party Committee added its own supplemental report on the draft regulations. Although its overall assessment was also favorable, describing social insurance as more "comprehensive and rational" than the current labor insurance program, the party report raised new concerns and questions. The two most important concerns were the overall cost of the new program and the limited capacity of the existing health care system, which was

33. Ibid.
34. Ibid.

deemed incapable of meeting the projected surge in demand. Shanghai's party leaders suggested gradual implementation to control the pace of spending increases to around 20 percent per year, as well as adding a provision to allow enterprises and organizations in financial difficulty to delay implementation of social insurance temporarily. Finally, the Shanghai Party Committee questioned whether handicraft cooperatives would ever have the financial capacity to sustain social insurance and raised the idea of setting up a separate program for them.[35]

The policy-making process continued to move quickly, with the All-China Federation of Trade Unions convening a national conference on labor insurance, welfare, and housing from May 21 to June 9, 1956. The policy conference received the endorsement of the top party leadership when Zhou Enlai met with the participants to encourage them to focus on improving workers' living standards by the end of the First Five-Year Plan.[36] In addition, the State Council extended labor insurance to commerce and several other industries to begin the process of expansion immediately.[37]

One of the top priorities of the policy-making conference was to discuss the reports from the municipal and provincial unions on the draft social insurance regulations. The agenda also went far beyond social insurance, taking a comprehensive view of welfare, including job placement, housing conditions, transportation problems, vocational training, health care, child care, and unemployment relief, now ostensibly the concern of the civil affairs bureaucracy.[38] In his speech at the conference, Shanghai union vicechairman Zhang Qi echoed Zhou Enlai's message by calling for the union to be less bureaucratic and more committed to improving workers' living standards.[39]

Following the national conference, a revised version of the draft social insurance regulations was issued in August 1956. In addition, a draft of detailed implementation regulations was also issued to solicit more feedback from lower levels of the union, party, and government

35. Ibid.
36. Wang Yu, et al., *Dangdai Zhongguo,* 135.
37. SMA, C1-2-2389.
38. SMA, A36-2-102c; Wang Yu, et al., *Dangdai Zhongguo,* 135.
39. SMA, C1-2-1839.

hierarchies.[40] The implementation regulations clarified the extent of the proposed social insurance system's population coverage, reiterating that there would be no size limit on employers and no distinction between permanent and temporary employees. Perhaps reflecting the influence of the Shanghai Party Committee's proposals, independent workers and the employees of handicraft cooperatives were now explicitly excluded from the main social insurance program in order to establish an alternative program more suitable for nonwage employees. In addition, a new provision was added allowing the implementation of social insurance to be delayed for enterprises in difficult financial conditions, as long as they obtained the approval of higher-level union authorities.

Although the detailed implementation regulations took a more cautious approach to welfare state expansion than the original proposal, the new social insurance system still promised to cover the entire urban workforce in two comprehensive programs. In addition, the new implementation regulations clarified that the new social insurance program would extend coverage to the countryside by enrolling all rural residents who were formally employed, whether by government agencies or by state farms. The rural majority working in the new collective farms fell into a similar category to urban handicraft and independent workers who were not wage workers. The alternative welfare program for urban cooperatives would presumably be relevant for rural cooperatives as well.

The new timetable for the expansion of the welfare state indicated that the deliberate rationing of the ruralization campaigns would be short. The unemployed would only have to wait until the end of 1957 for the welfare reforms that would transform China's narrow welfare state.

## *The Crisis in Eastern Europe*

When the CCP held its Eighth Party Congress in September 1956, party leaders such as Liu Shaoqi were triumphant that the urban revolution

40. SMA, C1-2-2159.

had gone so smoothly and peacefully. Looking back over the eleven years since the last party congress in 1945 fostered a deep sense of accomplishment among party leaders: in a little over a decade they had won the civil war, reunified the mainland, and fought the United States to a draw in Korea. Moreover, the Chinese Communists had been able to carry out their rural and urban social revolutions in just a few years and with much less bloodshed than their Soviet "big brother." Another point of pride was the revival of the Chinese economy, including the midcourse corrections to the First Five-Year Plan. Although China still faced many economic challenges to catch up to the Soviet Union, its political achievements overshadowed the precedent set by the Russian Revolution, with the civil war and famine that followed the Bolshevik seizure of power. The sense of the fragility of the CCP's political support in the cities that marked the early 1950s seemed to have been transformed by the speed of the urban revolution.

The self-satisfaction that CCP leaders expressed in September was soon compounded by deeper doubts about the Soviet model when they heard the news that Hungarians had staged a massive anti-communist insurrection in October 1956. Order was only restored after the Soviet Red Army invaded Hungary in November 1956. The Hungarian Uprising was the culmination of political unrest that had spread across Eastern Europe since Stalin's death in 1953. The Eastern European model of rapid socialist industrialization and welfare state development no longer looked so ideal, even if Eastern Europe had the highest living standards in the Communist world.

Khrushchev, the Soviet Union's new party chairman, blamed his predecessor for the unrest, denouncing Stalin's despotism as undermining support for communism. After hearing about Khrushchev's political diagnosis, Mao came to a different conclusion about the source of the problems in Eastern Europe. Rather than blame Stalin, Mao blamed the Soviet model itself. From Mao's perspective, the problems did not lie at the top of the regime in Stalin's personal rule, but at the bottom reaches of the new Stalinist party-states in Eastern Europe, where petty bureaucrats dominated the lives of ordinary people and alienated them from the regime. So rather than limit the power of party leaders, as Khrushchev had proposed, Mao called for expanding the freedom of people outside the party. In his famous "Hundred Flowers" speech in May 1956, Mao called for more opportunities for political participation for people outside the party. At the same time, he called for opening up political debate in China to accommodate ideas outside the bounds of official ideology. When the Hungarian Uprising took place, Mao saw it as further evidence that his political reform proposals needed to be adopted.[41]

## *The First Mass Rectification Campaign and the 1957 Strike Wave*

Mao's rhetoric became reality in the spring of 1957, when the CCP launched its first mass rectification campaign, an innovation of one of the most important kinds of campaigns in Chinese Communist governance. Rectification campaigns had originally been developed by the CCP in the 1940s as internal campaigns for party cadres to enforce discipline and improve ideological and policy indoctrination. The centerpiece of these closed-door campaigns was the practice of criticism and self-criticism, which brought cadres together in groups to criticize each other's actions and ideas. Ultimately, group criticism was supposed to culminate in self-criticism, when party members reflected on their past actions and thoughts, and resolved to hew more faithfully to party policies in the future.

In his February 1957 speech "On Contradictions," Mao proposed opening up the process to the public, allowing ordinary citizens to criticize government officials and party cadres in open meetings and make suggestions for reform. Mao argued that this form of communist democracy would help the Chinese overcome the kinds of problems plaguing Eastern Europe. Moreover, his confidence in the power of Chinese nationalism and the rapid success of the revolution led Mao to conclude that the problems so evident in Eastern Europe were not nearly as serious in China.[42]

41. MacFarquhar, *Origins of the Cultural Revolution*, vol. 1, 43–48.
42. Teiwes, *Politics and Purges*, 187–188.

It took several months for Mao to convince the rest of the CCP leadership to back the idea of a mass rectification campaign, since leaders like Liu Shaoqi feared that it would undermine the authority and legitimacy of the party. Another reason for his caution was that Shanghai's workers were already engaging in slowdowns, protests, and wildcat strikes in an effort to forestall the standardization of wages and welfare benefits. As the economic consequences of the urban revolution gradually became clear in 1956, workers were discovering that their hopes of sharing in the profits that their owners had given up so quickly were naive. Wage and benefit cuts in the process of standardization turned out to be many workers' reward from the socialization of industry. For workers, the urban revolution's most visible outcome was the bureaucratization of the command economy rather than the redistribution of property and income.

In April 1957, Liu Shaoqi spent nearly a week in Shanghai meeting with local officials and investigating the growing labor unrest in the city. Although Liu was reportedly reluctant to embrace Mao's political reforms, he was more open to Mao's economic ideas. On April 27, Liu gave a speech to Shanghai labor leaders urging union cadres to support their workers rather than try to repress them, in order to gain the workers' sympathy and loyalty.[43]

Apparently Liu Shaoqi and the other top leaders acquiesced to Mao's political proposals soon after that trip to investigate labor conditions in Shanghai. The new mass rectification campaign was quickly launched on May 1, 1957. Shanghai began its campaign by convening roundtable discussions with invited groups of intellectuals, business leaders, and other prominent citizens in early May. The meetings were initially hesitant and cautious, but after repeated encouragement from top CCP leaders, the invited participants gradually expressed more criticism.[44]

For example, Shanghai's capitalists began criticizing the socialization campaign they had led so enthusiastically just the year before. Li Kangnian, who owned and operated several different factories before 1956, criticized the regime for ignoring the proposal he had submitted to the Shanghai People's Congress to compensate capitalists for

43. MacFarquhar, *Origins of the Cultural Revolution*, vol. 1, 196–98.
44. Van Slyke, *Enemies and Friends*, 244.

their factories by giving them union membership and labor insurance. Instead, the CCP had falsely credited him with formulating the party's actual compensation policy, which was almost universally but quietly disliked by capitalists because the buyouts perpetuated their bad class status indefinitely. Other capitalists and managers complained in rectification meetings that they had do-nothing jobs in their former factories, with no responsibility, no authority, and absolutely no respect.[45]

Shanghai's workers were not as timid as their former employers. Rather than join in yet another series of roundtable discussions, Shanghai's workers seized the opportunity presented by the mass rectification campaign to turn their complaints into the biggest strike wave in Shanghai's long history of labor unrest. The spark that turned Shanghai's labor protests into a strike wave was a demonstration by apprentices, thousands of whom marched through the streets to protest a new regulation that suddenly extended their training and low pay by several years.[46] Workers from more than 975 factories across the city then leapt into action with slowdowns, strikes, and demonstrations of their own. The labor conflict took place largely in the newly socialized joint-owned enterprises, where the wage and welfare benefit standardization process was under way. According to an investigation of 545 protests, 42 percent were prompted by welfare problems, 35 percent involved wage demands, 6 percent opposed factory evacuations to the interior, and another 6 percent were caused by problems with apprenticeship programs.[47]

The most common kind of welfare conflicts stemmed from workers' efforts to protect the private welfare benefits that they had won from their companies in the strikes of the late 1940s and the Five Antis anticorruption campaign in 1952. The ongoing process of standardizing private and labor insurance contract benefits was the first step toward integration into the full labor insurance program. For example, the Ziyuan Battery Factory merged with a smaller factory with better benefits in 1956. When a single labor insurance contract was proposed based on the Ziyuan benefits, workers from the smaller factory went on strike

45. MacFarquhar, ed., *Hundred Flowers*, 197–98, 202.
46. SMA, B54-1-5b.
47. SMA, B54-1-5a.

to protect their privileges, declaring that "the main factory is imperialist, and our branch factory has been colonized."[48]

The conflicts were sharper when mergers redistributed the labor insurance reserve funds from one enterprise to another that lacked welfare benefits. For example, when the Yingyin Knitting Factory was forced to merge with a small papermaking company, the management from the knitting factory objected to extending their labor insurance program to the workers at the papermaking factory, since it threatened to eat up their reserves. The papermakers, however, protested against this discrimination and demanded equal treatment by their new state managers.[49]

Labor protests over welfare and wages sometimes escalated into demands for political reform. For example, the new management of the Shanghai Pen Factory decided to convene a workers' representative assembly to get the union's endorsement of their wage reform proposal. Before the assembly, however, the workers conducted a secret election to choose their own representatives. When the enterprise union refused to recognize the elected delegates, the workers held a mass meeting and criticized their union cadres for being undemocratic. The district-level union office ended up intervening to negotiate a compromise, with 80 percent of the delegates elected by the workers and the other 20 percent chosen by the existing union leadership.[50]

Although these solutions fit Lai Ruoyu's concept of worker participation in the union, other political demands were too radical for the union to accommodate, even in the context of a mass rectification campaign. Many workers and union cadres complained about Li Lisan's purge from the union leadership in 1951 and called for his return.[51] A small number of strikers took their political demands much further. Strikers at the Da Guang Ming Shirt Factory called for revolution, claiming: "The KMT was bad, so we overthrew the KMT. The CCP is even worse. Since liberation, our lives are hard and the CCP is exploit-

48. SMA, B54-1-2.
49. SMA, C1-2-2382.
50. SMA, B54-1-2.
51. SMA, C1-2-2255.

alive. We're going to heat up the furnace again."[52] Protesters from the Guangxin Dye Factory sought to prevent the relocation of their factory to the interior. After their petitions, street protests, and a hunger strike failed to produce results, they threatened to commit suicide en masse in order to instigate a "Hungarian Incident" in China.[53]

The most radical protests may have been carried out by workers, but the unemployed also seized the opportunities presented by the mass rectification campaign to take to the streets to protest. The largest group of protesters among the unemployed in the spring of 1957 came from the estimated 8,500 people who had returned to Shanghai from the Jiangxi reclamation project.[54] In addition, people from as far away as the remote northwestern frontier provinces also returned to join the campaign. For example, one-fourth of the people sent to Qinghai abandoned their jobs and returned to Shanghai, complaining loudly that they had been tricked into leaving for poorly paid jobs.[55] The returnees petitioned for the return of their Shanghai household registrations, along with new jobs and food rations.

The petitions escalated quickly into larger protests during the strike wave. On May 20, for example, twenty-eight Jiangxi returnees led a march to the Shanghai Labor Bureau, where they staged a sit-in to demand new jobs and the urban household registration status necessary for job placement. Labor bureau cadres quoted the protest leader as arguing: "The constitution guarantees freedom of movement. Why can't we move our household registration? Do you want us to try "big democracy" like the apprentices? We've been back for nine months, and you keep saying that you'll study the matter. If the labor bureau can't resolve the problem, we'll go to the Shanghai Party Committee. If they can't solve it, we'll go the center [in Beijing]. If they can't solve it, we'll go overseas!"[56]

The All-China Federation of Trade Unions responded to the strike wave by dispatching Wang Rong, the director of the national union's

52. SMA, B54-1-4.
53. Ibid; Perry, "Shanghai's Strike Wave," 11.
54. SMA, B54-1-2.
55. SMA, B54-1-5b.
56. SMA, B54-1-2.

Wage Bureau, and Li Xian, the director of the national Labor Insurance Bureau, to Shanghai. Following Lai Ruoyu's lead, they recommended a compromise to resolve the strike wave: responding to some of the strikers' economic and political demands in concrete ways but at the same time holding the line on policy in order to move gradually toward standardization of wages and welfare benefits. For example, Li Xian argued for extending labor insurance to all branches of newly merged enterprises as long as the total number of employees in the merged enterprise surpassed the hundred-person limit for the program. But he continued to recommend that smaller enterprises be limited to labor insurance contracts with lower benefits until social insurance could be implemented.[57]

Workers' political demands were more controversial. The calls for deposing the Communist Party were reported to Public Security, but both Lai Ruoyu and Wang Rong embraced many of the workers' demands for greater political participation in the union, even if greater union autonomy from party control was required to make that participation meaningful.[58] Lai's endorsement showed that his evolution from an outsider sent in by the party to rein in the union was complete: by 1957, he had become an insider championing the interests of the workers he represented.

But at the same time that union leaders were trying to regain some measure of leadership over the fast-moving strike wave, Shanghai Mayor Ke Qingshi took a different tack to resolve the crisis, establishing the innocuously named "Shanghai Municipal Temporary Work Committee" on May 23, 1957.[59] The new party committee was more daring in its response to the workers' economic demands than the national labor union leaders. Declaring that most of the economic demands were reasonable, the temporary committee blamed the messy socialization process for causing the strike wave, especially the push for standardizing wages and benefits.[60] The committee called for union cadres to lead the push for better wages and benefits but through offi-

57. SMA, C1-2-2382.
58. Harper, "Party and Unions," 105–6.
59. SMA, B54-1-1.
60. SMA, B54-1-6.

cial channels, such as petitions and negotiations, rather than through "extreme" behavior such as strikes.[61]

It is not clear that either Lai Ruoyu or Ke Qingshi had much influence over the union cadres they were trying to direct. Many union cadres across the city were demoralized by the strike wave and were trying to quit their posts rather than insert themselves more directly into the conflict.[62] The central CCP's decision to call an abrupt end to the rectification campaign on June 7 was a more important factor in taming the strike wave. The violent repression of student demonstrations in Wuhan on June 12–13 gave notice to protesters around the country that the rules had changed.[63] Calls for political reform would no longer be tolerated, and strikes and street protests were now risky tactics.

Despite the danger, the unemployed in Shanghai continued their demonstrations. On June 12, more than eighty unemployed protesters marched on the district government offices in Luwan and Zhabei, storming buildings, threatening cadres, and locking them in their offices. Soon afterward, seventy to eighty unemployed returnees started protesting at the Shanghai Bureau of Civil Affairs every day, overturning furniture and shouting slogans such as "We are Chinese, we demand food!"[64] Even people who had escaped from labor reform camps joined the demonstrations at the bureau of civil affairs. Although the police were called in to break up the sit-ins, cadres from the civil affairs bureau complained that their efforts were totally ineffective. When the protesters were put in detention, they used it as an opportunity to rest up and eat. As soon as they recovered, they escaped and went straight back to protesting.[65]

Workers were more responsive to the sudden change in the political climate. Ke Qingshi's strategy of responding to workers' economic but not political demands seems to have been followed. The strike wave began to ebb in mid-June without any serious political reforms to

61. SMA, B54-1-6.
62. Ibid; SMA B54-1-2.
63. MacFarquhar, *Origins of the Cultural Revolution*, vol. 1, 223–24; Teiwes, *Politics and Purges*, 232–33.
64. SMA, B54-1-2.
65. Ibid.

*Table 5.3.* Shanghai Labor Insurance and Contract Coverage, 1955–57

| Year | Labor insurance | Increase | Labor insurance contracts | Increase |
|------|-----------------|----------|---------------------------|----------|
| 1955 | 433,464 | 1% | 109,094 | 25% |
| 1956 | 560,680 | 29% | 369,094 | 238% |
| 1957 | 905,000 | 61% | 475,026 | 29% |

*Sources:* SMA, C1-2-2380; SMA, B31-1-59; SMA, C1-2-1764; SMA, C1-2-1768; SMA, C1-2-2384.

increase worker participation in either the union or enterprise management. But economic demands met with more success. With union cadres under pressure and having the power to make decisions on eligibility for labor insurance, labor insurance coverage surged, expanding 61 percent in 1957 (table 5.3). Since the Shanghai union's budget for labor insurance had been based on an estimated 4 percent increase in the number of workers covered, the small budget deficits from 1956 quickly escalated into a much bigger problem.[66] Labor insurance contracts also grew by 29 percent in 1957, consolidating and building on the surge in coverage that the program enjoyed in 1956. The labor unrest of 1956–57 may have been an ephemeral response to a brief moment of political liberalization, but it had a lasting impact on the Chinese welfare state.

The Shanghai Temporary Committee portrayed its few accommodations to demands for urban household registrations as concessions. For example, unemployed workers who were deemed too old or too sick to work were allowed to stay in Shanghai, as were people whose spouses had permanent jobs there.[67] But these exceptions to the ruralization policy are more properly viewed as corrections of overzealous recruitment during the campaign than as a significant policy change. The great majority of the protesters faced the choice of either returning to their land or their jobs in the interior, or hiding in Shanghai with friends or relatives without any regular income or rations of their own. In contrast to workers, the unemployed did not enjoy any long-term gains from their protests in 1957. Weak as the union was at this point—hated by many workers—and viewed as irrelevant by many party officials and enterprise managers—it played an important role

66. SMA, C1-2-2384.
67. SMA, B54-1-2.

in expanding labor insurance. The contrasting experiences of workers and the unemployed in resisting a new policy of economic constraint in 1955–57 showed that even having a weak union on your side was a significant advantage over those with no union at all.

The sudden, unexpected expansion of labor insurance coverage, however, may have come at the cost of more fundamental reform. At some point in the chaos of the Hundred Flowers mass rectification campaign and the crackdown that followed, the draft social insurance regulations were quietly withdrawn, and the policy process was suspended. The disappearance of social insurance from the political agenda in 1957 was not publicized. As late as March 1957, the Shanghai labor union was still ranking the implementation of social insurance as its top priority in its 1957 work plans.[68] In May, the director of the national Labor Insurance Division discussed social insurance as if it would be implemented soon. But when Premier Zhou Enlai reported on wage and welfare policy to the CCP Central Committee in September 1957, it became clear that a policy reversal had been made.[69]

In his speech, Zhou made no reference to social insurance (at least in the published versions of the report). Instead, he announced a different strategy for expanding China's welfare state than the one the CCP had been pursuing over the last three years. He declared that welfare policy for workers should be set in reference to the living standards of all Chinese people, including the peasant majority. Zhou also asserted that the first priority in welfare policy was to ensure that everyone, peasants and workers alike, had enough to eat. The logical outcome of the new commitment to equality and basic needs was a new welfare program for peasants rather than further increasing the gap between urban and rural living standards with social insurance. The only comment Zhou made in reference to labor insurance was to order the State Council to study how to incorporate party and government employees into the labor insurance program and eliminate their special free supply system, the one surviving reform from the draft 1956 social insurance regulations.[70] Less than two years after his self-criticism for failing to support

68. SMA, C1-2-2384.
69. Zhonggong zhongyang wenxian yanjiu shi, *Zhou Enlai,* 375.
70. Ibid.

Mao's acceleration of the economic reforms, Zhou Enlai and the proponents for greater balance and restraint in economic policy seemed to be dominant again.

Given the limited sources available on social insurance, we do not know why the policy was quietly dropped in 1957. One reason may have been economic, since the cost of social insurance would have been considerable. For example, in a city like Shanghai social insurance could have doubled the size of the labor insurance program at a point when its funds were already in deficit. Expansion on that scale would have had a major impact on the entire Second Five-Year Plan. More fundamentally, the long-promised prosperity that structural economic reform was supposed to unleash was still nowhere on the horizon. The labor shortages of the First Five-Year Plan were not simply delayed. They were a mirage.

Another reason may have been political. The Shanghai union's labor insurance division worried in 1957 that workers would continue to be dissatisfied even after the implementation of social insurance if expansion meant losing their special benefits.[71] Small sacrifices that paled in comparison to the demands placed on the unemployed were rejected by Shanghai's workers during the 1957 strike wave.

## The Anti-Rightist Campaign

The Anti-Rightist campaign of 1957–58 brought an end to the 1957 strike wave and permanently weakened the official labor union within the Communist regime. Ironically, the political mistake in launching a Hundred Flowers mass rectification campaign only ended up reinforcing Mao's power and helped to shape a new consensus behind his political and economic policies. In the summer of 1957, when Mao Zedong pulled back from the mass rectification campaign that he had energetically promoted since his "Let a Hundred Flowers Bloom" speech, he did so with the face-saving claim that his real intent had always

71. SMA, C1-2-2382.

been to lay a trap for the hidden enemies of the Chinese Communist regime. Under this guise, the CCP transformed the "Hundred Flowers" campaign into the Anti-Rightist campaign.[72] Rather than seek to reform the behavior of party cadres and government officials by soliciting feedback from people outside the party, the new phase of the mass rectification campaign sought to turn the tables in order to identify, purge, and punish critics of the Chinese Communist regime. "Rightists" were now considered to be class enemies on the basis of their political attitudes and actions, regardless of their actual class backgrounds.

The best-known targets of the new rectification campaign were capitalists, intellectuals, and government officials who had criticized the regime during the Hundred Flowers movement.[73] Once the rectification movement turned on them in the summer of 1957, these critics were in turn criticized by their colleagues in struggle meetings convened in their mass organizations and workplaces. But the campaign went much further than these well-known targets. We have only limited data on the scope of the movement, but what little data are available suggest that the Anti-Rightist campaign was the largest urban struggle campaign of the 1950s. The quotas for campaign targets ranged from 5 to 7 percent of the total membership of each work unit and mass association.[74] Another indication of the scale of the Anti-Rightist campaign in Shanghai comes from a district-level report that shows that nearly one-quarter of Shanghai's residents were targeted for investigation in the course of the movement.[75] Those unlucky enough to be labeled "Rightists" suffered punishments ranging from prison, to exile to the countryside, to loss of jobs and party membership, or demotion to lower-ranking positions.

As suggested by the scale of the campaign, it also affected the core social classes cultivated by the Communist regime. The labor union was one of the most prominent targets. The first step in the labor union campaign was a series of meetings at every level of the union hierarchy to announce a major policy reversal toward the strike wave, which was still simmering in the summer of 1957. Although the strikers were

72. MacFarquhar, *Origins of the Cultural Revolution*, vol. 1, 279–80.
73. Teiwes, *Politics and Purges*, 276.
74. White, *Policies of Chaos*, 143.
75. SMA, A20-1-81.

judged as being "essentially correct," the central party advanced a new explanation for the source of the problems in the 1956–57 strike wave. Rather than continue to blame the unrest on the messy socialization process, as both Lai Ruoyu and Ke Qingshi had done, the new diagnosis advanced during the Anti-Rightist campaign was that the union itself was the cause of the strikes. According to the new interpretation, the union's "subjective" and "bureaucratic" approach to labor unrest had fostered an attitude among workers that the state was responsible for meeting all of their needs. Strike demands that had been deemed reasonable as recently as May 1957 were recast as "irrational" before the year was out.[76] Both Ke Qingshi's and Lai Ruoyu's responses to the strike wave were now invalidated, but Lai and the union bore the blame for instigating the problem.

The revisionist view of the strike wave was extended back to the 1949 revolution, in response to the reemergence of Li Lisan's purge as an issue in the strike wave. Because union cadres and workers alike had complained about Li's dismissal six years earlier and demanded his return, the newly chastened national union leadership issued a report for the Anti-Rightist campaign that reviewed Li Lisan's mistakes in the founding of the Communist labor union. The report went to great length to detail and explain the reasons for Li Lisan's purge, emphasizing Li's emphasis on redistribution rather than production as one of his most serious errors. Although the labor insurance program itself was not described as a mistake, the report did criticize Li Lisan for prioritizing labor insurance over more fundamental tasks.[77]

The new diagnosis of the strike wave and the revival of the campaign against Li Lisan set the stage for yet another purge of the union's leadership. At the national level, Chairman Lai Ruoyu was heavily criticized during the Anti-Rightist campaign. Before he was punished, however, he died of cancer in May 1958. Wang Rong, director of the national union's Wage Department and the cadre who went to Shanghai to lead the union's response to the strike wave, was one of the most prominent victims of the campaign.[78]

76. SMA, C1-2-2391.
77. SMA, C1-2-2255.
78. Harper, "Party and Unions," 112–13.

To replace Lai, the CCP turned to Liu Ningyi, who was appointed chairman of the All-China Federation of Trade Unions in August 1958. Unlike Lai Ruoyu, Liu Ningyi came into the position with considerable experience in labor union politics. Liu had been chairman of the wartime base area union federation in the 1940s and had attended the founding of the World Federation of Trade Unions with Zhu Xuefan in 1945 (see chapter 1). Since 1949, Liu Ningyi had served as deputy chairman of the All-China Federation of Trade Unions and continued to focus on the federation's international work.[79] His promotion could not have come at a more difficult time.

Soon after the leadership changes at the top, the purge extended far down the union hierarchy, quickly becoming the biggest purge in the history of the Communist labor movement. In Shanghai, the union struggle campaign began in July 1957, when cadres began posting big-character posters criticizing union leaders at the Shanghai Federation of Trade Unions headquarters, a tactic that quickly spread to the city's industrial unions as well. Hundreds and in some places thousands of posters sparked several rounds of struggle meetings in which Rightists were publicly identified and criticized.[80] For many district and enterprise unions, the struggle phase of the campaign began in September 1957, and stretched well into 1958.

By the end of the campaign in the municipal headquarters, 245 union cadres were punished, including 69 who received criminal sentences and another 176 who suffered various forms of administrative punishment, such as labor reform, forced retirement, or being sent to the countryside.[81] An additional 226 were demoted and transferred out of Shanghai, which meant that 35 percent of the Shanghai Federation of Trade Unions' cadres had been punished over the course of the campaign.[82] Although Shanghai union chairman Zhong Min survived

79. Li Jiaqi, *Shanghai gongyun*, 816–17.
80. SMA, C1-2-5334.
81. SMA, C1-2-210.
82. Mark Frazier describes the Anti-Rightist campaign at the enterprise level as being relatively small, affecting only a minority of the workforce. Since his statistics include all employees and do not distinguish union cadres, union cadres were presumably an even smaller minority of the people punished. See Frazier, *Making of the Chinese Industrial Workplace*, 200.

and continued to lead the union, much of the rest of the municipal union's leadership was purged. For example, Guan Ruicai, the director of the municipal union's labor insurance bureau, was demoted and transferred to Jiangxi province.[83]

Liu Ningyi's main responsibility after taking over the leadership of the national union in 1958 was to carry out the third phase of the Anti-Rightist campaign: the complete reorganization of the national union under orders from the CCP Central Committee.[84] The orders required every level of the union organization to submit to the unqualified authority of the party committee at the same level, breaking up the complicated dual system of horizontal party and vertical union supervision that had been established by Lai Ruoyu's reforms. For Liu Ningyi, the reorganization must have been a strange coda to his long career in labor politics. In the 1940s, Liu's "democratic" base area unions, which were at least formally free from party control, had been so inspirational that they helped to convince Chinese Association of Labor chairman Zhu Xuefan to defect from the KMT. Now Liu was in charge of implementing the same kind of institutional controls over the union that the KMT had pioneered in the 1930s and 1940s.

The party's renewed assertion of direct control set the stage for the decentralization of the union down to the enterprise in 1958. Every level of the union organization, from the national headquarters down to the industrial, provincial, and municipal unions, was cut to the bare bones, transferring most of their remaining programs and responsibilities either laterally to the Labor Ministry or downward to the enterprise level of the union. The Shanghai Federation of Trade Unions lost 92 percent of its staff in the reorganization, leaving only ninety-three cadres and twenty workers to operate the union's municipal headquarters, the Workers Cultural Palace, the Sailors Club, and the Shanghai Sanatorium.[85] From that point forward, only enterprise unions were fully staffed to provide programs and services in the workplace. To all intents and purposes, the union was now a subsidiary of the party committee in each state-owned enterprise, with almost no reach beyond

83. SMA, C1-2-210.
84. Ibid; Lu Xiangxian and Liu Song, *Zhu Xuefan*, 203.
85. SMA, C1-2-210.

the confines of the factory floor. With this last remaining toehold in the workplace, labor was almost, but not completely, excluded from the Chinese Communist regime. Bottom-up pressure for welfare expansion may have continued to be strong, but policy makers in Beijing no longer felt it.

## Evaluating the Chinese Approach to Welfare State Expansion

Despite the effort to eliminate transitional welfare programs and temporarily constrain labor insurance in 1955–56, the welfare state expanded rapidly by 1957. The 1955 cuts in investment had a direct but temporary impact. Since employment in Shanghai declined 2 percent from 1954 levels, labor insurance saw its smallest increase in coverage in the short history of the program: just a 1 percent gain (table 5.3). As called for in the new economic development strategy of short-term restraint, most of the growth in 1955 came in cheaper labor insurance contracts, whose coverage increased 25 percent.

After the socialization of industry and the new investment drive in 1956, growth in the contract program surged. Coverage under labor insurance contracts more than tripled in a single year. There was also a sudden 29 percent increase in labor insurance coverage in 1956 for the same reasons. The rapid pace of socialization and the sudden expansion of the labor insurance and labor insurance contract programs in 1956 caught the Shanghai labor union unprepared. Based on predictions of declining employment, the Shanghai union's labor insurance department had budgeted for a program with just over 590 enterprises and 350,000 workers in 1956, a decline of nearly 20 percent from 1955 levels.[86] Instead of declining, employment surged 27 percent in 1956 with the new industrialization drive, and socialization brought an additional 378 employers into the program. As a result, Shanghai's labor insurance coverage increased 29 percent in 1956. For the first time in its short

86. SMA, C1-2-2384.

*Table 5.4.* Shanghai Welfare Coverage, 1955–57

| Year | Total beneficiaries | Percent change | Workforce coverage | Population coverage |
|------|--------------------|----------------|--------------------|---------------------|
| 1955 | 542,558 | -34% | 17% | 9% |
| 1956 | 930,276 | 71% | 26% | 15% |
| 1957 | 1,380,026 | 48% | 38% | 20% |

Sources: SMA, B127-1-53; SMA, C1-2-2380; SMA, B31-1-59; SMA, C1-2-1764; SMA, C1-2-1768; SMA, C2-1-2384; SMA, C1-2-2384; Shanghaishi tongji ju, *Shanghai shi guomin jingji.*

history, the Shanghai program ran a deficit of nearly one million yuan in 1956, forcing the union to dip into its labor insurance reserves to keep the program going.[87]

But the increases in 1956 paled in comparison to the gains in 1957, when labor insurance coverage surged 61 percent in the wake of the strike wave, the largest single-year gain in the program's history. Although growth in the labor insurance contract program slowed, The total reach of Shanghai's welfare state increased 73 percent in the final years of the First Five-Year Plan, In terms of total numbers, the expansion in beneficiaries in 1955–57 was 42 percent larger than the expansion in coverage that the CCP intentionally engineered in 1952–54, even after the elimination of most unemployment relief programs is taken into account.

Why did the welfare state expand so much? Welfare politics changed significantly in the mid-1950s. There was no top-down pressure for expansion outside of the push to develop the new social insurance policy. Moreover, the unemployed were demobilized, and significant numbers of them were physically removed from the city. Workers in particular were very eager for redistribution, but they were disappointed that they did not benefit materially from the urban revolution. In the newly egalitarian society created in 1956, both capitalists and the urban poor sought the welfare protections that workers enjoyed, but no cross-class alliances could be formed.

In this new context, the CCP's strategy of deliberately triaging welfare and jobs backfired. It was welfare state insiders who became the new obstacle. Their efforts to preserve their own privileges made it

87. SMA, C1-2-2382.

clear that there was a political cost to any kind of reform that standard-ized benefits. Since Chinese workers had the leverage to try to protect their interests through the union and in the workplace, they were able to seize the political opportunity that the mass rectification campaign provided them to voice their opposition. Workers' preferential incor-poration into the Chinese Communist regime in the labor union gave them the power to try to protect their narrow interests at the expense of the broader interests of welfare state outsiders.

In contrast, unemployed workers were less successful with their collective protests. Facing much weaker resistance from the unem-ployed after they had been demobilized and effectively cut off from the labor union, the Shanghai government was initially able to meet its ambitious campaign target of moving more than half a million people out of the city without facing the kind of collective protest that slow job placement had engendered a year or two beforehand. Still, unem-ployed workers with urban household registrations were able to resist ruralization much more effectively than rural migrants. While more than 33,000 unemployed workers with Shanghai household registra-tions moved into the interior to farm and do construction work, the majority of the urban unemployed stayed on and many continued to collect social relief.

Although the ruralization campaign and the new household regis-tration and rationing regulations did succeed in reducing Shanghai's urban population 8 percent in 1955, rural-urban migration quickly resumed in 1956 at a faster pace than before the new policy was put in place. The prospect of a job and the amenities of urban life were too promising for household registration and ration coupons to deter people from migration. By 1957, Shanghai's urban population rebounded to more than 6 million residents, and its total population neared 7 million.[88] The outcome of the 1955 ruralization campaign showed that physically moving people out of the city and denying them legal resi-dence was not enough to keep them in the countryside.

The quiet refusal to leave Shanghai or the quiet return to the city proved to be a more effective form of resistance than noisy demon-strations in front of the Shanghai Labor Bureau. After losing their

88. Shanghaishi tongji ju, *Shanghai shi guomin jingji*, 38

connection to the official labor union, the unemployed could not push policy makers to change their policies, but they could undermine their ability to implement them when tens of thousands and then hundreds of thousands of people simply refused to comply.

Chinese welfare reformers made the bold gambit in 1955 of making the rationing of welfare explicit, arguing the logic of short-term sacrifice for long-term gain. Whatever people thought of the logic, they were not willing to make the sacrifice. Individual resistance from the unemployed and collective resistance by workers prevented budget cuts and promoted expansion of the welfare state in ways policy makers had never intended. The rationing mechanisms of household registration and ruralization campaigns were insufficient in the face of bottom-up pressure for welfare state expansion. Neither the budget savings nor the long-promised labor shortages materialized, leading to the indefinite postponement of social insurance. The one continuity in welfare politics in the 1950s was that China suffered from too much enthusiasm for the welfare state rather than opposition to it.

# CHAPTER 6

# *Mao's Communes: Universal Welfare in the Great Leap Forward, 1958–62*

The goal of a broad welfare state remained distant in 1958, a year after Chinese welfare reformers had hoped to achieve one. The failure of two ambitious rounds of welfare reform left the problems of China's narrow welfare state essentially unchanged. Moreover, the indefinite postponement of social insurance made it clear that a Soviet-style welfare state was not going to be a solution to broadening welfare coverage in China any time soon. At the same time, the strikes and street protests in the spring of 1957 showed that Chinese were in no mood to wait. Workers wanted labor insurance and other benefits that they had come to regard as their due. The unemployed had more urgent demands: they wanted the jobs and welfare protections they had been promised in the new socialist command economy.

In Eastern Europe, the Soviet Union was responding to similar popular pressure to improve living standards with new subsidies to the region to finance wage hikes and better welfare benefits.[1] China faced a much bigger problem in trying to expand its narrow welfare state and without the prospect of outside help. Indeed, by 1958 outside influence on Chinese policy makers was declining quickly. As the relationship

---

1. Bunce, "Empire Strikes Back," 10–12.

between the Soviet Union and China deteriorated, Chinese policy makers increasingly looked inward for new ideas.

To achieve the goal of a broad welfare state, Chinese welfare reformers pioneered a new approach to extending coverage: commune welfare programs to meet the basic needs of all citizens. With a program design that placed a higher priority on coverage than benefits, commune welfare programs promised to make the expansion of coverage economically and administratively easier than for labor insurance. In addition, the new reforms placed the highest priority on covering the rural majority, seeking to close the urban/rural gap that the Chinese welfare state had deepened.

Although the politics behind these policies are harder to discern than for earlier periods, it is clear that political conditions were changing rapidly in the late 1950s. Top-down pressure for welfare reform did not ebb with the decline in Soviet influence on China. Commitment to the highest international standards remained strong in Beijing, and the radical Great Leap Forward development strategy provided a powerful new impetus for welfare reform. In Shanghai, bottom-up demand for welfare also remained high, but workers and the urban poor faced different opportunities and constraints. Despite the dismantling of the union at the end of the Anti-Rightist campaign, enterprise unions still provided workers with a form of preferential access to power that no other social groups enjoyed. The new communes were intended to become the new grassroots political institutions of the regime, incorporating all members on an equal basis, including the urban poor. But the relationship between enterprise unions and communes remained hazy. Unemployed workers were no longer completely excluded from the regime, but they did not have the same leverage as workers, who were members of both unions and communes.

Since the Chinese welfare state seemed to expand under almost any political conditions, the real question by 1958 was whether a radical new program design could help regulate its expansion to ensure its sustainability. Although it is hard to know whether the new policies received a fair test in the chaotic conditions of the Great Leap Forward, the radical inequalities they spawned had tragic consequences for Chinese society.

## *The Great Leap Forward Development Strategy*

The factional struggle in the CCP over economic development policy remained unresolved after the failures of the 1956 investment drive and the 1957 political crisis. Under Zhou Enlai's leadership in the State Council, work proceeded on a relatively conservative Second Five-Year Plan, which was more moderate in its ambitions and more stringent in its budget controls than its predecessor had been.[2] In the meantime, Chairman Mao doubled down on his acceleration strategy, calling for an entirely new approach to economic development based on the party's wartime mobilization experience in the 1940s.

Mao's political acumen was more important in settling the debate over the two strategies than the strength of his economic arguments. By switching sides to transform the Hundred Flowers campaign into the Anti-Rightist movement, Mao gained the backing of his critics in the party leadership and still maintained the obedience of his longtime supporters. With this new political consensus undergirded by fear of being labeled a Rightist, Mao was quickly able to forge a consensus on economic policy as well. At the second session of the Eighth CCP Congress in May 1958, Zhou Enlai and at least five other top economic officials carried out self-criticism, recanting their earlier opposition to big-push investment drives and other radical economic policies.[3] After their concessions, Mao had the power to override much of the policy-making process that had been carefully built up over the last decade. Economic policy was taken out of the hands of the economic planners, who were discredited by the failure of the Soviet model. In their place, Mao's personal decisions and ad hoc party conferences that gave a more prominent role to provincial and municipal officials formed the center of a new policy-making process.

Although the idea of an investment drive was not new, the scale of Great Leap Forward investment was unprecedented. Under Mao's pressure, capital investment accelerated more than 50 percent from

2. Teiwes and Sun, *China's Road*, 33–35.
3. Yang, *Calamity and Reform*, 34; MacFarquhar, *Origins of the Cultural Revolution*, vol. 2, 57.

1957 to 1958 and then another 35 percent in 1959.[4] The other elements of the new Great Leap Forward strategy were more fundamental departures from Soviet precedents. The first innovation was the new focus on agricultural production, which was considered to be the most significant constraint on the Chinese economy.[5] Rather than spend scarce capital on providing electricity, tractors, and fertilizer to farmers, the CCP sought to boost agricultural production by reorganizing collectives into much larger communes averaging nearly five thousand families each.[6] The communes mobilized labor for irrigation, flood control, and other infrastructure projects as a way to increase grain production on the cheap.

The second major departure from Soviet economic orthodoxy was decentralization of the economic planning system. Instead of trying to balance resources across different regions and different sectors of the economy to create a highly specialized and centralized national economy, the new decentralized approach to planning fostered more self-reliance within provinces and regions. The CCP Secretariat replaced the State Economic Planning Commission as the linchpin of the new system, making the party rather than the government the mechanism for integrating the command economy. Provincial party committees were authorized to retain more of their local profits and tax revenues and spend them according to their own perceptions of local needs.[7] In addition to abandoning the effort to balance resources across regions, Chinese policy makers also abandoned the effort to balance resources across industries. Most of the new investment was poured into the steel and iron industries, considered at the time to be the most significant bottleneck holding back industrialization. Although the backyard furnaces were the most visible aspect of the drive to increase steel and iron production, it was actually large-scale state-owned enterprises that garnered most of the new investment.[8]

4. Naughton, *Chinese Economy*, 63.
5. Riskin, *China's Political Economy*, 114–15.
6. MacFarquhar, *Origins of the Cultural Revolution*, vol. 2, 86; Yang, *Calamity and Reform*, 36.
7. MacFarquhar, *Origins of the Cultural Revolution*, vol. 2, 59–60; Teiwes and Sun, *China's Road*, 58–59.
8. Howe, "Industrialization," 175–76.

The Great Leap Forward development strategy was clear about its goals but flexible and often vague about the means of achieving those ends. For example, the goal of matching British steel production was precise and measurable. But rather than rely on the comprehensive plans and detailed regulations of a Soviet-style command economy, the new Maoist approach favored inspiring bottom-up enthusiasm for hard work and austere living conditions. Planning targets became aspirational goals rather than tools for economic coordination, and political slogans such as "more, better, faster, cheaper" replaced regulations to communicate the new policies to the grass roots.

The Great Leap Forward was the most expansive development strategy the Chinese Communist regime ever tried. The idea that breaking through the constraints on grain and steel production would quickly lead to broad-based, self-sustained industrialization fostered a new perspective among Chinese policy makers on the welfare state. Rather than viewing welfare spending as a form of consumption, they began to view it as a form of investment that would help unleash the productivity of China's workforce.

## Commune Welfare Policy

China's ambitious Great Leap Forward welfare policies also marked a complete departure from the Soviet model. The new goal was not welfare for industrial workers or the urban population but universal welfare programs that reached every citizen, urban and rural alike. In this new Maoist vision, communes would provide simpler and more egalitarian forms of welfare protection focused on basic needs rather than income protection. Another key difference in the new programs was that communes were intended to be decentralized and flexible rather than standardized and bureaucratic. Local officials could decide which services and benefits to offer in their communes in response to their citizens' needs and desires rather than follow the dictates of central planners in Beijing.

The new commune welfare policies emerged in the spring and summer of 1958 in a loose policy-making process that involved more propaganda than planning. One source of inspiration for the new commune policy came from several local experiments in mobilizing labor for water conservancy projects in Hubei, Henan and Anhui.[9] Another source of ideas was the party's wartime experience of developing rural base areas. Innovations from the 1940s that proved influential in 1958 included mobilizing labor for economic development, a flexible and decentralized approach to governance, and the free supply system of providing in-kind benefits to party members.[10]

Little is known about welfare policy-making in this period beyond the broad contours of the economic policy debates. The All-China Federation of Trade Unions was not involved, nor was the Ministry of Civil Affairs. Mao's personal intervention was decisive, and even his casual comments could take on the authority of law. His supporters were able to catch his attention on his investigation tours and at roving policy conferences, where people from the propaganda department had as much likelihood of being heard on economic policy as anyone with experience in planning or production. Policy debates, let alone opposition to ideas that had already been endorsed by Mao, were limited in the wake of the Anti-Rightist campaign.

The kinds of welfare programs that Mao and other central party leaders promoted for the new communes included canteens, day care centers, homes for the elderly, and basic health care.[11] Commune canteens were seen as an effective way to meet people's most basic need for food, ensuring that everyone would have enough to eat. Day care centers for children and residential homes for the elderly were portrayed as collective institutions to care for the most vulnerable members of society. Finally, health clinics to provide basic care and health education were portrayed as a way to stretch the limited resources and expertise of China's existing health care system. Once basic needs were met, theoretically the elderly and disabled would not need pensions or an elaborate bureaucracy to distribute them.[12]

---

9. MacFarquhar, *Origins of the Cultural Revolution*, vol. 2, 77; Luo Pinghan, *Da guo fan*, 1–6.
10. Chang, *Power and Policy*, 99–100.
11. Zeng Xueji and Guo Yifan, *Renmin gongshe*, 3–4; Su Wei, *Renmin gongshe*, 7.
12. Su Wei, *Renmin gongshe*, 26.

Another key difference from Soviet policies was that the fundamental purpose of commune welfare programs was egalitarian. Instead of establishing comprehensive benefits from the beginning and then gradually expanding coverage to more of the population, communes were designed to start offering the most basic services to everyone and then gradually expand those services until they met people's full needs.[13] In this regard, commune welfare followed the same principle of program design as citizen pensions. But in contrast to citizen pension programs, no entitlements to welfare benefits were created; instead each commune was supposed to tailor its benefits to local needs and resources.

Although the communes were a dramatic policy innovation, the new initiative was not seen as replacing China's existing welfare state—at least not in the short term. Unlike the elimination of unemployment relief in 1955, the new Maoist approach to welfare reform did not sacrifice preexisting programs in order to find the resources for new commune welfare programs. Instead, labor insurance and social relief were allowed to continue, and the commune welfare programs were added on top of the existing welfare state. The new approach was premised on the idea that commune welfare programs were an investment in the mobilization of labor rather than a new form of consumption. For example, day care centers freed up housewives to enter the labor force, and canteens freed up everyone from the daily chores of shopping, cooking, and cleaning. Propagandists tried to quantify the amount of labor liberated by the commune canteens, asserting that they saved each commune member three hours of housework per day, savings that they estimated would increase the nation's entire labor force by the equivalent of one-third.[14] Expanding production, rather than budget cuts, would finance China's welfare reforms.

In the new Maoist vision of welfare state development, the old welfare state would gradually shrink in size and importance in the long run, as the new commune programs improved their benefits and services. Eventually, the old welfare state would be eliminated—not because it was too expensive but because it would no longer be

13. Zeng Xueji and Guo Yifan, *Renmin gongshe*, 3–4; Su Wei, *Renmin gongshe*, 7–8.
14. Su Wei, *Renmin gongshe*, 4.

needed in a new communal welfare society where everyone's needs were met.[15]

CCP leaders promoted the new welfare policies in the spring and summer of 1958 in speeches, articles, and highly publicized tours of local development and welfare projects. This propaganda push culminated in a new policy issued at the CCP's Beidaihe Conference in August 1958 that officially endorsed the commune as the basic unit of local government and economic planning.[16] Since the resolution on communes was vague about welfare, most of the new Great Leap Forward welfare policies were introduced informally through news articles, model commune charters, and pamphlets rather than the national regulations that mandated previous welfare programs.

The ephemeral nature of these tools of communication and the unclear authority they conveyed did not inhibit policy makers' ambitions. In speeches and essays, Mao and other top CCP leaders envisioned the new communes as the building blocks of the new political regime and socialist society that they wanted to create. Their goal was to integrate political administration, economic management, and military defense into a single unit at the local level. In addition to becoming the basic unit of the state and the economy, the communes were also designed to displace the family as the key institution of local society.[17] In this conception, welfare programs were not the product of the political regime; they were an integral part of it. For example, canteens were seen as central institutions in the new commune regime: welfare providers that fulfilled the most basic human needs, political arenas where organizational meetings and ideological training could be conducted, and social institutions that could build community and broaden people's relationships beyond the scope of the family.[18] Similarly, day care served a welfare function in caring for young children, an important economic function in freeing up women to enter the work-

15. Zeng Xueji and Guo Yifan, *Renmin gongshe*, 2–3; Su Wei, *Renmin gongshe*, 7; SMA, C1-2-3118a.
16. Chan, *Mao's Crusade*, 79–81; MacFarquhar, *Origins of the Cultural Revolution*, vol. 2, 85–87; Luo, *Da guo fan*, 19–20.
17. Zeng Xueji and Guo Yifan, *Renmin gongshe*, 1; Yang Jisheng, *Mubei*, vol. 2, 660; Luo Pinghan, *Da guo fan*, 24–25.
18. Su Wei, *Renmin gongshe*, 5.

force, as well as a political role in educating young children in socialist values. As a result, welfare work was viewed as inherently political in nature. Recruiting welfare workers was supposed to be first and foremost a political task, and the job qualifications promoted for commune welfare workers included class status, education, political reliability, and skills in organizing political meetings.[19] Experience in cooking, child care, or other aspects of the welfare service provided was secondary to political considerations.

Since with hindsight we know their disastrous outcome, it is hard to know whether to take Great Leap Forward welfare policies seriously, just as it is difficult to view the new economic policies as a viable development strategy. But if we try to view these welfare reforms in the context of China's economic and political problems in 1958, as a group they represent an innovative and ambitious new approach to welfare state expansion. What looked like caution in the withdrawal of the social insurance regulations in 1957 was actually a prelude to a much more radical effort to expand the Chinese welfare state.

## The Early Urban Communes in Shanghai

How did the new Great Leap Forward welfare policies play out on the ground? In the countryside, the policy-making and implementation processes were completely intertwined, with communes established before and during the August 1958 Beidaihe Conference that endorsed the new commune policies.[20] In most large cities, the communes were not implemented for two years, a reflection of both the higher priority placed on the countryside and the greater discretion provided to urban political leaders.

Shanghai mayor and party secretary Ke Qingshi's political position had improved considerably with the Great Leap Forward. Although his policy response to the 1957 strike wave had been repudiated in the

19. Gongqingtuan Liaoning sheng weiyuanhui bangongshi, *Zuo dang de hao zhushou*, 9–11.
20. Yang, *Calamity and Reform*, 36.

Anti-Rightist campaign, his call for responding to workers' economic rather than political demands fit with the new political climate. As an early supporter of Mao, Ke gained more prominence at the national level, including a promotion to the Politburo in 1958.[21] In addition, the new decentralization policies gave him more discretion at home. He used both sources of power to advance Shanghai's interests as well as his own career.

The new investment drive was the first Great Leap Forward policy implemented in the cities. It quickly transformed Shanghai's economy, allowing local party leaders to reverse many of the limits that the First Five-Year Plan had imposed on the city's growth. With control over local revenues, Ke Qingshi built up the city's state-owned enterprises in the steel and iron industries so that within a few short years the city's heavy industries grew large enough to overshadow the light consumer industries that had always been the mainstay of Shanghai's economy.[22] In addition, the municipal government loosened budget constraints on almost all state-owned enterprises in an effort to meet rapidly increasing production targets, leading to a broad-based surge in both production and employment.

Shanghai did not jump onto the commune bandwagon until October 1958, by which point 99 percent of the Chinese countryside had been reorganized into communes (or at least claimed to have done so). After the new commune policy was announced at Shanghai's Third People's Congress in October 1958, all of Shanghai's rural counties and some urban districts immediately began the process of organizing communes. But at that point, rumors spread that the communes were going to collectivize all property, including personal property. Bank runs and panic buying of food and other necessities started before the month was out, threatening to shut down Shanghai's economy.[23] Similar problems emerged in Beijing and a few other major cities.[24] To quell the crisis, Ke Qingshi postponed the implementation of the urban communes indefinitely, a decision endorsed by Mao and the rest of the

21. MacFarquhar, *Origins of the Cultural Revolution*, vol. 2, 62.
22. Howe, "Industrialization," 160, 173–77; Xiong Yuezhi et al., *Shanghai tongshi*, vol. 12, 90–92.
23. Xiong Yuezhi et al., *Shanghai tongshi*, vol. 11, 168; Li Duanxiang, *Chengshi*, 81.
24. Chan, *Mao's Crusade*, 88, 94–95.

top CCP leadership at the party's Zhengzhou Conference in November 1958. At this early point in the Great Leap Forward, popular resistance to the communes and their welfare programs prompted a quick response from CCP leaders.

As a result, Shanghai residents saw more continuity than change in welfare policy in the first few years of the Great Leap Forward. Two smaller social policy initiatives in education and health care were implemented in 1958. In response to the call for popular mobilization for development, local activists and district cadres began organizing new schools, since the public school system had not yet been able to meet the high demand for education.[25] The new grassroots schools (*minban xuexiao*) were small and informal, often housed in apartments, offices, police stations, warehouses, and temples. Many of the teachers were housewives and youths with limited education themselves—often just a junior high school education. As a result, the education provided in most grassroots schools was limited to basic literacy, mathematics, and political education, without the advanced classes, art, music, and physical education that the public schools offered. For adults, factories and industrial bureaus set up "Red and Expert" vocational schools to provide more specialized training in short-term training courses. The new schools were financed by student fees that were sometimes higher than the fees charged by public schools.

Mobilization for health care was more organized. The 1958 campaign to "Eliminate the Four Pests" led district governments across the city to set up Red Cross health stations (*hong shizi hui weisheng zhan*).[26] Staffed by health workers given short medical courses on first aid, hygiene, and the symptoms of common infectious diseases, the health stations were supplemented by larger numbers of Red Cross volunteers. Together they carried out public health education, setting up educational exhibits, lecturing over neighborhood public address systems, and organizing hygiene classes for children. The volunteers also carried out health surveillance, which entailed monitoring the cleanliness of their neighbors, as well as reporting suspected cases of infectious diseases such as cholera, measles, and hepatitis to local

25. SMA, B105-7-1180.
26. SMA, A31-2-70.

hospitals. But their most dramatic activity was to lead public health campaign drives. For example, one health station in Nanshi district was commended for mobilizing the residents of one of the district's worst slums for a major clean-up campaign, sweeping off roofs, disinfecting open sewers, and hauling out nearly 1,300 pounds of garbage.[27]

The only other welfare policies implemented in Shanghai during the first phase of the Great Leap Forward were new variations of the policies adopted in 1955: ruralizing the unemployed and constraining the growth of the labor insurance program. A massive new ruralization campaign was launched in 1958, with a campaign target of permanently moving 900,000 people out of Shanghai. Once again, the Shanghai Party Committee set the goal of limiting Shanghai's urban population to the size of Moscow, still considered an urban model at a time when so many other aspects of Soviet influence were being abandoned.[28] At the same time, the national household registration regulations were revised in an effort to close the last loophole in the comprehensive household registration system that was set up in 1955. The new 1958 regulation required any person who wanted to move to receive permission from government officials at both ends of the move, including the target destination.[29] The new process was intended to give urban officials the tools they needed to meet their population quotas.

The 1958 ruralization campaign targeted the unemployed and recent rural migrants, and also identified many new groups for evacuation. At the top of the list were Rightists and other groups that had been labeled politically suspect, including landlords, rich peasants, counterrevolutionaries, and other so-called bad elements. In addition, a vague and flexible category of the "dregs of the old society" (*qu shehui zhazi*) was targeted for evacuation, a group that included petty criminals, religious practitioners, and vagrants, among others.[30] Shanghai's district governments gave widely different estimates of the number of "dregs" living in their jurisdictions, ranging from 3,000 to 50,000

27. Ibid.
28. SMA, B168-1-885.
29. Cheng and Selden, "Origins and Social Consequences," 663.
30. SMA, A20-1-81.

people.[31] The campaign also targeted people who still earned their living through the market, such as small venders, itinerant peddlers, and domestic servants. A more surprising addition to the campaign's target list was social relief recipients, including even disabled recipients involved in various self-help production programs in the city.[32]

The ruralization campaign was the first step in preparation for organizing urban communes. District commune implementation plans aimed to sort out which residents should be included in the urban communes and which residents should be excluded.[33] For example, the district plans for setting up the urban communes describe the Anti-Rightist campaign as laying the foundation for the communes by separating out "impure" elements before collectivization.[34] The Shanghai Bureau of Civil Affairs carried out the Anti-Rightist campaign among the unemployed in 1958, identifying thirty-two criminals, forty counterrevolutionaries, and more than nine hundred "bad elements" who were singled out for criminal and civil punishments such as being sent to labor camps in the countryside.[35]

The Anti-Rightist campaign seems to have succeeded in preventing any large-scale protests against the ruralization campaign despite the kind of activism the unemployed displayed in 1957. After potential ringleaders who might orchestrate resistance to the campaign had been punished, the ruralization campaign was launched among the unemployed. But the lack of collective action in 1958–59 did not mean that there was no individual resistance, especially among the people with some measure of political and social legitimacy. Educated youth proved to be especially adept at avoiding their assigned fate. The city only managed to recruit one-fourth of the total quota of educated youth targeted for evacuation in 1958 and then abandoned the effort entirely in 1959.[36] Unemployed workers and recent rural migrants had more difficulty escaping ruralization, but they continued to turn

31. Ibid., See, for example: Jiangning qu, 2; Penglai qu, 2.
32. SMA, A20-1-81; SMA B168-1-538.
33. SMA, A20-1-81.
34. Ibid., See, for example: Yulin qu.
35. SMA, B168-1-538.
36. SMA, B168-1-885; B168-1-888.

around and go back to Shanghai in significant numbers. For example, a 1959 investigation of recent rural migrants in detention discovered almost 11,000 people who had been evacuated from the city at least once before.[37]

Over the course of the Great Leap Forward, the ruralization campaigns were gradually institutionalized as an ongoing and permanent program. The shelter system to detain people targeted for evacuation expanded significantly in 1959, when each district government established its own shelter to supplement the municipal shelter operated by the Bureau of Civil Affairs.[38] The lane and alley residents committees staffed the new shelter system, mobilizing housewives and social relief recipients to investigate detainees and take care of them until they were sent back. New bureaucratic procedures were established to review the household registration, employment status, and political history of every person detained for ruralization. In addition, civil affairs cadres from each of the surrounding provinces were sent to Shanghai to help carry out investigations of migrants and coordinate the evacuations. Finally, the transportation bureau set aside daily quotas of train and ship tickets to transport people out of Shanghai.[39] Mao's assault on government bureaucracy in the Great Leap Forward did not extend to the growing detention and removal system.

While the ruralization campaigns were expanding and becoming more institutionalized, labor insurance was essentially frozen in the early phase of the Great Leap Forward. As the new Great Leap Forward investment in heavy industry gathered pace, state-owned enterprises expanded through both mergers and new hires. Over the course of 1958, another 653 enterprises in Shanghai grew large enough to pass the hundred-employee threshold to qualify for labor insurance. Out of that group, 151 enterprises immediately applied to the Shanghai Federation of Trade Unions to implement labor insurance. Their enterprise party committees expressed strong support for the applications, arguing that mergers made administering different labor insurance contract

37. SMA, B168-1-892a.
38. SMA, B168-1-892b.
39. SMA, B168-1-905.

programs in one enterprise difficult.[40] Even if the labor union was only an enterprise-level organization at that point, it could still exert pressure on the party-state at the grass roots.

Above the grassroots level, however, workers had no leverage whatsoever. Even though the enterprises worked through the party hierarchy and even though each application clearly met the requirements of the labor insurance regulations, the reformed Shanghai Federation of Trade Unions now advocated freezing the labor insurance program by stopping the enrollment of new enterprises and employees. The Shanghai union made the argument that labor insurance did not fit the new approach to economic development in the Great Leap Forward.[41] But rather than follow either the provisions of the labor insurance regulations or the new commune policies in such an uncertain environment, the municipal union referred the applications to the government industrial bureaus that supervised each enterprise.

When those government agencies also failed to make a decision, the Shanghai union consulted with both the Labor Ministry and the national union headquarters in Beijing. The national union agreed with the policy of freezing enrollment in labor insurance but was just as reluctant to make any decision without explicit party backing.[42] As a result, the enterprise applications remained in limbo while the Great Leap Forward raced on. It was Ke Qingshi and the Shanghai Party Committee that finally made the decision in September 1959, ordering the implementation of labor insurance in all enterprises with more than one hundred employees as stipulated in the labor insurance regulations.[43]

The first phase of the Great Leap Forward in 1958–59 saw only partial implementation of the new commune welfare policies. Shanghai's rural areas saw the implementation of commune canteens and day care centers, but communes were not organized in most urban areas, nor were many new welfare programs put in place. Expansion of labor insurance to new enterprises was suspended owing to indecision more than anything else. It was the new 1958–59 ruralization campaign that

40. SMA, C1-2-3118b.
41. Ibid; SMA, C1-2-3118a.
42. SMA, C1-2-3397.
43. SMA, C1-2-3118c.

saw the most progress in the early phase of the Great Leap Forward, relocating 523,650 people out of Shanghai and into the interior.[44] Moreover, new regulations and a fledgling new bureaucracy were put in place to enforce population quotas. However, neither the new campaigns nor the new population control bureaucracy were effective at constraining Shanghai's population growth, which reached new heights in 1958–59. Despite the egalitarian thrust of the Great Leap Forward, both decentralization of investment and ruralization reinforced urban privilege.

## *The Lushan Plenum and Full Implementation of the Urban Communes*

Before the Great Leap Forward's first year was out, the new development strategy was already creating an economic crisis in the countryside. Grain production plummeted in 1959, while production targets and procurement quotas soared. Labor mobilization for infrastructure and industrial projects came at a cost to planting, reducing the acreage sown in 1959 rather than expanding it. In addition, work incentives in the enlarged communes disappeared, as the connection between labor and income grew more and more attenuated. In this context, the free supply system and the all-you-can-eat policies in many commune canteens led to the rapid erosion of grain reserves.[45] New policies to limit grain rations in the canteens came too late to preserve grain supplies in many places, and government grain procurement quotas based on bogus production figures remained unchanged. As a result, famine spread to ten provinces in the spring of 1959.[46]

Shanghai was not directly affected by the famine developing in the countryside. But as people fled from the famine regions in 1959, news of the terrible conditions in rural communes began to spread by word of mouth.[47] In April 1959, the Shanghai Party Committee convened

44. SMA, B168-1-888.
45. Yang, *Calamity and Reform*, 37.
46. Ibid, 46.
47. SMA, B168-1-892a.

an enlarged party meeting with the cadres who worked on population control to convince them that their sympathy with refugees' claims about the devastation in the countryside was misplaced.[48] The official explanation for the migrants' behavior was that they were not fleeing famine but were rather seeking to shirk the hard work the rural communes were mobilizing during traditional slack times. Rather than ease up on the ruralization program, as had been done in the past when natural disasters struck, the new policy was to continue to round up rural migrants and return them to the countryside. The propaganda campaign was also extended to the broader public in order to quell rumors about the economic crisis.[49]

The confrontation between Mao Zedong and Marshal Peng Dehuai at the Lushan Plenum in July 1959 ensured that there would be no effective government response to the growing crisis. A war hero and Minister of Defense, Peng Dehuai used his political capital to try to convince Mao to change direction. In a private letter to the chairman, Peng cited reports of famine coming from local officials and ordinary citizens to question the astronomical production statistics reported by the provinces.[50] Mao's response was to denounce Peng as a traitor and to purge him from the party and military leadership. In doing so, Mao decisively settled any inner-party debate over what was happening in the countryside in favor of the preposterous production figures reported by provincial officials. Whether out of faith in Mao's leadership or fear of being purged like Peng Dehuai, the rest of the top CCP leaders quickly rallied to Mao's side.

In the wake of the Lushan Plenum, every aspect of the Great Leap Forward intensified. The investment drive accelerated again. At the same time, grain procurement continued to the point of leaving little or nothing for peasants to eat or plant in many provinces, and little relief was provided to the famine regions.[51] In addition, the Anti-Rightist campaign was revived, leading to the punishment of 7.35 million more cadres, party members, and ordinary citizens as

48. SMA, B168-1-892b.
49. SMA, B168-1-892c.
50. MacFarquhar, *Origins of the Cultural Revolution*, vol. 2, 213–216.
51. Dali Yang, *Calamity and Reform*, 52–53.

Rightists in 1959–60.[52] Finally, commune policies were also revived. For example, rural communes that had closed their canteens were pressured into reopening them in late 1959. The decision to implement the urban communes in the spring of 1960 was part of the radical push to keep the Great Leap Forward going, even as its difficulties mounted.[53]

Although most Shanghai residents had little sense of the severity of the economic problems in the countryside, the revival of the Anti-Rightist campaign made it clear that criticism of party policy was dangerous. This time implementation of the urban communes in March 1960 was rapid and comprehensive, without any bank runs or other signs of resistance. Shanghai's urban districts were each divided into four to six communes, which organized all urban residents who did not already have jobs and who were therefore not members of a work unit. The districts had already identified their targets for organization into the new communes during the 1958 ruralization campaign: more than 640,000 adults in good political standing who did not have formal employment. According to their reports, the target population represented 67 percent of the total adult population in Shanghai who could work but did not have regular jobs.[54]

All commune welfare programs were implemented immediately, without the kind of effort to determine local needs, wants, or resources that the 1958 policies had envisioned. It is hard to know whether to trust the reports on commune welfare during the Great Leap Forward, given what we now know about pervasive lying in economic production statistics in this period. However, the fact that many sources document large and growing deficits incurred by commune welfare programs suggests that at least some of the data were not manufactured to please higher-ranking officials.

According to these reports, Shanghai's largest new welfare program was the commune canteens, which served 1.5 million people up to three

52. MacFarquhar, *Origins of the Cultural Revolution*, vol. 3, 179.

53. Yang, *Calamity and Reform*, 52–53; Li Duanxiang, *Chengshi*, 81

54. SMA, A20-1-23. Capitalists and certain groups of intellectuals were excluded from the communes along with the so-called dregs of society. See Yang Jisheng, *Mubei*, vol. 2, 653–54.

*Table 6.1.* Shanghai Commune Meals and Relief Handouts, 1958–63

| Year | Social relief handouts | Commune meals | Total | Percent change | Population coverage |
|---|---|---|---|---|---|
| 1958 | 501,296 | 0 | 501,296 | -54% | 7% |
| 1959 | 248,733 | 0 | 248,733 | -50% | 2% |
| 1960 | 172,009 | 13,200,042 | 13,372,051 | 5,235% | 127% |
| 1961 | 135,602 | 10,458,621 | 10,594,223 | -21% | 100% |
| 1962 | 211,131 | 2,500,894 | 2,712,025 | -74% | 26% |
| 1963 | 402,473 | 0 | 402,473 | -85% | 4% |

*Sources:* SMA, A20-1-23; SMA, A20-1-38; SMA, A20-1-77; SMA, B168-1-712; SMA, B168-1-716; SMA, B168-1-717; SMA, B168-1-726; SMA, B168-1-732.

meals a day by June 1960 (table 6.1).[55] Initially, there was an effort to integrate factory canteens with the neighboring community. For example, in April 1960 a state-owned machine factory in Luwan district merged its factory canteen with five small commune canteens in the surrounding neighborhoods to create a large integrated canteen on the factory grounds. The experiment did not last longer than a week, since long lines and the chaotic comings and goings of the neighborhood residents delayed the workers' meals and disrupted discipline within the plant. Moreover, elderly residents struggled to make it up the stairs to reach the second-floor factory canteen.[56]

After such early experiments, the separation of factory canteens and the development of small and medium neighborhood canteens quickly became the norm across the city, since the smaller canteens were better able to manage problems with lines, sufficient seats, and cooking equipment. Most canteens provided simple meals of rice and other grains with vegetables, with a few specialized canteens in the city for people with dietary restrictions, such as Muslims.[57] The canteens quickly reached their high point of service provision in the summer and early fall of 1960. Studies of the communal canteens carried out

55. SMA A20-1-23.
56. SMA, A20-1-51.
57. SMA, A20-1-53.

in 1961 explained the surge in popularity in terms of a combination of political pressure, the elimination of informal vegetable markets, and the policy of allowing all the relatives of commune workers to eat for free.[58] While there was little open resistance to the commune canteens, local residents directed a steady barrage of complaints about the quality of the food to canteen workers.[59] As diners told researchers working for the Shanghai Party Committee, the people from Ningbo and the people from Yangzhou did not like to eat the same dishes.[60] More to the point, no one liked to eat bad food.

The second largest commune welfare program comprised the day care centers set up by the lane and alley residents committees. At the high point of the communes in June 1960, more than 377,000 children were cared for in the new day care centers, which the districts estimated to be 84 percent of all children under seven years of age.[61] More than 34,000 day care workers cared for an average of eleven children each. Most day care centers were set up in residents' homes or in the resident committees' offices or warehouses. Despite the ad hoc setting, most centers were large, averaging 150 children. Many of the parents of the children placed in the new day care centers were newly mobilized housewives who were going to work in the communes and lacked any grandparents or older children to take care of the younger children at home. Parents were required to pay fees for child care, but the day care programs never broke even and required subsidies from district governments to operate.[62]

The new grassroots schools were incorporated into the urban communes in March 1960 as a collective welfare program. They were nearly as large as the day care program, serving more than 278,000 students in June 1960.[63] Most students were in primary school, but the urban communes also ran high schools, night schools, and "Red and Expert" vocational schools as well. Their consolidation as commune

58. SMA, A20-1-51b.
59. SMA, A20-1-53.
60. SMA, A20-1-51b.
61. SMA, A20-1-23.
62. SMA, A20-1-37. For example, this budget report shows that Shanghai's communal day care programs received 12 percent of their funding from the government in 1961.
63. SMA, A20-1-23.

welfare programs increased party scrutiny of their operations but also gave them access to government subsidies, which allowed the communes to standardize and improve teachers' wages.[64] Red Cross health stations were also formally incorporated into the urban communes as their primary health program in March 1960, although their operations were still primarily coordinated by the public health bureau and local hospitals.

The fifth welfare program offered by the communes was newly established in 1960: social welfare (*shehui fuli*) services. Rather than an expansion of welfare, these programs essentially collectivized the last remnants of the private market in the cities. Their services included laundry, repairs, small stores, tailors, barbers, plumbers, and electricians.[65] In addition to skilled artisans forced to work for the urban communes rather than sell their services privately, mobilized housewives were also pressed into service. The housewives' services prompted many complaints that they lacked the necessary skills, for example, giving bad haircuts and damaging delicate silks they were supposed to be cleaning. Shanghai's social welfare service programs never provided data on the number of people they served, but they were the third largest employer among the commune welfare programs, with more than 36,000 employees by June 1960.[66]

These five programs—canteens, day care, education, health stations, and social welfare services—were the core of the new Great Leap Forward approach to welfare. But probably the most important welfare function served by the urban communes was a massive public jobs program for the unemployed. Commune jobs paid stipends and limited welfare benefits that were far lower than the wages and benefits available through regular employment, but they were more generous than any previous unemployment relief program. With stipends that averaged 20 yuan per month, the new urban commune employees were making approximately half the income of an average industrial worker in a state-owned enterprise.

The scale of commune employment was significant—surpassing the

64. SMA, B105-7-1180.
65. SMA, A20-1-23; SMA, A20-1-51c.
66. SMA, A20-1-51c.

*Table 6.2.* Shanghai Unemployment Programs, 1958–63

| Year | Commune employment | Increase | Evacuations |
|------|--------------------|----------|-------------|
| 1958 | 0 | 0% | 235,892 |
| 1959 | 0 | 0% | — |
| 1960* | 365,521 | 9% | — |
| 1961 | 296,738 | -19% | 270,000 |
| 1962 | 227,882 | -23% | 254,000 |
| 1963 | 0 | -100% | — |

*1960 jobs compared to 1953 unemployment registration.
Sources: SMA, A20-1-23; SMA, A20-1-38; SMA, A20-1-77; SMA, B168-1-910, SMA, B168-1-915.

previous peak during the 1953 Universal Job Placement program (table 6.2). The five commune welfare programs together employed nearly 119,000 people, amounting to 26 percent of total commune employment. The largest source of commune employment was "shock" labor teams that were sent to state-owned and cooperative enterprises as temporary workers, as well as lane and alley production groups that did handicraft work in homes and offices. The residential production groups' primary products included paper boxes, bamboo products, and textiles such as hand-spun yarn. A smaller group of workers were employed by commune factories. The city transferred forty-seven small enterprises and factory workshops employing more than 10,000 workers to the urban communes in 1960. Another 33,000 people worked in new factories established by the urban communes, producing iron, lead, copper, and chemicals such as ethyl alcohol. Commune factory workers accounted for about 12 percent of urban commune production jobs.[67]

Commune workers' responses to their new public works jobs varied widely, shaped in large part by their economic interests. For the unemployed, stipends were a significant improvement in their income and commune jobs provided more status then being a social relief recipient. For self-employed workers and domestic servants, however, the new jobs often came at a significant cost to their standard of living. For example, a nanny in Zhabei district was inspired by the campaign to quit her job of more than ten years to join a production team in her commune. Her

67. SMA, A20-1-23.

wages were slightly lower in her new job, and she now had to pay all her living costs on her own, leaving her unable to support herself, much less continue to send remittances to her family in the countryside.[68] Zhabei district carried out a study of the income of former self-employed workers after their incorporation into the urban communes that showed 72 percent of them suffered significant income losses.[69]

Since many commune jobs went to housewives and other members of larger households, they did help to achieve one of the goals of the urban communes: boosting household income. One study on the impact of the Great Leap Forward on employment and income showed that nearly 60 percent of a sample of Shanghai households had two or more members with jobs in 1960, up from less than 20 percent in 1957.[70] As a result, the number of households with incomes of less than 10 yuan per month fell from one-third of many districts' population to 10 percent after the urban communes were implemented.[71]

The addition of urban commune welfare programs and employment to the preexisting labor insurance and social relief programs meant that 1960 marked the peak expansion of the urban welfare state in the Mao era. However controversial the commune welfare programs may have been, they rapidly expanded coverage to the majority of Shanghai's population.[72]

## *The Crisis of the Great Leap Forward Famine*

Shanghai may have had the economic resources and political support (or acquiescence) necessary for comprehensive implementation of commune welfare programs, but the radical turn in the Great Leap Forward only deepened China's economic crisis. At the same time that the urban welfare state reached its peak in 1960, the Great Leap

68. SMA, A20-1-60.
69. Ibid.
70. SMA, A20-1-51a.
71. Ibid.
72. Luo Pinghan, *Da guo fan*, 3. Rural communes reached broad coverage in 1958.

Forward famine reached its depths in the countryside.[73] This tragedy could not persist for long. The soft budget constraints that fueled the economy reached their ultimate limit in 1960 when urban food supplies began running short for the first time. It was only at this point that the radicals in Beijing finally acknowledged that the grain shortage was real. Mao was reported to have given up eating meat to express his solidarity with the people who did not have enough to eat.[74]

The initial response to the crisis was tepid. The central CCP issued a new policy to encourage rural communes to reduce their nonfarming activities in order to expand grain production.[75] In addition, urban grain rations were cut and grain imports began, all in an effort to ease the urban food shortage. But these efforts were too little and too late. By December 1960, all of China's major cities, including Shanghai, had gone through their grain reserves.[76]

The economic crisis in the winter of 1960–61 led to much bigger policy changes. Grain imports expanded significantly, and grain procurement quotas in the countryside were slashed.[77] In addition, the CCP recentralized control over the economic planning system, reining in the provincial and municipal party committees.[78] After the restoration of the planners, the central CCP abruptly shut the Great Leap Forward investment drive down in June 1961, with sharp budget cuts and orders to lay off 20 million industrial workers nationwide.[79] At the same time, rural communes were finally given the authority to shut down their canteens, after investigations by central CCP leaders had revealed that they were almost universally despised. Zhou Enlai reported to Mao that peasants were greeting the closure of the canteens as their "second liberation," on a par with their first liberation from the landlords.[80]

The urban communes, however, did not shut down their canteens or

73. Yang, *Calamity and Reform*, 53.
74. Yang Jisheng, *Mubei*, vol. 1, 564–65.
75. Teiwes and Sun, *China's Road*, 215–16.
76. Lardy, "Chinese Economy," 385; Brown, *City versus Countryside*, 67.
77. MacFarquhar, *Origins of the Cultural Revolution*, vol. 3, 14, 27; Yang, *Calamity and Reform*, 66.
78. MacFarquhar *Origins of the Cultural Revolution*, vol. 3, 16.
79. Ibid., 32; Yang Jisheng, *Mubei*, vol. 2, 746.
80. MacFarquhar, *Origins of the Cultural Revolution*, vol. 3, 49.

any of their welfare programs. The reason they survived the 1961 budget cuts are not clear.[81] But participation in commune welfare programs declined markedly as pressure to use them eased and new fees for their services were imposed. The canteens saw the most precipitous decline in participation, feeding more than 1.6 million people at their peak in August 1960 and then dropping more than 50 percent over the following year. A study of one commune in Luwan district conducted for the Shanghai Party Committee in the summer of 1961 showed that most residents were only eating lunch in the canteens, and 28 percent of residents were eating all three meals at home.[82] Part of the reason for the decline was simply less political pressure, allowing more freedom to choose the convenience of the canteen or the quality of home cooking. But another important reason for declining participation was the food shortage. Interviews with residents showed that they had calculated that they could stretch their limited rations further by cooking at home and at the same time gain control over how they divided up their food among family members. The report concluded that the canteens were a problem in a time of food shortages, both because they wasted scarce resources and because they generated political dissatisfaction with the regime.

Urban commune production jobs declined by 27 percent in this period, and a new category of laid-off commune workers "waiting" for new jobs was created for more than 70,000 of these former employees. The rest of Shanghai was hit much harder by the budget cuts. More than 215,000 jobs were lost in the city, leading to an 8 percent drop in total employment in 1961, more than four times worse than the last recession in 1955.[83]

As the central CCP leaders continued their investigations into famine conditions in the countryside and sham accounting methods in industry, they realized that the 1961 funding cuts were inadequate to resolve the crisis. At the Seven Thousand Cadres Conference in January 1962, Mao and other top CCP leaders finally admitted that some mistakes had been made in the Great Leap Forward, but attributed most of them to poor implementation. In other words, local officials,

81. SMA, A20-1-38.
82. SMA, A20-1-51b.
83. SMA, A20-1-38; Shanghi tongji ju, ed. *Shanghai shi guomin jingji*, 46.

rather than central party leaders, took the blame for the economic crisis.[84] Mao Zedong gave an apology of sorts for his mistakes and allowed other CCP leaders to take over day-to-day management of the party-state, but he did not step down. Similarly, Mayor Ke Qingshi confessed to making errors in the massive investment drive but nothing more serious. Since the steel production drive consolidated Shanghai's industrial sector after the sharp cuts in investment in the mid-1950s, in some ways Ke's "error" was actually one of his lasting achievements. He continued as both Shanghai's first party secretary and a member of the Politburo.

In the wake of the conference, the central CCP ordered another round of budget cuts and layoffs of 10 million workers nationwide. The second round of budget cuts in 1962 led to the loss of another 310,700 jobs in Shanghai, which amounted to another 12 percent reduction in the size of Shanghai's workforce. When combined with the layoffs in 1961, almost all of the increase in Shanghai's labor force in the Great Leap Forward had been eliminated. The massive layoffs of 1961–62 followed a "last-in, first-out" policy, targeting new employees hired after 1957, especially the rural migrants who still had connections in the countryside. The underlying principle of the new rationing policy for jobs and welfare privileges was to sacrifice promises made to newcomers in favor of protecting the guarantees that had already been given to welfare state insiders.[85]

The second severe round of budget cuts finally led to the dismantling of the urban commune welfare programs. The canteens, day care centers, social welfare services, and health care stations were all shut down in June 1962, a full year after the end of the rural programs. Almost all of the staff in the commune welfare programs and production teams were immediately laid off.[86] The only urban commune welfare programs to survive were the grassroots schools that predated the communes and were still largely financed by tuition fees. Moreover, they were able to prove that demand for their services was strong and

84. MacFarquhar, *Origins of the Cultural Revolution*, vol. 3, 170–71.
85. Xiong Yuezhi et al., *Shanghai tongshi*, vol. 11, 178–79; Perry and Li, *Proletarian Power*, 104.
86. SMA, A20-1-70; Li Duanxiung, *Chengshi*, 139.

that the majority of their graduates passed the entrance exams to the next level in the education system. As a result, they were transferred to the Department of Education for reorganization and incorporation into the public education system.[87]

The only production jobs that survived the communes were in the forty-seven enterprises that had been transferred from the municipal government to the urban communes in 1960. Two years later, only thirty-one were still in operation. Among the survivors, the city government reclaimed only fifteen factories owing to difficulties in securing adequate supplies and electricity to keep them in operation.[88] No one but the commune workers may have mourned the loss of the commune welfare programs, but the end result of the 1961–62 budget cuts was the elimination of almost all of the expansion in the Chinese welfare state during the Great Leap Forward.

## Institutionalizing Ruralization

The huge budget cuts in 1961–62 were followed by rapid escalation of the ruralization campaigns. Nationwide, the party set a goal of ruralizing the 30 million people laid off in 1961–62, but kept the scale of the program secret.[89] Sending people to the countryside in the middle of a rural famine was a reversal of traditional famine policy of allowing refugees to go to cities to seek shelter and food. But Zhou Enlai and other CCP leaders who promoted ruralization calculated that the unemployed workers would be able to at least partially grow their own food, reducing the procurement burden on the rural communes.[90]

To meet these goals required going beyond the recent rural migrants

87. Ibid.
88. SMA, A20-1-69.
89. MacFarquhar, *Origins of the Cultural Revolution*, vol. 3, 204; Brown, *City versus Countryside*, 85; Luo Pinghan, *Da Qianxi*, 139–140, 172; Lu Yilong, "1949 nian hou," 125. The national campaign targets cited by different sources vary from 15 to 30 million. Estimates of the actual results of the campaigns vary from 16 to 29 million.
90. MacFarquhar, *Origins of the Cultural Revolution*, vol. 3, 30; Yang Jisheng, *Mubei*, vol. 2, 745–46.

hired during the Great Leap Forward, so the 1961–62 ruralization campaigns also targeted long-term urban residents, including urban commune workers. The former housewives who staffed the commune welfare programs were encouraged to go back to doing housework, and production workers were encouraged to support themselves by doing their own handicraft production and repair services.[91] But commune workers who did not have another employed worker in their household were targeted for ruralization regardless of their household registration status.

Recent high school and junior high school graduates were a particularly vulnerable group, since they needed a job to secure their own urban residency. In addition to sending educated youth to work in Xinjiang and reclaim land in Jiangxi as had been done in the past, the Shanghai Labor Bureau and the Higher Education Bureau worked together to recruit students for a new Communist Labor University (Gongchanzhuyi laodong daxue) in the mountains of Jiangxi. Combining farm work with educational classes, the school was open to Shanghai youth aged seventeen to twenty-five with at least a junior high education. Of all the unattractive options offered to educated youth in the early 1960s, the Communist Labor University at least offered the hope of continuing their education in some way.[92]

Including the laid-off workers, educated youth, and rural migrants detained for lacking migration permits, more than 270,000 people were evacuated from Shanghai in 1961.[93] Another 254,000 people were moved out of Shanghai in 1962.[94] For the first time since they began in 1955, the city's ruralization campaigns met their full targets. This new success in implementation did not mean that the campaigns' targets accepted their fate quietly. Laid-off workers tried desperately to resist ruralization. At the No. 9 Cotton Mill in Shanghai, for example, workers attacked the cadres sent to carry out the lay-offs, tearing

91. SMA, A20-1-70.
92. Xiong Yuezhi et al., *Shanghai tongshi*, vol. 11, 180.
93. Shen Zhi and Li Tao, *Shanghai laodong*, 113; Xiong Yuezhi et al., *Shanghai tongshi*, vol. 13, 148; SMA, B168-1-910.
94. Shen Zhi and Li Tao, *Shanghai laodong*, 113; Xiong Yuezhi et al., *Shanghai tongshi*, vol. 13, 148–50; SMA, B168-1-915.

the cadres' clothes and going to their houses to steal food from them. Others tried to appeal to the cadres' sympathies, volunteering to work for free if they could keep their labor insurance benefits and urban residency status.[95]

Although the changes in the household registration system, the detention system, and ruralization campaigns had been gradual, their cumulative impact was decisive. The completion of the household registration regulations in 1958 finished the national infrastructure for comprehensive population control. Shanghai's construction of a permanent detention shelter system during the 1958–59 ruralization campaigns provided the beginnings of the bureaucracy to enforce the regulations. The next key change was a major decline in the rate of migration to Shanghai in the winter of 1960–61.[96]

The reasons for the shift are not entirely clear. In the last quarter of 1960, the Shanghai Bureau of Civil Affairs reported that the number of rural migrants detained for evacuation suddenly dropped 72 percent. The cadres in charge of the detention and evacuation system at the time had no explanation for the sudden change, and they anticipated that the numbers would soon increase again because of the "natural disaster" taking place in the countryside.[97] Instead, the decline was permanent. Stricter enforcement of the household registration system in the countryside helps to account for the shift. Local studies of villages and counties in the famine regions have revealed that many rural cadres reversed their policies toward migration by 1960, switching from facilitating migration to trying to prevent and punish it.[98] At the extreme, there are also examples of rural officials arresting and even attacking villagers trying to flee. Lower levels of rural-urban migration from 1961 onward put much less pressure on Shanghai's fledgling population control system.

At that point, the Shanghai Bureau of Civil Affairs carried out a major reorganization of its detention system, centralizing the district shelters under its control to cope with the 1961 budget cuts. Although

---

95. Frazier, *Making of the Chinese Industrial Workplace*, 219.
96. SMA, B168-1-900; SMA, B168-1-572.
97. SMA, B168-1-900; Yang Jisheng, *Mubei*, vol 2, 949.
98. Thaxton, *Catastrophe and Contention*, 163–66; Li, *Fighting Famine*, 360–62.

two-thirds of the 204 employees in the municipal and district shelters were laid off, the detention shelters' capacity remained unaffected.[99] In fact, the bureau viewed the staff reductions as a way to improve the program, since most of the staff in the district shelters were former housewives and social relief recipients. Policemen and many other government officials had been complaining that the district staff made too many mistakes in their investigations of the detainees, especially mistakes in identifying people with political problems.[100] Evaluations of the streamlined program's performance in 1962 concluded that it had improved with more professional employees, resulting in fewer mistaken detentions, fewer escapes, and more effective political education.[101]

The impact of all these incremental changes was that the 1962 ruralization campaign differed fundamentally from all the ruralization campaigns that had preceded it, resulting for the first time in a long-term reduction in Shanghai's urban population. In 1962, Shanghai's urban population fell 1 percent. Shanghai's population did not immediately rise again the following year as happened after past ruralization campaigns, but instead leveled off at 6.4 million.[102] Ruralization campaigns and strict enforcement of the household registration system became the long-term unemployment policy of the Maoist welfare state.

## Consolidating the Urban Welfare State

Although unemployed workers had little luck in resisting their ruralization in 1961–62, their employed counterparts had more political leverage in the workplace. At the most basic level, their leverage was evident in the survival of the labor insurance program through the recession and massive budget cuts that eliminated commune welfare. In fact, the mass layoffs of 1961–62 contributed to a sharp increase in welfare

99. SMA, B168-1-182.
100. SMA, B168-1-900.
101. SMA, B168-1-572.
102. Shanghaishi tongji ju, *Shanghai shi guomin jingji*, 22. Shanghai's total population leveled off at nearly 10.6 million people in this period.

spending. The Shanghai labor union's labor insurance reserve funds had been running large surpluses again during the Great Leap Forward investment drive, since most of the new enrollees in the program were young enough to provide additional contributions without making many claims for benefits. After the layoffs began in 1961, however, the Shanghai labor insurance program began running a monthly deficit. Early retirements were one important reason. Many of the workers targeted for layoffs chose to retire early rather than accept a new job or farm work in the interior, strengthening their claim to urban residency and ensuring that they would have an ongoing source of income, no matter how small. For example, the Shenxin No. 9 Cotton Mill laid off 15 percent of its workforce, which affected far more employees than the recent hires during the Great Leap Forward. For workers who had worked long enough, early retirement with partial benefits was clearly preferable to being sent to the countryside.[103]

The impact on the labor insurance program was immediate, putting the program in deficit. As stipulated in the labor insurance regulations, the national union headquarters in Beijing dipped into the national reserve funds and provided the Shanghai union with 4.5 million yuan to cover the shortfall in 1961. In 1962, the national subsidy to the Shanghai labor insurance program doubled.[104]

It was at this point that the central government formulated a new set of revisions to the labor insurance regulations to stabilize the program after the dramatic expansion and drastic cuts of the Great Leap Forward. One particularly difficult legacy of the investment drive was that many of the new enterprises created through mergers were still operating multiple different labor insurance contract programs side by side. Another problem was that there were still large numbers of temporary workers even after the layoffs of 1961–62.[105]

When the Shanghai Federation of Trade Unions convened round-table discussions with cadres and workers to provide feedback on the draft revisions, it encountered very different reactions. Temporary workers who managed to stay on after the layoffs of 1961–

103. Frazier, *Making of the Chinese Industrial Workplace*, 218–19.
104. SMA, C1-2-3795.
105. SMA, C1-2-3628; SMA, C1-2-3627.

62 clamored for reclassification, claiming "we do the same work as permanent workers and make the same contribution, so we should have the same benefits."[106] But they no longer found many allies. Union cadres at the grassroots level still expressed concern in these discussions over the inequalities in wages and benefits within enterprises and among different enterprises. But the attitudes of ordinary workers had changed decisively. In contrast to their generosity in the 1950s, permanent workers voiced new opposition to any expansion of coverage at a time when "natural disasters" were causing so many economic difficulties.[107] When resources were so constrained that people were worried for their very survival, the solidarity that had marked the interactions between welfare state insiders and outsiders earlier in the decade disappeared.

The 1962 revisions to the labor insurance regulations consolidated the program in the workplace. The new regulations authorized state-owned enterprises with multiple labor insurance and contract programs to unify them into a single program. At the same time, the cities that stopped expanding labor insurance during the Great Leap Forward were ordered to implement the program in all firms that had grown past the hundred-worker size limit, just as Shanghai had done in 1959. The new regulations also clarified the status of collective enterprises to exclude them from labor insurance, regardless of their size or financial status.[108] The practical effect of this policy change was to transform the labor contract program from a temporary measure into a permanent program for collective enterprises with lower benefits than full labor insurance. Taken together, the new policies standardized labor insurance in state-owned enterprises and labor insurance contracts in collective enterprises, equalizing benefits across all permanent employees within those enterprises. The distinction between permanent and temporary employees, however, was maintained.

The 1962 reforms reversed the slide in labor insurance and contract coverage caused by the 1961–62 layoffs. In Shanghai, labor insurance coverage grew at a steady rate of 6 to 7 percent per year from 1963 to 1965 after the program was consolidated (table 6.3). Nationwide, labor

106. SMA, C1-2-3628.
107. Ibid.
108. SMA, C1-2-4303.

*Table 6.3.* Shanghai Labor Insurance and Contract Programs, 1958–63

| Year | Labor insurance | Increase | Labor insurance contracts | Increase |
|------|-----------------|----------|---------------------------|----------|
| 1958 | 1,086,088 | 20% | 580,000 | 21% |
| 1959 | 1,160,823 | 7% | 576,000 | -17% |
| 1960 | 1,350,000 | 16% | 480,000 | -28% |
| 1961 | 1,275,000 | -6% | 345,966 | -10% |
| 1962 | 1,161,000 | -9% | 312,864 | -4% |
| 1963 | 1,235,979 | 6% | 301,233 | -4% |

*Sources:* SMA, C1-2-4414; SMA, C1-2-3391; SMA, C1-2-3627.

insurance coverage also increased 6 percent after the new regulations were issued.[109] By 1965, Shanghai's labor insurance program had recovered to match its previous high point in 1960.

The importance of the labor union's last remaining toehold in the workplace is suggested by the impact of the 1962 labor insurance revisions on the program's operating deficits. Rather than close the program's funding gap, the new revisions only increased the cost of the program. By 1964, the Shanghai Federation of Trade Unions had increased its annual request for subsidies to 10 million yuan.[110] The preferential incorporation of labor led to the involution of the Chinese welfare state in the crisis of the Great Leap Forward famine, a dynamic in which every improvement in benefits for welfare state insiders put the expansion of coverage that much farther out of reach for welfare state outsiders.

In this context, where the difference between employment and unemployment determined people's fates—where they could live, what kind of work they could do, and how they could survive the economic crisis—jobs and all the privileges that came with them became the ultimate resource for patronage politics. It did not take party and union leaders long to realize how much power they wielded—and to use it to buttress their positions and the regime along with it. For example, workers at Shanghai No. 2 Cotton Mill complained that the vice chairman of their enterprise union wielded her control over food and welfare

109. Ibid.
110. SMA, C1-2-4753.

funds unfairly during the famine: "Not only is she constantly eating herself—in the canteen, in the kindergarten, in workers' rooms—but she also has control over the workers' hardship fund. Workers must give her gifts . . . and do housework for her."[111] Over time, control over jobs and welfare benefits became a source of patronage that became entrenched as a powerful form of clientelism centered on the workplace. A former worker interviewed in the 1970s described how patronage operated in his factory: "[Workshop leaders] use their control of housing, jobs for relatives, and loans to control workers. For [emergency] loans, you have to...get the group leader's approval, and then shop leaders have a meeting to decide.[112]

Labor insurance was not the only urban welfare program to expand in the early 1960s. Social relief not only survived the economic crisis intact but grew rapidly. Program administrators in the Shanghai Bureau of Civil Affairs loosened the very restrictive eligibility standards they had used during the Great Leap Forward investment drive. After years of declining enrollment and distributions of relief, both suddenly increased more than 50 percent in 1962. Expansion continued at a faster pace after the economy began to recover in 1963, with the caseload more than doubling from 1961 levels. Social relief became a permanent and growing part of the urban welfare state in the early 1960s.[113]

The hierarchy of the labor insurance program, labor insurance contracts, and social relief constituted China's permanent urban welfare state. All three programs grew at a steady, relatively moderate pace after 1962, in the midst of the worst recession since the 1949 takeover. This pattern of development suggests that the bifurcation of the Chinese economy was complete, protecting and privileging the urban population to different degrees while leaving the unemployed and the rural population to fend for themselves. The ironic outcome of the ambitious new effort to promote economic equality in the Great Leap Forward was the entrenchment of deeper inequalities in the Chinese welfare state.

111. Frazier, *Making of the Chinese Industrial Workplace*, 229.
112. Walder, *Communist Neo-Traditionalism*, 99.
113. Fan Jingsi, ed., *Shanghai minzheng*, 391–92

## *Evaluating the Great Leap Forward Welfare Reforms*

The politics of welfare reform were deceptively easy during the Great Leap Forward. Without any political opposition or rival claims on new resources from welfare state insiders, the CCP was able to implement its new commune welfare programs in almost every local community, first in the countryside in 1958 and then in the cities in 1960. And without any economic limits on the expansion of these programs, whether imposed by markets or by central planners, the CCP was briefly able to construct a nearly universal commune-based welfare state. This temporary achievement, however, came at the expense of China's economic collapse. The long-term impact of the Great Leap Forward welfare reforms stemmed from their failure rather than the ephemeral programs they created.

Looking at coverage in Shanghai over the entire Great Leap Forward period from 1958 to 1962 reveals the impact of its policy swings on its urban welfare state. The growth in coverage in its core welfare programs was rapid from 1958 to 1960, surging to 51 percent of Shanghai's total workforce in a period of rapid job growth (table 6.4). Thanks to the investment drive and all the new commune jobs, unemployment fell considerably, perhaps as low as 2 percent of the urban population.[114]

If we take the commune canteens into account, Shanghai achieved a broad welfare state in 1960. The scale of the commune canteens is highlighted by the comparison to Shanghai's previous food distribution programs. In 1953 in the wake of the Universal Job Placement program, 1.2 million handouts of relief rice and cash grants were provided over the course of the year. By 1960, the commune canteens claimed to feed as many people every month, making the program more than eleven times as large. Even if these figures were exaggerated, half this expansion would constitute a significant expansion in coverage. For the first time, most of the urban population had guaranteed access to food, with the noted exception of the more than 200,000 unemployed urbanites considered unsuitable for incorporation into the communes, largely due to political problems.[115]

114. SMA, A20-1-51
115. SMA, A20-1-23. A good proportion of these excluded urbanites, however, were members of larger households with some other source of income and food rations.

*Table 6.4.* Shanghai Welfare Coverage, 1958–62

| Year | Total beneficiaries | Percent change | Workforce coverage | Population coverage |
|------|---------------------|----------------|--------------------|---------------------|
| 1958 | 1,666,088 | 21% | 42% | 22% |
| 1959 | 1,736,823 | 4% | 43% | 17% |
| 1960 | 2,185,521 | 26% | 51% | 21% |
| 1961 | 1,917,704 | -12% | 46% | 18% |
| 1962 | 1,701,746 | -11% | 42% | 16% |

*Sources:* SMA, C1-2-4414; SMA, C1-2-3391; SMA, C1-2-322; SMA, A20-1-23; SMA, A20-1-38; SMA, A20-1-77; Shanghaishi tongji ju, *Shanghai shi guomin jingji.*

The brief moment of broad coverage in 1960 began to erode in the wake of budget cuts in 1961. After the commune welfare programs were dismantled, the 1962 labor insurance revisions and social relief adjustments stabilized Shanghai's welfare state coverage at 42 percent of Shanghai's workforce and 16 percent of the total population (table 6.4). This level of significant but narrow welfare coverage proved long lasting.

Mao and the other policy makers involved in creating the commune welfare programs sought to make 1958 the turning point in the development of the Chinese welfare state, marking the transition to universal coverage. Their welfare reforms were the most ambitious of anything tried in this era, but they were also the most transient, leaving almost no lasting trace. Instead, 1962 proved to be the turning point that had lasting consequences. This year not only saw the demise of the urban communes and their welfare programs; it was also the year in which the labor insurance and social relief programs were consolidated, and the ruralization campaigns were transformed into a permanent bureaucratic system of population control. The result was an unequal welfare state providing very different benefits and levels of protection for different groups among the urban population and imposing nearly complete exclusion of the unemployed and the rural majority.

Why were the commune welfare programs such an unmitigated failure? The first and most obvious problem was that they were too expensive to sustain. Shanghai's urban communes made little or no effort to tailor their welfare programs to local resources. The canteens, which were supposed to be the first and most basic of the commune welfare programs, were not self-financed as policy makers had envisioned in 1958. Moreover, the entire suite of welfare programs that policy makers proposed for gradual implementation was implemented at once with no regard to local needs or resources. The high degree of standardization in communal welfare programs suggests the repression of the Anti-Rightist campaign was as effective in ensuring compliance as national regulations and a bureaucracy to enforce them. When large-scale new programs were added on top of the continuing labor insurance and social relief programs, the increase in welfare spending during the Great Leap Forward was substantial. If Shanghai could afford to subsidize its programs with its new control over local revenues, few other local governments could.

In contrast to the Great Leap Forward's non-existent budget constraints, the 1962 welfare reforms provided an effective rationing mechanism to regulate the expansion of the Chinese welfare state. Ruralization and the household registration system kept access to the Maoist welfare state in line with the resources necessary to sustain it. Cities such as Shanghai still needed subsidies from the national union to support benefits for their older workforce, but the financial foundations of labor insurance were more secure from the early 1960s onward. The other rationing mechanism invented in the Great Leap Forward famine was the last-in, first-out policy employed in the 1961–62 budget cuts. Like ruralization, this policy was also long lasting. After the crisis eased, the same principle was applied to subsequent budget cuts in the labor insurance and labor insurance contract programs, protecting the entitlements of the people already in the system by cutting the benefits of new hires. Over time, the policy of last-in, first-to-receive-benefit-cuts created an elaborate hierarchy of benefits within the labor insurance program for different age cohorts. Decades later, this rationing policy still privileged the pre-1957 "revolutionary" generation with the best wages and benefits in the workforce.[116]

In addition to soft budget constraints, another important reason for the failure of commune welfare programs was lack of popular support. The canteens were the heart of the problem. Even in a period of tight food rations, almost no one in Shanghai wanted the food that

116. Davis, "Unequal Chances," 242.

the canteens served. Political pressure and the inducement of free food temporarily elicited widespread participation in the canteens. But as soon as the pressure eased, Shanghainese showed their preference for cooking their own meals. The fact that only the educational programs survived the dismantling of the urban communes suggests that political support for these programs was just as important for their durability as their economic sustainability.

If political support is necessary for welfare institutions to endure, the contrast between commune welfare programs and the rest of the Maoist welfare state is puzzling. The inequalities and exclusions of the Chinese welfare state caused considerable political unrest in the 1950s; why were even deeper inequities accepted by the people disadvantaged by them in the 1960s?

One important factor in stabilizing China's narrow welfare state was the change in policy makers' attitudes toward welfare reform. The idea that welfare spending posed a trade-off with economic development became a lasting principle of Chinese welfare policy. The original promise to create a broad welfare state was never revoked, but it was indefinitely postponed. There were no more top-down attempts to expand the reach of the Chinese welfare state in the Mao era; indeed there were no more attempts to expand its reach in the Deng era that followed. The welfare policy failures of the 1950s and early 1960s left a lasting legacy of cautious conservatism among CCP policymakers. Without new reforms, ordinary people had few opportunities to contest the limits of the Chinese welfare state.

Extreme scarcities in the early 1960s may also have helped transform popular attitudes toward China's narrow, unequal welfare state in the cities. Although workers still seemed sanguine about expanding the welfare state in the future, in the short term tight economic constraints made them concerned first and foremost with protecting their own benefits. As patronage over jobs, welfare benefits, housing, and rations increasingly came to define urban politics, the working class grew increasingly concerned with protecting its privileges in the workplace. Even the inequalities among labor insurance, collective labor contracts, and social relief paled in comparison to the threat of ruralization. Welfare state outsiders in the cities, such as temporary workers, may never have accepted their inequitable treatment after all the promises that had been made to them, but the harsh repression embodied in the population control system ensured that they valued the privileges they still had left to them, even if it was just urban residency. It was the combination of privilege and repression that finally stabilized the narrow Maoist welfare state, giving it strong popular support from the Communist regime's urban constituencies.

The unemployed no doubt vehemently opposed their exile to the countryside. Their physical exclusion, however, ensured that they could not come to the cities to engage in street protests to redress the inequities of the Chinese welfare state. Living in a city, even visiting a city, became a privilege in the 1960s that the CCP controlled and could dole out to its most loyal supporters. Access to the one political arena that the CCP had difficulty controlling in the 1950s—the street—was now the preserve of an urban elite.

In many ways, the mature Maoist welfare state was more the product of failure than of design. The failures of egalitarianism in the Great Leap Forward led to the institutionalization of a narrow and unequal welfare state in a moment of crisis. Ruralization of the urban unemployed became a permanent policy rather than a temporary measure. The labor insurance contract program followed a similar trajectory. Combined with the consolidation and expansion of labor insurance and social relief, the hierarchy and the limits of the Maoist welfare state were institutionalized in 1962 in a way that proved to be enduring.

CONCLUSION

# China's Narrow Welfare State
## in Comparative Perspective

What lessons can we draw from the Maoist welfare state to help understand the development of narrow welfare states in other countries? Although China's revolutionary politics and radical welfare reforms were highly unusual, the problems that challenged Chinese welfare reformers were not. The difficulties posed by the high cost of expanding social insurance coverage in a poor economy were faced by almost all developing countries in the postwar period. But China had the advantage of strong political forces pushing for a broad welfare state. International influence, political mobilization strategies, and economic development policy all contributed to strong top-down leadership in welfare reform. The reforms were quickly embraced by strong societal support from workers and the urban poor. Furthermore, the social revolution eliminated potential political opposition to welfare reform from capitalists.

Despite such advantages, China's three major welfare reform initiatives in the 1950s failed to attain the goal of broad coverage. Balancing strong political demand for welfare and limited resources in a social insurance welfare state proved to be too difficult to achieve. A missing ingredient in the reforms was state capacity to regulate the expansion of coverage in a way that was both economically sustainable and politically acceptable. A further problem stemmed from the preferential incorporation of labor, which turned into an obstacle to the expansion of coverage as workers' efforts to protect their privileges increasingly came at the expense of welfare state outsiders. If Mao's China was not able to overcome these problems, despite the considerable political and social forces pressing for welfare reform, its experience suggests that the mismatch between program design and economic and political conditions poses a fundamental constraint on the development of the welfare state in other settings as well.

This conclusion summarizes lessons that can be drawn from the Maoist welfare state, including the role of globalization, the politics surrounding its founding, and the attempts to expand its reach. The Chinese case is then compared to both developing and advanced industrial countries to identify potential solutions to the problem of narrow welfare states. The last part of the chapter examines the implications of these lessons for welfare reform in China today.

## *The Role of Globalization in Chinese Welfare Politics*

International influence played a central role in China's welfare politics from the 1920s onward. Chinese policy experts in universities and international organizations such as the International Labour Organization disseminated knowledge about European policy innovations, shaping political agendas in China even before an effective central state had been established. International influence had an even greater impact in the 1940s and 1950s, when welfare policy was incorporated into foreign policy in the Second World War and the Cold War. The international consensus that formed in the 1920s and 1930s in favor of social insurance had a profound impact on Chinese policy debates, precluding consideration of alternative program designs easier to implement in predominantly agricultural economies. Chinese policy debates centered on the question of when social insurance should be adopted, not whether it was the best choice.

A distinctive feature of Chinese welfare politics in this period of political instability was the lack of clear boundaries between international relations and domestic politics. International influence occurred not only in global hubs such as Geneva and Moscow; Chinese activists also brought it home to wield as a weapon in domestic politics. Policy makers such as Li Lisan turned their foreign expertise into political capital. International organizations such as the ILO provided a valuable source of legitimacy, and foreign labor unions such as the CIO offered resources that reshaped Chinese labor politics at the grass roots.

Blurry boundaries reflected China's place in the international order in the eras of imperialism and superpower competition. The globalization of welfare policies in that period was not a process of dissemination among equal units, as policy diffusion is often conceptualized.[1] The attraction of welfare state pioneers like Germany and Denmark was greater in Beijing and Buenos Aires than in Washington, D.C. Similarly, the ILO was not as important an influence on the European countries that dominated the organization as it was on countries that were relegated to the back benches. The biggest deterrent to the adoption of new welfare programs in China was semicolonialism rather than the level of economic development or the strength of domestic political opposition. Placing the globalization of the welfare state in the context of European, Soviet, and American power in the twentieth century is essential in explaining different patterns of diffusion.[2]

China's historical experience suggests that the form that ideas take powerfully affects their diffusion. Both the welfare state and the ideal of universal coverage had strong normative and political appeal in the postwar era. Yet welfare state legislation spread much more widely than reform policies to expand coverage. Comparing the globalization of different sets of policies suggests that the ILO's development of a coherent policy package for the welfare state may have contributed to its wider spread. The appealing simplicity of the

---

1. Dobbin et al., "Global Diffusion"; Weyland, "Theories of Policy Diffusion"; Rogers, *Diffusion of Innovations*; Berry, "Sizing Up State Policy."
2. Treating countries as equal units that exist over this entire period is standard in research on the early phase of the globalization of welfare policy. See, for example, Collier and Messick, "Prerequisites vs. Diffusion"; Orenstein, *Privatizing Pensions*; Strang and Chang, "ILO and the Welfare State."

message of universal coverage was not matched in the policies developed to achieve that goal, which were complex and varied for different program designs.

Comparing the diffusion of coverage reforms among capitalist and communist countries during the Cold War reinforces the importance of policy legibility. The Soviet Union developed a consistent set of policies for welfare reform and linked them to its advice on economic development. It exported both policy packages to almost all communist countries, including China, in the 1940s and 1950s. The ILO, however, formulated vague and sometimes contradictory guidelines for welfare reform at the same time that it set clear goals for coverage. Since many capitalist countries ruled by governments that promoted the welfare state failed to adopt reforms to expand coverage, more than ideology or political interests were at stake. The legibility of policy ideas also matters.

Simpler, more standardized policy packages may have the potential to spread further, but their very simplicity can render them more difficult to implement under widely different conditions. The Chinese Communists faithfully carried out the Soviet model of welfare reform in the early 1950s, yet the same policies yielded the opposite results: exacerbating China's labor surplus rather than resolving any putative labor shortages. Similarly, the global diffusion of social insurance has led to the development of narrow, unequal welfare states in the developing world that in many respects are mirror opposites to the relatively progressive welfare states found in the advanced industrial countries. One-size-fits-all policies may facilitate wide diffusion, but the same quality can undermine their effectiveness.

## *War and the Founding of the Chinese Welfare State*

The adoption of new welfare programs for workers by the Nationalist and Communist parties in the 1940s and early 1950s showed that China's low level of economic development was no obstacle to adopting major social policy initiatives. Even the Nationalist government, which struggled to revive the economy and sustain its operations in the 1940s, did not hesitate to expand the scope of its responsibilities. More surprising, the Chinese Civil War did not prove to be an impediment to the founding of the Chinese welfare state—instead it turned out to be a catalyst. Military competition sparked political competition, leading both parties to adopt new welfare programs for the areas under their control.

The Chinese policy-making process was defined by competitive mobilization rather than redistributive bargaining. The main line of conflict was between two rival political parties competing for political and military dominance, not between two rival classes seeking to renegotiate their share of income. Making promises, claiming credit, and avoiding blame were more important than tilting the balance of power between capital and labor. As a result, strong top-down pressure for new welfare programs was not accompanied by strong bottom-up pressure for welfare protection. In an era of strike waves and almost continuous labor unrest, Chinese workers demanded higher wages and protection from the ravages of hyperinflation. In China, welfare was not the outcome of the incorporation of social forces into politics; it was instead a tool to facilitate their mobilization.

The differences in the welfare politics promoted by the Nationalist and Communist regimes are not easily captured by broad regime-type categories. Both parties were Leninist organizations, both established state-corporatist institutions to incorporate capital and labor into the regime, and at least in this transitional period they both promoted cross-class alliances among capital, labor, and the unemployed. The differences in the kind of corporatism created by the Nationalist and Communist regimes were most significant at the grassroots level. Moreover, it was only at the local level that social forces had a meaningful opportunity to participate in welfare politics by cooperating with or resisting the party's welfare agenda.

At the grass roots, two differences between the political parties' implementation of their welfare programs for workers stand out as explanations for the CCP's relative success in building a welfare state: the degree of internal party discipline and the structure of political participation in program implementation. The KMT effort was propelled by factional competition within the regime, but the same forces undermined the sustainability of the new programs. Demonstrations and counterdemonstrations orchestrated by factional rivals undermined the reputation of new welfare initiatives. In addition, the fast-moving competition for control among factions led to quick abandonment of new programs in favor of starting over with even newer ones, making it hard to consolidate any of them. In contrast, the CCP sought to limit factionalism within the party and focused on external competition with the KMT and labor racketeers for workers' loyalty. Communist political leaders with their own popular constituencies, such as Zhu Xuefan and Li Lisan, respected the limits of the roles assigned to them by the party. Furthermore, they were reassigned before they could consolidate their personal sources of power. As a result, CCP implementation efforts were cumulative, promoting the institutionalization of new programs.

The second important difference between the two parties lay in  the kind of political participation they permitted in the implementation and administration of their welfare programs. In keeping with its rhetoric about fostering a cross-class coalition, the KMT allowed participation by both capital and labor in its Worker Welfare program, which was institutionalized in corporatist enterprise committees. As a result, capitalists were able to use their new leverage to block both programs and benefits. Although the CCP adopted the same cross-class rhetoric under the guise of New Democracy, it was very selective about which programs and institutions provided real, as opposed to symbolic, political participation. In the new labor insurance program, workers were given meaningful participation in implementation, even determining each other's eligibility. But capitalists were given as little scope as possible for action and were subject to considerable intimidation as well. The preferential incorporation of labor over capital had a significant impact on implementation of the labor insurance program, propelling it to more than ten times the size of the KMT precedent in a matter of months. Although these forms of preferential incorporation of labor were not institutionalized, they had a profound impact on the scale of the Communist welfare programs.

As a result of the parties' top-down policy process, redistributive conflict was relatively marginal to the politics of the founding of the Chinese welfare state. Redistributive bargaining took place only during implementation and only at the grassroots level. The KMT institutionalized redistributive bargaining in its corporatist worker welfare committees. The CCP, however, tried to sidestep the politics of redistribution as much as possible. It was telling that the targets of the labor insurance struggle campaign were not capitalists, but instead the CCP's rival labor organizers on the factory floor. Competitive mobilization was a bigger threat to Communist implementation efforts than resistance from the employers who financed the new welfare programs.

The conditions that promoted nondemocratic political competition in China included war, national emergencies, and weak internal controls within the ruling party. Since these same conditions made institutionalizing the state more difficult, they were as likely to contribute to the collapse of the regime as they were to the foundation of a lasting welfare state. The sudden demise of the Nationalist regime only a few years after its first major welfare initiatives is a case in point. Although the Communist Party avoided that fate, its welfare state was weakly institutionalized at its founding, with a bureaucracy beginning to form only after the program had already been implemented and the first benefits distributed. The weak bureaucratic infrastructure of both the worker welfare and labor insurance programs suggests that there were few institutional continuities between them. The much smaller size of the KMT Worker Welfare program also limited the scope of any potential institutional continuities.[3] Beyond defining a challenging context for welfare reform with the choice of program design and the timing of its adoption, the wartime origins of China's welfare state left no lasting constraints on its development.

3. Much of the earlier research on the Chinese workplace has focused on the minority of companies with worker welfare programs: Frazier, *Making of the Chinese Industrial Workplace*; Bian, *Making of the State Enterprise System*; Bray, *Social Space and Governance*; Perry, "From Native Place to Workplace"; and Lü, "Minor Public Economy."

# *The Painful Expansion of the Chinese Welfare State*

Although China's low level of economic development did not inhibit policy makers from adopting a labor insurance program, it did impose lasting constraints on the pace of its expansion. Even with steady economic growth for most of the 1950s, job growth was slow and government budgets remained tight. Within these constraints, however, the social revolution carried out in the 1950s transformed the structure of inequality in Chinese society quickly and completely.

The political dynamics surrounding welfare reform also changed quickly in the early 1950s. Top-down pressure for welfare reform remained strong throughout the decade, but the motives behind it changed. After labor organizers were eased out of power at the head of China's official Communist labor union, economic planners took over the welfare policy-making process. In place of political strategies to mobilize working-class support for the regime, China's changing economic development strategies provided new impetus for welfare reform. Top-down pressure did not ease up in the transition; the CCP's ambitious development strategies served to expand the goals of welfare reform.

Another major change in the early 1950s was a rapid surge in bottom-up political demand for welfare. The sudden turnaround in citizens' expectations for the welfare state in the early 1950s was striking. Ignorance about welfare policies and programs among ordinary workers in the late 1940s and early 1950s had been pervasive, and one can only assume that the nonworking urban poor were less savvy about the differences among worker welfare, labor insurance, and unemployment relief. Once labor insurance was implemented, however, workers and nonworkers alike began to notice the differences, whether through personal experience or through neighborhood gossip. Labor insurance's most important advantage for China's young workforce was the access to health care it provided. But once older workers began to retire and draw pensions, the full significance of labor insurance's privileges started to sink in.

The mere existence of welfare programs would have gradually led to increasing awareness of the attractions of the Chinese welfare state as well as the hierarchies within it. But probably the most important factor shaping the political demand for welfare in the 1950s was the CCP's extensive propaganda efforts. Workers and the urban poor did not need to figure out the contours of the new welfare state on their own. The Chinese Communist leadership raised everyone's expectations by promising good jobs with full benefits in a matter of a few years. The rapid turnaround in public opinion in the early 1950s added considerable pressure for reforms to expand coverage.

China's first attempt at expansion followed the Soviet model: temporarily using cheaper, more easily administered welfare programs like unemployment relief to broaden coverage immediately. In the meantime, policy makers sought to engineer massive expansion of formal sector employment in order to permanently incorporate people outside the formal sector into the welfare state on an equal basis. The Soviet approach to welfare state expansion quickly won wide political support in urban China. Despite high levels of income inequality, both workers and the unemployed embraced the reforms. Moreover, capitalists posed no resistance to the expansion of welfare after their first searing experience with a struggle campaign. As a result, enrollment in the Universal Job Placement program soared and new benefits were created in many private firms.

Because the resources needed to engineer rapid expansion of formal sector employment were lacking, disappointment quickly turned the unemployment program into a political liability. The unemployed contested their unequal treatment through collective protest. Although they gained only token responses to their demands, the unemployed soon turned enthusiasm for unemployment relief into resentment over unfulfilled promises. Intensifying the gap between expectations and reality, the command economy suddenly rendered the implicit rationing of access to labor insurance very visible. By trying to eliminate the labor market and replace it with a single government bureaucracy for labor allocation, the impersonal, decentralized rationing carried out by employers was replaced by a single bureaucracy staffed by cadres who had the power to determine people's fates. Once the unemployed protested against the labor bureau to demand jobs and welfare, they politicized the rationing that had been in place from the beginning of the labor insurance program.

Although the CCP lacked resources to buy off political opposition, it enjoyed more power and discretion than most governments. It used these advantages to try radical alternatives to expand the welfare state. The first effort in 1955 sought to adapt the Soviet model by replacing unemployment relief with ruralization of the unemployed, following the same logic of adopting temporary measures until structural economic reform could facilitate the expansion of labor insurance. By sending the unemployed into the interior and reinvesting relief funds in new industries, the policy sought to accelerate economic growth. Rationing was deliberate this time, with no compensation for those who were forced to wait for jobs and labor insurance. Indeed, the CCP tried to win popular support for the logic of making short-term sacrifices for long-term gains. The Communists failed to convince the unemployed to support the policy, but the effective exclusion of unemployed workers from the labor union allowed the CCP to implement its policy reversal in 1955–56 without facing the same kind of collective resistance that the unemployment relief program had generated a few years earlier. The decline in partisan political competition and the elimination of underground labor organizations ensured that the unemployed had few options for collective resistance, even as they clung to their recently acquired identities as unemployed workers.

At the same time, the urban revolution was completed, eliminating capitalists as a potential source of political opposition to welfare reform and creating a much more egalitarian society. Labor continued to be effectively incorporated into the regime through the official labor union. Using their leverage through the labor union and the Hundred Flowers campaign, workers challenged the limits of the welfare state in the 1957 strike wave. Workers were successful in expanding coverage within the existing program and protecting many of their private benefits as well. The cost of their success was the CCP's withdrawal of the new social insurance regulations proposed in 1956, which would have extended coverage to the entire urban workforce and laid the foundation for a broad welfare state. Without any direct conflict between workers and the urban poor, preferential incorporation of labor had become an obstacle to the expansion of coverage.

The Great Leap Forward was another attempt to break through the constraints on the Chinese economy and the welfare state. Commune welfare programs represented a completely different approach to expanding the welfare state, more similar in some respects to citizen pension programs. By creating new, less expensive welfare programs such as commune canteens, the CCP gave up on the goal of extending full labor insurance benefits to the entire population. In contrast to other developing countries, Chinese welfare reformers sought to achieve universal coverage through commune welfare programs rather than limit the new programs to specific groups excluded from social insurance. With the continuation of labor insurance and the addition of new universal programs on top of it, workers gained new benefits and lost none of their old ones. The CCP simply abandoned rationing altogether.

Top-down pressure for welfare reform escalated during the Great Leap Forward as fear of punishment in the Anti-Rightist campaign impelled party cadres to implement the new Maoist vision of welfare reform. Although bottom-up pressure for welfare reform was muted by dislike of the commune canteens, the unemployed benefited from new jobs in the commune welfare programs and were incorporated into the new communes as urban residents. Their positions were not equal to the union membership that regular workers enjoyed, but dismantling the national labor union structure in the Anti-Rightist campaign closed the gap in political access to some degree.

Shanghai briefly achieved universal coverage in its food programs in 1960 (fig. C.1).[4] This achievement, however, came at the cost of undermining the sustainability of the welfare state—and indeed the entire economy along with it. Soft budget constraints were a bigger obstacle to expanding coverage than the preferential incorporation of labor.

In the crisis of the Great Leap Forward famine, the new commune welfare programs were completely dismantled, and the temporary austerity policies first tried in 1955 were made permanent.[5] Ruraliza-

4. China probably achieved broad coverage in 1958–59, before many rural commune canteens were shut down.
5. This finding supports Naughton's identification of the Great Leap Forward famine

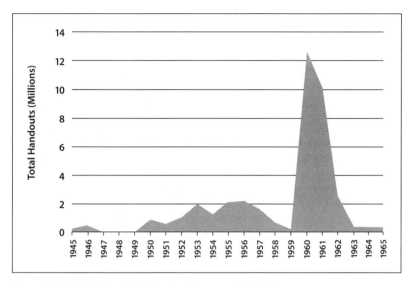

*Figure C.1* Shanghai Food Distribution Programs, 1945–65

*Sources:* SMA, A20-1-23; SMA, A20-1-38; SMA, A20-1-77; SMA, B127-1-53; SMA, B168-1-510; SMA, B168-1-512; SMA, B168-1-521; SMA, B168-1-712; SMA, B168-1-716; SMA, B168-1-717; SMA, B168-1-726; SMA, B168-1-732; SMA, B168-1-880; SMA, B168-1-910; SMA, B168-1-915; Shanghaishi tongji ju, ed., *Shanghai shi guomin jingji.*

tion of the unemployed and strict enforcement of the household registration system stabilized the labor insurance program. The household registration system became China's long-term solution to the problem of unemployment, forming a critical element of the Maoist welfare state.

Any remaining solidarity between workers and the unemployed evaporated in the midst of food shortages and massive layoffs. As the perception of scarcity turned redistribution into a zero-sum struggle, union leaders and workers alike sought to preserve their benefits rather than help welfare state outsiders. The contrasting fates of welfare state insiders and outsiders in the wake of these policy changes could hardly have been more extreme. In the ruralization campaigns in 1961–62, millions of unemployed workers were sent to the countryside to fend for themselves. In contrast, welfare state insiders saw their privileges

---

as the key turning point in the development of the Chinese workplace. See Naughton, "Danwei."

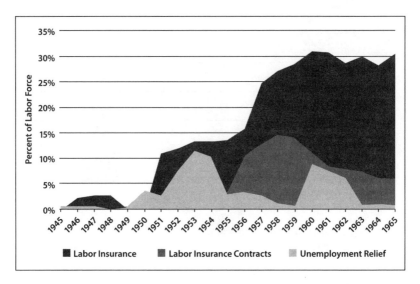

*Figure C.2* Shanghai Welfare Coverage, 1945–65

Sources: Shanghai zonggonghui, *1948 laogong nianjian*, 25–28, 75; Shanghai shi, *Shehui xingzheng tongji*, 75; Shanghai shi, *1946 Shanghai nianjian*, N19; Li Jianhua, "Zhanhou Shanghai shi ," 4–5; Shanghaishi tongji ju, *Shanghai shi guomin jingji*; SMA: A20-1-23; A20-1-38; A20-1-77; B127-1-15; B127-1-19; B127-1-53; B168-1-510; B168-1-511; B168-1-512; B168-1-521; B168-1-712; B168-1-880; B31-1-59; C1-2-322; C1-2-601; C1-2-1117; C1-2-1431; C1-2-1764; C1-2-1768; C1-2-2380; C1-2-2384; C1-2-3627; C1-2-3391; C1-2-4414.

reinforced in the 1962 labor insurance revisions, at the cost of increasing deficit spending. Although labor's political leverage had been reduced, its remaining toehold in state-owned enterprises was precisely the point where workers wielded the most power over production. The importance of this remnant of preferential incorporation was evident in the deepening gulf between welfare state insiders and outsiders.

Rationing reached full form in the early 1960s, transforming welfare politics at the grass roots from protest politics into patronage politics. With the hope of significantly changing the contours of the welfare state through welfare reform gone, the only remaining access to the welfare state was through the job placement bureaucracy and enterprise unions. Cadres' power to choose whom to privilege and whom to exclude came to define not just welfare politics, but urban politics more broadly for much of the Maoist era (fig. C.2).[6]

6. Walder, *Communist Neo-Traditionalism*; Whyte and Parish, *Urban Life*; Davis, "Unequal Chances."

*Table C.1.* Conditions Shaping the Expansion of Coverage in the Chinese Welfare State

| | Soviet transitional reforms 1952–54 | Chinese austerity reforms 1955–58 | Maoist commune reforms 1958–62 |
|---|---|---|---|
| Top-down pressure | high | mixed | very high |
| Political incorporation | labor and urban poor in equal coalition | preferential access for labor; urban poor excluded | labor and urban poor in unequal coalition |
| Predicted outcome | major expansion | no expansion | minor expansion |
| Actual outcome | minor reform coverage +46% | no reform coverage +62% | major reform coverage +23% |

Placing the three failed reform attempts side by side shows that the hypothesis that an equal coalition between workers and the unemployed will produce the most extensive gains in coverage is too simplistic (table C.1). In the Chinese case, there was sufficient top-down and bottom-up pressure to expand welfare coverage. Moreover, it took both top-down welfare reforms and bottom-up political demands to produce significant, lasting gains in welfare coverage. Even so, the preferential incorporation of labor over welfare state outsiders like the unemployed could turn into an obstacle to expansive welfare reform when the priorities of welfare state insiders took precedence over those of outsiders.

The failures of Chinese attempts to expand coverage demonstrate the difficulties of striking a balance between strong political demands for welfare and scarce economic resources. Reducing demands for welfare through repressive measures such as the ruralization campaigns was possible, but completely eliminating preferential incorporation for the Chinese Communist regime's key constituency was not. Loosening budget constraints was a far more tempting option, since it did not generate the same kind of political opposition. But it proved economically disastrous.

The Great Leap Forward famine led Chinese political leaders to abandon the effort to create a broad welfare state. The crisis also made urban workers very conservative, concerned above all else with maintaining their precarious privileges and passing them on to their children. Both at the top and at the grass roots of the Chinese

Communist regime there was strong political support for maintaining the inequalities at the heart of the welfare state. The exiled urban poor and the rural majority were no more compliant than they had been in the 1950s. But the household registration system ensured that they could do little to change their fate.

The scarcity of welfare protection only enhanced the value people placed on it. Even the upheavals of the Cultural Revolution, when almost every other urban institution came under assault, did not shake the foundations of labor insurance in state-owned enterprises. It was not the strength of workplace institutions that defined the limits of China's welfare state; instead it was the narrow reach of labor insurance that strengthened the institution of the workplace.

## Distinctive Features of the Chinese Case

Some distinctive features of the Chinese case provide insight into the fundamental dynamics of welfare state expansion. Taken together, the treatment of capitalists, elimination of the labor market, and rapid changes in inequality all rendered China's revolutionary welfare politics unusual among countries with narrow welfare states. First, the CCP's expropriation of capitalists removed one of the main sources of opposition to welfare state expansion. Without the political interference from economic elites found in other countries, the Chinese case highlights labor's contradictory role in welfare politics. The preferential incorporation of labor over capital facilitated the founding of the welfare state, providing the political support necessary for wide implementation. But after that point, the preferential incorporation of labor became an obstacle to the expansion of coverage. The alliance between workers and other social classes was fragile. With the realization that welfare reform was a zero-sum game, the politics of rationing developed and the solidarity between workers and the unemployed evaporated. Labor used its political advantage over the urban poor to protect its own interests, further widening the gap between welfare state insiders and outsiders. This vicious cycle led to the involution of the welfare state, with every increase in benefits making the expansion of coverage that much more difficult.

The second distinctive feature of Chinese politics in the 1950s was the elimination of the labor market, which highlights the role of rationing in the expansion of coverage. Rationing mechanisms are one of the primary ways in which the level of economic development affects welfare coverage. In social insurance welfare states in capitalist economies, the labor market serves as one of the main gatekeepers to welfare protection. It is a decentralized mechanism that most people take for granted since it appears to ration access on a meritocratic basis. Once the Chinese Communists eliminated the labor market, however, rationing for the welfare state could no longer fade into the background. Although the new job placement bureaucracy tried to adhere to meritocratic norms in allocating labor based on education and skill, the inconsistencies and injustices of their decisions quickly became politicized. In the more developed communist countries, labor shortages ensured that bureaucratic labor allocation did not generate the same kind of conflict. But due to China's huge imbalance in the demand and supply of jobs, the CCP ultimately resorted to population controls through the household registration system as a rationing mechanism for its welfare state. Forcibly reducing the urban population to a level the formal sector of the economy could sustain was a crude but effective measure to regulate the demand for jobs and welfare.

The third unusual aspect of welfare reform in revolutionary China were the rapid swings in economic inequality in the 1950s, providing a test case to assess the impact of inequality on the politics of redistribution. Examining how workers and the unemployed responded to changing cross-class coalitions offers an indirect measure of how inequality shaped incentives.

The evidence in the Chinese case is contradictory. With high levels of income inequality in the early years of the welfare state, workers expressed enthusiasm for redistribution and generosity toward the welfare needs and concerns of the unemployed. This pattern of high inequality and cross-class cooperation in the politics of redistribution corresponds to the findings from research on advanced industrial democracies.[7] Yet a decade later in the Great Leap Forward famine, extreme inequalities in access to food and jobs destroyed any semblance of cooperation between workers and the unemployed.[8] The inequalities in the two periods were very different, with capitalists enjoying the privileges of wealth in the early 1950s and ordinary workers enjoying the privileges of security in the early 1960s. Even after taking these variations in the nature of inequality and the privileged class into account, the Chinese case complicates the comparative debate rather than settling it. But it does offer an alternative explanation: economic scarcity.

Changing perceptions of scarcity provide a parsimonious explanation of the rise and fall of cross-class cooperation in Chinese welfare politics. The anticipation of ample resources in the early 1950s fueled cooperation between workers and the unemployed. The recession of the mid-1950s changed people's perceptions, and workers grew more competitive with the urban poor in welfare politics. The competition between them eased in the late 1950s when the Great Leap Forward again raised expectations of rapid economic growth and prosperity. Once extreme scarcity hit in the early 1960s, however, the competition took on the dynamics of a zero-sum struggle. Scarcity provides a simpler explanation of the changing dynamics of Chinese welfare politics in the 1950s than either the level or the nature of income inequality. It might also serve to reconcile the contradictory findings about class segmentation and welfare coalitions in Western Europe and Latin America.[9]

7. See, for example, Kenworthy and Pontusson, "Rising Inequality." Because of the CCP's top-down manipulation of coalitions, the Chinese case does not offer insight into inequality's impact on the role of segmented classes in coalition formation. See Baldwin, *Politics of Social Solidarity*; Mesa-Lago, *Social Security in Latin America*.
8. See, for example, Mares and Carnes, "Social Policy in Developing Countries."
9. Baldwin, *Politics of Social Solidarity*; Mesa-Lago, *Social Security in Latin America*.

## Comparing China to Other Developing Countries

In addition to expropriating capitalists and eliminating labor markets, radical reforms like ruralization and commune canteens set the Chinese case apart, with few counterparts among other developing countries. But the problems that prompted these experiments were common elsewhere as well. Because social insurance was considered the gold standard in program design in the postwar period when most developing countries founded their welfare states, almost all developing countries experienced the tension between low levels of economic development and the high cost of expanding coverage.

Since most developing countries never undertook reforms to expand coverage, the causes behind their narrow welfare states are not a mystery. Limited policy diffusion, state officials who do not take the lead in welfare reform, weak bottom-up pressure for inclusion, and economic elites who oppose the expansion of coverage provide obvious explanations for their failure of ambition. For these countries, the Chinese case simply stands as a warning that political ambition alone will not overcome the limits of a narrow welfare state.

But for those developing countries that did attempt major reforms to expand welfare coverage in the postwar period, there are striking parallels to the Chinese case even in places never touched by revolution. Moreover, since some of those countries managed to achieve broad coverage under challenging economic and political conditions, the comparisons point to possible solutions to the problem of narrow welfare states.

One common feature of welfare reformers in the developing world is the preferential incorporation of labor. The spread of corporatist institutions from Europe to Latin America, the Middle East, and parts of Asia in the 1930s and 1940s brought with it a strong preference for mobilizing and incorporating workers over farmers and other social classes.[10] As a corporatist institution itself, the ILO has played a central role in promoting corporatism in welfare policy making and administration.

10. Schmitter, "Still the Century of Corporatism?"; Chirot, "Corporatist Model"; Collier, "Trajectory"; Molina and Rhodes, "Corporatism."

When corporatist institutions were created under authoritarian regimes without other points of access to the policy-making process, the advantage that organized labor gained over farmers and the urban poor was significantly greater than in democratic regimes.

The preferential incorporation of labor across markedly different political regimes helps to explain some of the parallels in welfare politics under Latin American populism and Chinese communism in the postwar period. In Brazil and Argentina, for example, populist authoritarian political leaders mobilized workers into official labor unions in the 1930s and 1940s.[11] In both countries, social insurance programs were created for the mobilization drive rather than emerging as an outcome of it. The ideology and the goals of Latin American and Chinese top-down mobilization efforts were in some ways polar opposites, but the policies and the process were fundamentally similar.

After Brazil and Argentina democratized in the postwar period, their corporatist unions survived with their privileges largely intact. In addition, unions were well placed to take advantage of the new democratic arenas opened to popular political participation. As populist politicians used welfare policy to campaign among the urban poor and other welfare state outsiders, they generated greater demand for welfare. In Argentina, three reforms to extend coverage were adopted in the unstable period of democratic rule after the Second World War.[12] Each expansion of coverage was accompanied by improvements of benefits for welfare state insiders, aptly described as the "massification of privilege."[13] As a result, spending escalated much faster than the growth in coverage. In Brazil, heightened political demand for welfare was evident in five major welfare reform bills proposed in the fifteen years after democratization. But when Brazil finally adopted the 1960 Social Insurance Act, all the provisions to expand coverage were eliminated in response to pressure from physicians groups, bankers, and organized labor.[14] Instead, benefits for welfare state insiders

11. Malloy, *Politics of Social Security*, 100–103; Velloso Cardoso de Oliveira, "Social Security in Brazil," 382; Collier and Collier, *Shaping the Political Arena*, 333–39.
12. Mesa-Lago, *Social Security in Latin America*, 165.
13. Ibid., 206.
14. Malloy, *Politics of Social Security*, 100–103; Velloso Cardoso de Oliveira, "Social Security in Brazil," 385–86.

were increased dramatically, further undermining the fiscal strength of the programs.

To explain such counterintuitive outcomes, scholars have focused on the absence of alliances between labor and other popular social classes, arguing that in Latin America's highly unequal societies organized labor had few interests in common with other social forces.[15] Other scholars have posited an alliance between organized labor and capitalists.[16] But the ways in which both Brazil and Argentina achieved broad welfare coverage in the 1970s suggest the preferential incorporation of labor may have been more important in limiting coverage than weak popular alliances or elite-labor coalitions. It was military governments, not democratically elected politicians, that were responsible for extending coverage to people without pensions (1971) in Argentina and to domestic workers (1971) and rural farm workers (1972) in Brazil. Moreover, the reforms were adopted in the wake of the reform and the repression of their official labor movements.[17] Regime change and the weakening of labor's privileges paved the way for welfare reforms to achieve broad coverage in Brazil and Argentina.

These comparisons suggest that labor's contradictory role in welfare reform is not peculiar to China or to communist regimes. The preferential incorporation of labor cut across many different kinds of political regimes in the twentieth century and helps explain the prevalence of narrow welfare states in so many of them. Latin American populist regimes also highlight the importance of rationing mechanisms to ensure the sustainability of the welfare state. The soft budget constraints of the 1950s and 1960s bankrupted Brazil's and Argentina's social insurance programs, even without aiming for universal coverage as China attempted in the Great Leap Forward. Deficit spending in social insurance programs combined with wage indexation to protect workers' income from inflation fueled hyperinflation and currency crises. Although Latin American economic crises were not as severe as

15. Mesa-Lago, *Social Security in Latin America*; Weyland, *Democracy without Equity*.
16. Cardoso and Helwege, "Populism, Profligacy, and Redistribution"; Mares and Carnes "Social Policy."
17. Malloy, *Politics of Social Security,* 129; Malloy and Parodi, "Politics, Equity and Social Security Policy"; Mesa-Lago, *Social Security in Latin America*, 166–67, 206.

China's economic collapse, they contributed to the demise of democratic rule in the 1960s. State capacity to regulate expansion in line with resources over the long term is essential to the achievement of a broad welfare state.

Outside their experiments with soft budget constraints, Latin American welfare states adopted a variety of rationing mechanisms to regulate the expansion of coverage. Most Latin American countries used labor markets as an external mechanism to ration access to the welfare state. They also developed political mechanisms to ration access more narrowly than the market alone. For example, policies limiting the scope of implementation by geographic region or economic sector were used in Colombia and Central America.[18] Often intended to be a temporary measure to implement social insurance gradually, many of these policies became permanent, whether owing to bureaucratic inertia or through explicit policy decisions. State tolerance of informal sector employment, rather than enforcing labor and welfare regulations, may represent another rationing mechanism. State capacity to regulate the expansion of the welfare state is critical to ensuring its long-term viability, but rationing mechanisms can also become obstacles to the expansion of welfare coverage long after economic constraints have eased.

Comparisons among the Chinese and Latin American welfare states show that broad coverage can be achieved in developing countries with social insurance welfare states. Strong state leadership in welfare reform was vital for attempting expansive welfare reform in each case. No particular cross-class coalition was necessary for the expansion of coverage, but the preferential incorporation of labor posed an obstacle to welfare reform, especially when resources were scarce and redistribution came to be seen as a zero-sum struggle. These comparisons also indicate that state capacity to regulate the expansion of the welfare state to ensure sustainability is vital for both welfare reform and the survival of the welfare state. Through repeated attempts at welfare reform, both Brazil and Argentina managed to combine all three ingredients by the early 1970s: strong state leadership, relatively equal access to the policy process, and an effective rationing mechanism. China had strong state

18. SSA, *Social Security Programs 1961*, 136, 146; SSA, *Social Security Programs 1979*, 50, 174.

leadership in welfare reform in the 1950s but privileged labor over the unemployed and failed to develop a rationing mechanism to regulate expansion effectively. By the time a crude but effective rationing mechanism was put in place in the 1960s, party leaders had given up on welfare reform.

## Comparing China to the Advanced Industrial Countries

The context for welfare reform was much more favorable in the advanced industrial countries, with far higher levels of economic development and stable democratic regimes that did not privilege labor to the same degree as many nondemocratic regimes. But the Chinese case reveals additional reasons why the path to broad coverage has been easier for the advanced industrial countries. The first was lower levels of political demand for welfare, especially before the Second World War. European workers may have been more knowledgeable about the advantages of the welfare state than their Chinese counterparts, but political demands from the middle classes and other groups were tempered by pro-market, antiwelfare ideologies such as liberalism.[19] In addition, the church often opposed welfare state expansion to protect its own role in charity and social services.[20] Neither political ideology nor religion moderated demand for welfare in China.

With less demand for rapid expansion of welfare coverage, the advanced industrial countries still had a greater state capacity to ration access to ensure sustainability. Most European social insurance programs adhered strictly to the "insurance principle" before the Great Depression and the Second World War. The insurance principle required that beneficiaries receive their entitlements only after a career of contributions to the program. This rationing mechanism kept commitments in line with resources over the long term and spurred the development of actuarial analysis that further enhanced state

19. Baldwin, *Politics of Social Solidarity*, 103–4, 158; Alesina and Glaeser, *Fighting Poverty.*
20. Kahl, "Religious Roots."

capacity. When the insurance principle was relaxed after the Second World War to achieve universal coverage, the advanced industrial countries not only had more resources to devote to their programs, but they also enjoyed greater capacity to regulate expansion. Actuarial analysis, dedicated tax revenues, and welfare bureaucracies capable of administering a rationing process equitably are mechanisms to align new commitments with available resources. Ironically, the states with the greatest capacity to ration access to the welfare state had the least need to do so.

## Implications for the Future

Today China is once again at the forefront of welfare reform in the developing world. After more than thirty years of caution, Chinese Communist Party leaders are pushing to achieve ambitious new goals in welfare reform. The contemporary Chinese reforms come in the context of a worldwide surge in welfare reforms to expand coverage that began in the 1990s and accelerated in the 2000s. Both Asia and Latin America are leading the new trend, and several African countries have also joined in.[21]

A milestone in the development of China's welfare state came in 2010, with the passage of the Social Insurance Law. The legislation was the culmination of the social insurance reform first put forward in 1956. After almost forty years in limbo, the proposal was revived in 1994. Internal party debates, solicitation of public feedback over the Internet, and review by the National People's Congress delayed passage of the law by another sixteen years. On first reading, the 2010 Social Insurance Law is much more ambitious than its predecessor, calling for a universal welfare state and directly addressing the welfare needs of the rural population.

But, in fact, the 2010 law is a social insurance law in name only, since

---

21. Huber and Stephens, *Democracy and the Left*; SSA, *Social Security Programs 2012–13*; Barrientos et al., *Social Assistance in Developing Countries Database*; Mares and Carnes, "Social Policy."

it does not specify any particular program design, much less mandate a social insurance program. Most significant, it does not create any new entitlements. For example, the provision on population coverage does not define what the term "coverage" means or set eligibility standards of any kind.[22] Similarly, although the law calls for old-age pensions, it does not specify what benefits should be provided. The contrast to the original 1951 Labor Insurance Regulations is stark, since the earlier regulations clearly mandated a social insurance program with legal entitlements to specific lifetime benefits.

Despite the shortcomings of the 2010 law as a social insurance policy, there are indications that the current round of welfare reform marks a turning point in the development of the Chinese welfare state. Perhaps more important than the new legislation was the announcement at the CCP's Sixth Plenum in 2006 of the target date of 2020 to achieve universal coverage in China's social security programs.[23] Evidence that the goals were more than window dressing came in 2008, when a new push was announced to reach universal coverage in health care by 2012. Three years later, the CCP announced that the goal had been achieved ahead of schedule with nationwide implementation of urban and rural health insurance programs.[24]

China's contemporary welfare reforms have been driven by top-down pressure from the CCP leadership. The revival of CCP interest in welfare reform in the 1990s stemmed initially from a new economic development strategy based on privatization of bankrupt state-owned enterprises. To facilitate privatization, structural welfare reforms transformed the workplace welfare system into a government-administered social insurance system.[25] These welfare reforms maintained benefits for retirees and workers forced into early retirement, but they also laid the institutional foundations for expanding coverage beyond the workplace. The first step came in 1997 with a pension reform that extended coverage to all enterprises.[26] Then in 1999 a new social assistance (*dibao*) program

22. Zhonghua renmin gongheguo, "Shehui baoxian fa."
23. Chinese Communist Party, "Communique of the Sixth Plenum."
24. Yip and Hsiao, "China's Health Reform."
25. Frazier, *Socialist Insecurity*; Beland and Yu, "A Long Financial March."
26. Xie Jianhua and Ba Feng, *Shehui baoxian faxue*, 132–33.

for the urban poor was created, China's first major welfare program for the urban poor since the 1950s.[27]

The CCP leaders who came to power in 2003 viewed welfare reform as more than a means to an end. Having risen through the ranks in party and government posts in the poor, less-developed interior, they promised efforts to reduce both regional and urban-rural inequality.[28] While remaining committed to rapid economic development, Hu Jintao and Wen Jiabao made reducing income inequality and improving living standards in the countryside goals in their own right. Hu and Wen were responsible for setting the goal of achieving a universal welfare state by 2020.

The first step in the expansion of the social safety net for the elderly in the countryside came in 2007, when a rural social assistance program was implemented nationwide, providing better benefits and broader coverage for poor elderly households than the former rural Five Guarantee (*wubao*) program.[29] With the rural program in place to complement the urban program established earlier, China completed the implementation of the first national social assistance program in its history. The second step in the push to achieve universal coverage came in 2009, when the New Rural Pension Scheme was piloted in two hundred counties.[30] Although achieving universal coverage in old-age pensions had seemed impossible to many Chinese policy analysts only a few years earlier, the implementation schedule was accelerated several times over the next few years, until Premier Wen Jiabao announced that China had achieved national implementation of rural pensions in July 2012, before the next leadership transition took place.[31]

Although there is local variation, most of the new rural pension programs are voluntary programs with government subsidies to create financial incentives to participate.[32] Impressive as the rapid implementation of this program is, the goal of universal coverage remains ambig-

27. Solinger, "Path Dependency Re-examined"; Solinger, "Urban Dibao."
28. Lam, *Chinese Politics.*
29. Tang Jun, "Chengxiang dibao zhidu," 15.
30. Guowuyuan, "Guanyu kaizhan xinxing."
31. Wen Jiabao, "Zai quanguo xinxing nongcun he chengzhen jumin."
32. Yang et al., "Social Security for China's Rural Aged."

uous, as more than a century of experience with voluntary pension programs around the world has shown that they usually suffer from low participation rates, especially among the poor. Comparative evidence suggests that national implementation of a voluntary pension program is unlikely to achieve broad coverage, much less universal coverage, even with financial incentives in place.

But when we step back to consider the economic and political conditions for welfare reform in China today, there are many reasons for optimism. The context for welfare reform has probably changed more dramatically in China than in any other country in the developing world. Economic constraints have been eased by more than thirty years of rapid economic development, making China a middle-income country with a per capita GDP that approached half of the world average in 2010, up from only one-fifth of the world average in 1950.[33] Moreover, the Chinese economy industrialized in the process, reducing agriculture's share of the workforce to below 50 percent by 2004.[34]

Another key change from the 1950s to the 2000s is that Chinese policy makers now show considerable flexibility in program design. One benefit of the vague 2010 Social Insurance Law is that it does not foreclose other program designs that are more likely to achieve broad coverage. In addition, the Chinese government has been experimenting with a variety of welfare program designs at the local level rather than importing the latest international model. The experiments help policy makers understand how the programs can be adapted to local conditions as well as gain firsthand knowledge about the tradeoffs that they pose. Their change in attitude is not the result of declining international influence; Chinese government officials and academics are more closely connected than ever to transnational policy networks, including the ILO, the World Bank, and the Asian Development Bank. But Chinese policy makers have also grown more critical, selectively adopting foreign models and paying much greater attention to adapting them to local conditions. Voluntary social insurance is probably not the route to universal coverage in China, but the new flexibility in program design could well lead to the adoption of programs more likely to achieve that goal.

33. Maddison, *World Economy.*
34. Naughton, *Chinese Economy*, 152.

Counterintuitive as it may sound, the final change in the political context for welfare reform is that the power and position of organized labor have declined precipitously. The privatization reforms in the late 1990s for small and medium state-owned enterprises undermined the institutional underpinnings of labor's preferential incorporation. As a result, workers and pensioners in state-owned enterprises were reduced to trying to hang on to their pensions rather than improve on them. Moreover, with the bankruptcy of their employers, retirees had every reason to support the expansion of coverage to new groups of welfare state outsiders, since they needed their ongoing contributions to finance their own continued benefits. The direction of redistribution has been reversed.

While top-down pressure for welfare reform increased significantly in the 1990s and 2000s, it is not clear that bottom-up demand has increased as fast. Although migrant workers are now being recruited into the official labor union, farmers still lack peasant associations or some other formal means of incorporation into the regime. Moreover, public opinion surveys show mixed attitudes toward welfare. Not surprisingly, there is continued strong support for welfare in urban areas, including for the idea of expanding coverage.[35] But the few surveys we have of rural residents and migrant workers show considerable suspicion regarding whether government welfare programs could help solve their problems, possibly as a legacy of China's regressive welfare state.[36] One of the lessons of the 1950s, however, is that experience with welfare programs can quickly generate demand for inclusion. The national implementation of old-age pensions may not achieve universal coverage by the 2020 goal, but it is likely to create conditions under which political demand for welfare expansion will increase. Direct experience and publicity for the new programs could create more bottom-up pressure for welfare reform.

The conditions that led to the failure of welfare reform and the development of a narrow welfare state in China have now changed fundamentally. More resources, more flexibility in program design, and a weakened working class define a context in which the urban

---

35. Frazier, *Socialist Insecurity.* 153–54.
36. Whyte, *Myth of the Social Volcano,* 50–51, 130–31.

poor and rural farmers are more likely to gain entry into the Chinese welfare state. Although doubts persist about the state's capacity to regulate the expansion of the welfare state to ensure long-run sustainability, there are more rationing mechanisms in place compared to during the Maoist welfare state.[37] In addition to continuation of the household registration system, the revival of labor markets and improvements in government agencies' expertise in statistical and economic analysis have strengthened state capacity.

Given their weak legal status, it is still too soon to tell whether and how China's new welfare programs will ameliorate poverty or reduce income inequality. Reaching these outcomes will depend on continued expansion of coverage to reach all citizens, as well as continued improvement and standardization in benefits. Devolution of the power to set benefit levels and tax contributions to the provincial, municipal, and the county levels renders the Chinese welfare state extremely decentralized and its benefits highly unequal. The CCP's current leadership could elect to ease up on the expansion of coverage, leave low benefits in place, or shut down the new programs entirely; only time will tell whether reforms will continue until universal coverage is achieved.

With its national social assistance program and broad welfare coverage in health care and pension programs, the new Chinese welfare state can be expected to reduce poverty, especially in the countryside. But unless there are major policy changes, the Chinese welfare state will not be as progressive as the European welfare states or even the American welfare state. As in Latin America, the long-term legacy of a narrow welfare state in China may be the persistence of high levels of inequality long after the limits of narrow coverage are overcome.

37. For doubts, see Frazier, *Socialist Insecurity*, 12–13.

# Bibliography

## Archives: Shanghai Municipal Archives (SMA)

A20-1-23. Zhonggong Shanghai shiwei. Chengshi renmin gongshe gongzuo lingdao xiaozu中共上海市委城市人民公社工作领导小组 (Shanghai Party Committee Urban Commune Leadership Small Group); Shanghai shi tongji ju 上海市统计局 (Shanghai Municipal Statistical Bureau). "Chengshi renmin gongshe zuzhi qingkuang tongji yuebao" 城市人民公社组织情况统计月报 (Monthly statistical reports on the organization and conditions of the urban people's communes). 1960.

A20-1-37. Zhonggong Shanghai shiwei. Chengshi renmin gongshe gongzuo lingdao xiaozu. "Chengshi renmin gongshe tongji ziliao" 城市人民公社统计资料 (Urban commune statistics). 1961.

A20-1-38. Zhonggong Shanghai shiwei. Chengshi renmin gongshe gongzuo lingdao xiaozu; Shanghai shi tongji ju. "Guanyu 1961 nian chengshi renmin gongshe zuzhi qingkuang tongji biao" 关于1961年城市人民公社组织情况统计表 (Statistical reports on the organization and conditions of the urban people's communes in 1961). 1961.

A20-1-51a. Zhonggong Shanghai shiwei. Chengshi renmin gongshe gongzuo lingdao xiaozu; Shanghai shehui kexue yuan. "Guanyu Liyuan diqu jumin jingji shenghuo de diaocha" 关于丽园地区居民经济生活的调查 (An investigation of the living conditions of the residents of Liyuan District). 1961.

A20-1-51b. Zhonggong Shanghai shiwei. Chengshi renmin gongshe gongzuo lingdao xiaozu; Shanghai shehui kexue yuan 上海社会科学院 (Shanghai Academy of Social Sciences). "You guan Liyuan diqu jumin chifan fangmian jige wenti de diaocha ziliao" 有关梨园地区居民吃饭方面几个问题的调查资料 (An investigation into some problems the residents have with food in Liyuan district). 1961.

A20-1-51c. Zhonggong Shanghai shiwei. Chengshi renmin gongshe gongzuo lingdao xiaozu; Shanghai shehui kexue yuan. "Liyuan diqu shenghuo fuwu shiye de diaocha" 丽园地区生活服务事业的调查 (An investigation into Liyuan District's daily living service enterprises) 1961.

A20-1-53. Zhonggong Shanghai shiwei. Chengshi renmin gongshe gongzuo lingdao xiaozu; Zhonggong Huangpu qu Guangdong lu jiedao diaocha gongzuo zu 中共黄埔区广东陆街道调查工作组 (Huangpu District Party Committee Guangdong Rd investigation work group). "Guanyu Guangdong lu jiedao gonggong shitang de diaocha" 关于广东陆街道公共食堂的调查 (An investigation of the Guangdong Rd commune canteens). 1961.

A20-1-60. Zhonggong Shanghai shiwei. Zhabei qu wei chengshi renmin gongshe lingdao xiaozu bangongshi 闸北区委城市人民公社领导小组办公室 (Zhabei District Party Committee Urban People's Commune Leadership Small Group Office). "Guanyu jiedao lining zuzhi qilaide geti laodongzhe de diaocha baogao (caogao)" 关于街道里弄组织起来的个体劳动者的调查报告（草稿） (Preliminary report on an investigation into the organization of independent workers in the lanes and alleys). 1961.

A20-1-69. Zhonggong Shanghai shiwei. Chengshi renmin gongshe gongzuo lingdao xiaozu. "Guanyu xiafang gongchang qingkuang de diaocha baogao" 关于下放工厂情况的调查报告 (Report on the conditions of decentralized factories). 1962.

A20-1-70. Zhonggong Shanghai shiwei, Chengshi renmin gongshe gongzuo lingdao xiaozu. "Guanyu tiaojian lining jiti shiye de yijian baogao" 关于调减里弄集体事业的意见报告 (Opinions about streamlining lane and alley collective enterprises). 1962.

A20-1-77. Zhonggong Shanghai shiwei. Chengshi renmin gongshe lingdao xiaozu. Shanghai shi tongji ju. "Guanyu jiedao linong zuzhi qingkuang tongji biao" (Statistical reports on conditions in lane and alley organizations). 1962.

A20-1-81. Zhonggong Shanghai shiwei. Gequ quwei lining gongzuo xiaozu 各区区委里弄工作小组 (Lane and Alley Party Committee Small Group). "Guanyu jianli chengshi renmin gongshe zhunbei gongzuo jihua" 关于建立城市人民公社准备工作计划 (Plans for the preparatory work to establish the urban people's communes). Oct.–Nov. 1958.

A31-2-70. Zhonggong Shanghai shiwei. Nanshi qu 南市区 (Nanshi district). "Sanpailou weishengzhan xianjin jingyan zongjie 三拍漏卫生站先进经验总结 (Summary report on Sanpailou Hygiene Station's advance). March 22, 1960.

A36-2-102a. Zhonggong Shanghai shiwei. Gongye zhengzhi bu 工业政治部 (Industry & Political Bureau). "Guanyu shiye gongren wenti" 关于失业工人问题 (Unemployed workers' problems). 1956.

A36-2-102b. Zhonggong Shanghai shiwei. Gongye zhengzhi bu. "Guanyu laodong jiuye wenti de baogao" 关于劳动就业问题的报告 (Report on job placement problems). 1956.

A36-2-102c. Zhonggong Shanghai shiwei. Gongye zhengzhi bu. "Guanyu xin heyingchang gongren jieji ruogan wenti" 关于新合营厂工人阶级若干问题 (Some problems among the working class in new joint-owned enterprises). 1956.

B25-1-1. Shanghai shi renmin weiyuanhui renkou bangongshi 上海市人民委员会人口办公室 (Shanghai Municipal People's Committee Population Office). "Guanyu jiaqiang benshi hukou dengji yu jianshao renkou de zhishi" 关于加强本市户口管理与逐步紧缩人口的指示（草稿）(Draft orders on strengthening household registration and population reduction). 1955.

B31-1-59. Shanghai shi tongji ju上海市统计局 (Shanghai Statistical Bureau). "Guanyu 1949–1962 Shanghai shi guomin jingji tongji" 关于1949–1962上海市国民经济统计 (Statistics on Shanghai's economy 1949–1962). 1963.

B54-1-2. Shanghai shi renmin weiyuanhui, linshi gongzuo weiyuanhui 上海市临时工作委员会 (Shanghai Municipal People's Committee, Temporary Work Committee)."Qingkuang fanying"情况反映 (Situation reports). 1957.

B54-1-4. Shanghai shi renmin weiyuanhui, linshi gongzuo weiyuanhui. "Qu baogao" 区报告 (District reports). 1957.

B54-1-5a. Shanghai shi renmin weiyuanhui, linshi gongzuo weiyuanhui, bangongshi. "Wu, liu yuefen chuli zhigong naoshi wenti de qingkuang baogao" 五,六月份处里职工闹事问题的情况报告 (Report on conditions in resolving labor disturbances and problems in May and June). October 29, 1957.

B54-1-5b. Shanghai shi renmin weiyuanhui, linshi gongzuo weiyuanhui. "Laodongju wu, liu yuefen chuli zhigong naoshi wenti de gongzuo baogao" 劳动局五,六月份处理职工闹事问题的工作报告 (Labor's Bureau's work report on resolving labor disturbances and problems in May and June). July 15, 1957.

B54-1-6. Shanghai shi renmin weiyuanhui, linshi gongzuo weiyuanhui. Shanghai shi gonghui lianhehui. "Wu, liu yuefen Shanghai bufen zhigong naoshi de qingkuang baogao" 五,六月份上海部分职工闹事的情况报告 (Report on conditions in the labor disturbances among some Shanghai workers in May and June). September 7, 1957.

B105-7-1180. Shanghai shi jiaoyu ju 上海市教育局 (Shanghai Municipal Education Bureau). "Guanyu Zhabei qu minban xiaoxue de qingkuang huibao" 关于闸北区民办学校的情况汇报(Report on the conditions of the grassroots primary schools in Zhabei district). June 27, 1961.

B127-1-10. Shanghai shi laodong ju 上海市人民政府劳动局 (Shanghai Municipal Labor Bureau). "Laodongju yinianlaide gongzuo gaikuang" 劳动局一年来的工作概况 (Survey of the bureau's work over the last year). 1950.

B127-1-15. Shanghai shi laodong ju 上海市劳动局 (Shanghai Municipal Labor Bureau). "Jiuge yue gongzuo jiankuang" 九个月工作简况 (Preliminary nine-month work report). 1951.

B127-1-19. Shanghai shi laodong ju. "1952 nian gongzuo zongjie baogao" 1952年工作总结报告 (1952 summary work report). 1952.

B127-1-29. Shanghai shi laodong ju. "1953 nian gongzuo zongjie baogao" 1953年工作总结报告 (1953 summary work report). 1953.

B127-1-53. Shanghai shi laodong ju. "Shanghai shi shiye gongren jiuji tongji ziliao" 上海市失业工人救济统计资料 (Shanghai unemployment relief statistics). 1955.

B127-1-54. Shanghai shi laodong ju. "1955 nian gongzuo zongjie baogao" 1955年工作总结报告 (1955 summary work report). 1955.

B127-1-1186. Shanghai shi laodong ju. "Guanyu Shanghai shi 1951 nian gongchang qiye shixing laodong baoxian" 关于上海市1951年工厂企业实行劳动保险 (Implementing labor insurance in Shanghai's industrial enterprises in 1951). 1951.

B127-1-1432. Shanghai shi laodong ju. "Shanghai shi shiye gongren jiji fenzi dahui" 上海市失业工人积极分子大会 (Shanghai Municipal Unemployed Worker Activists Congress). 1956.

B127-1-1930. Shanghai shi laodong ju. "Guanyu shiye gongren jiuji gongzuo you minzheng bumen jieguande lianhe tongzhi" 关于失业工人救济工作由民政部门接管的联合通知 (Joint notice on the Ministry of Civil Affairs' takeover of unemployment relief). 1956.

B127-2-16. Shanghai shi laodong ju. "Fa shiye gongren dengji gongzuo" 发失业工人登记工作 (Carrying out unemployment registration work). 1951.

B129-2-6. Shanghai shi shiye gongren jiuji weiyuanhui 上海市失业工人救济委员会 (Shanghai Municipal Unemployment Relief Commission). "Shiye gongren daibiao huiyi" 失业工人代表会议 (Unemployed Workers' Representative Congress). 1951.

B129-2-16a. Shanghai shi shiye gongren jiuji weiyuanhui. "Diaocha Maochangdan chang gonghui jiuji fafang gongzuo baogao" 调查茂昌蛋厂工会救济发放工作报告 (Investigation report on the relief work of the Maochangdan factory union). 1951.

B129-2-16b. Shanghai shi shiye gongren jiuji weiyuanhui. "Jiefang qian shiye gongren dengji banfa 解放前失业工人登记办法 (Methods for registering unemployed workers [laid off] before liberation). 1951.

B129-2-16c. Shanghai shi shiye gongren jiuji weiyuanhui. "Shuqi xuexi ban zongjie" 暑期学习班总结 (Summary report on the summer study classes). 1951.

B129-2-16d. Shanghai shi shiye gongren jiuji weiyuanhui. "5 yue 7 ri dengji ke kuoda huiyi" 五月七日登记科扩大会议 (May 7 enlarged meeting of the Registration Division). 1951.

B129-2-16e. "Fa shiye gongren dengji gongzuo dianxing jieshao" 发失业工人登记证工作典型介绍 (An introduction to doing model unemployment registration work). 1951.

B131-1-2. Shanghai laodong jiuye weiyuanhui 上海劳动就业委员会 (Shanghai Job Placement Committee). "Guanyu laodong jiuye gongzuo de baogao" 关于劳动就业工作的报告 (Job placement work report); "Guanyu guanche zhongyang laodong jiuye gongzuo xin fangzhen de baogao" 关于贯彻中央劳动就业工作新方针的报告 (Revised report on implementing the Central Job Placement Committee's new policy). 1953.

B131-1-7. Shanghai laodong jiuye weiyuanhui. Zhengwuyuan jiuye laodong weiyuanhui 政务院劳动就业委员会 (State Administrative Council Job Placement Committee). "Guanyu shiye renyuan tongyi dengji banfa" 关于失业人员统一登记办法 (Methods for universal unemployment registration). 1952.

B131-1-8. Shanghai laodong jiuye weiyuanhui. Shanghai laodong ju fen dangzu 上海劳动局分党组 (Shanghai Labor Bureau Party Branch). "Dui jige youguan laodong jiuye wenti de yijian" 对几个有关劳动就业问题的意见 (Suggestions on some job placement registration problems). 1953.

B131-1-11. Shanghai laodong jiuye weiyuanhui. Shanghai shi laodongju fen dangzu 上海市劳动局分党组 Shanghai Municipal Labor Bureau Party Branch. "Guanyu benshi shiye renyuan zuzhi ji laodong jiuye jingchang gongzuo bianzhi yijian de shuoming" 关于本市失业人员组织及劳动就业经常工作编制意见的说明 (Explanation for suggestions on the organization of unemployed workers and the regular operation of the job placement system). July 18, 1953.

B131-2-4. Shanghai laodong jiuye weiyuanhui; Zhongyang renmin zhengfu laodong bu dangzu 中央人民政府劳动部党组 (Central Labor Ministry Party Group). "Guanyu muqian laodong jiuye gongzuo baogao" 关于目前劳动就业工作报告 (Job placement work report). 1954.

B168-1-182. Shanghai shi minzheng ju. Zhonggong weiyuanhui 上海市民政局中共委员会 (Shanghai Civil Affairs Bureau Party Committee). "Shanghai shi shourong qiansong gongzuo jigou bianzhi fangan" 上海市收容迁送工作机构编制方案 (Plan for reorganizing Shanghai's shelter and evacuation work"). 1961.

B168-1-510. Shanghai shi minzhengju 上海市民政局 (Shanghai Municipal Civil Affairs Bureau). "Shanghai shi minzheng gongzuo tongji 1949-53" 上海市民政工作统计1949-53 (Shanghai civil affairs statistics 1949-53). 1953.

B168-1-511. Shanghai shi minzheng ju. "1954 nian Shanghai shi minzheng gongzuo tongji" 1954年上海市民政工作统计 (Shanghai civil affairs statistics 1954). 1954.

B168-1-512. Shanghai shi minzhengju. "Shanghai shi minzheng gongzuo tongji ziliao 1955" 上海市民政局统计资料 (Shanghai civil affairs statistics 1955). 1955.

B168-1-521. Shanghai shi minzheng ju. "Shanghai shi minzheng ju gongzuo tongji ziliao 1956" 上海市民政局统计资料 (Shanghai civil affairs statistics 1956). 1957.

B168-1-538. Shanghai shi minzheng ju. "1958 Shanghai minzhengju baogao" 1958年上海市民政工作总结. (1958 summary work report). 1959.

B168-1-572. Shanghai shi minzhengju. "1962 nian Shanghai shi mingzhengju gongzuo baogao" 1962年上海市民政局工作总结 (1962 work report). 1963.

B168-1-712. Shanghai shi minzhengju. "Shanghai shi shinian minzheng gongzuo tongji 1949-59" 上海市十年民政工作统计 (Ten years of Shanghai civil affairs work statistics 1949-59). 1959.

B168-1-716. Shanghai shi minzheng ju. "1960 nian shehui jiuji" 1960年社会救济 (Social relief 1960). 1960.

B168-1-717. Shanghai shi minzheng ju. "1961 nian shehui jiuji" 1961年社会救济 (Social relief 1961). 1961.

B168-1-726. Shanghai shi minzheng ju. "1962 nian shehui jiuji" 1962年社会救济 (Social relief 1962). 1962.

B168-1-732. Shanghai shi minzheng ju. "1963 nian shehui jiuji" 1963年社会救济 (Social relief 1963). 1963.

B168-1-862. Shanghai shi minzheng ju. Zhengxie Shanghai shi weiyuanhui 政协上海市委员会 (Chinese People's Consultative Conference, Shanghai Municipal Committee). "Guanyu jinsuo Shanghai renkou wenti de qingkuang he yijian" (Opinions and circumstances surrounding the problem of reducing Shanghai's population). (August 25, 1955).

B168-1-880. Shanghai shi minzhengju. "Guanyu wailai renkou qingkuang he yijian de baogao" 关于外来人口情况和意见的报告 (Report on the conditions and opinions of the rural migrant population).1957.

B168-1-885. Shanghai shi minzhengju. Shanghai shi renmin weiyuanhui 上海市人民委员会 (Shanghai Municipal Committee). "Guanyu dongyuan chengshi shengyu laodongli zhiyuan shehui zhuyi nongye jianshe de gongzuo de chubu jihua" 关于动员城市剩余劳动力支援社会主义农业建设的工作的初步计划 (Preliminary plan to mobilize surplus urban labor to support the socialization of agriculture). 1958.

B168-1-888. Shanghai shi minzhengju dangzu 上海市民政局党组 (Shanghai Municipal Civil Affairs Bureau Party Group). "Guanyu renkou gongzuo de qingkuang baogao" 关于人口工作的情况报告 (Report on population control work). 1958.

B168-1-892a. Shanghai shi minzheng ju. Shanghai shi renmin weiyuanhui. "Guanyu zhizhi nongcun laodongli mangmu liuru chengshi de gongzuo de qingkuang baogao" 关于制止农村劳动力盲目流入城市的工作的情况报告 (Report on stopping blind migration of rural labor power into cities). 1959.

B168-1-892b. Shanghai shi minzheng ju. Zhizhi nongcun laodongli mangmu liuru benshi diaocha zu 制止农村劳动力盲目流入本市调查组 (Investigation small group to stop the blind migration of rural labor power into Shanghai). "Guanyu waidi liuru benshi de nongcun laodongli huixiang shengchan de gongzuo baogao" 关于外地流入本事的农村劳动力回乡生产的工作报告 (Report on work to evacuate rural migrants to return to agricultural production). 1959.

B168-1-892c. Shanghai shi minzheng ju. "Guanyu zhizhi nongcun laodongli mangmu liuru chengshi de gongzuo baogao" 关于制止农村劳动力盲目流入城市的工作报告 (Report on stopping the blind migration of rural labor power into the city). 1959.

B168-1-900. Shanghai shi minzhengju. "1960 nian shourong qiansong wailai renkou huixiang shengchan gongzuo zongjie" 1960年收容迁送外来人口回乡生产工作总结(初稿) (Summary report on shelter and ruralization work in 1960 for populations from outside Shanghai [draft]). 1961.

B168-1-905. Shanghai shi minzhengju. "Shourong qiansong gongzuo qingkuang" 收容迁送工作情况 (Shelter and evacuation work conditions). 1960.

B168-1-910. Shanghai shi minzheng ju. "1962 nian shourong qiansong gongzuo" 1962年收容遣送工作 (Shelter and evacuation work 1962). 1962.

B168-1-915. Shanghai shi minzheng ju. "1963 nian shourong qiansong gongzuo" 1963年收容遣送工作 (Shelter and evacuation work 1963). 1963.


C1-1-210. Shanghai shi zonggonghui 上海市总工会 (Shanghai Federation of Trade Unions. "Shiwei guanyu shixing gonghui quanli xiafang de tongzhi" 市委关于实行工会权力下放的通知 (Notice on the Municipal Party Committee's decentralization of union authority). 1958.

C1-1-322. Shanghai shi zonggonghui 上海市总工会 (Shanghai Federation of Trade Unions). "1965 niandu gonghui gongzuo" 1965年度工会工作 (1965 Union Work Report). 1966.

C1-2-323. Shanghai shi zonggonghui. "Shi waishang qiye laodong baoxian diaocha tongji" 市外商企业劳动保险调查统计 (A statistical investigation into labor insurance in foreign firms). 1950.

C1-2-328. Shanghai shi zonggonghui. "Waishang qiye laobao qingkuang" 外商企业劳保情况 (Labor insurance conditions in foreign enterprises). 1950.

C1-2-331. Shanghai shi zonggonghui. "Ge zhongyao chanye laobao fuli gaikuang" 格重要产业劳保福利概况 (Labor insurance and welfare conditions in each major industry). 1950.

C1-2-332a. Shanghai shi zonggonghui. "Guanyu taolun laobao tiaoli caoan de zongjie baogao" 关于讨论劳保条例草案的总结报告 (Summary report on discussions about the draft labor insurance regulations). 1950.

C1-2-591a. Shanghai shi zonggonghui. "Guanyu laodong baoxian kapian zhunbei gongzuo zongjie baogao" 关于劳动保险卡片准备工作总结报告 (Summary report on labor insurance card registration preparatory work). 1951.

C1-2-591b. Shanghai shi zonggonghui. "Guanyu laodong baoxian shishi qingkuang zonghe baogao" 总情况关于劳动保险实施合报告 (Summary report on the implementation of labor insurance). 1951.

C1-2-601. Shanghai shi zonggonghui. "Guanyu laodong baoxian shishi tongji ziliao" 关于劳动保险实施统计资料 (Statistical materials on labor insurance implementation). 1951.

C1-2-606. Shanghai shi zonggonghui. "Guanyu juban laodong baoxian xunlian" 关于举办劳动保险训练 (Carrying out labor insurance training). 1951.

C1-2-609. Shanghai shi zonggonghui. Zhonghua quanguo zonggonghui 中华全国总工会 (All-China Federation of Trade Unions). "Laodong baoxian bu zuzhi tongze (caoan)" 劳动保险部组织通则（草案） (Organizational rules for the Labor Insurance Department [Draft]). 1951.

C1-2-846. Shanghai shi zonggonghui. "Wujin gongye" 五金工业 (The metalllurgical industry). 1952.

C1-2-849. Shanghai shi zonggonghui. Zhonghua quanguo zonggonghui. "Dui guanyu shengyu laodong baoxian jijin zhi shiyong banfa ji qita wenti buchong yijian" 对关于剩余劳动保险基金之使用办法及其他问题补充意见 (Opinions on using the labor insurance reserve funds and other supplementary issues). 1952.

C1-2-1114. Shanghai shi zonggonghui. "Laodong baoxian gongzuo baogao" 劳动保险工作报告 (Labor insurance work report) 1953.

C1-2-1117. Shanghai zonggonghui. "Guanyu laodong baoxian qiye zhifu fei" 关于劳动保险企业支付费 (Enterprise labor insurance spending). 1953.

C1-2-1118. Shanghai zonggonghui. "Shehui baoxian gangling chubu caoan" 社会保险纲领初步草案 (Preliminary draft social insurance principles). 1953.

C1-2-1431. Shanghai zonggonghui. "Laobao jijin zhi biao" (Labor insurance reserve spending tables). 1954.

C1-2-1764. Shanghai shi zonggonghui. "1955 nian laodong baoxian gongzuo baogao" 1955年劳动保险工作报告 (1955 labor insurance work report). 1955.

C1-2-1768. Shanghai shi zonggonghui. "1955 laodong baoxian jijin tongji biao" 1955 劳动保险基金统计表 (1955 labor insurance reserve fund statistical reports). 1955.

C1-2-1839. Shanghai shi gonghui lianhehui. "Zhang Qi zai quanzong laodong baoxian shenghuo zhuzhai gongzuo huiyi shang de fayan" (Zhang Qi's speech at the ACFTU conference on workers' labor insurance, livelihood and housing work). May 24, 1956.

C1-2-1840. Shanghai shi zonggonghui. Zhonghua quanguo zonggonghui. "Quanguo gonghui gongzuo shiernian guihua gangyao" 全国工会工作十二年规划纲要（草案）(Draft twelve-year national program for union work). 1956.

C1-2-2159. Shanghai shi zonggonghui. "Guanyu xiugai Zhonghua renmin gongheguo laodong baoxian tiaoli de jidian shuoming (caoan)" 关于修改中华人民共和国劳动保险条例的几点说明（草　案）(An explanation of the draft revisions to the PRC Labor Insurance Regulations). 1956.

C1-2-2255. Shanghai shi zonggonghui. Zhonghua quanguo zonggonghui. "Guanyu 1951 nian 12 yue quanzong dangzu kuoda huiyi youguan wenti de jieshi" 关于1951年12月全总党组 矿扩大会议有关问题的解释 (An explanation of the problems at the December 1951 national union enlarged party meeting). 1957.

C1-2-2322. Shanghai shi zonggonghui. "1953 nian fandui jingji zhuyi yundong" (1953 年反对经济主义运动) (The 1953 campaign against economism). 1957.

C1-2-2380. Shanghai shi gonghui lianhehui laodong baoxian bu 上海市工会联合会劳动保险部 (Shanghai Federation of Trade Unions Labor Insurance Department). "1956 nian gonghui laodong baoxian gongzuo zongjie ji 1957 nian gongzuo guihua (chugao)" 1956年工会劳动保险工作总结及1957年工作规划（初稿）(1956 Union Labor Insurance Department work report and 1957 draft work plan). 1957.

C1-2-2382. Shanghai shi gonghui lianhehui laodong baoxian bu. "Laodong baoxian wenti de gaijin yijian" 劳动保险问题的改进意见(Suggestions for reforming some labor insurance problems). 1957.

C1-2-2384a. Shanghai shi gonghui lianhehui 上海市工会联合会 (Shanghai Federation of Trade Unions). "Laodong baoxian wenti" 劳动保险问题 (Problems with labor insurance). 1957.

C1-2-2384b. Shanghai shi gonghui lianhehui. "1957 niandu laodong baoxian jin shouzhi yusuan shuoming baogao" 1957年度劳动保险金收支预算说明报告 (Report on the 1957 labor insurance reserves revenue, spending, and budget). September 13, 1957.

C1-2-2389. Shanghai shi gonghui lianhehui laodong baoxian bu. Zhonghua quanguo zonggonghui laodong baoxian bu 中华全国总工会劳动保险部 (All-China Federation of Trade Unions Labor Insurance Department). "1957 nian quanzong baoxian bu gongzuo yaodian" 1957年全总保险部工作要点, (Priorities for 1957 national union labor insurance work). 1957.

C1-2-2391. Shanghai shi gonghui lianhehui. "Shi gonglian baoxian buzhang Zhang Lin tongzhi zai chuanda quanguo gonghui jiji fenzi laodong baohu gongzuo huiyi fayan" 市工联保险部长张林同志在传达全国工会积极分子劳动保护工作会议发言 (Municipal union labor department director  Zhang Lin's speech at the AFCTU work conference for work safety activists. 1957.

C1-2-3118a. Shanghai shi gonghui lianhehui. "Guanyu gaijin laodong baoxian zhidu de yijian (caogao)" 关于改进劳动保险制度的意见（草稿）(Draft suggestions for reforming the labor insurance system). 1958.

C1-2-3118b. Shanghai shi gonghui lianhehui. "1958, 1959 nian laodong baoxian jijin zhichu tongji biao" (Statistical reports on 1958–59 labor insurance reserve spending). 1959.

C1-2-3118c. Shanghai shi gonghui lianhehui. Shiwei laodong gongzi weiyuanhui 市委劳动工资委员会 (Shanghai Party Committee Labor and Wage Committee). "Guanyu zeng bai ren yi shang gongchang qiye shishi laodong baoxian wenti de tongzhi" 关于新增百人以上工厂企业实施劳动保险问题的通知 (Notice on the problem of implementing labor insurance in industrial enterprises that recently have grown to more than one hundred employees). 1959.

C1-2-3391. Shanghai shi zonggonghui. "1959–1960 nian laodong baoxian feiyong shouzhi tongji biao" 1959, 1960年度劳动保险费用收支统计表 (1959–1960 Labor insurance revenue and expenditure statistics). 1960.

C1-2-3627. Shanghai shi zonggonghui. "Guanyu laodong baoxian shishi fanwei diaocha baogao" 关于劳动保险实施范围调查报告 (Report on the scope of labor insurance implementation). 1961.

C1-2-3397. Shanghai shi zonggonghui. Shanghai shi zonggonghui, Shenghuo bu 生活部 (Shanghai General Labor Union, Living Conditions Department). "Guanyu laodong baoxian ruogan wenti de yijian" 关于劳动保险若干问题的意见 (Some suggestions about some labor insurance problems). 1960.

C1-2-3628. Shanghai shi zonggonghui, Shenghuo bu. "Guanyu linshigong he fei gonghuiyuan de laodong baoxian daiyu wenti de baogao (chugao)" 关于临时工和非工会员的劳动保险待遇问题的报告（初稿）. (Draft report on problems with labor insurance benefits for temporary workers and non-union members). N.d.

C1-2-3795. Shanghai shi zonggonghui. "Guanyu shenqing laodong baoxian tiaoji jin de baogao" 关于申请劳动保险调剂金的报告 (Report on the application for labor insurance supplemental funding). 1962.

C1-2-4303. Shanghai shi zonggonghui, Shenghuo bu. "Guanyu shixing laodong baoxian tiaoli qingkuang, wenti he yijian de baogao (caogao)" 关于实施劳动保险条例情况问题和意见的报告（草稿）(Draft report on suggestions and questions on the conditions for implementation of the labor insurance regulations). 1963.

C1-2-4414. Shanghai shi zonggonghui. "1958 nian–1964 nian gonghui gongzuo jiben qingkuang zonghe tongjibiao" 1958年–1964年工会工作基本情况综合统计表 (Summary statistics on union work and basic conditions 1958–1964". 1965.

C1-2-4753. Shanghai shi zonggonghui. "Tongji yuebao" 统计月报 (Monthly statistical reports). 1963.

C1-2-5334. Shanghai shi zonggonghui. Shangye gonghui zhengfeng lingdao xiaozu 商业工会整风领导小组 (Commercial union rectification leadership small group). "Shangye gonghui zhengfeng yundong yange" 商业工会整风运动沿革 (Development of the Anti-Rightist campaign in the commercial union). 1958.

Q6-7-13. Shanghai shi shiye gongren linshi jiuji weiyuanhui 上海市失业工人临时救济委员会 (Shanghai Municipal Committee for Temporary Relief for Unemployed Workers). "Yingshang dianche gongsi" 英商电车公司 (British Commercial Tramway Company). 1948.

Q6-7-578. Shanghai shi shiye gongren linshi jiuji weiyuanhui. "Shiye gongren linshi jiuji tiaoli" 失业工人临时救济条例" (Program for temporary relief for unemployed workers). "Shehui bu shoufuqu shiye gongren linshi jiuji banfa gangyao"

社会部收复区失业工人临时救济办法纲要 (Ministry of Social Affairs outline of temporary relief methods for unemployed workers in returned districts). 1946.

Q201-2-31. Shanghai shi shanghui 上海市商会 (Shanghai Municipal Chamber of Commerce). "Jiuji Shanghai shi shiye gongren lianxi huiyi" 救济上海市失业工人联席会议 (Joint meeting with the Shanghai Unemployed Worker Relief [Committee]). 1945.

## Secondary Sources

Abel, Christopher, and Colin M. Lewis. "Exclusion and Engagement: A Diagnosis of Social Policy in Latin America in the Long Run." In Abel and Lewis, eds., *Exclusion and Engagement: Social Policy in Latin America*. London: Institute of Latin American Studies, University of London, 2002.

Adam, Jan. "Social Contract." In Adam, ed., *Economic Reforms and Welfare Systems in the USSR, Poland, and Hungary: Social Contract in Transformation*. Basingstok: Palgrave Macmillan, 1991.

Agarwala, A. N. "The Social Security Movement in India." *The Economic Journal* 56:224 (Dec. 1946): 568–82.

Ahmad, Ehtisham, and Athar Hussein. "Social Security in China: A Historical Perspective." In Ahmad et al., eds., *Social Security in Developing Countries*. Oxford: Clarendon Press, 1991.

Alber, Jens. "Continuities and Changes in the Idea of the Welfare State." *Politics and Society* 16:4 (1988): 451–68.

Alesina, Alberto, and Edward L. Glaeser. *Fighting Poverty in the US and Europe: A World of Difference*. Oxford: Oxford University Press, 2004.

Avelino, George, David S. Brown, and Wendy Hunter. "The Effect of Capital Mobility, Trade Openness, and Democracy on Social Spending in Latin America, 1980–1999." *American Journal of Political Science* 49:3 (2005): 625–41.

Ayusawa, Iwao Frederick. *International Labor Legislation*. New York NY: Columbia University Press, 1920.

Bachman, David. *Bureaucracy, Economy and Leadership in China: The Institutional Origins of the Great Leap Forward*. Cambridge: Cambridge University Press, 1991.

Baldwin, Peter. *The Politics of Social Solidarity: Class Bases of the European Welfare State, 1875–1975*. Cambridge: Cambridge University Press, 1990.

Barrientos, Armando. *Pension Reform in Latin America*. Brookfield, VT: Ashgate, 1998.

Berry, Frances. "Sizing Up State Policy Innovation Research." *Policy Studies Journal* 22:3 (1994): 442–56.

Beveridge, William. *Social Insurance and Allied Services*. London: HMSO, 1942.

Bian, Morris L. *The Making of the State Enterprise System in Modern China: The Dynamics of Institutional Change*. Cambridge MA: Harvard University Press, 2005.

Blyth, Mark. *Great Transformations: Economic Ideas and Institutional Change in the Twentieth Century*. Cambridge: Cambridge University Press, 2002.

Bo Yibo. *Ruogan zhongda juece yu shijian de huigu*, vol.1. Beijing: Zhonggong zhongyang dangxiao chubanshe, 1991.

Boli, John, and George M. Thomas. "World Culture in the World Polity: A Century of International Non-Governmental Organization." *American Sociological Review* 62:2 (1997): 171–90.

Bras, Marcel. "15th Anniversary of the WFTU." *International Bulletin of the Trade Union and Working Class Press*, no. 24 (Oct. 15–31, 1960).

Bray, David. *Social Space and Governance in Urban China: The Danwei System from Origins to Reform*. Stanford CA: Stanford University Press, 2005.

Briggs, Asa. "The Welfare State in Historical Perspective." *European Journal of Sociology* 2:2 (1961): 221–58.

Brooks, Sarah M. "Interdependent and Domestic Foundations of Policy Change: The Diffusion of Pension Privatization around the World." *International Studies Quarterly* 49:2 (2005): 273–94.

———. *Social Protection and the Market in Latin America: The Transformation of Social Security Institutions*. Cambridge: Cambridge University Press, 2009.

Brown, Jeremy. *City versus Countryside in Mao's China: Negotiating the Divide*. Cambridge: Cambridge University Press, 2012.

Buckley, Cynthia, and Dennis Donahue. "Promises to Keep: Pension Provision in the Russian Federation." In Mark G. Field and Judyth L. Twigg, eds., *Russia's Torn Safety Nets: Health and Social Welfare during the Transition*. New York NY: St. Martin's Press, 2000.

Bunce, Valerie. "The Empire Strikes Back: The Evolution of the Eastern Bloc from a Soviet Asset to a Soviet Liability." *International Organization* 39:1 (1985): 1-46.

Cardoso, Eliana, and Ann Helwege. "Populism, Profligacy, and Redistribution." In Rudiger Dornbusch and Sebastian Edwards, eds., *The Macroeconomics of Populism in Latin America*. Chicago IL: University of Chicago Press, 1991.

Carlton, Frank Tracy. *The History and Problems of Organized Labor*. Boston: D. C. Heath, 1911, 1920.

Castles, Francis G. *The Working Class and Welfare: Reflections on the Development of the Welfare State in Australia and New Zealand, 1890–1980*. Wellington, NZ: Allen and Unwin, 1985.

Chan, Alfred L. *Mao's Crusade: Politics and Policy Implementation in China's Great Leap Forward*. Oxford: Oxford University Press, 2001.

Chang, Carsun. *Third Force in China*. New York: Bookman Associates, 1952.

Chang, Parris H. *Power and Policy in China*. University Park PA: Pennsylvania State University Press, 2nd ed., 1978.

Chen, Janet Y. *Guilty of Indigence: The Urban Poor in China, 1900–1958*. Princeton NJ: Princeton University Press, 2012.

Chen Lisong. "Jianada shehui anquan zhidu." *Shehui gongzuo tongxun* 3:2 (1946): 26–29.

Chen Shousun. *Shehui wenti cidian*. Shanghai: Minzhi shuju, 1929.

Cheng, Tiejun, and Mark Selden, "The Origins and Social Consequences of China's Hukou System." *China Quarterly*, no. 139 (Sept. 1994): 644–68

Chiang, Yung-chen. *Social Engineering and the Social Sciences in China*. Cambridge: Cambridge University Press, 2001.

Chinese Communist Party. "Communique of the Sixth Plenum of the 16th CPC Central Committee." October 12, 2006. http://english.peopledaily.com.cn/200610/12/eng20061012_310923.html.

Chinese National Relief and Rehabilitation Administration. *CNRRA: Purpose, Functions, Organization*. [Shanghai]: The Administration, 1946.

Chirot, Daniel. "The Corporatist Model and Socialism." *Theory and Society* 9:2 (1980): 363–81.

Chu, Hsueh-fan. "Are the Workers in China Divided?" *China Weekly Review* 105:2 (Mar. 8, 1947): 37–38.

Clark, Mary A. *Gradual Economic Reform in Latin America: The Costa Rican Experience*. Albany NY: State University of New York Press, 2001.

Coble, Parks. *Facing Japan: Chinese Politics and Japanese Imperialism, 1931–1937*. Cambridge MA: Council on East Asian Studies, Harvard University, 1991.

Cochran, Sherman. *Big Business in China: Sino-Foreign Rivalry in the Cigarette Industry, 1890–1930*. Cambridge MA: Harvard University Press, 1980.

Cohen, Wilbur J. "The First Inter-American Conference on Social Security." *Social Security Bulletin* 5:10 (October 1942): 4–7.

Collier, David. "Trajectory of a Concept: 'Corporatism' in the Study of Latin America." In Peter H. Smith, ed., *Latin America in Comparative Perspective: New Approaches to Methods and Analysis*. Boulder CO: Westview Press, 1995.

Collier, David, and Richard Messick. "Prerequisites vs. Diffusion: Testing Alternative Explanations of Social Security Adoption." *American Political Science Review* 69:4 (1975): 1299–1315.

Collier, Ruth Berins, and David Collier. *Shaping the Political Arena*. Princeton: Princeton University Press, 1991.

Commons, John R., and John B. Andrews. *Principles of Labor Legislation*. New York NY: Harper, 2nd ed., 1916.

Congress of Industrial Unions. *CIO News*, 1941–47.

Cuban Economic Research Project. *Social Security in Cuba*. Miami FL: University of Miami, 1964.

Cutright, Phillips. "Political Structure, Economic Development, and National Social Security Programs." *American Journal of Sociology* 70:5 (1965): 537–50.

Davis, Deborah. "Chinese Social Welfare: Policies and Outcomes." *China Quarterly*, no. 119 (Sept. 1989): 577–97.

———. "Unequal Chances, Unequal Outcomes: Pension Reform and Urban Inequality." *China Quarterly*, no. 114 (June 1988): 223–42.

Deacon, Bob et al. *Global Social Policy: International Organizations and the Future of Welfare*. Thousand Oaks CA: Sage Publications, 1997.

Dillon, Nara. "Middlemen in the Chinese Welfare State: The Role of Philanthropists in Refugee Relief in Wartime Shanghai." *Studies in Comparative International Development* 46:1 (2011).

————. "New Democracy and the Demise of Private Charity in Shanghai." In Jeremy Brown and Paul G. Pickowicz, eds., *Dilemmas of Victory: The Early Years of the People's Republic of China*. Cambridge MA: Harvard University Press, 2007.

————. "The Politics of Philanthropy: Social Networks and Refugee Relief in Shanghai, 1932–1949." In Dillon and Jean C. Oi, eds., *At the Crossroads of Empires: Middlemen, Social Networks and State Building in Republican Shanghai*. Stanford CA: Stanford University Press, 2008.

Dirlik, Arif. "Mass Movements and the Left Kuomintang." *Modern China* 1:1 (Jan. 1975): 46–74.

Dixon, John. *The Chinese Welfare System, 1949–79*. New York NY: Praeger, 1981.

————. *Social Security in Global Perspective*. Westport, CT: Praeger, 1999.

Dixon, John, and Hyung-shik Kim, eds. *Social Welfare in Asia*. London: Croom Helm, 1985.

Dobbin, Frank, Beth Simmons, and Geoffrey Garrett. "The Global Diffusion of Public Policies: Social Construction, Coercion, Competition, or Learning?" *Annual Review of Sociology* 33 (2007): 449–72.

Dongbei xingzheng weiyuanhui. "Dongbei gongying qiye zhanshi zanxing laodong baoxian tiaoli." *Dongbei xingzheng gongbao* (Shenyang), no. 1948.

Durán-Valverde, Fabio. "Anti-Poverty Programmes in Costa Rica: The Non-Contributory Pension Scheme." Extension of Social Security Paper No. 8. Geneva: International Labour Office, 2002.

Eastman, Lloyd. *Seeds of Destruction: Nationalist China in War and Revolution, 1937–1949*. Stanford CA: Stanford University Press, 1984.

Eckstein, Harry. "Case Study and Theory in Political Science." In Fred I. Greenstein and Nelson W. Polsby, eds., *Handbook of Political Science*, vol. 7. Reading MA: Addison-Wesley, 1975.

Endres, Anthony M., and Grant A. Fleming. *International Organizations and the Analysis of Economic Policy, 1919–1950*. Cambridge: Cambridge University Press, 2002.

Epstein, Israel. *Notes on Labor Problems in Nationalist China*. New York NY: Institute of Pacific Relations, 1949.

Esping-Andersen, Gøsta. *The Three Worlds of Welfare Capitalism*. Princeton NJ: Princeton University Press, 1990.

————, ed. *Welfare States in Transition: National Adaptations in Global Economies*. Thousand Oaks CA: Sage Publications, 1996.

Ewig, Christina. *Second-Wave Neoliberalism: Gender, Race, and Health Sector Reform in Peru*. University Park PA: Pennsylvania State University Press, 2010.

Fan Jingsi, et al. ed., *Shanghai minzheng zhi*. Shanghai: Shanghai shehui kexue yuan chubanshe, 2000.

Ferdinand, Peter, and Martin Gainsborough, eds. *Enterprise and Welfare Reform in Communist Asia*. London: Frank Cass, 2003.

Finnemore, Martha. "International Organizations as Teachers of Norms: The United Nations Educational, Scientific, and Cultural Organization and Science Policy." *International Organization* 47:4 (1993): 565–97.

Flora, Peter. *Growth to Limits: The Western European Welfare States since World War II*, vol. 4. New York NY: Walter de Gruyter, 1987.

Flora, Peter, and Jens Alber. "Modernization, Democratization and the Development of Welfare States in Western Europe." In Peter Flora and Arnold J. Heidenheimer, eds., *The Development of Welfare States in Europe and America*. New Brunswick, NJ: Transaction Publishers, 1981.

Flora, Peter, and Arnold J. Heidenheimer, eds. *The Development of Welfare States in Europe and America*. New Brunswick, NJ: Transaction Publishers, 1981.

Fones-Wolf, Elizabeth. "Labor and Social Welfare: The CIO's Community Services Program, 1941–1956." *Social Service Review* 70:4 (1996): 613–34.

Frazier, Mark W. *The Making of the Chinese Industrial Workplace: State, Revolution, and Labor Management*. Cambridge: Cambridge University Press, 2002.

———. *Socialist Insecurity: Pensions and the Politics of Uneven Development in China*. Ithaca NY: Cornell University Press, 2010.

Fung, Edmund S. K. *In Search of Chinese Democracy: Civil Opposition in Nationalist China, 1929–1949*. Cambridge: Cambridge University Press, 2000.

Gao, Qin. "Redistributive Nature of the Chinese Social Benefit System: Progressive or Regressive?" *China Quarterly*, no. 201 (March 2010): 1–19.

Gardner, John. "The Wu-fan Campaign in Shanghai: A Study in the Consolidation of Urban Control." In A. Doak Barnett, ed., *Chinese Communist Politics in Action*. Seattle: University of Washington Press, 1969.

George, Vic, and Nick Manning. *Socialism, Social Welfare and the Soviet Union*. London: Routledge and Kegan Paul, 1980.

Ghai, Dharam. "Social Security: Learning from Global Experience to Reach the Poor." *Journal of Human Development* 4:1 (2003): 125–50.

Gil, Indermit S., Truman Packard, and Juan Yermo. *Keeping the Promise of Social Security in Latin America*. Stanford CA: Stanford University Press, 2005.

Gillion, Colin, et al. eds. *Social Security Pensions: Development and Reform*. Geneva: International Labour Office, 2000.

Gongqingtuan Liaoning sheng weiyuanhui bangongshi. *Zuo dang de hao zhushou: Gongqingtuan nongcun zuzhi xiezhu dang gaohao renmin gongshe jiti fuli shiye de jingyan*. Shenyang: Liaoning renmin chubanshe, 1959.

Gonzalez-Vega, Claudio, and Victor Hugo Cespedes. "Costa Rica." In Simon Rottenberg, ed., *Costa Rica and Uruguay: The Political Economy of Poverty, Equity and Growth*. Oxford: Oxford University Press, 1993.

Gordon, Linda, ed. *Women, the State, and Welfare*. Madison WI: University of Wisconsin Press, 1990.

Gough, Ian, and Geof Wood et al., eds. *Insecurity and Welfare Regimes in Asia, Africa and Latin America: Social Policy in Development Contexts*. Cambridge: Cambridge University Press, 2008.

Gu, Edward X. "Dismantling the Chinese Mini-Welfare State? Marketization and the Politics of Institutional Transformation, 1979–1999." *Communist and Post-Communist Studies* 34, (2001): 91–111.

Guoji laodong ju. *Yazhou laogong yubei huiyi.* Shanghai: Guoji laodong ju, Zhongguo fenju, 1948.

Guomin zhengfu caizheng bu zhuhu diaocha huojia chu. *Shehui baoxian.* Laogong wenti congshu, vol. 14. Shanghai: Guomin zhengfu caizheng bu zhuhu diaocha huojia chu, 1928.

Guowuyuan. "Guanyu kaizhan xinxing nongcun shehui yanglao baoxian shidian de zhidao yijian." *Guofa,* no. 32 (2009). http://www.gov.cn/zwgk/2009-09/04/content_1409216.htm.

Haas, Peter M. "Epistemic Communities and International Policy Coordination." *International Organization* 46:1 (1992): 1–35.

Haggard, Stephan, and Robert R. Kaufman, *Development, Democracy, and Welfare States: Latin America, East Asia and Eastern Europe.* Princeton NJ: Princeton University Press, 2008.

Harper, Paul. "The Party and the Unions in Communist China." *China Quarterly,* no. 37 (Jan.–March 1969): 84–119.

Havinden, Michael, and David Meredith. *Colonialism and Development: Britain and its Tropical Colonies, 1850–1960.* Oxford: Routledge, 1993.

Heclo, Hugh. *Modern Social Politics in Britain and Sweden.* New Haven CT: Yale University Press, 1974.

Hicks, Alexander. *Social Democracy and Welfare Capitalism: A Century of Income Security Policies.* Ithaca NY: Cornell University Press, 1999.

Hills, John, John Ditch, and Howard Glennerster. "Introduction." In *Beveridge and Social Security: An International Retrospective.* Oxford: Oxford University Press, 1994.

Holzmann, Robert, David A. Robalino, and Noriuki Takayama, eds. *Closing the Coverage Gap: Role of Social Pensions and Other Retirement Income Transfers.* Washington DC: World Bank, 2009.

Honig, Emily. *Sisters and Strangers: Women in the Shanghai Cotton Mills, 1919–1949.* Stanford CA: Stanford University Press, 1986.

Horie Kiitsu. *Shiye wenti.* Trans. Liu Baoshu. Zhongguo Guomindang zhongyang dangbu shencha shehui wenti congshu. Shanghai: Taipingyang shudian, 1928.

Howard, Joshua H. *Workers at War: Labor in China's Arsenals, 1937–1953.* Stanford, CA: Stanford University Press, 2004.

Howe, Christopher. *Employment and Economic Growth in Urban China 1949–1957.* Cambridge: Cambridge University Press, 1971.

———. "Industrialization under Conditions of Long-Run Population Stability: Shanghai's Achievement and Prospect." In Howe, ed., *Shanghai: Revolution and Development in an Asian Metropolis.* Cambridge: Cambridge University Press, 1981.

Huabei zonggonghui choubei weiyuanhui, ed. *Di liuci quanguo laodong dahui jueyi.* Zhongyuan xinhua shudian, 1949.

Huber, Evelyne, and John D. Stephens. *Democracy and the Left: Social Policy and Inequality in Latin America*. Chicago IL: University of Chicago Press, 2012.

Immergut, Ellen. *Health Politics: Interests and Institutions in Western Europe*. Cambridge: Cambridge University Press, 1992.

India, B.P. Adarkar Committee. *Report on Health Insurance for Industrial Workers*. New Delhi: Government of India Press, 1949.

India, Planning Commission. *First Five-Year Plan: People's Edition*. Delhi: Ministry of Information and Broadcasting, 1953.

International Labour Organization (ILO). *The ILO Yearbook 1932*. Geneva: Albert Kundig, 1933.

———. *The ILO Yearbook 1934–35*, vol. 1. Geneva: Albert Kundig, 1935.

———. *The International Labour Organisation and Social Insurance*. Geneva: International Labour Office, 1925.

———. "The International Labour Organisation and Social Insurance." *International Labour Review* 11:6 (June 1925): 763–83.

———. NORMLEX Database. www/ilo.org/dyn/normlex

———. "Post-War Trends in Social Security." *International Labour Review* 59:6 (1949) 668–83.

———. "The Seventeenth Session of the International Labour Conference" *International Labour Review* 28:3 (September 1933): 317–51.

———. "The Sixteenth Session of the International Labour Conference" *International Labour Review* 26:2 (August 1932): 151–98.

———. *Social Security: A New Consensus*. Geneva: International Labour Organization, 2001.

———. "The Thirty-fifth Session of the International Labour Conference." *International Labour Review* 66:4 (1952): 281–317.

———. "The Twenty-sixth Session of the International Labour Conference." *International Labour Review* 50:1 (July 1944): 1–39.

———. *World Labour Report 2000*. Geneva: International Labour Organization, 2000.

———. *World Social Security Report 2010/11*. Geneva: International Labour Organization, 2010.

Israel, John, and Donald W. Klein. *Rebels and Bureaucrats: China's December 9ers*. Berkeley CA: University of California Press, 1976.

Jain, Shashi. "Basic Social Security in India." In Wouter van Ginneken, ed., *Social Security for the Excluded Majority: Case Studies of Developing Countries* (pp.37–38) Geneva: International Labour Organization, 1999.

James, Estelle. "Coverage under Old Age Security Programs and Protection for the Uninsured: What Are the Issues?" In Nora Lustig, ed., *Shielding the Poor: Social Protection in the Developing World*. Washington, DC: Brookings Institution Press, 2001.

Jin Yufan. *Laodong baoxian fa yuanlun*. Shanghai: Donghua tushu gongsi, 1935.

Kahl, Sigrun. "The Religious Roots of Modern Poverty Policy: Catholic, Lutheran, and Reformed Protestant Traditions Compared." *European Journal of Sociology* 46:1 (April 2005): 91–126.

Kallgren, Joyce. "Social Welfare and China's Industrial Workers." In A. Doak Barnett, ed., *Chinese Communist Politics in Action*. Seattle WA: University of Washington Press, 1969.

Kaple, Deborah A. *Dream of a Red Factory: The Legacy of High Stalinism in China*. Oxford: Oxford University Press, 1994.

Kaufman, Robert, and Alex Segura-Ubiergo. "Globalization, Domestic Politics, and Social Spending in Latin America: A Time-Series Cross-Section Analysis 1973–97." *World Politics* 53:4 (2001): 553–87.

Kenworthy, Lane. "Do Social-Welfare Policies Reduce Poverty? A Cross-National Assessment." *Social Forces* 77:3 (1999): 1119–39.

Kenworthy, Lane, and Jonas Pontusson. "Rising Inequality and the Politics of Redistribution in Affluent Countries." *Perspectives on Politics* 3:3 (2005): 449–71.

Lam, Willy Wo-Lap. *Chinese Politics in the Hu Jintao Era*. Armonk NY: M. E. Sharpe, 2006

Lamson, Herbert Day. *Social Pathology in China: A Source Book for the Study of Problems of Livelihood, Health, and the Family*. Shanghai: Commercial Press, 1935.

Lardy, Nicholas R. "Centralization and Decentralization in China's Fiscal Management." *China Quarterly*: 61 (March 1975): 25–60.

———. "The Chinese Economy under Stress, 1958–1965." In Roderick MacFarquhar and John K. Fairbank, eds., *The Cambridge History of China*, vol. 14. Cambridge: Cambridge University Press 1987.

———. *Economic Growth and Distribution in China*. Cambridge: Cambridge University Press, 1978.

Lee, Leo Ou-fan, and Andrew Nathan. "The Beginnings of Mass Culture: Journalism and Fiction in the Late Ch'ing and Beyond." In David Johnson, Andrew J. Nathan, and Evelyn S. Rawski, eds., *Popular Culture in Late Imperial China*. Berkeley CA: University of California Press, 1985.

Levine, Steven I. *Anvil of Victory*. New York NY: Columbia University Press, 1987.

Lewis, Colin M. "Social Insurance in the Argentine: Ideology and Policy." In Christopher Abel and Lewis, eds., *Welfare, Poverty and Development in Latin America*. Basingstoke: Macmillan, 1993.

Lewis, Colin M., and Peter Lloyd-Sherlock. "Social Insurance Regimes: Crisis and 'Reform' in the Argentine and Brazil since c. 1900." Working Paper 68/02. London: Department of Economic History, London School of Economics, 2002.

Li Baosen. *Laodong baoxian fa ABC*. Shanghai: ABC congshu she, 1931.

Li Duanxiang. *Chengshi renmin gongshe yundong yanjiu*. Changsha: Hunan renmin chubanshe, 2006.

Li Guicai, ed. *1948–1988 Zhongguo gonghui sishinian ziliao xuanbian*. Shenyang: Liaoning renmin chubanshe, 1990.

Li, Hua-Yu. *Mao and the Economic Stalinization of China, 1948–53*. Lanham, MD: Rowman and Littlefield, 2006.

Li Jianhua. "Zhanhou Shanghai shi zhi shiye jiuji." *Shehui yuekan* 2:3 (March 1947): 4–6.

Li Jiaqi, ed. *Shanghai gongyun zhi.* Shanghai: Shanghai shehui kexue yuan chubanshe, 1997.

Li, Lillian M. *Fighting Famine in North China: State, Market, and Environmental Decline, 1690s–1990s.* Stanford, CA: Stanford University Press, 2007.

Li Lisan. "Guanyu Zhonghua renmin gongheguo laodong baoxian tiaoli caoan de jidian shuoming." *Laodong gongbao,* vol. 8 (March 1951).

Li Qiong. "Minguo shiqi shehui baoxianchu tan." *Huazong keji daxue xuebao* 2006:82–86.

Li Rongting. *Shehui baoxian gailun.* Shanghai: Lixin kuaiji tushu yongpin she, 1953.

Li Weihan. *Huiyi yu yanjiu.* Vol. 2 Beijing: Zhonggong dangshi ziliao chubanshe, 1986.

Liang, Yung-chang. *The Kuomintang and the Chinese Worker.* Taiwan: China Cultural Service, 1954.

Lieberthal, Kenneth G. "Mao versus Liu? Policy Towards Industry and Commerce, 1946–49." *China Quarterly,* no. 47 (July–Sept. 1971): 494–520.

Lin Ping, ed. *Quanguo diliuci laodong dahui.* Dalian: Dalian dazhong shudian, 1948.

Loh, Robert, and Humphrey Evans. *Escape From Red China.* New York NY: Coward-McCann, 1962.

Lu Jingshi. *Zhongguo laodong zhengce zhi lilun yu shiji.* Taiwan sheng zhengfu shehui chu, 1954.

Lu Xiangxian, ed. *Zhongguo laodong xiehui jianshi.* Shanghai: Shanghai renmin chubanshe, 1987.

Lu Xiangxian and Liu Songbin. *Zhu Xuefan zhuan.* Beijing: Tuanjie chubanshe, 2005.

Lü, Xiaobo. "Minor Public Economy: The Revolutionary Origins of the Danwei." In Lü and Elizabeth J. Perry, eds., *Danwei: The Changing Chinese Workplace in Historical and Comparative Perspective.* Armonk, NY: M. E. Sharpe, 1997.

Lü, Xiaobo, and Elizabeth J. Perry, eds. *Danwei: The Changing Chinese Workplace in Historical and Comparative Perspective.* Armonk, NY: M. E. Sharpe, 1997.

Lu Yilong, "1949 nian hou de Zhongguo huji zhidu: Jiegou yu bianqe." *Beijing daxue xuebao* 39:2 (2002).

Lu Zhushu. *Shiye wenti yanjiu.* Shanghai: Zhongyang tushuju, 1927.

Luo Pinghan. *Da guo fan: Gonggong shitang shimo.* Nanning: Guangxi renmin chubanshe, 2007.

Luo Pinghan, *Da qianxi: 1961–63 niande chengzhen renkou jingjian.* Nanning: Guangxi renmin chubanshe, 2003.

Ma Chaojun. *Zhongguo laogong wenti.* Shanghai: Minzhi shuju, 1927.

Ma Junwu. *Shiyeren ji pinmin jiuji zhengce.* Shanghai: Shangwu yinshuguan, 1929.

Ma, Tehyun. "A Chinese Beveridge Plan: The Discourse of Social Security and the Post-War Reconstruction of China." *European Journal of East Asian Studies* 11:2 (2012): 329–49.

MacFarquhar, Roderick, ed. *The Hundred Flowers Campaign and the Chinese Intellectuals.* New York NY: Praeger, 1960.

———. *The Origins of the Cultural Revolution,* vol. 1: *Contradictions among the People 1956–1957.* New York NY: Columbia University Press, 1974.

———. *The Origins of the Cultural Revolution,* vol. 2: *The Great Leap Forward 1958–1960.* New York NY: Columbia University Press, 1983.

———. *The Origins of the Cultural Revolution,* vol. 3: *The Coming of the Cataclysm 1961–66.* New York NY: Columbia University Press, 1997.

Maddison, Angus. *The World Economy: A Millennial Perspective.* Paris: Organisation for Economic Co-operation and Development 2006.

Madrid, Raul. *Retiring the State: The Politics of Pension Privatization in Latin America and Beyond.* Stanford CA: Stanford University Press, 2003.

Malloy, James M. *The Politics of Social Security in Brazil.* Pittsburgh PA: University of Pittsburgh Press, 1979.

Malloy, James M. and Carlos A. Parodi, "Politics, Equity and Social Security Policy in Brazil: A Case-Study of Statecraft and Citizenship, 1965–85." In Christopher Abel and Colin M. Lewis, eds., *Welfare, Poverty and Development in Latin America.* Basingstoke: Macmillan Press, 1993.

Mao Qihua. "Luetan jiefang zhanzheng shiqi Shanghai gongren yundong de yixie qingkuang" [A summary discussion of conditions in the Shanghai labor movement during the war of liberation]. *Shanghai gongyunshi yanjiu ziliao* no. 2 (1982).

Mares, Isabela. "Social Protection around the World." *Comparative Political Studies* 38:6 (2005): 623–51.

Mares, Isabela, and Matthew Carnes. "Social Policy in Developing Countries." *Annual Review of Political Science* 12:1 (2009): 93–113.

Martin, Brian G. *The Shanghai Green Gang: Politics and Organized Crime 1919–1937.* Berkeley CA: University of California Press, 1996.

Meisner, Maurice. *Mao's China and After.* 3rd ed. New York NY: The Free Press, 1999.

Mesa-Lago, Carmelo. *Ascent to Bankruptcy: Financing Social Security in Latin America.* Pittsburgh PA: University of Pittsburgh Press, 1989.

———. *Changing Social Security in Latin America.* Boulder CO: Lynne Rienner, 1994.

———. *Social Security and the Prospects for Equity in Latin America.* Washington DC: World Bank, 1991.

———. *Social Security in Latin America: Pressure Groups, Stratification and Inequality.* Pittsburgh PA: University of Pittsburgh Press, 1978.

Midgley, James. *Social Security and Inequality in the Third World.* New York NY: Wiley, 1984.

Molina, Oscar, and Martin Rhodes. "Corporatism: The Past, Present, and Future of a Concept." *Annual Review of Political Science* 5:1 (2002): 305–31.

Mouton, Pierre. *Social Security in Africa: Trends, Problems and Prospects.* Geneva: International Labour Office, 1975.

Müller, Katharina. *The Political Economy of Pension Reform in Central-Eastern Europe.* Northampton MA: Edward Elgar, 2000.

———. *Privatising Old-Age Security: Latin America and Eastern Europe Compared.* Northampton MA: Edward Elgar, 2003.

Mulligan, Casey B. et al. "Do Democracies Have Different Public Policies Than Non-Democracies?" *Journal of Economic Perspectives* 18:1 (2003): 51–74.

Naughton, Barry. *The Chinese Economy.* Cambridge MA: MIT Press, 2007.

———. "Danwei: The Economic Foundations of a Unique Institution." In Xiaobo Lü and Elizabeth J. Perry, eds., *Danwei: The Changing Chinese Workplace in Historical and Comparative Perspective.* Armonk, NY: M. E. Sharpe, 1997.

O'Brien, Kevin J. *Reform without Liberalization: China's National People's Congress and the Politics of Institutional Change.* Cambridge: Cambridge University Press, 1990.

Oliveira, Moacir Veloso Cardoso de. "Social Security in Brazil." *International Labour Review* 84:1 (1961): 376–93.

Orenstein, Mitchell. *Privatizing Pensions: The Transnational Campaign for Social Security Reform.* Princeton NJ: Princeton University Press, 2008.

Parish, William L., and Martin King Whyte. *Village and Family in Contemporary China.* Chicago IL: University of Chicago Press, 1978.

Paukert, Felix. "Social Security and Income Redistribution: Comparative Experience." In Everett M. Kassalow, ed., *The Role of Social Security in Economic Development.* Social Security Administration Research Report 27. Washington, D.C.: Government Printing Office, 1968.

Pepper, Suzanne. *Civil War in China: The Political Struggle, 1945–1949.* Berkeley CA: University of California Press, 1978.

Perry, Elizabeth J. "From Native Place to Workplace: Labor Origins and Outcomes of China's Danwei System." In Xiaobo Lü and Perry, eds. *Danwei: The Changing Chinese Workplace in Historical and Comparative Perspective.* Armonk, NY: M. E. Sharpe, 1997.

———. *Patrolling the Revolution: Worker Militias, Citizenship, and the Modern Chinese State.* Lanham, MD: Rowman and Littlefield, 2005.

———. *Shanghai on Strike: The Politics of Chinese Labor.* Stanford: Stanford University Press, 1993.

———. "Shanghai's Strike Wave of 1957." *China Quarterly,* no. 137 (March 1994): 1–27

Perry, Elizabeth J., and Li Xun. *Proletarian Power.* Boulder CO: Westview Press, 1997.

Pierson, Paul. *Dismantling the Welfare State? Reagan, Thatcher, and the Politics of Retrenchment.* Cambridge: Cambridge University Press, 1994.

Porter, Robin. *Industrial Reformers in Republican China.* Armonk, NY: M. E. Sharpe, 1994.

Qian Lijun. "Shanghai jiefang chuqi de zhenya fangeming yundong." In Li Zhuanhua. ed., *Shanghai jiefang chuqi de shehui gaizao.* Beijing: Zhonggong dangshi chubanshe, 1999.

Quadagno, Jill. *The Color of Welfare: How Racism Undermined the War on Poverty.* Oxford: Oxford University Press, 1994.

Quanguo zonggonghui. *Guojia shehui baoxian: Sulian gonghui gongzuo shouce.* Trans. Zhonghua quanguo zonggonghui Ewen fanyi shi. Beijing: Gongren chubanshe, 1954.

————. *Sulian gonghui de shehui baoxian gongzuo.* Shanghai: Laodong chubanshe, 1951.

————. "Zhongyang renmin zhengfu zhengwuyuan fabu guanyu jiuji shiye gongren zhishi." *Laodong gongbao* (March 1950), 9–13.

Reed, Christopher A. *Gutenberg in Shanghai: Chinese Print Capitalism, 1876–1937.* Honolulu HI: University of Hawai'i Press, 2004.

Rein, Martin, Barry L. Friedman, and Andreas Wörgotter, eds. *Enterprise and Social Benefits after Communism.* Cambridge: Cambridge University Press, 1997.

Remington, Thomas F. *The Politics of Inequality in Russia,* Cambridge: Cambridge University Press, 2011.

Ren Yuanyuan. *Shehui baoxian lifa zhi qushi.* Shanghai: Qun xue she, 1936.

Rimlinger, Gaston V. *Welfare Policy and Industrialization in Europe, America, and Russia.* New York: Wiley, 1971.

Riskin, Carl. *China's Political Economy: The Quest for Development since 1949.* Oxford: Oxford University Press, 1987.

Rodgers, Daniel T. *Atlantic Crossings: Social Politics in a Progressive Age.* Cambridge MA: Belknap Press of Harvard University Press, 1998.

Rodrik, Dani. *Has Globalization Gone Too Far?* Washington, DC: Institute for International Economics, 1997.

————. "Why Do More Open Economies Have Bigger Governments?" *Journal of Political Economy* 106:5 (1998): 997–1032.

Rofman, Rafael. "Social Security Coverage in Latin America." Social Protection Discussion Paper Series. Washington DC: World Bank, 2005.

Rogaski, Ruth. *Hygienic Modernity: Meanings of Health and Disease in Treaty-Port China.* Berkeley CA: University of California Press, 2004

Rogers, Everett. *Diffusion of Innovations.* New York NY: Free Press, 1995.

Rosenberg, Mark B. "Social Security Policymaking in Costa Rica: A Research Report." *Latin American Research Review* 14:1 (1979): 116–33.

Ross, Michael. "Is Democracy Good for the Poor?" *American Journal of Political Science* 50:4 (2006): 865–74.

Rubinow, I. M. *Social Insurance.* New York NY: Henry Holt, 1916.

Rudra, Nita. *Globalization and the Race to the Bottom in Developing Countries: Who Really Gets Hurt?* Cambridge: Cambridge University Press, 2008.

Schmitter, Philippe C. "Still the Century of Corporatism?" In Schmitter and Gerhard Lembruch, eds., *Trends Toward Corporatist Intermediation.* London UK: Sage, 1979.

Segura-Ubiergo, Alex, *The Political Economy of the Welfare State in Latin America.* Cambridge: Cambridge University Press, 2007.

Selden, Mark. *The Political Economy of Chinese Socialism.* Armonk, NY: M. E. Sharpe, 1988.

Selznick, Philip. *The Organizational Weapon.* New York NY: McGraw-Hill, 1952.

Shanghai shi. *1946 Shanghai shi nianjian.* Shanghai: Zhonghua shuju, 1946.

Shanghai shi. *Shanghai shi shehui xingzheng tongji.* Shanghai: Shehui ju, 1948.

Shanghaishi tongji ju, ed. *Shanghai shi guomin jingji he shehui fazhan lishi tongji ziliao (1949–2000)*. Beijing: Zhongguo tongji chubanshe, 2001.

Shanghai zonggonghui. *Liangnian laide gongren yundong*. 1951.

Shao Xinshi, and Deng Ziba, eds. *Shanghai shi laogong nianjian, 1948*. Shanghai: Dagong tongxunshe, 1948.

Shehui bu. *Laogong fagui*. Shanghai: Shehui bu Jing-Hu qu tepaiyuan banshichu, 1945.

———. *Shehui fagui huibian*. Shanghai: Shehui bu Jing-Hu qu tepaiyuan banshichu, 1945.

———. "Yingguo shehui anquan jihua." *Shehui gongzuo tongxun* 2:9 (1945).

Shen Yixing et al., eds. *Shanghai gongren yundong shi*. Shenyang: Liaoning renmin chubanshe, 1998.

Shen Zhi and Li Tao, eds. *Shanghai laodong zhi*. Shanghai: Shanghai shehui kexue yuan chubanshe, 1998.

Shyu, Lawrence N. "China's Wartime Parliament: The People's Political Council 1938–45." In Paul K. T. Sih, ed., *Nationalist China during the Sino-Japanese War, 1937–45*. Hicksville NY: Exposition Press, 1977.

Simmons, Beth, and Zachary Elkins. "The Globalization of Liberalization: Policy Diffusion in the International Political Economy." *American Political Science Review* 98:1 (2004): 171–89.

Skocpol, Theda. *Protecting Soldiers and Mothers: The Political Origins of Social Policy in the United States*. Cambridge MA: Belknap Press of Harvard University Press, 1992.

Smeeding, Timothy, and Katherine Ross Phillips. "Social Protection for the Poor in the Developed World." In Nora Lustig, ed., *Shielding the Poor: Social Protection in the Developing World*. Washington D.C.: Brookings Institution Press, 2001.

Smeeding, Timothy M., Lee Rainwater, and Gary Burtless. "U.S. Poverty in a Cross-National Context." In Sheldon Danziger and Robert Haveman, eds., *Understanding Poverty*. New York: Russell Sage Foundation, 2001.

Snyder, Richard. "Scaling Down: The Subnational Comparative Method." *Studies in Comparative International Development* 36:1 (2001): 93–110.

So, Bennis Wai-yip. "The Policy-Making and Political Economy of the Abolition of Private Ownership in the Early 1950s: Findings from New Material." *China Quarterly*, no. 171 (Sept. 2002): 682–703.

Social Security Administration (SSA). *Social Security Programs Throughout the World 1961*. Washington, D.C.: U.S. Department of Health, Education, and Welfare, 1961.

———. *Social Security Programs Throughout the World 1979*. Washington, D.C.: U.S. Department of Health and Human Services, 1980.

———. *Social Security Programs Throughout the World 1999*. Washington D.C.: Social Security Administration, 1999.

Social Security Board (SSB). *An Outline of Foreign Social Insurance and Assistance Laws*. Washington, D.C.: Federal Security Agency, 1940.

Solinger, Dorothy J. "Path Dependency Re-examined: Chinese Welfare Policy in the Transition to Unemployment." *Comparative Politics* 38:1 (2005): 83–101.

———. "The Urban Dibao: Guarantee for Minimum Livelihood or for Minimal Turmoil?" In Fulong Wu and Chris Webster, eds , *Marginalization in Urban China: Comparative Perspectives*. New York NY: Palgrave Macmillan, 2010.

Steinmetz, George. *Regulating the Social: The Welfare State and Local Politics in Imperial Germany*. Princeton NJ: Princeton University Press, 1993.

Strang, David, and Patricia Mei Yin Chang. "The International Labor Organization and the Welfare State: Institutional Effects on National Welfare Spending, 1960–80." *International Organization* 47:2 (1993): 235–62.

Su Wei. *Renmin gongshe: Zenyang banhao jiti fuli shiye*. Beijing: Tongsu duwu chubanshe, 1959.

Subrahmanya, R. K. "Extension of Social Insurance Schemes in the Formal Sector." In Wouter van Ginneken, ed., *Social Security for All Indians*. Oxford: Oxford University Press, 1998.

Svensson, Marina. *Debating Human Rights in China: A Conceptual and Political History*. Lanham, MD: Rowman and Littlefield, 2002.

Tang Chunliang. *Li Lisan zhuan*. Harbin: Heilongjiang renmin chubanshe, 1984.

Tang Jun. "Chengxiang dibao zhidu: lishi, xianzhuang yu qianzhan." *Hongqi wengao*, no. 18 (2005): 14–17.

Tarrow, Sidney. *Power in Movement: Social Movements and Contentious Politics*. Cambridge: Cambridge University Press, 2nd ed., 1998.

Teiwes, Frederick C. *Politics and Purges in China: Rectification and the Decline of Party Norms 1950–1965*. White Plains NY: M.E. Sharpe, 1979.

———. *Politics at Mao's Court: Gao Gang and Party Factionalism in the Early 1950s*. Armonk, NY: M. E. Sharpe, 1990.

Teiwes, Frederick C., and Warren Sun. *China's Road to Disaster: Mao, Central Politicians, and Provincial Leaders in the Unfolding of the Great Leap Forward, 1955–1959*. Armonk, NY: M.E. Sharpe, 1999.

Thaxton, Ralph A., Jr. *Catastrophe and Contention in Rural China*. Cambridge: Cambridge University Press, 2008.

Thelen, Kathleen. "How Institutions Evolve: Insights from Comparative Historical Analysis." In James Mahoney and Dietrich Rueschemeyer, eds., *Comparative Historical Analysis in the Social Sciences*. Cambridge: Cambridge University Press, 2003.

———. *How Institutions Evolve: The Political Economy of Skills in Germany, Britain, the United States, and Japan*. Cambridge: Cambridge University Press, 2004.

Thomas, Albert. À *la recontre de l'Orient: Notes de voyages, 1928–1929*. Geneva: Société des amis d'Albert Thomas, 1959.

Timmins, Nicholas. *The Five Giants: A Biography of the Welfare State*. London: HarperCollins Press, 1995.

Tone, Andrea. *The Business of Benevolence: Industrial Paternalism in Progressive America*. Ithaca NY: Cornell University Press, 1997.

United Nations Relief and Rehabilitation Administration. *UNRRA in China 1945–1947*. Washington, D.C.: UNRRA, 1948.

Usui, Chikako. "Welfare State Development in a World System Context: Event History Analysis of First Social Insurance Legislation among 60 Countries, 1880–1960." In Thomas Janoski and Alexander Hicks, eds., *The Comparative Political Economy of the Welfare State.* Cambridge MA: Cambridge University Press, 1994.

van Ginneken, Wouter, ed. *Social Security for the Excluded Majority: Case Studies of Developing Countries.* Geneva: International Labour Office, 1999
Van Slyke, Lyman P. *Enemies and Friends: The United Front in Chinese Communist History.* Stanford CA: Stanford University Press, 1967.
Villars, C. "Social Security Standards in the Council of Europe: The ILO Influence." *International Labour Review* 118:3 (May-June 1979): 343–54.

Wagner, Augusta. *Labor Legislation in China.* Peking: Yenching University, 1938.
Wakeman, Frederic. "Cleanup: The New Order in Shanghai." In Jeremy Brown and Paul G. Pickowicz, eds., *Dilemmas of Victory: The Early Years of the People's Republic of China.* Cambridge MA: Harvard University Press, 2007.
Walder, Andrew. *Communist Neo-Traditionalism: Work and Authority in Chinese Industry.* Berkeley CA: University of California Press, 1986.
Wales, Nym. *The Chinese Labor Movement.* New York NY: John Day Co., 1945.
Wang, Fei-ling. *Organizing through Division and Exclusion: China's Hukou System.* Stanford CA: Stanford University Press, 2005.
Wang Yaoshan. "Huiyi jieguan Shanghai de zhunbei gongzuo." In Shi Hongzi, ed., *Jieguan Shanghai qinli ji.* Shanghai: Shanghai shi zhengxie wenshi ziliao bianji bu, 1997.
Wang Yongxi et al, eds. *Zhongguo gonghui shi.* Beijing: Zhonggong dangshi chubanshe, 1992.
Wang Yu et al. *Dangdai Zhongguo gongren jieji he gonghui yundong jishi 1949–1988.* Shenyang: Liaoning daxue chubanshe, 1989.
Wen Jiabao. "Zai quanguo xinxing nongcun he chengzhen jumin shehui yanglao baoxian gongzuo zongjie biaozhang dahui shangde jianghua." *Renmin Ribao* (October 13, 2012). http://www.cusdn.org.cn/news_detail.php?id=220174.
Weyland, Kurt. *Democracy without Equity: Failures of Reform in Brazil.* Pittsburgh PA: University of Pittsburgh Press, 1996.
———. "Theories of Policy Diffusion: Lessons from Latin American Pension Reform." *World Politics* 57:2 (2005): 262-295.
WFTU (World Federation of Trade Unions). *Information Bulletin,* nos. 13–14 (39–40) (July 1947).
———. *Information Bulletin,* nos. 19–20 (69–70) (Aug. 1948).
———. *Report of Activity of the World Federation of Trade Unions.* Paris: Presented to the Second World Trade Unions Congress, October 15, 1945–April 30, 1949.
———. *The World Federation of Trade Unions 1945–1985.* Prague: World Federation of Trade Unions, 1985.
White, Lynn T., III. *Policies of Chaos: The Organizational Causes of Violence in China's Cultural Revolution.* Princeton NJ: Princeton University Press, 1989.
Whyte, Martin King. *Myth of the Social Volcano: Perceptions of Inequality and Distributive Justice in Contemporary China.* Stanford CA: Stanford University Press, 2010.

Whyte, Martin King, and William L. Parish. *Urban Life in Contemporary China.* Chicago IL: University of Chicago Press, 1984

Wibbels, Erik, and John S. Alquist. "Development, Trade, and Social Insurance." *International Studies Quarterly* 55:1 (2011): 125–49.

Wilensky, Harold. *The Welfare State and Equality: Structural and Ideological Roots of Public Expenditures.* Berkeley CA: University of California Press, 1975.

Wolf, Charles, Jr. *Markets or Governments: Choosing between Imperfect Alternatives.* Cambridge MA: MIT Press, 1988.

Wong, Joseph. *Healthy Democracies: Welfare Politics in Taiwan and South Korea.* Ithaca NY: Cornell University Press, 2004.

World Bank. *Averting the Old Age Crisis.* Oxford: Oxford University Press, 1994.

———. *China: The Health Sector.* Washington DC: World Bank, 1984.

Wu Li. "Jianguo chuqi dang guanyu jiuye wenti de zhengce." *Zhonggong dangshi ziliao,* no. 52. Beijing: Zhonggong dangshi chubanshe, 1994.

Wu, T'ien-wei. "Contending Political Forces during the War of Resistance." In James C. Hsiung and Steven I. Levine, eds., *China's Bitter Victory: The War with Japan 1937–1945.* Armonk, NY: M. E. Sharpe, 1992.

Xie Jianhua and Ba Feng. *Shehui baoxian faxue.* Beijing: Beijing daxue chubanshe, 1999.

Xie Zhenmin. *Zhonghua minguo lifashi.* [Nanjing]: Zhengzhong shuju, 1937.

Xiong Yuezhi, et al. *Lao Shanghai: Ming ren, ming shi, ming wu da guan.* Shanghai: Shanghai renmin chubanshe, 1997.

———. *Shanghai tongshi,* vol. 7 *Minguo zhengzhi.* Shanghai: Shanghai renmin chubanshe, 1999.

———. *Shanghai tongshi,* vol. 11: *Dangdai jingji.* Shanghai: Shanghai renmin chubanshe, 1999.

———. *Shanghai tongshi,* vol. 12: *Dangdai zhengzhi.* Shanghai: Shanghai renmin chubanshe, 1999.

———. *Shanghai tongshi,* vol. 13: *Dangdai shehui.* Shanghai: Shanghai renmin chubanshe, 1999.

Yang, Dali. *Calamity and Reform in China: State, Rural Society, and Institutional Change since the Great Leap Famine.* Stanford: Stanford University Press, 1996.

Yang Jisheng. *Mubei: Zhongguo liushi niandai de da jihuang jishi.* Hong Kong: Tiandi tushu youxian gongsi, 2008.

Yang, Kuisong, "Reconsidering the Campaign to Suppress Counterrevolutionaries," *China Quarterly,* no. 193 (2008): 102–21.

Yang Zhi. *Sulian laodong baoxian zhidu.* Shanghai: Shijian chubanshe, 1951.

Yashar, Deborah. J. "Civil War and Social Welfare: The Origin of Costa Rica's Competitive Party System." In Scott Mainwaring and Timothy Scully, eds., *Building Democratic Institutions: Party Systems in Latin America.* Stanford: Stanford University Press, 1995.

Ye Zhonghao. "Huang'an xian suweiai zhengfu shehui baoxianju jishi." *Hubei dang'an,* no. 12 (2002).

Yeh, Wen-hsin. "The Republican Origins of the Danwei: The Case of Shanghai's Bank of China." In Xiaobo Lü and Elizabeth J. Perry, eds., *Danwei: The Changing Chinese Workplace in Historical and Comparative Perspective*. Armonk, NY: M. E. Sharpe, 1997.

Yingguo zhu Hua dashiguan. *Beifolizhi shehui baoxian ji youguan shiye*. Chongqing: Yingguo zhu Hua dashiguan xinwen chu, 1944.

Yu Jianting. *Chen Yun yu dongbei de jiefang*. Beijing: Zhongyang wenxian chubanshe, 1998.

Zeng Xueji and Guo Yifan. *Renmin gongshe jiti shiye wenti jieda*. Chengdu: Sichuan renmin chubanshe, 1959.

Zhang Jinping. "Dadong yanchang shijian de zhenxing." *Shanghai Dangshi* vol. 3 (1989): 31–35.

Zhang Yapei, ed. *Shanghai gongshang shetuan zhi*. Shanghai: Shanghai shehui kexue yuan, 2001.

Zhang Yongmao. *Jiekesiluofake de shehui baoxian*. Shanghai: Zhonghua shuju, 1950.

Zhonggong Shanghai shi zuzhi bu. *Shanghai shi zhengquan xitong, difang junshi xitong, tongyi zhanxian xitong, quanzhong tuanti xitong*. Shanghai: Shanghai renmin chubanshe, 1991.

Zhonggong zhongyang wenxian yanjiu shi. *Jianguo yilai zhongyao wenxian*, vols. 1–3. Beijing: Zhongyang wenxian chubanshe, 1992.

———. *Zhou Enlai jingji wenxuan*. Beijing: Zhongyang wenxian chubanshe, 1993.

Zhongguo Guomindang. *Zhongguo Guomindang di liuci quanguo daibiao dahui ziliao jiyao*. Chongqing: Zhongxin chubanshe, 1945.

Zhongguo shehui kexue yuan. *Zhonghua renmin gongheguo jingji dang'an 1949–1952. Laodong gongzi he zhigong fuli juan*. Beijing: Zhongguo shehui kexue chubanshe, 1994.

———. *Zhonghua renmin gongheguo jingji dang'an ziliao xuanbian 1953–1957: Laodong gongzi he zhigong fuli juan*. Beijing: Zhongguo wujia chubanshe, 1998.

Zhonghua renmin gongheguo. "Shehui baoxian fa 2010." http://www.npc.gov.cn/npc/xinwen/2010-10/28/content_1602435.htm.

———. *Shehui baoxian fagui xuanbian*. Beijing: Zhongguo fazhi chubanshe, 1995.

Zhongyang dang'anguan, ed. *Zhonggong zhongyang wenjian xuanji*. Beijing: Zhonggong zhongyang dangxiao chubanshe, 1989.

Zhu Hua et al. *Shanghai yibai nian*. Shanghai: Shanghai renmin chubanshe, 1999.

# Glossary

All-China Federation of Trade Unions (ACFTU) 全国总工会

An Futing 安辅庭

Anti-Rightist Campaign 反右派运动

Bao Huaguo 包华国

Bo Yibo 薄一波

Campaign to Suppress Counterrevolutionaries 镇压反革命运动

Chen Yi 陈毅

Chiang Kaishek 蒋介石

Chinese Association of Labor 中国劳动协会

Chinese Communist Party 中国共产党

Civil Affairs Ministry 民政部

Deng Xiaoping 邓小平

dibao 低保

Du Yuesheng 杜月笙

economism 经济主义

Gongchan zhuyi laodong daxue 共产主义劳动大学

Great Leap Forward (da yuejin) 大跃进

Great Leap Forward famine 三年困难时期

Green Gang (qingbang) 青帮

Gu Zhenggang 谷正纲

hong shizi hui weishengzhan 红十字会卫生站

household registration system 户口制度

Hu Jintao 湖锦涛

Hundred Flowers movement 百花齐放 整风运动

Jiang Jingguo 蒋经国

jiuguo yundong 救国运动

Ke Qingshi 柯庆施

Kuomintang 国民党

Lai Ruoyu 赖若愚

Li Fuchun 李富春

Li Kangnian 李康年

Li Lisan 李立三

Li Weihan 李维翰

Li Xian 李仙

lianluozhan 联络站

Liu Changsheng 刘长生

Liu Ningyi 刘宁一

Liu Shaoqi 刘少奇

liumang 流氓

Lu Jingshi 陆京士

Ma Chaojun 马超俊

Mao Zedong 毛泽东

May Thirtieth Movement 五卅运动

Meigong Tang 美工堂

minban xuexiao 民办学校

minzhu gaige 民主改革

National Salvation Movement 救国运动

Pan Hannian 潘汉年
Peng Dehuai 彭德怀
People's Liberation Army 人民解放军
qu shehui zhazi 社会渣滓
quanmiande laodong jiuye 全面的劳动就业
quanyi 全异
Rao Shushi 饶漱石
Rong Yiren 荣毅仁
Shanghai Business Federation 上海市工商联合会
Shanghai Chamber of Commerce 上海总商会
Shanghai Civil Affairs Bureau 上海民政局
Shanghai Federation of Trade Unions 上海总工会，上海市工会联合会
Shanghai General Labor Union (KMT) 上海市总工会
Shanghai Labor Bureau 上海劳动局
Shanghai Municipal Council 上海市参议会
Shanghai Party Committee 上海公共市委
Shanghai People's Congress 上海人民代表会
Shanghai Social Affairs Bureau 上海社会局
Shanghai Temporary Committee 上海临时委员会

Shanghai Unemployed Workers' Congress 上海失业工人代表会
Shanghai Workers' Congress 上海工人代表会
shehui jiuji 社会救济
Sheng Pihua 盛丕华
Social Affairs Ministry 社会部
Sun Yatsen 孙中山
syndicalism 工团主义
Three Antis Five Antis movement 三反五反运动
Universal Job Placement program 全面的劳动就业
Wang Rong 王榕
wangpai 王牌
Wen Jiabao 温家宝
Wu Guozhen 吴国祯
Wu Kaixian 吴开先
Wu Shaoshu 吴绍澍
wubao 五保
xiafang 下放
Yang Fan 杨帆
Zhang Qi 张祺
Zhong Min 钟民
Zhou Enlai 周恩来
Zhou Xuexiang 周学湘
Zhu Xuefan 朱学范

# Index

Alber, Jens, 18
All-China Federation of Trade Unions
(ACFTU), 127, 152–53, 157, 168,
234, 265, 278; Anti-Rightist campaign,
221–24; campaign against economism, 175–76; industrial union reform,
204–5; purge of Li Lisan, 149–50,
175, 214, 222; response to 1957 strike
wave, 215–16; role in labor insurance
policy, 124–25, 129–31, 174–75, 243,
259–60; role in social insurance policy,
206–9; role in unemployment policy,
128; Seventh National Labor Congress,
177–78; Sixth National Labor Congress, 122–24
An Futing, 120
Anti-Rightist Campaign, 230, 231,
234, 238, 241, 265, 278; first phase,
220–25; second phase after the Lushan
Plenum, 245–46
Argentina, 12, 286–88

Baldwin, Peter, 18, 21–22
Bao Huaguo, 64
Beveridge Report, 59–60, 66
Bo Yibo, 165, 176

Brazil, 12, 286–88
broad coverage. *See* broad welfare state
broad welfare state, 30, 154, 198, 266,
268, 277, 285; in Argentina and
Brazil, 286–88; causes, 18–24, 25–28,
35–36, 288–90; in China, 75, 161–62,
192–93, 229–30, 263–64, 278n4,
281, 291–95; in communist countries,
63, 70–76; in Costa Rica, 68–69;
definition, 11; geography, 12–13; in
Germany, 67–68; obstacles, 15–17,
35–36; in Soviet Union, 72–74

Campaign to Suppress Counterrevolutionaries, 140, 142, 145, 153
Chen Yi, 136, 173, 177, 185
Chiang Kaishek, 80, 81, 106, 112
Chinese Association of Labor, 93, 101,
114, 119, 120, 224; connections to
CIO, 87, 112; founding, 81–82; impact of the Second Sino-Japanese War,
82–85; move to Hong Kong, 106–7;
merger with ACFTU, 122–23, 127;
Twenty-Three Demands, 98–100, 106;
worker welfare program, 88–90

Chinese Civil War, 31–32, 79, 113, 121, 148, 170, 210; CCP takeover of Shanghai, 132–35; in the Cold War, 62; end of the war, 128; impact on CCP welfare programs, 151–54; impact on KMT welfare programs, 114–17; KMT retreat, 113, 126; KMT takeover of Shanghai, 91–93; political competition, 118–19, 124, 126–28; 157–58, 272; preconditions, 91

Chinese Communist Party (CCP), 2, 4–6, 29, 157–58, 168, 181, 271, 295; alliance with KMT, 54; Anti-Rightist campaign, 220–24, 245–46; Campaign to Suppress Counter-revolutionaries, 140–42; comparison to KMT, 31–32, 151–54, 272–74; in the Chinese Civil War, 113, 126, 134, 140–41, 158; economic development policy, 159–60, 193–95, 231–233; Eighth Party Congress, 209–10; in the Great Leap Forward, 231–39, 245, 252–55; Hundred Flowers mass rectification campaign 211–19; impact on welfare coverage, 151–54, 186–91, 225–28, 263–67; Jiangxi soviet welfare, 56–57; in the Korean War, 128, 148, 158, 163, 174–75; labor insurance, 138–44, 173–174; Lushan Plenum, 245; at the 1946 Political Consultative Conference, 98–99; party-union relations, 148–50, 176–78, 204–5, 221–25; political competition with KMT, 98–99, 108–9, 112, 118–31, 272–74; repression by KMT, 54–55, 82; in the Second Sino-Japanese War, 80, 91, 118–19; in the Second World War, 91; Seven Thousand Cadres Conference, 253–54; socialization of industry, 202–4; Sufan Campaign, 185–86; takeover of Shanghai 132–35; Three Antis-Five Antis Campaign, 163–66; unemployment policy, 136–38, 145–48, 169–72, 184; welfare reform, 75, 161–62; 195–98, 205–9; 233–35; 275–84; 290–92; in the WFTU, 61, 224.

Chinese National Relief and Rehabilitation Agency, 61, 89
Chinese Nationalist Party. *See* KMT
citizen pensions, 10, 18, 30, 42, 46, 59, 66, 235
Civil Affairs Ministry (CCP), 202, 234
CNRRA. *See* Chinese National Relief and Rehabilitation Program
Cold War, 41, 62, 63, 65, 66, 67, 69, 76, 124, 269, 271
Colonialism. *See* imperialism
command economy, 2, 6, 19, 163, 205, 206, 276; definition, 159–60; in the Great Leap Forward, 232–33; labor union in, 163, 175, 205; transition to, 159–60, 194–95, 197, 212; welfare in, 161–62, 170–71, 206
commune canteens, 234–36, 243–44, 246–49, 252–54 263–66, 278, 285
commune day care, 234, 243, 248–49, 254
commune health stations, 239, 249, 254
commune schools, 239, 248–49, 254
commune social welfare services, 249, 254
commune welfare, 230, 233–37, 246, 249–51, 253–55, 256, 263–66, 278
Congress of Industrial Organizations (CIO), 86–88, 112, 276
corporatism, 24, 27, 31–33, 72, 79, 169; CCP corporatism, 131, 134, 148–50, 153, 166, 178, 272–74; in developing countries, 285–86; in the ILO, 285; KMT corporatism, 85–86, 88, 90–93, 131, 272–74
Costa Rica, 12, 68, 69
Czechoslovakia, 70, 75, 157

democracy, 23–24, 44; China's democracy movement, 49, 83, 98–100, 107; direct democracy, 72, 211, 251; labor democracy, 72, 83, 123, 177–78; New Democracy, 123, 134, 139, 166, 178, 273; Tutelary Democracy, 83–84, 99
demogrant pensions. *See* citizen pensions
Deng Xiaoping, 175, 266

Denmark, 41–43, 270
disability insurance, 2, 9, 46, 52, 64, 71, 73, 90, 126, 130, 161
Du Yuesheng, 82, 87, 99

economic development, 76, 197; China's level of economic development, 30, 32, 57, 270–71, 275–80, 293; Chinese economic development policy, 192–95, 231–33, 291–92; impact of economic development policy on welfare, 21, 27, 29, 188, 225, 233–36, 266, 268; impact of the level of economic development on welfare, 15–17, 19, 26, 32, 35, 283, 285, 289; role of unions in economic development, 175–78, 204–5; Soviet economic development policy, 158–60
economism, 150, 150n79, 176–78, 189

First Five-Year Plan, 220, 238; beginning, 175–180; 192; end, 205–206, 208, 226; policies, 159–62; preparation, 159, 169, 171–74; publication, 198–99, 203; revisions, 185–86, 187, 190, 192–93, 195, 197, 210; Soviet plan, 73–4; welfare in the Indian plan, 67
First Sino-Japanese War, 44
Flora, Peter, 18
Frazier, Mark, 5, 86n20, 223n82, 274n3

Germany, 40–44, 67, 69, 270
grassroots schools. *See* commune schools
Great Britain. *See* United Kingdom
Great Leap Forward, 6, 29, 267; commune welfare policy 230, 233–37; economic development policy, 231–33; impact on labor insurance, 242–43, 259–62; investment drive, 237–38, 242, 245; Lushan Plenum, 245; retrenchment, 252–53, 254–56; as a turning point, 264; urban communes 238–40, 246–51. *See also* Great Leap Forward famine

Great Leap Forward famine, 244–45 252, 261, 265, 278, 281, 284
Green Gang, in the Campaign to Suppress Counterrevolutionaries, 140–41, 144, 152–153; role in KMT labor unions, 82, 87, 92, 94, 99, 104, 273
Gu Zhenggang, 108

Haggard, Stephen, 21, 23
household registration system, 215, 218, 242, 265, 279, 282, 295; enforcement, 256–58; in the 1955 ruralization campaign, 199–201, 227–28; in the 1961–62 ruralization campaign, 256–58; regulations, 197, 240
Hu Jintao, 292
Huber, Evelyne, 23
Hundred Flowers mass rectification campaign, 211–19, 220–21, 227, 231, 277
Hungarian Uprising, 210–11, 215
Hungary, 157, 210–11

imperialism, 44–45, 62, 76, 145–146, 148, 197; impact on China, 44, 48, 53, 55–56, 78, 80–81, 91, 270
India, 12, 47, 60, 64, 67, 179
inequality, 8–9, 19, 22–23, 28, 69; in China, 1–3, 7, 33, 35, 188, 191, 275–76, 282–84
International Federation of Trade Unions, 64
international influence, 20–21, 25, 27, 39–47, 58–69, 76–77; on China, 29–30, 32, 35, 41, 44–45, 47–57, 61–62, 65, 70–77, 78–79, 86–87, 89, 293, 268–71, 293
International Labour Organization (ILO), 12, 14, 50; founding 45–46; influence on China, 47–49, 55–57, 61, 63–65, 269–71, 293; 1947 Asian Regional Conference, 63–64; role of Chinese Association of Labor, 61, 81, 100, 120–22; Second World War, 58–59, 60–61; standards 11, 46, 47, 55–56, 61, 63–65, 269–71, 293

Jiang Jingguo, 112–13

Kaufman, Robert, 21, 23
Ke Qingshi, 185, 216–17, 222, 237–38, 243, 254
Khrushchev, 210
Korean War, 31–32, 118, 128, 148, 158, 163, 175, 180
Kuomintang (KMT), 29, 146, 170, 172, 182, 189, 214, 224; Chinese Civil War, 113, 126, 134, 140–41; collapse, 112–113; comparison to CCP, 31–32, 118–19, 132–39, 143–44, 147, 148–50, 151–54, 199, 272–274; competition with the CCP, 120–22, 140–41; established central government, 48–49; factionalism, 93, 116, 132–33, 273; First Party Congress, 54–57; impact on welfare coverage, 114–17; Korean War, 128; labor politics, 82–83, 86–90, 100–101, 120–22, 123–32; 1948 Currency Reform, 112–13; 1947 Wage Freeze, 107–9; Political Consultative Conference, 98–99; Second World War, 58–59, 61, 78–81, 84–85; in Taiwan, 32, 67, 126, 128, 131; takeover of Shanghai, 91–94, 95, 96

labor insurance, 31, 40, 63, 75, 147, 150, 177, 222, 224, 258; CCP labor insurance implementation, 138–44, 273–74; CCP labor insurance policy, 129–32; CCP Northeast provisional labor insurance policy, 125–26; coverage, 2, 151–54, 187–88, 225–26, 251, 264–67; in the Great Leap Forward, 235, 240, 242–43; KMT labor insurance policy, 126–27; in the 1957 strike wave, 213–14, 216, 218–20; 1956 draft social insurance regulations, 206–9; 1953 labor insurance revisions, 173–76; 1962 labor insurance revisions, 259–61; rationing access, 35, 190, 240, 257, 276–77, 279–82; relationship to other welfare programs, 161–62, 195–97, 229–30, 262; as a

social insurance program, 30, 49–51, 73–74; in the Soviet Union, 73–74
labor insurance contracts, 161–62, 169, 177, 188, 216, 225, 260, 262
labor rackets. *See* Green Gang
Lai Ruoyu, 175–76, 204–5, 214, 216–17, 222–24
Li Baosen, 50
Li Fuchun, 149, 159, 186
Li Kangnian, 212
Li Lisan, 157–59, 167, 170, 175, 178, 183, 186, 270, 273; Chairman of the CCP, 122; controversy over purge from the ACFTU, 153, 176, 214, 222; exile to the Soviet Union, 122, 270; role in founding the ACFTU, 122–24, 133; role in labor insurance policy, 125–26, 129–31; role in May 30th Movement, 81–82; role in unemployment relief policy, 128; purge from the ACFTU, 149–50
Li Weihan, 181
Li Xian, 216
Liu Changsheng, 133, 136, 164–65, 175–76
Liu Ningyi, 61, 223–24
Liu Shaoqi, 57, 149, 209, 212
Lu Jingshi, 83, 85–86, 88, 99–100, 126–27, 126fn20; in Shanghai, 81–82, 92–97, 101–2, 106–8
Lu Xiaobo, 5
Lu Zhushu, 50
Lushan Plenum, 245

Ma Chaojun, 49–50
Mao Zedong, 2, 4, 189; Anti–Rightist movement, 220–21; commune policy, 233–36; economic development policy, 194, 202–3, 205–6, 231–33; Hundred Flowers campaign, 210–12; response to the crisis in Eastern Europe, 210–12; role in Great Leap Forward, 231, 234, 236, 238, 242, 245, 252–54, 264; role in policy process, 149, 167–68, 194, 202–3, 231–36, 238–39, 245, 252–53
Marshall, George, 98

maternity benefits, 2, 9, 52, 65, 71, 90, 126, 130
May Thirtieth Movement, 81, 108, 122
Mesa-Lago, Carmelo, 22

narrow welfare state, 29, 69, 80, 104, 209, 229; in Argentina and Brazil, 285–88; causes, 4–6 15–25, 35–36, 268–69, 270–71, 282–90; in contemporary China, 14, 290–95; definition, 11, 14; in developing countries, 15, 62–63, 285–89; geography, 12–13; in India, 67; in Maoist China, 1–2, 4–6, 35–36, 114–115, 151–52, 186–88, 264–67, 274–282; in the Soviet Union, 72, 75; in Taiwan, 67
National Labor Congresses (CCP), 123–24, 177–78
National Salvation Movement, 80–84
Naughton, Barry, 6, 278n5
New Democracy (CCP). *See* democracy
1911 Revolution, 44
noncontributory flat-rate pensions. *See* citizen pensions

old-age pensions, 10, 291, 292. *See also* citizen pensions; provident funds; social insurance
Opium Wars, 44
organized crime. *See* Green Gang

Pan Hannian, 185
Peng Dehuai, 245
People's Liberation Army (PLA), 113, 124, 126, 128, 132, 137
Perry, Elizabeth, 5
Philadelphia Conference (ILO), 60–61
political coalitions, 21–25, 27–28, 33–35, 43, 68; CCP's cross-class coalition, 119, 133–34, 136, 139–41, 145–48; CCP's exclusion of capitalists, 203–4; CCP's exclusion of the unemployed, 182–84, 200–201, 240–41; CCP's weakening of labor, 222–25; KMT's cross-class coalition, 84–86, 92–93, 102–4, 115–16

program design, 30, 75, 124, 161, 271, 274, 285; diffusion, 42–43, 46–47, 50–51, 53, 58, 269; impact on the expansion of coverage, 18–19, 25–26; program types, 10, 10n26, 230, 233–235
protest, 79–80, 134, 201, 229, 241, 246, 280; KMT bans on protest, 85, 107; KMT labor protests, 89, 96, 100–101, 108–9, 116–17, 273; by unemployed workers, 96, 100–101, 167–68, 181–84, 190, 212–18, 227, 256–57, 276; *See also* strike wave
provident funds, 10, 16, 22n57, 26n67, 67

Rao Shushi, 185–86
rationing, 17, 36; in advanced industrial countries, 190, 283, 289–90; consolidation of rationing mechanism in China, 254, 265, 280–83, 295; deliberate rationing in China, 195–98, 209, 228, 254, 276–77; in developing countries, 287–89; failure of rationing in China, 179–82, 225–28, 251–53, 278; politicization of rationing in China, 190–91, 283
Red Cross health stations. *See* commune health stations
Ren Yuanyuan, 50–51
Romania, 43, 70, 75
Rong Yiren, 164, 166
Roosevelt, Eleanor, 64
ruralization, 285; definition, 196, 196fn5; impact of the 1958–59 campaign, 240–44, 245, 256; impact of the 1955 campaign, 198–202, 218, 227–28; impact of the 1961-62 campaign, 256–58, 266, 270–81; institutionalization, 242, 255–58, 264; rationing, 196–97, 209, 264–65, 277

Schulter, John, 112
Second Five-Year Plan, 220, 231
Second Sino-Japanese War, 31, 56, 58, 62, 96; beginning of the war; 80; end

of the war, 91–94; impact on the CCP, 80, 118–19, 126, 197; impact on the KMT, 79, 80–86, 86n20

Second World War, 9, 18, 269; in China, 5, 78–79, 84, 86n20, 91, 117, 119, 126; impact on policy diffusion, 41, 58–62, 76; as a turning point, 41, 58–60, 67, 74, 144, 286, 289–90

semicolonialism. *See* imperialism

Shanghai Business Federation (CCP), 133–34, 163, 178, 189, 203, 212

Shanghai Chamber of Commerce (KMT), 92–95, 113, 115

Shanghai Civil Affairs Bureau (CCP), 182, 217, 234, 241–42, 257, 262

Shanghai Federation of Trade Unions (SFTU)(CCP), Anti-Rightist campaign, 223–25; campaign against economism, 176–77; founding 133–35; Great Leap Forward, 242–43; purges, 175–76; role in labor insurance, 138, 140, 142–44, 258–61; role in 1957 strike wave, 214–218; role in policy making, 129–30, 173–74, 207–8, 259–60; role in unemployment relief, 135–36, 145–48, 184; Three Antis-Five Antis campaign, 164–69

Shanghai General Labor Union (KMT), 82, 92–93, 95, 101–2, 107–9, 140

Shanghai Labor Bureau (CCP), 135, 184, 256; role in job placement, 180–81, 190, 215, 227; role in labor insurance, 138–39; role in unemployment relief, 166–67

Shanghai Municipal Council (KMT), 93, 134

Shanghai Party Committee (CCP), 165, 215, 248, 253; ruralization policy, 198, 240, 244; welfare policy recommendations, 173–74, 207–9, 243

Shanghai People's Congress (CCP), 134, 212, 238

Shanghai Social Affairs Bureau (KMT), 96–97, 101, 103, 107–8

Shanghai Temporary Committee (CCP), 216–18

Shanghai Unemployed Workers' Congress (CCP), 145–46, 148

Shanghai Worker Welfare Committee (KMT), 100–102, 105, 107–10, 115, 140

Shanghai Workers' Congress (CCP), 135, 177

Sheng Pihua, 133

Social Affairs Ministry (KMT), 83–85, 92, 94, 97, 121

social assistance, 8, 10fn26, 19, 292, 295. *See also* social relief

social insurance, 7, 22, 30, 226, 228, 229, 237, 283; in Argentina & Brazil, 286–88; CCP social insurance policy, 1–2, 5, 54, 56–57, 118, 154, 162, 205–9, 219–220; comparison to citizen pensions, 9–10, 18–19; comparison to KMT Workplace Welfare program, 138; in Costa Rica, 68–69; diffusion, 39, 42–43, 47, 49–57, 58–61, 69–70, 269–71; diffusion to China, 50–57, 70–77; draft Social Insurance regulations (1956), 205–9, 219–220; endorsement by the ILO 46; expansion of coverage, 18–19, 26, 35–36, 63–64, 268, 278, 285–89; in Germany 42, 67–68; KMT socialist insurance policy, 54–56, 78, 90, 98–99, 121, 126–27, 131; policy standards, 46, 64–67; program design, 9–10, 16, 18–19; Social Insurance Law (2010) 290–291, 293. *See also* labor insurance

social pensions. *See* citizen pensions

social relief, 162; and commune welfare, 235, 250–51, 258; consolidation, 262, 264–67; coverage, 186–88, 201–2, 247, 264–65; implementation, 167, 183; policy, 162; and ruralization, 200, 227, 241

social security. *See* social insurance

socialization of industry, 33, 165, 203

Soviet economic development strategy, 158–61, 188, 190, 192–94

Soviet model of welfare reform, 70–76, adaptation of the Soviet model,

192–93, 277; end of Soviet influence,
233; Soviet influence on China, 70, 75,
161–62, 170, 207, 271, 276
Soviet Union, 12, 30, 57, 125, 157,
190; in the Cold War, 62, 64; and Li
Lisan, 122; response to the Hungarian
Uprising, 210, 229–30; Sino-Soviet
Friendship Treaty, 70; Sino-Soviet
split, 229–30. *See also* Soviet economic
development strategy; Soviet model of
welfare reform
Stalin, 210
Stalinist development strategy. *See* Soviet
economic development strategy
state capacity, 15, 28, 33, 138, 268, 288–
90, 295; definition, 17, 35–36, 288
Stephens, John, 23
strike wave, 100, 116, 272; global 1919
strike wave, 45; Shanghai 1957 strike
wave, 213–20, 220–22, 226, 237–38,
277; Shanghai 1948–49 strike wave,
111, 134, 135; Shanghai 1949–50
strike wave, 148; Shanghai 1946–47
strike wave, 102, 105, 108
Sun Yatsen, 54
Sweden, 43–44, 46, 57, 66
Sweetland, Monroe, 87
syndicalism, 150, 176

Thomas, Albert, 48
Three Antis, Five Antis Campaign, 163;
beginning of, 163–164; definition,
163fn8; impact on unemployment
relief, 167–68, 181–82, 184; impact
on welfare benefits, 168–69, 186–87,
213; party-led phase, 165–66; political
impact, 175–76, 178, 189, 198, 203;
union-led phase, 164–65
Tutelary Democracy (KMT). *See* democracy

Unemployed Workers Congress. *See*
Shanghai Unemployed Workers'
Congress
unemployment insurance, 52, 71

unemployment relief, 78, 86, 150, 173,
208; CCP implementation, 135 38,
147–48, 275–77; CCP policy 128,
131, 147; commune employment,
249–51; coverage, 151–53, 186–88;
Jiangxi soviet experiment, 57, 118;
KMT implementation, 91, 93–97,
101, 109–11, 114–17, 121; KMT policy, 88, 90, 131; Soviet policy, 19, 74,
162; Three Antis–Five Antis emergency
relief, 166–68; transition to social
relief, 196, 201–2; unemployed workers congress, 145–46; Universal Job
Placement implementation, 178–84,
190–91; Universal Job Placement
policy, 169–72. *See also* protest
United Kingdom, 42, 45, 51, 59, 79
United Nations, 60, 62, 64
United Nations Relief and Rehabilitation
Administration (UNRRA), 61, 88–89,
91, 95, 101, 110
universal coverage. *See* universal welfare
state
Universal Declaration of Human Rights,
64
Universal Job Placement program, 192,
195, 263, 276; coverage, 186–88; failure, 182–85, 190–91; implementation,
178–81; policy, 169–72
universal welfare state, 14, 15, 39, 41,
73, 290; definition, 11; diffusion of
the idea of universal welfare states,
58–60; diffusion of reforms to achieve
universal coverage, 63–69, 270–71;
geography, 12; goal in contemporary
China, 291–92; goal in the Great Leap
Forward, 233, 264, 278; invention of
reforms to achieve universal coverage,
46; role of reform in achieving universal welfare states, 18–19

Walder, Andrew, 6
Wang Rong, 215–16, 222
Wen Jiabao, 292

Worker Welfare program, 78, 91, 93, 153, 274n3, 275; Chinese Association of Labor programs, 87; comparison to labor insurance, 138–39, 143, 151, 273–74; coverage in Shanghai, 114–16; 117, 121, 125, 131; factionalism, 88–90, 107–110; implementation in Shanghai, 101–5; KMT programs, 88–90; U.S. programs, 86–87

World Federation of Trade Unions (WFTU), 61–62, 64–65, 120–22, 127, 176, 223

Wu Guozhen, 108

Wu Kaixian, 97, 99, 101

Wu Shaoshu, 96

Xie Zhengfu, 61

Yang Fan, 185

Zhang Pengjun, 64

Zhang Qi, 208

Zhong Min, 176, 223

Zhou Enlai, 159; role in economic development policy 159, 194, 203, 219–20, 231; role in food policy 252, 255; role in social insurance policy 208, 219; role in unemployment relief policy 169–72

Zhou Xuexiang, 92

Zhu Xuefan, 108, 109, 133, 150, 224, 273; appointed director of the Chinese Association of Labor, 81–83; chairman of the Shanghai General Labor Union 83, 92; defection to the CCP, 111–12; defection to Hong Kong, 106–7; in the ILO, 61, 100; in the May 30th Movement, 81–82; in the National Salvation movement, 82–83; rivalry with Lu Jingshi, 81–83, 85–86, 88–90, 92–95, 101; at the Sixth National Labor Congress, 122–24; Twenty–three Demands, 98–100; in the U.S., 87; in the WFTU 120–22, 127, 223

*Harvard East Asian Monographs*
(most recent titles)

189. Susan Daruvala, *Zhou Zuoren and an Alternative Chinese Response to Modernity*
191. Kerry Smith, *A Time of Crisis: Japan, the Great Depression, and Rural Revitalization*
192. Michael Lewis, *Becoming Apart: National Power and Local Politics in Toyama, 1868–1945*
193. William C. Kirby, Man-houng Lin, James Chin Shih, and David A. Pietz, eds., *State and Economy in Republican China: A Handbook for Scholars*
194. Timothy S. George, *Minamata: Pollution and the Struggle for Democracy in Postwar Japan*
195. Billy K. L. So, *Prosperity, Region, and Institutions in Maritime China: The South Fukien Pattern, 946–1368*
196. Yoshihisa Tak Matsusaka, *The Making of Japanese Manchuria, 1904–1932*
197. Maram Epstein, *Competing Discourses: Orthodoxy, Authenticity, and Engendered Meanings in Late Imperial Chinese Fiction*
199. Haruo Iguchi, *Unfinished Business: Ayukawa Yoshisuke and U.S.-Japan Relations, 1937–1952*
200. Scott Pearce, Audrey Spiro, and Patricia Ebrey, *Culture and Power in the Reconstitution of the Chinese Realm, 200–600*
201. Terry Kawashima, *Writing Margins: The Textual Construction of Gender in Heian and Kamakura Japan*
202. Martin W. Huang, *Desire and Fictional Narrative in Late Imperial China*
203. Robert S. Ross and Jiang Changbin, eds., *Re-examining the Cold War: U.S.-China Diplomacy, 1954–1973*
204. Guanhua Wang, *In Search of Justice: The 1905–1906 Chinese Anti-American Boycott*
205. David Schaberg, *A Patterned Past: Form and Thought in Early Chinese Historiography*
206. Christine Yano, *Tears of Longing: Nostalgia and the Nation in Japanese Popular Song*
207. Milena Doleželová-Velingerová and Oldřich Král, with Graham Sanders, eds., *The Appropriation of Cultural Capital: China's May Fourth Project*
208. Robert N. Huey, *The Making of 'Shinkokinshū'*
209. Lee Butler, *Emperor and Aristocracy in Japan, 1467–1680: Resilience and Renewal*

210. Suzanne Ogden, *Inklings of Democracy in China*
211. Kenneth J. Ruoff, *The People's Emperor: Democracy and the Japanese Monarchy, 1945–1995*
212. Haun Saussy, *Great Walls of Discourse and Other Adventures in Cultural China*
213. Aviad E. Raz, *Emotions at Work: Normative Control, Organizations, and Culture in Japan and America*
214. Rebecca E. Karl and Peter Zarrow, eds., *Rethinking the 1898 Reform Period: Political and Cultural Change in Late Qing China*
215. Kevin O'Rourke, *The Book of Korean Shijo*
216. Ezra F. Vogel, ed., *The Golden Age of the U.S.-China-Japan Triangle, 1972–1989*
217. Thomas A. Wilson, ed., *On Sacred Grounds: Culture, Society, Politics, and the Formation of the Cult of Confucius*
218. Donald S. Sutton, *Steps of Perfection: Exorcistic Performers and Chinese Religion in Twentieth-Century Taiwan*
219. Daqing Yang, *Technology of Empire: Telecommunications and Japanese Expansionism in Asia, 1883–1945*
220. Qianshen Bai, *Fu Shan's World: The Transformation of Chinese Calligraphy in the Seventeenth Century*
221. Paul Jakov Smith and Richard von Glahn, eds., *The Song-Yuan-Ming Transition in Chinese History*
222. Rania Huntington, *Alien Kind: Foxes and Late Imperial Chinese Narrative*
223. Jordan Sand, *House and Home in Modern Japan: Architecture, Domestic Space, and Bourgeois Culture, 1880–1930*
224. Karl Gerth, *China Made: Consumer Culture and the Creation of the Nation*
225. Xiaoshan Yang, *Metamorphosis of the Private Sphere: Gardens and Objects in Tang-Song Poetry*
226. Barbara Mittler, *A Newspaper for China? Power, Identity, and Change in Shanghai's News Media, 1872–1912*
227. Joyce A. Madancy, *The Troublesome Legacy of Commissioner Lin: The Opium Trade and Opium Suppression in Fujian Province, 1820s to 1920s*
228. John Makeham, *Transmitters and Creators: Chinese Commentators and Commentaries on the Analects*
229. Elisabeth Köll, *From Cotton Mill to Business Empire: The Emergence of Regional Enterprises in Modern China*
230. Emma Teng, *Taiwan's Imagined Geography: Chinese Colonial Travel Writing and Pictures, 1683–1895*
231. Wilt Idema and Beata Grant, *The Red Brush: Writing Women of Imperial China*
232. Eric C. Rath, *The Ethos of Noh: Actors and Their Art*
233. Elizabeth Remick, *Building Local States: China during the Republican and Post-Mao Eras*
234. Lynn Struve, ed., *The Qing Formation in World-Historical Time*
235. D. Max Moerman, *Localizing Paradise: Kumano Pilgrimage and the Religious Landscape of Premodern Japan*

236. Antonia Finnane, *Speaking of Yangzhou: A Chinese City, 1550–1850*
237. Brian Platt, *Burning and Building: Schooling and State Formation in Japan, 1750–1890*
238. Gail Bernstein, Andrew Gordon, and Kate Wildman Nakai, eds., *Public Spheres, Private Lives in Modern Japan, 1600–1950: Essays in Honor of Albert Craig*
239. Wu Hung and Katherine R. Tsiang, *Body and Face in Chinese Visual Culture*
240. Stephen Dodd, *Writing Home: Representations of the Native Place in Modern Japanese Literature*
241. David Anthony Bello, *Opium and the Limits of Empire: Drug Prohibition in the Chinese Interior, 1729–1850*
242. Hosea Hirata, *Discourses of Seduction: History, Evil, Desire, and Modern Japanese Literature*
243. Kyung Moon Hwang, *Beyond Birth: Social Status in the Emergence of Modern Korea*
244. Brian R. Dott, *Identity Reflections: Pilgrimages to Mount Tai in Late Imperial China*
245. Mark McNally, *Proving the Way: Conflict and Practice in the History of Japanese Nativism*
246. Yongping Wu, *A Political Explanation of Economic Growth: State Survival, Bureaucratic Politics, and Private Enterprises in the Making of Taiwan's Economy, 1950–1985*
247. Kyu Hyun Kim, *The Age of Visions and Arguments: Parliamentarianism and the National Public Sphere in Early Meiji Japan*
248. Zvi Ben-Dor Benite, *The Dao of Muhammad: A Cultural History of Muslims in Late Imperial China*
249. David Der-wei Wang and Shang Wei, eds., *Dynastic Crisis and Cultural Innovation: From the Late Ming to the Late Qing and Beyond*
250. Wilt L. Idema, Wai-yee Li, and Ellen Widmer, eds., *Trauma and Transcendence in Early Qing Literature*
251. Barbara Molony and Kathleen Uno, eds., *Gendering Modern Japanese History*
252. Hiroshi Aoyagi, *Islands of Eight Million Smiles: Idol Performance and Symbolic Production in Contemporary Japan*
253. Wai-yee Li, *The Readability of the Past in Early Chinese Historiography*
254. William C. Kirby, Robert S. Ross, and Gong Li, eds., *Normalization of U.S.-China Relations: An International History*
255. Ellen Gardner Nakamura, *Practical Pursuits: Takano Chōei, Takahashi Keisaku, and Western Medicine in Nineteenth-Century Japan*
256. Jonathan W. Best, *A History of the Early Korean Kingdom of Paekche, together with an annotated translation of* The Paekche Annals *of the* Samguk sagi
257. Liang Pan, *The United Nations in Japan's Foreign and Security Policymaking, 1945–1992: National Security, Party Politics, and International Status*
258. Richard Belsky, *Localities at the Center: Native Place, Space, and Power in Late Imperial Beijing*
259. Zwia Lipkin, *"Useless to the State": "Social Problems" and Social Engineering in Nationalist Nanjing, 1927–1937*
260. William O. Gardner, *Advertising Tower: Japanese Modernism and Modernity in the 1920s*
261. Stephen Owen, *The Making of Early Chinese Classical Poetry*

## Harvard East Asian Monographs

262. Martin J. Powers, *Pattern and Person: Ornament, Society, and Self in Classical China*
263. Anna M. Shields, *Crafting a Collection: The Cultural Contexts and Poetic Practice of the Huajian ji* 花間集 (*Collection from among the Flowers*)
264. Stephen Owen, *The Late Tang: Chinese Poetry of the Mid-Ninth Century (827–860)*
265. Sara L. Friedman, *Intimate Politics: Marriage, the Market, and State Power in Southeastern China*
266. Patricia Buckley Ebrey and Maggie Bickford, *Emperor Huizong and Late Northern Song China: The Politics of Culture and the Culture of Politics*
267. Sophie Volpp, *Worldly Stage: Theatricality in Seventeenth-Century China*
268. Ellen Widmer, *The Beauty and the Book: Women and Fiction in Nineteenth-Century China*
269. Steven B. Miles, *The Sea of Learning: Mobility and Identity in Nineteenth-Century Guangzhou*
270. Man-hung Lin, *China Upside Down: Currency, Society, and Ideologies, 1808–1856*
271. Ronald Egan, *The Problem of Beauty: Aesthetic Thought and Pursuits in Northern Song Dynasty China*
272. Mark Halperin, *Out of the Cloister: Literati Perspectives on Buddhism in Sung China, 960–1279*
273. Helen Dunstan, *State or Merchant? Political Economy and Political Process in 1740s China*
274. Sabina Knight, *The Heart of Time: Moral Agency in Twentieth-Century Chinese Fiction*
275. Timothy J. Van Compernolle, *The Uses of Memory: The Critique of Modernity in the Fiction of Higuchi Ichiyō*
276. Paul Rouzer, *A New Practical Primer of Literary Chinese*
277. Jonathan Zwicker, *Practices of the Sentimental Imagination: Melodrama, the Novel, and the Social Imaginary in Nineteenth-Century Japan*
278. Franziska Seraphim, *War Memory and Social Politics in Japan, 1945–2005*
280. Cynthia J. Brokaw, *Commerce in Culture: The Sibao Book Trade in the Qing and Republican Periods*
281. Eugene Y. Park, *Between Dreams and Reality: The Military Examination in Late Chosŏn Korea, 1600–1894*
282. Nam-lin Hur, *Death and Social Order in Tokugawa Japan: Buddhism, Anti-Christianity, and the Danka System*
283. Patricia M. Thornton, *Disciplining the State: Virtue, Violence, and State-Making in Modern China*
284. Vincent Goossaert, *The Taoists of Peking, 1800–1949: A Social History of Urban Clerics*
286. Charo B. D'Etcheverry, *Love after* The Tale of Genji: *Rewriting the World of the Shining Prince*
287. Michael G. Chang, *A Court on Horseback: Imperial Touring & the Construction of Qing Rule, 1680–1785*
288. Carol Richmond Tsang, *War and Faith: Ikkō Ikki in Late Muromachi Japan*
289. Hilde De Weerdt, *Competition over Content: Negotiating Standards for the Civil Service Examinations in Imperial China (1127–1279)*

290. Eve Zimmerman, *Out of the Alleyway: Nakagami Kenji and the Poetics of Outcaste Fiction*

291. Robert Culp, *Articulating Citizenship: Civic Education and Student Politics in Southeastern China, 1912–1940*

292. Richard J. Smethurst, *From Foot Soldier to Finance Minister: Takahashi Korekiyo, Japan's Keynes*

293. John E. Herman, *Amid the Clouds and Mist: China's Colonization of Guizhou, 1200–1700*

294. Tomoko Shiroyama, *China during the Great Depression: Market, State, and the World Economy, 1929–1937*

295. Kirk W. Larsen, *Tradition, Treaties and Trade: Qing Imperialism and Chosŏn Korea, 1850–1910*

296. Gregory Golley, *When Our Eyes No Longer See: Realism, Science, and Ecology in Japanese Literary Modernism*

297. Barbara Ambros, *Emplacing a Pilgrimage: The Ōyama Cult and Regional Religion in Early Modern Japan*

298. Rebecca Suter, *The Japanization of Modernity: Murakami Haruki between Japan and the United States*

299. Yuma Totani, *The Tokyo War Crimes Trial: The Pursuit of Justice in the Wake of World War II*

301. David M. Robinson, ed., *Culture, Courtiers, and Competition: The Ming Court (1368–1644)*

302. Calvin Chen, *Some Assembly Required: Work, Community, and Politics in China's Rural Enterprises*

303. Sem Vermeersch, *The Power of the Buddhas: The Politics of Buddhism During the Koryŏ Dynasty (918–1392)*

304. Tina Lu, *Accidental Incest, Filial Cannibalism, and Other Peculiar Encounters in Late Imperial Chinese Literature*

305. Chang Woei Ong, *Men of Letters Within the Passes: Guanzhong Literati in Chinese History, 907–1911*

306. Wendy Swartz, *Reading Tao Yuanming: Shifting Paradigms of Historical Reception (427–1900)*

307. Peter K. Bol, *Neo-Confucianism in History*

308. Carlos Rojas, *The Naked Gaze: Reflections on Chinese Modernity*

309. Kelly H. Chong, *Deliverance and Submission: Evangelical Women and the Negotiation of Patriarchy in South Korea*

310. Rachel DiNitto, *Uchida Hyakken: A Critique of Modernity and Militarism in Prewar Japan*

311. Jeffrey Snyder-Reinke, *Dry Spells: State Rainmaking and Local Governance in Late Imperial China*

312. Jay Dautcher, *Down a Narrow Road: Identity and Masculinity in a Uyghur Community in Xinjiang China*

313. Xun Liu, *Daoist Modern: Innovation, Lay Practice, and the Community of Inner Alchemy in Republican Shanghai*

314. Jacob Eyferth, *Eating Rice from Bamboo Roots: The Social History of a Community of Handicraft Papermakers in Rural Sichuan, 1920–2000*

315. David Johnson, *Spectacle and Sacrifice: The Ritual Foundations of Village Life in North China*

316. James Robson, *Power of Place: The Religious Landscape of the Southern Sacred Peak (Nanyue 南嶽) in Medieval China*

317. Lori Watt, *When Empire Comes Home: Repatriation and Reintegration in Postwar Japan*

318. James Dorsey, *Critical Aesthetics: Kobayashi Hideo, Modernity, and Wartime Japan*

319. Christopher Bolton, *Sublime Voices: The Fictional Science and Scientific Fiction of Abe Kōbō*

320. Si-yen Fei, *Negotiating Urban Space: Urbanization and Late Ming Nanjing*

321. Christopher Gerteis, *Gender Struggles: Wage-Earning Women and Male-Dominated Unions in Postwar Japan*

322. Rebecca Nedostup, *Superstitious Regimes: Religion and the Politics of Chinese Modernity*

323. Lucien Bianco, *Wretched Rebels: Rural Disturbances on the Eve of the Chinese Revolution*

324. Cathryn H. Clayton, *Sovereignty at the Edge: Macau and the Question of Chineseness*

325. Micah S. Muscolino, *Fishing Wars and Environmental Change in Late Imperial and Modern China*

326. Robert I. Hellyer, *Defining Engagement: Japan and Global Contexts, 1750–1868*

327. Robert Ashmore, *The Transport of Reading: Text and Understanding in the World of Tao Qian (365–427)*

328. Mark A. Jones, *Children as Treasures: Childhood and the Middle Class in Early Twentieth Century Japan*

329. Miryam Sas, *Experimental Arts in Postwar Japan: Moments of Encounter, Engagement, and Imagined Return*

330. H. Mack Horton, *Traversing the Frontier: The Man'yōshū Account of a Japanese Mission to Silla in 736–737*

331. Dennis J. Frost, *Seeing Stars: Sports Celebrity, Identity, and Body Culture in Modern Japan*

332. Marnie S. Anderson, *A Place in Public: Women's Rights in Meiji Japan*

333. Peter Mauch, *Sailor Diplomat: Nomura Kichisaburō and the Japanese-American War*

334. Ethan Isaac Segal, *Coins, Trade, and the State: Economic Growth in Early Medieval Japan*

335. David B. Lurie, *Realms of Literacy: Early Japan and the History of Writing*

336. Lillian Lan-ying Tseng, *Picturing Heaven in Early China*

337. Jun Uchida, *Brokers of Empire: Japanese Settler Colonialism in Korea, 1876–1945*

338. Patricia L. Maclachlan, *The People's Post Office: The History and Politics of the Japanese Postal System, 1871–2010*

339. Michael Schiltz, *The Money Doctors from Japan: Finance, Imperialism, and the Building of the Yen Bloc, 1895–1937*

340. Daqing Yang, Jie Liu, Hiroshi Mitani, and Andrew Gordon, eds., *Toward a History beyond Borders: Contentious Issues in Sino-Japanese Relations*

341. Sonia Ryang, *Reading North Korea: An Ethnological Inquiry*

342. Shih-shan Susan Huang, *Picturing the True Form: Daoist Visual Culture in*

Harvard East Asian Monographs

Traditional China

343. Barbara Mittler, *A Continuous Revolution: Making Sense of Cultural Revolution Culture*
344. Hwansoo Ilmee Kim, *Empire of the Dharma: Korean and Japanese Buddhism, 1877–1912*
345. Satoru Saito, *Detective Fiction and the Rise of the Japanese Novel, 1880–1930*
346. Jung-Sun N. Han, *An Imperial Path to Modernity: Yoshino Sakuzō and a New Liberal Order in East Asia, 1905–1937*
347. Atsuko Hirai, *Government by Mourning: Death and Political Integration in Japan, 1603–1912*
348. Darryl E. Flaherty, *Public Law, Private Practice: Politics, Profit, and the Legal Profession in Nineteenth-Century Japan*
349. Jeffrey Paul Bayliss, *On the Margins of Empire: Buraku and Korean Identity in Prewar and Wartime Japan*
350. Barry Eichengreen, Dwight H. Perkins, and Kwanho Shin, *From Miracle to Maturity: The Growth of the Korean Economy*
351. Michel Mohr, *Buddhism, Unitarianism, and the Meiji Competition for Universality*
352. J. Keith Vincent, *Two-Timing Modernity: Homosocial Narrative in Modern Japanese Fiction*
354. Chong-Bum An and Barry Bosworth, *Income Inequality in Korea: An Analysis of Trends, Causes, and Answers*
355. Jamie L. Newhard, *Knowing the Amorous Man: A History of Scholarship on* Tales of Ise
356. Sho Konishi, *Anarchist Modernity: Cooperatism and Japanese-Russian Intellectual Relations in Modern Japan*
357. Christopher P. Hanscom, *The Real Modern: Literary Modernism and the Crisis of Representation in Colonial Korea*
358. Michael Wert, *Meiji Restoration Losers: Memory and Tokugawa Supporters in Modern Japan*
359. Garret P. S. Olberding, ed., *Facing the Monarch: Modes of Advice in the Early Chinese Court*
360. Xiaojue Wang, *Modernity with a Cold War Face: Reimagining the Nation in Chinese Literature Across the 1949 Divide*
361. David Spafford, *A Sense of Place: The Political Landscape in Late Medieval Japan*
362. Jongryn Mo and Barry Weingast, *Korean Political and Economic Development: Crisis, Security, and Economic Rebalancing*
363. Melek Ortabasi, *The Undiscovered Country: Text, Translation, and Modernity in the Work of Yanagita Kunio*
364. Hiraku Shimoda, *Lost and Found: Recovering Regional Identity in Imperial Japan*
365. Trent E. Maxey, *The "Greatest Problem": Religion and State Formation in Meiji Japan*
366. Gina Cogan, *The Princess Nun: Bunchi, Buddhist Reform, and Gender in Early Edo Japan*
367. Eric C. Han, *Rise of a Japanese Chinatown: Yokohama, 1894–1972*
368. Natasha Heller, *Illusory Abiding: The Cultural Construction of the Chan Monk Zhongfeng Mingben*

369. Paize Keulemans, *Sound Rising from the Paper: Nineteenth-Century Martial Arts Fiction and the Chinese Acoustic Imagination*

370. Simon James Bytheway, *Investing Japan: Foreign Capital, Monetary Standards, and Economic Development, 1859–2011*

371. Sukhee Lee, *Negotiated Power: The State, Elites, and Local Governance in Twelfth-Fourteenth China*

372. Foong Ping, *The Efficacious Landscape: On the Authorities of Painting at the Northern Song Court*

373. Catherine L. Phipps, *Empires on the Waterfront: Japan's Ports and Power, 1858–1899*

374. Sunyoung Park, *The Proletarian Wave: Literature and Leftist Culture in Colonial Korea, 1910–1945*

375. Barry Eichengreen, Wonhyuk Lim, Yung Chul Park, and Dwight H. Perkins, *The Korean Economy: From a Miraculous Past to a Sustainable Future*

376. Heather Blair, *Real and Imagined: The Peak of Gold in Heian Japan*

377. Emer O'Dwyer, *Significant Soil: Settler Colonialism and Japan's Urban Empire in Manchuria*

378. Martina Deuchler, *Under the Ancestors' Eyes: Kinship, Status, and Locality in Premodern Korea*

379. Joseph R. Dennis, *Writing, Publishing, and Reading Local Gazetteers in Imperial China, 1100–1700*

380. Catherine Vance Yeh, *The Chinese Political Novel: Migration of a World Genre*

381. Noell Wilson, *Defensive Positions: The Politics of Maritime Security in Tokugawa Japan*

382. Miri Nakamura, *Monstrous Bodies: The Rise of the Uncanny in Modern Japan*

383. Nara Dillon, *Radical Inequalities: China's Revolutionary Welfare State in Comparative Perspective*

384. Ma Zhao, *Runaway Wives, Urban Crimes, and Survival Tactics in Wartime Beijing, 1937-1949*

385. Mingwei Song, *Young China: National Rejuvenation and the* Bildungsroman, *1900-1959*

386. Christopher Bondy, *Voice, Silence, and Self: Negotiations of Buraku Identity in Contemporary Japan*

387. Seth Jacobowitz, *Writing Technology in Meiji Japan: A Media History of Modern Japanese Literature and Visual Culture*

388. Hilde De Weerdt, *Information, Territory, and Elite Networks: The Crisis and Maintenance of Empire in Song China*

389. Elizabeth Kindall, *Geo-Narratives of a Filial Son: The Paintings and Travel Diaries of Huang Xiangjian (1609–1673)*

390. Matthew Fraleigh, *Plucking Chrysanthemums: Narushima Ryūhoku and Sinitic Literary Traditions in Modern Japan*

391. Hu Ying, *Burying Autumn: Poetry, Friendship, and Loss*

392. Mark E. Byington, *The Ancient State of Puyŏ in Northeast Asia: Archaeology and Historical Memory*

393. Timothy J. Van Compernolle, *Struggling Upward: Worldly Success and the Japanese Novel*